QUANTUM MYSTICISM

Where Science Meets Spirituality

D.R. T STEPHENS

S.D.N Publishing

Copyright © 2023 (Updated 2025) S.D.N Publishing

All rights reserved

The characters and events portrayed in this book are fictitious. Any similarity to real persons, living or dead, is coincidental and not intended by the author.

No part of this book may be reproduced, or stored in a retrieval system, or transmitted in any form or by any means, electronic, mechanical, photocopying, recording, or otherwise, without express written permission of the publisher.

ISBN: 9798864007587

CONTENTS

Title Page
Copyright
General Disclaimer — 1
Foreword — 3
Chapter 1: Introduction: Exploring Science And Spirit — 5
Chapter 2: Foundations of Quantum Mechanics — 15
Chapter 3: Spiritual Frameworks of Interconnection — 25
Chapter 4: Wave-Particle Duality and Spiritual Paradox — 36
Chapter 5: Quantum Entanglement and Oneness — 47
Chapter 6: Observer Effect and Consciousness — 58
Chapter 7: Schrödinger's Cat: The Mystery of Being and Non-Being — 68
Chapter 8: Quantum Tunneling and Miracles — 78
Chapter 9: Heisenberg's Uncertainty and Free Will — 88
Chapter 10: Superposition and Multiple Realities — 98
Chapter 11: The Holographic Principle and Wholeness — 108
Chapter 12: Quantum Cosmology and Creation Myths — 119
Chapter 13: Hidden Variables and Karmic Laws — 129
Chapter 14: Quantum Healing and Energy Work — 140
Chapter 15: Quantum Chaos and Spiritual Disorder — 150
Chapter 16: Synchronicity and Quantum Correlations — 160

Chapter 17: The Anthropic Principle and Purpose 171
Chapter 18: Non-locality and Akashic Records 181
Chapter 19: Everett's Many-Worlds and Reincarnation 191
Chapter 20: Quantum Teleportation and Astral Travel 201
Chapter 21: Ethics in Quantum Mysticism 212
Chapter 22: Quantum Computing and the Mind of God 223
Chapter 23: Consciousness Studies: The Next Frontier 234
Chapter 24: Metaphysical Implications of Quantum Physics 245
Chapter 25: Quantum Mysticism in Popular Culture 256
Chapter 26: Technological Horizons & Spiritual Insight 266
Chapter 27: Cultural and Historical Roots of Quantum Mysticism 277
Chapter 28: Reappraising Materialism and Physical Reality 288
Chapter 29: Future Directions in Quantum Spirituality 299
Chapter 30: Philosophy of Science and Spiritual Praxis 310
Chapter 31: Critiques & Debates in Quantum Spirituality 320
Chapter 32: Bridging Quantum Concepts into Daily Life 331
Chapter 33: Synthesis: The Evolving Tapestry 341
Chapter 34: Conclusion: Unraveling the Cosmic Web 351
Bibliography 354
THE END 375

GENERAL DISCLAIMER

This book is intended to provide informative and educational material on the subject matter covered. The author(s), publisher, and any affiliated parties make no representations or warranties with respect to the accuracy, applicability, completeness, or suitability of the contents herein and specifically disclaim any implied warranties of merchantability or fitness for a particular purpose.

The information contained in this book is for general information purposes only and is not intended to serve as legal, medical, financial, or any other form of professional advice. Readers should consult with appropriate professionals before making any decisions based on the information provided. Neither the author(s) nor the publisher shall be held responsible or liable for any loss, damage, injury, claim, or otherwise, whether direct or indirect, consequential, or incidental, that may occur as a result of applying or misinterpreting the information in this book.

This book may contain references to third-party websites, products, or services. Such references do not constitute an endorsement or recommendation, and the author(s) and publisher are not responsible for any outcomes related to these third-party references.

In no event shall the author(s), publisher, or any affiliated parties be liable for any direct, indirect, punitive, special, incidental, or other consequential damages arising directly or indirectly from any use of this material, which is provided "as is," and without warranties of any kind, express or implied.

By reading this book, you acknowledge and agree that you assume all risks and responsibilities concerning the applicability and consequences of the information provided. You also agree to indemnify, defend, and hold harmless the author(s), publisher, and any affiliated parties from any and all liabilities, claims, demands, actions, and causes of action whatsoever, whether or not foreseeable, that may arise from using or misusing the information contained in this book.

Although every effort has been made to ensure the accuracy of the information in this book as of the date of publication, the landscape of the subject matter covered is continuously evolving. Therefore, the author(s) and publisher expressly disclaim responsibility for any errors or omissions and reserve the right to update, alter, or revise the content without prior notice.

By continuing to read this book, you agree to be bound by the terms and conditions stated in this disclaimer. If you do not agree with these terms, it is your responsibility to discontinue use of this book immediately.

FOREWORD

"Not only is the Universe stranger than we imagine, it is stranger than we can imagine." —J.B.S. Haldane

If, like me, you have immense curiosity and reverence for the mysteries of existence, then I invite you to embark on this journey through Quantum Mysticism. Together we will explore a profound dialogue between realms often viewed as opposites: the rigorous empiricism of quantum physics and the transcendent insights of spirituality. It will challenge your understanding of reality and inspire wonder at the interconnectedness of all things.

Quantum physics invites us to peer into a world where the very fabric of reality is probabilistic, fluid, and interconnected. Whereas spiritual traditions across cultures have long intuited a cosmos unified by patterns of harmony, consciousness, and transcendence. These insights resonate deeply with the revelations of modern physics.

This book is about finding the common ground science and spirituality share in their quest for truth. These explorations don't provide definitive answers but inspire new questions, provoke thought, and nurture a sense of awe.

As you journey through these thought provoking ideas, I hope you find intellectual stimulation and a deeper appreciation for the profound unity underlying existence.

May it leave you as enchanted by the mysteries of life as the many philosophers, poets, scientists and scholars who have sought to unravel them across the ages.

    D.R.T. Stephens

CHAPTER 1: INTRODUCTION: EXPLORING SCIENCE AND SPIRIT

"The most beautiful experience we can have is the mysterious. It is the fundamental emotion that stands at the cradle of true art and true science." – Albert Einstein

Welcome to an intriguing journey through a realm that has baffled scientists and mystics alike: the confluence of quantum physics and spirituality. While at first glance, the empiricism of quantum physics seems irreconcilable with the metaphysical domain of spirituality, deeper inquiry often reveals striking similarities. Indeed, both disciplines ask grand questions about existence, interconnectedness, and the fabric of reality.

The Complexity of Quantum Physics

Quantum physics, a foundational theory in modern science, was formulated in the early 20th century. It postulates a counterintuitive, non-classical way of understanding reality at the most fundamental levels. From quantum entanglement to wave-particle duality, the concepts in quantum theory often seem as mystical and elusive as the esoteric principles found in ancient spiritual texts. It is a field that is as rigorous and mathematical as it is puzzling and paradoxical. Research continues to explore topics like superposition, non-locality, and quantum tunneling, which despite their scientific trappings, often venture into the realms of the inexplicable.

Origins of Quantum Mysticism: How
Early Twentieth Century Physics
Sparked Philosophical Questions

The turn of the twentieth century saw a major shift in scientific understanding, fueled by new discoveries in physics that radically challenged traditional beliefs. At the center of this revolution was quantum physics, a field that not only changed the course of scientific thought but also connected powerfully with ancient philosophical and spiritual questions. This merging of science and metaphysics, known as quantum mysticism, owes its origins to the groundbreaking theories and discoveries that arose during this key period.

The conceptual underpinning of quantum mechanics was laid in 1900 by Max Planck, who introduced the quantum, a theoretical leap that addressed abnormalities in blackbody radiation. Planck unintentionally lay the framework for a science that would overturn deterministic Newtonian physics by proposing that energy be quantized—existing in discrete packets rather than as a continuous flow. Shortly after, Albert Einstein's 1905 explanation of the photoelectric phenomenon solidified the concept of quantization by exposing light's particle-like nature. These early discoveries pointed to a reality that was significantly more fragmented and perplexing than previously thought.

The early decades of the twentieth century saw an avalanche of discoveries that upended the classical world's predictability. Niels Bohr's 1913 model of the atom introduced the concept of discrete energy levels, which challenged classical mechanics' assumption of continuity. Meanwhile, Werner Heisenberg's uncertainty principle and Erwin Schrödinger's wave equation demonstrated a probabilistic dimension to subatomic particle behavior. These advances marked the end of a mechanistic universe regulated by absolute predictability, and the emergence of a reality molded by probabilities, dualities, and uncertainties.

As these quantum occurrences challenged intuition, they also drew connections with long-held spiritual and philosophical traditions. The concept of wave-particle duality, for example, questioned the notion of fixed identities, reflecting non-dualistic ideas found in Hinduism and Buddhism, where phenomena are seen to be both different and interdependent. Similarly, the principle of uncertainty corresponded to philosophical teachings emphasizing the impermanence and unpredictability of the material world. Such analogies began to weaken the distinction between scientific inquiry and spiritual thought, paving the way for a more expansive discussion.

This junction is exemplified by quantum entanglement, a phenomena described in 1935 by physicists including Einstein, Boris Podolsky, and Nathan Rosen. Entanglement refers to the immediate correlation between two particles, regardless of distance, implying a non-local interconnectedness that contradicts traditional concepts of causation. Einstein first regarded this phenomena as "spooky action at a distance," but it later became a cornerstone of quantum mechanics and a source of intrigue for those investigating metaphysical themes of unity and oneness. Philosophical traditions that emphasize the linked aspect of existence, such as Advaita Vedanta and Taoism, found unexpected resonance with this scientific principle.

The cultural and philosophical ramifications of quantum mechanics were not lost on the scientists who pioneered the discipline. Philosophical traditions had a significant impact on figures such as Bohr, Schrödinger, and Heisenberg. Schrödinger, for example, was profoundly influenced by the Upanishads, ancient Hindu literature that investigate the unity of consciousness and the universe. His thoughts on the "oneness" of reality indicate a purposeful integration of his scientific understanding with spiritual insights, a pattern shared by other quantum pioneers. This interaction of ideas demonstrated quantum mechanics' capacity to not only explain physical occurrences but also to investigate questions of existence and meaning.

At the same time, quantum mechanics called into question classical physics' deterministic foundations, sparking new philosophical discussions about free will, causation, and the nature of reality. The probabilistic character of quantum occurrences implied that the future was not completely predetermined, which was consistent with existential and spiritual discourses emphasizing choice and freedom. This philosophical change influenced not only physics, but also spurred artists, writers, and philosophers from all disciplines to wrestle with the implications of a universe governed by probability rather than certainty.

The public's interest in quantum mechanics expanded as its implications were popularized by scientists and philosophers. Fritjof Capra's The Tao of Physics (1975) bridged the gap between physics and spiritual philosophy, captivating the interest of readers anxious to investigate the interdependence of science and mysticism. Capra's synthesis found connections between quantum theories and Eastern spiritual traditions, presenting them as complimentary ways of understanding reality. Although such interpretations were criticized for oversimplifying or distorting scientific principles, they emphasized quantum mechanics' lasting attraction as a tool for philosophical inquiry.

Despite its transforming impact, quantum mysticism is still a disputed area, with detractors cautioning against confusing metaphorical analogies with empirical facts. Scholars and scientists underline the significance of explaining quantum phenomena with rigor and precision, warning against the dangers of pseudoscience. Nonetheless, the connections between quantum mechanics and spiritual traditions have prompted multidisciplinary discussions, advocating a holistic approach to comprehending the intricacies of reality.

At its root, the origins of quantum mysticism highlight the fundamental interconnection of human research. The early twentieth-century quantum mechanics discoveries not only transformed physics, but also prompted humanity to reconsider age-old issues about the nature of reality, consciousness, and existence. Quantum physics continues to inspire a better understanding of the secrets that create the universe and our role within it by merging scientific rigour with philosophical investigation.

Bridging Separate Worlds: Why Some See Quantum Theory as Aligned with Spiritual Concepts

At the junction of quantum theory and spiritual thought, a unique discourse emerges, in which two seemingly distinct areas converge on similar issues about reality, existence, and consciousness. Quantum mechanics, with its paradoxical principles and profound ramifications, calls orthodox materialist frameworks into question. Simultaneously, many spiritual traditions have long dealt with comparable difficulties, providing insights that are consistent with quantum notions. This convergence has spurred a rising interest in investigating how the frameworks of science and spirituality might complement one other in fundamental ways.

Quantum mechanics has transformed the scientific knowledge of reality by proposing rules that contradict conventional logic. Its foundation is built on concepts such as wave-particle duality, uncertainty, and entanglement, all of which challenge deterministic world beliefs. These concepts challenge the Newtonian idea of a predictable, clockwork universe, replacing it with a probabilistic and linked reality. For example, the dual nature of light and matter—as both waves and particles—emphasizes the fluidity of existence, which has parallels in spiritual teachings emphasizing the coexistence of opposites or dualities.

The acknowledgment of the elusive nature of reality is a common theme throughout spiritual traditions. Many Eastern philosophies, including Hinduism, Buddhism, and Taoism, have long held that the material world is an illusion, or maya—an impermanent projection of a deeper, unseen truth. This concept is echoed by quantum mechanics, which is probabilistic in nature and relies on the observer to shape outcomes. The idea that particles exist in superposition, inhabiting several states at the same time until seen, contradicts spiritual teachings about reality's impermanence and fluidity.

The observer effect, a fundamental principle of quantum physics, has sparked considerable philosophical and spiritual interest. In studies such as the double-slit test, the presence of an observer impacts whether particles behave as waves or discrete particles, showing the interconnectedness of consciousness and reality. This has prompted some to believe that awareness may actively shape the universe. Spiritual traditions, particularly those emphasizing mindfulness and awareness, position consciousness at the heart of existence, implying that reality reflects the observer's inner state. While quantum theory does not expressly allow such metaphysical interpretations, the parallels have piqued the interest of both scientists and mystics.

Quantum entanglement presents yet another striking link between science and spirituality. This phenomenon, in which particles remain attached regardless of distance, challenges traditional concepts of locality and causality. Einstein famously described this as "spooky action at a distance," but entanglement has been experimentally confirmed, emphasizing the universe's interconnectedness. Entanglement resonates strongly with spiritual traditions that emphasize unity and interconnectedness, such as the Buddhist concept of Indra's Net or the Upanishadic idea of all existence being one. These connections have motivated some to investigate whether quantum interconnectedness might serve as a scientific foundation for spiritual concepts of unity.

However, there is some disagreement over how to connect quantum mechanics and spirituality. Critics argue that attempts to reconcile the two frequently oversimplify or misrepresent scientific concepts, leading to what some refer to as "quantum mysticism." Misinterpretations of quantum theory, such as claims that thoughts can directly influence physical outcomes via quantum processes, lack empirical support. Scientists warn against confusing figurative analogies with solid data, stressing the importance of distinguishing between speculative philosophy and proven physics.

Despite these criticisms, the interplay between quantum physics and spirituality provides rich ground for interdisciplinary inquiry. Both domains are concerned with serious existential concerns, such as what reality is. How does consciousness develop? What is the relationship between a person and the universe? Quantum physics and spirituality provide a deeper understanding of the universe and humanity's place within it by engaging in these shared inquiry.

Niels Bohr, a physicist, created the concept of complementarity, which provides a suitable foundation for connecting quantum physics to spirituality. Complementarity implies that seemingly opposing perspectives, such as wave and particle explanations of light, can be correct depending on the circumstances. This principle exemplifies spiritual acceptance of paradox, in which opposites coexist in harmony to reflect a deeper reality. This concept is embodied by Taoism's yin-yang dualism, which emphasizes the interdependence of opposites in making the whole.

Quantum mechanics calls into question reductionist scientific perspectives that strive to explain events by breaking them down into smaller, isolated components. Instead, quantum theory portrays a tightly interwoven reality in which the whole cannot be fully comprehended by examining its constituents separately. This holistic viewpoint is consistent with spiritual traditions that emphasize the interdependence of all things, promoting a change from materialism to a more integrated worldview.

Modern intellectuals and scholars have attempted to broaden this conversation by incorporating quantum insights into broader philosophical and spiritual frameworks. Fritjof Capra's famous work, The Tao of Physics, examines analogies between quantum mechanics and Eastern mysticism, proposing that both provide complimentary viewpoints on fundamental truths. Similarly, David Bohm's implicate order theory proposes that the cosmos functions as a cohesive whole, with an underlying order manifesting as visible phenomena. Bohm's views, while not universally accepted in physics, have resonated with spiritual beliefs in a cosmic oneness that underpins existence's multiplicity.

The relationship between quantum mechanics and spirituality has practical ramifications for how people live their lives. Recognizing the unpredictability and interdependence inherent in quantum concepts can encourage humility, flexibility, and adaptability. Spiritual practices that foster mindfulness, compassion, and a sense of oneness can help to reinforce this worldview, enabling people to navigate life with greater awareness and connectivity. These ideas, taken together, call for a change away from rigid, deterministic thinking and toward a more fluid, dynamic understanding of existence.

The convergence of quantum theory and spiritual notions reflects humanity's long-standing yearning to grasp the nature of reality and its deeper meaning. While quantum physics gives a scientific foundation for delving into the universe's fundamental building elements, spirituality provides a prism through which to understand the significance of these discoveries for consciousness, purpose, and connection. By connecting these disparate worlds, we obtain a deeper and more nuanced understanding of the mysteries that define our existence.

Scope of This Journey: Major Themes We Will Explore, From Entanglement to Consciousness

The study of quantum physics and its potential connections with spirituality transports us into a world of great intricacy and awe. This journey is about more than just the intersection of two fields; it's about delving into the deep fabric of ideas that question our view of reality. As we traverse this interaction, certain basic themes will emerge as focus points, forming the dialectic between quantum mechanics and spiritual thought. Entanglement, wave-particle duality, awareness, and the philosophical consequences of uncertainty are among the issues explored. Each provides a distinct perspective from which we might reinvent our role in the universe.

Entanglement has emerged as one of quantum physics' most interesting phenomena. Entanglement is a scientific term that defines a scenario in which particles remain coupled regardless of distance, so that the state of one particle instantly influences the state of another. This contradicts the traditional concept of locality, which holds that things can only interact through physical proximity or unambiguous causal links. Entanglement has been empirically demonstrated and is essential in quantum computing and cryptography. Beyond its technological implications, entanglement is profoundly ingrained in spiritual traditions that value interconnectivity. The Buddhist idea of Indra's Net, a huge network in which each node reflects the others, is similar to the holistic view provided by entangled particles. Through this lens, entanglement calls into question the boundaries of personality, implying that separation may be an illusion concealing a deeper connection.

Another fundamental element is reality's intrinsic duality. Wave-particle duality, the principle that phenomena such as photons and electrons can behave like waves or particles depending on how they are measured, is introduced by quantum mechanics. This duality defies classical categorization and compels us to reconsider the strict binaries that frequently determine our worldview. Similarly, spiritual traditions commonly accept paradoxical dualities, such as the divine's simultaneous transcendence and immanence, or the interplay of yin and yang. Both science and spirituality encourage us to transcend beyond reductive thinking, cultivating an openness to the coexistence of opposites. Accepting duality allows us to obtain a better grasp of the richness and nuance of existence.

The concept of consciousness connects quantum mechanics and spirituality. In quantum physics, the observer effect emphasizes measurement's perplexing role in determining a system's state. Observation appears to condense the probabilistic wave function into a single reality, posing fundamental problems regarding the link between consciousness and the physical world. While the scientific community's interpretations of this phenomenon differ greatly, it has spurred philosophical arguments about the nature of awareness and its potential role in influencing reality. Consciousness has long been central to spiritual teachings, with many defining it as the essential foundation of existence. The primacy of consciousness, whether expressed as the universal mind, Atman, or the interconnected web of awareness, provides a common foundation for discussion between quantum theory and spirituality.

Uncertainty, as expressed in Heisenberg's uncertainty principle, is also a major theme. According to this principle, certain attributes, such as position and momentum, cannot be measured with arbitrary precision at the same time. This essential constraint calls into question classical conceptions of determinism and predictability, implying that uncertainty is an unavoidable component of the universe. Uncertainty is frequently accepted as a path to enlightenment in spiritual systems, particularly those based on Eastern thought. The Tao Te Ching, for example, extols the merits of embracing the unknown and flowing with life's inherent volatility. Both quantum mechanics and spirituality provide avenues to humility and adaptation by acknowledging uncertainty as a fundamental element of reality rather than a defect.

As we explore deeper into these ideas, it becomes clear that the conversation between quantum physics and spirituality is about discovering complimentary insights rather than replacing one framework with another. Both disciplines need us to question our beliefs, push the boundaries of our knowledge, and remain open to the great mysteries that define our reality. This journey will investigate these intersections through a series of interconnected discussions, analyzing how quantum theory principles relate to and differ from spiritual perspectives. By delving into these topics, we hope to shed light on how science and spirituality may complement one another, opening up fresh perspectives on the universe and our place within it.

CHAPTER 2: FOUNDATIONS OF QUANTUM MECHANICS

"Nature loves to hide." – Heraclitus

Quantum mechanics is founded on ideas that question conventional understandings of reality, providing the framework for a scientific revolution in the early twentieth century. These principles—Planck's constant, wave-particle duality, and superposition—are not only fundamental to contemporary physics, but they also raise wider philosophical problems about the nature of existence and the relationship between perception and reality.

Planck's constant, indicated by hhh, originated as a solution to a major physics problem in the late nineteenth century. Scientists struggled at the time to explain blackbody radiation behavior, notably the ultraviolet disaster anticipated by classical physics. Max Planck proposed in 1900 that energy is quantized rather than continuous. According to his theory, energy is released or absorbed in discrete packets known as quanta, with each quantum equal to the frequency of the radiation. This connection is formally represented as E=hvE = h \nuE=hv, where EEE is the energy, hhh is Planck's constant, and ν uv is the frequency. The discovery of Planck's constant not only answered the blackbody radiation problem, but it also heralded the beginning of quantum mechanics. It proposed that the cosmos functions on discrete units at its most fundamental level, which differed significantly from classical physics' continuous assumptions.

Wave-particle duality further transformed scientific thinking by demonstrating that particles like electrons and photons have both wave-like and particle-like qualities depending on how they are perceived. This idea was initially proved by the double-slit experiment, in which particles traveling through two slits generated a wave-like interference pattern. However, when measured or witnessed, these identical particles behaved as distinct entities. The duality destroyed the traditional divide between particles and waves, combining two previously different categories into a more complex reality. Wave-particle duality called into question physicists' intuitive understandings of matter and energy, leading them to admit that these things could not be clearly defined. Furthermore, this idea raised philosophical problems regarding the observer's involvement in constructing reality—a subject that continues to resurface in talks connecting science and spirituality.

Superposition extends wave-particle duality by proposing that a quantum system can exist in numerous states at the same time until measured or seen. This notion is illustrated by Schrödinger's thought experiment, in which a hypothetical cat in a closed box is both alive and dead until the box is opened. Superposition is theoretically defined using a wave function, which reflects the probability of all conceivable quantum system states. When seen, the wave function collapses into a single state, raising important concerns about the nature of reality and awareness' role in influencing events. The concept of superposition emphasizes quantum mechanics' stochastic character, which contrasts dramatically with conventional physics' deterministic structure.

Collectively, these principles illustrate the quantum world's non-intuitive and paradoxical features. They question the traditional principles of objectivity, determinism, and separability, providing a new framework for comprehending occurrences that contradict common sense. Planck's constant, for example, emphasizes the granularity of energy, whereas wave-particle duality blurs the distinctions between seemingly opposing events, and superposition demonstrates the coexistence of possibilities. Together, they depict a dynamic and probabilistic reality rather than one that is fixed or unchanging.

These concepts have far-reaching ramifications, impacting fields such as philosophy, biology, and psychology. Planck's finding of quantized energy has analogs in cognitive science, where discrete neuronal firings influence perception and reasoning. Wave-particle duality is similar to philosophical arguments regarding existence's dualities, such as the interaction of mind and body or material and spiritual. Similarly, the principle of superposition corresponds to concepts of potentiality and choice, implying that reality itself may be more flexible and contingent than previously thought.

Quantum mechanics, through these fundamental laws, opens the door to more general metaphysical problems. The quantization of energy compels us to reexamine the fundamental building elements of reality, sparking discussions concerning the nature of existence and the beginnings of the cosmos. Wave-particle duality calls into question the concept of separateness, implying a deeper oneness underneath the apparent variety of forms. Superposition, with its emphasis on probabilities and possibilities, prompts a reconsideration of causation, determinism, and event interconnectivity.

These concepts have also spurred technological and experimental developments. Planck's constant supports quantum computing and spectroscopy, allowing for exact measurements at minuscule sizes. Wave-particle duality is critical to the development of electron microscopy and photonic devices, but superposition is essential in quantum information theory, allowing for phenomena like quantum entanglement and teleportation. The actual implementations of these ideas illustrate that they are relevant not only to abstract theory, but also to the technical advancements that shape modern civilization.

While the mathematical and experimental components of these principles are solidly grounded in empirical research, their larger implications encourage us to consider fundamental concerns about the nature of reality. Quantum physics questions the classical worldview, replacing certainty with uncertainty, determinism with chance, and separateness with interconnection. This paradigm shift is consistent with many spiritual traditions that emphasize the dynamic, interrelated, and impermanence of life.

Exploring these concepts takes us into a region where science and philosophy meet, providing complementary viewpoints on the universe's secrets. The quantized nature of energy, the duality of matter and waves, and the superposition of states all push us to embrace a more intricate, interrelated, and intriguing reality than we had previously envisioned. These principles serve as the foundation for quantum physics, leading us through a domain that defies intuition while providing significant insights into the fabric of reality. They remind us that the universe is more than just a collection of items; it is a dynamic interplay of forces, probabilities, and interactions that invites us to perpetually broaden our understanding of the cosmos.

Uncertainty and Measurement: How Heisenberg Destroyed Classical Determinism

Werner Heisenberg's introduction of the uncertainty principle in 1927 transformed scientists' understanding of measurement and the inherent constraints of observation in quantum physics. This notion not only represented a break from classical physics' deterministic worldview, but it also lay the groundwork for quantum theory's probabilistic character. Heisenberg's uncertainty principle became a cornerstone of quantum mechanics and an ongoing philosophical controversy because it challenged the long-held idea that accurate knowledge of a system's state was always available.

The uncertainty principle asserts that some physical qualities, such as location and momentum, cannot be exactly measured at the same time. The mathematical expression is $\Delta x \cdot \Delta p \geq \hbar/2$, where Δx represents uncertainty in location, Δp represents uncertainty in momentum, and $\hbar$ is the reduced Planck's constant. This equation demonstrates that attempting to reduce uncertainty in one attribute always increases uncertainty in the other. Unlike measurement mistakes in conventional physics, this uncertainty is inherent in the quantum system and represents a basic component of reality rather than experimental equipment limits.

Heisenberg's conceptual breakthrough was tremendous. Classical physics, which was founded on Newtonian mechanics, held that with enough information about a system's beginning state, its future behavior could be predicted with absolute certainty. This deterministic paradigm underlay most of scientific development in the 18th and 19th centuries, providing a feeling of order and predictability in the cosmos. The uncertainty principle, on the other hand, broke this sense of certainty, exposing that the tiny world follows completely different laws. In quantum physics, the process of measuring disrupts the system, making it difficult to get complete knowledge of all its attributes at the same time.

This challenge to determinism goes beyond practical measuring issues and into the fundamental essence of reality. Heisenberg's observations suggest that the cosmos is inherently probabilistic at its heart. For example, the location and momentum of an electron are probabilities defined by a wave function rather than fixed values waiting to be discovered. When the wave function is measured, it collapses to a precise value, but the particle remains in a state of potentiality. The probabilistic nature of quantum systems adds unpredictability, which calls deterministic interpretations of cause and effect into question.

The uncertainty principle also raises fascinating concerns about how the observer shapes reality. In classical physics, measurement was viewed as a passive process of discovery that revealed preexisting truths about a system. However, in quantum physics, measurement actively influences the outcome and collapses the wave function. This interplay between observer and observed calls into question the conventional distinction between subject and object, implying a participatory cosmos in which reality is not completely independent of our perceptions. Such notions are consistent with philosophical and spiritual traditions that emphasize the interdependence of the observer and the observed, obscuring the difference between thought and matter.

Heisenberg's principle has far-reaching consequences that affect subjects like as philosophy, psychology, and epistemology. Philosophically, the uncertainty principle calls for a rethinking of traditional concepts of causation and objectivity. It implies that, at its most fundamental level, reality may be about dynamic interactions and probabilities rather than fixed things. This transition is similar to Eastern ideologies like Buddhism and Taoism, which emphasize impermanence, interconnection, and the illusory nature of permanent identities. These traditions, such as quantum physics, advocate a mindset that values ambiguity and flexibility over rigid certainty.

The uncertainty principle has been used as a metaphor in psychology to explain human behavior and decision making. Measurement of one attribute of a particle upsets another, and attempts to examine and describe parts of human identity or experience might change those qualities as well. This metaphor emphasizes the intricacy and interconnection of human systems, in which actions, ideas, and emotions are inextricably linked and defy easy, deterministic explanation.

Epistemologically, Heisenberg's principle questions the limitations of human knowledge as well as the assumptions that underpin scientific investigation. It reminds us that science is more than just a tool for discovering absolute facts; it is also a framework for creating models that resemble reality within the restrictions of observation and measurement. The uncertainty principle thus promotes humility in scientific efforts by accepting the inherent limitations of our techniques as well as the potential of occurrences beyond our current comprehension.

The uncertainty principle has both challenged and fueled technological advancement. For example, the concept restricts measurement precision, such as electron microscope resolution and atomic clock stability. At the same time, it has spurred progress in quantum technologies such as quantum computing and quantum cryptography. Quantum computers use the probabilistic nature of quantum states to do computations well beyond the capability of conventional systems, whereas quantum cryptography uses the idea to construct secure communication protocols that are resistant to eavesdropping. These examples highlight how theoretical discoveries from the uncertainty principle have been transformed into practical advancements with far-reaching ramifications for technology and society.

Despite its revolutionary influence, the uncertainty principle has sparked debate and misinterpretation. Some have confused it with philosophical relativism, which implies that all facts are equally uncertain or subjective. In actuality, the principle is a precise mathematical statement regarding the behavior of quantum systems that does not imply that knowledge or truth is wholly subjective. Others have attempted to apply the theory to metaphysical realms, relating it to concepts like free will or awareness. While such interpretations are fascinating, they are still hypothetical and should be addressed with caution to avoid mixing scientific discoveries with unjustified extrapolations.

In order to reconcile the uncertainty principle with wider philosophical and spiritual frameworks, a balance of rigor and openness is required. The concept encourages us to challenge deterministic assumptions and embrace a more complex view of reality, but it does not replace evidence-based reasoning and critical inquiry. By recognizing the distinction between scientific truth and philosophical conjecture, we may appreciate the profound insights of the uncertainty principle without misrepresenting its meaning or relevance.

When we consider Heisenberg's legacy, it becomes evident that the uncertainty principle is more than just a technical aspect of quantum physics. It is a prism through which we may investigate the boundaries of knowledge, the interaction between observation and reality, and the ever-changing nature of existence. It encourages us to see uncertainty as a basic element of the cosmos, full of possibilities and linkages, rather than a defect or constraint. As a result, it provides a more in-depth understanding of quantum puzzles and their resonance with timeless philosophical problems about the nature of reality, knowing, and existence.

Non-Classical Insights: Why Quantum Ideas Defy Common Sense.

Quantum physics significantly altered humanity's perception of reality by offering notions that contradict conventional wisdom and daily experience. Quantum mechanics functions in a realm characterized by probabilities, superpositions, and intrinsic uncertainties, as opposed to classical mechanics, which follows predictable routes and interactions according to intuitive principles. These occurrences challenge how people generally view the world because they violate the deterministic, linear, and macroscopic frameworks that are common in everyday life.

Non-classical insights in quantum mechanics emerged in the early twentieth century as experimental observations showed phenomena that classical theories could not explain. Planck's quantized energy levels, the wave-particle duality of light proven in the double-slit experiment, and Heisenberg's uncertainty principle all revealed a microscopic realm that acts on principles that are foreign to macroscopic logic. These findings ushered in a paradigm change, compelling physicists to devise new conceptual frameworks to characterize particle and wave behavior, as well as the complicated interplay between them.

One of the most perplexing parts of quantum physics is the idea of wave-particle duality, which holds that phenomena such as photons and electrons have both particle-like and wave-like features depending on how they are perceived. When light passes through a diffraction grating, it behaves like a wave, resulting in an interference pattern, yet when detected individually by sensors, it behaves like discrete particles. This duality contradicts classical assumptions, which hold that things are either particles or waves but not both. The potential of quantum entities to emerge in different ways depending on the observing situation highlights a fundamental aspect of quantum mechanics: reality is dependent on measurement and observation.

Superposition adds another degree of intricacy to quantum mechanics. In classical systems, items exist in discrete states; a coin is either heads or tails, and a car is either parked or driving. Particles in quantum systems can live in a superposition of states, embodying numerous possibilities at the same time, until an observation pushes the system to a particular state. Schrödinger's thought experiment with a cat that is both alive and dead until the box is opened exemplifies the perplexing implications of superposition. This idea supports technologies like quantum computing, in which qubits use superposition to execute computations tenfold quicker than traditional bits. However, for most people, the concept of anything being in two conflicting situations contradicts common sense.

Einstein describes entanglement as "spooky action at a distance," and it is another significant divergence from classical thought. When two particles get entangled, their characteristics stay interdependent regardless of distance between them. Measuring one particle's state instantly identifies the condition of the other, even if they are light years distant. This behavior contradicts traditional intuitions about locality and causality, which hold that interactions should occur through direct touch or at fixed speeds. Entanglement has been empirically validated in various studies and is an important component of developing technologies such as quantum encryption. However, the implications for reality's interconnection call into question strongly held concepts of separateness and independence.

Quantum mechanics stands apart from conventional frameworks due to its probabilistic aspect. Quantum mechanics is based on probabilities, whereas Newtonian physics uses deterministic equations to predict precise events. The wave function, which is important to quantum theory, defines a particle's chance of being detected in different states rather than its actual position or route. An electron in an atom, for example, does not orbit the nucleus in the same way that a planet orbits a star; instead, it lives as a cloud of possibilities, its exact position unknown until measured. This probabilistic viewpoint necessitates a reconsideration of cause-and-effect linkages, implying that randomness is an inherent aspect of the cosmos rather than a limitation of human understanding.

Another important non-classical understanding is how perception shapes reality. Measurements in classical physics show objective features that exist irrespective of the observer. In quantum physics, measurement compresses the wave function and chooses a precise outcome from a set of probabilities. This active participation of the observer has spurred philosophical disputes concerning the nature of reality and the distinction between the observer and the observed. Some interpretations, such as the Copenhagen interpretation, hold that reality is ambiguous until viewed, whilst others, such as the many-worlds interpretation, propose that all conceivable outcomes occur in parallel universes, with observation selecting which branch of reality is experienced.

These nontraditional concepts call into question not just scientific understanding, but also philosophical and cultural systems. Classical physics offered a mechanical worldview in which the cosmos worked like a clockwork machine, regulated by deterministic principles. This viewpoint encouraged belief in predictability, control, and the separation of thought and matter. In contrast, quantum physics includes uncertainty, connectivity, and the active role of observation, leading to a more dynamic and relational picture of reality. These observations are consistent with philosophical traditions that emphasize the fluidity and interconnection of life, such as Buddhism and Taoism, which have long rejected fixed dualities and linear causality.

The contradictory character of quantum mechanics highlights the limitations of human perception, which evolved to traverse a macroscopic world ruled by classical physics. Our brains are trained to see objects as having fixed places, time as flowing uniformly, and causation as linear. In contrast, the quantum universe functions on sizes and principles that contradict our intuitive classifications. This mismatch emphasizes the significance of mathematical abstraction and experimental verification in increasing scientific knowledge, as human intuition alone is unable to comprehend the complexity of the quantum world.

Quantum mechanics has sparked fresh research into the nature of knowledge and reality. What does the fact that particles do not have defined attributes until measured suggest about the existence of an objective reality independent of observation? Can the cosmos be viewed as inherently probabilistic, or are there hidden variables that restore determinism on a deeper level? These topics are still being debated, showing quantum theory's significant philosophical implications.

Despite its difficulties to intuition, quantum mechanics has been extraordinarily effective in describing natural occurrences and allowing technological advances. It serves as the theoretical underpinning for semiconductors, lasers, MRI machines, and quantum computers, among other developments. These practical examples show that, while quantum notions are difficult to grasp, they provide strong tools for explaining and manipulating reality's basic principles.

The non-classical discoveries of quantum physics urge a greater appreciation for the universe's secrets and the changing character of human understanding. They remind us that reality is considerably more complex and dynamic than we initially realize, prompting us to broaden our intellectual frontiers and embrace the unknown. Quantum physics reshapes the scientific landscape by contradicting traditional intuition, inspiring new ways of thinking about existence, interconnection, and the limitations of cognition.

CHAPTER 3: SPIRITUAL FRAMEWORKS OF INTERCONNECTION

"As above, so below; as within, so without." – Attributed to Hermes Trismegistus (from the "Emerald Tablet")

Throughout history, ancient spiritual traditions have endeavored to explain the interconnectedness of reality, providing deep insights into the oneness of all things and the unseen forces that hold the world together. Long before current quantum physics, these traditions defined ideas of unity and causality that are still relevant today, such as entanglement, superposition, and nonlocality. Exploring the teachings of Hinduism, Buddhism, and mystical Judaism reveals that these systems of thought explored the secrets of life with depth and insight, inspiring both spiritual searchers and scientific explorers.

Hinduism's notion of cosmic oneness is deeply nuanced thanks to the idea of Brahman, the fundamental, formless truth that underpins all creation. The Upanishads depict Brahman as an endless and indivisible essence that manifests in the universe's many forms while remaining beyond them. The Chandogya Upanishad famously says, "Tat Tvam Asi" ("You Are That"), confirming the intrinsic oneness of the individual soul (Atman) and the universal soul (Brahman). This concept implies a basic interconnectivity that is consistent with the quantum principle of entanglement, in which particles remain associated across long distances, functioning as if they are part of a single unified system. The Hindu notion of Maya, or illusion, adds to the paradoxical aspect of quantum reality by positing that the plurality and separateness observed in the material world are distortions of the underlying oneness.

Krishna adds to this interrelated awareness in the Bhagavad Gita by introducing the concept of karma, which is a web of deeds and repercussions that extends beyond individual lifetimes. Karma is more than just a moral framework; it is an awareness of the intimately intertwined fabric of reality, in which each action has ripple effects that affect the entire. This causal chain is conceptually similar to hidden variables in quantum physics, in which outcomes can be influenced by unseen elements beyond immediate experience. By emphasizing the oneness of all creatures and the interconnection of their acts, Hinduism anticipated the present scientific view that the cosmos is a dynamic interaction of forces and relationships rather than separate individuals.

Buddhism's interdependent origination philosophy, known as Pratītyasamutpāda, explores the concept of oneness and hidden energies. According to this view, all phenomena develop in dependence on other phenomena, ruling out the possibility of autonomous existence. The renowned image of Indra's Net, adopted from Mahayana Buddhism, eloquently portrays this concept: the cosmos is shown as an infinite web of jewels, each reflecting the other in a limitless interplay of light and connectedness. This picture is intimately associated with the quantum concept of nonlocality, in which particles are connected in ways that contradict classical separateness. The interwoven gems represent how all creatures are interrelated, with each portion reflecting the whole—an theory that is intriguingly similar to contemporary physics' holographic principle.

The Buddhist worldview also emphasizes impermanence and the emptiness (Shunyata) of intrinsic existence, which are consistent with quantum physics' probabilistic character. In the quantum realm, particles exist as probabilistic wave functions rather than fixed things, expressing potentialities that only collapse into definite states when seen. Similarly, in Buddhism, phenomena are viewed as devoid of essential essence, existing only as temporary combinations of causes and circumstances. This viewpoint promotes a dynamic understanding of reality, one that is constantly altered by interactions and processes—a position that has startling similarities in the shifting interpretations of quantum systems.

Mystical Judaism, especially as articulated in the Kabbalistic tradition, provides profound insights into the oneness of existence and the unseen forces at work in the universe. The notion of Ein Sof, the limitless and unfathomable source of all being, is central to Kabbalah thinking. Ein Sof transcends all duality, being as the ultimate oneness from whence the plurality of creation emerges. The ten Sefirot, or divine characteristics, are the channels via which the infinite shows itself in the finite universe, resulting in a framework of interrelated forces that maintain and modify existence. This hierarchical yet unified view of creation is reminiscent of the layered intricacies of quantum systems, in which various components emerge from underlying fields and interactions.

Kabbalistic teachings also explore the concepts of hiddenness and disclosure, a duality that reflects the quantum link between observation and reality. The Zohar, a basic Kabbalistic literature, defines heavenly light as hidden and disclosed via the processes of creation, comparing the universe to a garment that both conceals and displays the divine essence. This interplay of concealment and manifestation is analogous to quantum physics' wave-particle duality, in which particles reveal various parts of their existence according on the observable context. Furthermore, the Kabbalistic belief in Tikkun Olam, or world repair, emphasizes people' interwoven obligation to harmonize with the cosmic order, which is consistent with the relational concept of quantum entanglement.

The reoccurring notion of oneness runs throughout these traditions, implying a remarkable connection with quantum physics' basic principles. However, it is critical to understand the distinctions in intent and approach between spiritual insights and scientific hypotheses. While quantum physics gives mathematically precise explanations of physical occurrences, spiritual teachings provide interpretative frameworks for comprehending the nature of existence and humanity's role within it. The shared ability to question preconceptions, broaden perception, and inspire wonder is what binds these fields together, not their equivalent.

The intersection of traditional spiritual teachings and quantum physics also creates new opportunities for multidisciplinary research. Researchers and philosophers have used these traditions' metaphors and concepts to explore concerns regarding consciousness, causation, and the nature of reality. For example, the notion of interconnection has affected ecological and ethical discourses, advocating comprehensive approaches to solving global concerns. Similarly, the focus on hidden forces has sparked new research into the interaction of mind and matter, as seen by the growing areas of quantum cognition and integrative medicine.

While it is easy to draw direct similarities between spiritual teachings and quantum physics, use caution to prevent oversimplification or distortion. Spiritual and scientific languages have diverse functions and work in various paradigms. However, their shared themes of oneness, interconnectedness, and hidden complexity imply that they are complimentary rather than incompatible, with each providing vital insights into the mysteries of existence.

Ancient insights from Hinduism, Buddhism, and mystical Judaism weave a complex tapestry of ideas that are consistent with quantum physics findings. These traditions show a profound and everlasting view of reality by delving into oneness, hidden powers, and interconnectedness. By combining these teachings with quantum physics concepts, we are urged to broaden our viewpoint, appreciating the beauty and complexity of a reality that defies categorization. This interaction between ancient knowledge and modern science continues to spark new questions and possibilities, paving the way for a more comprehensive understanding of the universe and our role in it.

Mystical Oneness: Teachings on the Cosmic Mind or Universal Essence

Throughout human history, numerous spiritual traditions have relied on the concept of mystical oneness, which is the belief of one interrelated cosmic essence or mind that connects all things together. It provides fundamental insights into the nature of reality, our role in it, and the possibility of transcending imagined boundaries between ourselves and world. Mystical teachings on oneness have arisen separately throughout civilizations, yet they share an underlying unity that is consistent with developing insights in current physics, notably quantum mechanics. Examining the viewpoints presented by various spiritual frameworks allows us to better understand how these concepts contribute to our understanding of interconnectivity and life.

The Upanishads in Hindu philosophy provide one of the most extensive examinations of oneness through the notion of Brahman. Brahman, described as the ultimate, unchanging reality, is the universe's source and essence. The link between Brahman and Atman, or individual soul, exemplifies the fundamental oneness of all reality. This relationship is emphasized in the Sanskrit phrase "Tat Tvam Asi," which means "You Are That," emphasizing the unity of human awareness with the global essence. Such teachings blur the line between observer and observed, implying that distinctions in the material world are illusions, or Maya, that obscure the undivided essence of Brahman.

This concept of oneness is strikingly similar to the present understanding of quantum fields, in which particles are no longer viewed as distinct entities but as excitations within a common underlying field. Just as the Upanishads describe the cosmos as a manifestation of Brahman, quantum field theory depicts the universe as an interwoven tapestry of energy, with each particle interconnected to the whole. Although their frameworks differ, Hindu mysticism and quantum physics share a view of reality as essentially unified.

Buddhism's teaching of interdependent origination, known as Pratītyasamutpāda, expands on the concept of mystical oneness. This principle holds that all phenomena develop in dependence on other phenomena, denying the concept of an autonomous self or essence. Shunyata, or emptiness, is a Mahayana Buddhist doctrine that asserts that all things lack fundamental existence and exist solely via their interactions with other phenomena. This idea of interconnectivity is consistent with the scientific theory of entanglement, in which particles impact one another instantly, regardless of distance. Just as Shunyata indicates a relational rather than inherent identity, quantum entanglement calls into question traditional ideas of location and separation.

The metaphor of Indra's Net, a key picture in Mahayana Buddhist thinking, provides a vivid representation of oneness. Each node in this infinite network is a diamond that reflects all other jewels, representing the interconnectedness and interdependence of all creatures and occurrences. The reflections inside reflections underline that the whole is present in each portion, echoing current physics' holographic principle, which holds that every piece of the world stores information about the whole. This deep discovery encourages reflection on the inseparability of life and the false nature of personal boundaries.

Through the teachings of Kabbalah, mystical Judaism adds a rich story to the discussion of cosmic oneness. This tradition is centered on the notion of Ein Sof, the endless and limitless heavenly source. Ein Sof transcends all duality and embodies the purest expression of oneness. The Sefirot, which symbolize the divine's expression in the corporeal world, emerge from Ein Sof. This emanation process corresponds to the unfolding of the cosmos in scientific cosmology, where basic rules and constants give rise to the universe's structure and complexity.

The Kabbalistic concept of divine sparks imbedded in all creation underlines the importance of connection. According to Lurianic Kabbalah, the duty of mankind is Tikkun Olam, or "repairing the world," which entails identifying and uplifting these sparks back to their origin. This spiritual practice exemplifies a sense of togetherness and a responsibility to align with the cosmic order. This is analogous to the idea of coherence in physics, in which systems preserve order and unity despite seeming chaos. Kabbalah mirrors the quantum notion that all diversity is based on a linked reality by highlighting the hidden divine nature in all things.

Sufism, Islam's mystical offshoot, provides a different perspective on oneness through the notion of Tawhid, or God's unity. Sufi poetry and teachings honor the disintegration of the ego and the union of the individual soul with the divine. Rumi, a famous Sufi poet, beautifully explains this union: "You are not a drop in the ocean; you are the entire ocean in a drop." This picture is consistent with reality's holographic aspect, in which each piece carries the essence of the whole. The Sufi path entails transcending the illusion of separation in order to recognize the underlying oneness of all things, a realization that shares conceptual parallels with quantum non-locality and the interconnectedness of matter and energy.

Indigenous spiritual traditions stress the interconnection of life and the universe. Many Native American cosmologies see the Earth, sky, and all living things as part of a holy unity. The Lakota term Mitákuye Oyás'iŋ, which means "All My Relations," embodies this worldview by acknowledging the connection of all creation. This holistic worldview promotes respect, responsibility, and harmony with nature, reflecting the ecological implications of quantum connection. Indigenous knowledge, by recognizing the inherent oneness of all existence, echoes quantum understanding of a cosmos bound together by unseen threads of connectivity.

Despite their disparate cultural and philosophical settings, these faiths share an acknowledgment of oneness as an essential part of life. This insight calls into question the reductionist assumption that reality can only be completely grasped by examining its constituent pieces. Instead, it encourages an integrated viewpoint that recognizes the connected and dynamic aspect of existence. The connection between spiritual teachings and quantum principles does not imply equality, but rather a common ability to inspire wonder and deepen our understanding of the universe.

When tackling the fundamental mysteries of life, both modern science and spirituality face linguistic and conceptual framework restrictions. Quantum mechanics, with its counterintuitive occurrences and probabilistic character, has unveiled a world that conventional physics could never have envisioned. Mystical traditions, via poetic and symbolic representations, also push the frontiers of comprehension, asking us to see beyond appearances and accept the interconnection of all things.

The interplay between mystical oneness and quantum physics opens up new avenues for interdisciplinary research. It invites scientists, philosophers, and spiritual searchers to work together to find the fundamental truths that link us. By combining traditional wisdom ideas with modern science, mankind may achieve a more comprehensive and harmonious knowledge of the cosmos and our role within it.

Revisiting Core Beliefs: How These

Perspectives Reflect Quantum's Interconnectedness

The connections between spiritual traditions emphasizing oneness and the interrelated phenomena revealed by quantum physics have prompted serious reassessment of long-held assumptions. The concept that reality exists as a unified, interconnected whole, rather than discrete components, is central to these analogies. By examining spiritual and scientific frameworks via this lens, we discover common truths that contradict materialism and reductionist worldviews, providing a more complete explanation of life.

Interconnectivity is one of the most noticeable junctions. Entanglement, for example, demonstrates in quantum physics that particles may impact one another instantly, even when separated by great distances. This contradicts traditional conceptions of separateness and locality, implying that the cosmos functions as a cohesive system. Similarly, spiritual traditions from many cultures have long stressed the interconnection of all life. Indigenous worldviews, for example, see the Earth as a living creature, with each element interrelated and important to the whole. This is consistent with quantum entanglement's argument that no entity exists in isolation.

The Buddhist notion of interdependent origination strengthens the concept of relational existence. According to this doctrine, all phenomena emerge from other phenomena, producing a web of relationships that determine their character. This viewpoint is consistent with the quantum finding that particles are characterized not only by their inherent qualities, but also by how they interact with other particles. In this sense, both quantum physics and Buddhist philosophy reject the concept of autonomous things, instead portraying reality as a complex network of dynamic interactions.

Revisiting key ideas demonstrates a mutual appreciation for contradiction and ambiguity. Quantum physics has challenged deterministic interpretations of reality by presenting probabilistic outcomes and the notion of uncertainty. According to Heisenberg's uncertainty principle, certain attributes, such as location and momentum, cannot be precisely measured at the same time. This intrinsic unpredictability calls into question the conventional wisdom that the cosmos is completely knowable and predictable. Similarly, spiritual traditions have always welcomed existence's mystery and paradoxes. Taoism, for example, emphasizes the Tao's intrinsic dualities, in which opposites like as light and dark are interrelated and inseparable. This is consistent with quantum physics' dual particle-wave nature, in which light and matter may behave as both waves and particles depending on how they are perceived.

This overlap also applies to issues of awareness and the observer's involvement in constructing reality. Quantum physics has demonstrated that the process of measuring compresses a particle's wave function, defining its state. This observer effect has been linked to spiritual traditions that emphasize the importance of observation and awareness in developing one's worldview. According to Advaita Vedanta, the character of reality is determined by the observer's awareness, implying a direct connection between consciousness and the material universe. While the scientific community is still split on the significance of the observer effect, the parallels with spiritual discoveries demonstrate a common interest in understanding the interaction between thought and matter.

The linked aspect of existence is also consistent with the notion of global oneness found in mystical traditions. According to Kabbalah, the cosmos is an emanation of Ein Sof, the limitless and indivisible divine source. This corresponds to the theory in quantum physics that all particles arise from a common quantum field, which unifies the universe at its most fundamental level. Similarly, the Sufi notion of Tawhid, or God's oneness, stresses that all visible world divides are deceptive, since everything ultimately reflects a single divine nature. These teachings challenge dualistic worldviews and promote a broad perspective of reality that transcends apparent bounds.

By reviewing these spiritual and scientific viewpoints, we are urged to reexamine interrelated ethical systems. The recognition of oneness in quantum physics and spirituality stresses a shared responsibility for the collective whole. In quantum jargon, particle interdependence emphasizes the importance of cooperative systems, as shown in ecological applications of quantum principles. Similarly, spiritual traditions promote harmony and balance, encouraging people to act in ways that support and enhance the interrelated web of life. These ideas motivate a change from individualism to a relational ethos, in which the well-being of the whole is prioritized.

Modern interpretations of these analogies have also spurred disputes about the boundaries of comparison and the dangers of confusing metaphor with scientific theory. Spiritual language frequently employs poetic and symbolic phrases, whereas science is based on actual data and tested theories. Critics warn against extrapolating quantum ideas into the spiritual sphere, noting that it can obfuscate science' solid basis. However, this discourse has also created new opportunities for interdisciplinary research, enabling scientists, philosophers, and spiritual thinkers to have important talks about the nature of reality.

The merging of quantum and spiritual viewpoints calls into question reductionist frameworks that attempt to describe complex events simply through their constituent components. Instead, these intersections foster holistic methods that take into account the emergent features of interrelated systems. This trend is especially noticeable in domains such as quantum biology, where researchers are investigating how quantum processes underpin life's intricacies, from photosynthesis to enzyme function. By linking disciplines, these investigations reveal the underlying connection that underpins both scientific and spiritual worldviews.

When we examine our underlying beliefs, quantum physics and spirituality both compel us to confront existential concerns about identity and purpose. If reality is inherently interrelated, the self cannot be seen as a separate entity, but rather as part of a larger totality. This discovery has transformational ramifications for how people see their place in the cosmos. Spiritual traditions stress this change via activities that foster harmony, such as meditation, prayer, and rituals that recognize interconnectedness. Similarly, quantum physics questions the concept of separation by showing the profound connections that weave the fabric of existence.

Reconsidering key ideas in light of quantum mechanics and spiritual discoveries opens up possibilities for reconciling science and spirituality. While these realms function under unique paradigms, their overlapping themes of interconnectivity, contradiction, and relational existence point to a complementing conversation rather than a destructive dichotomy. This synthesis promotes a more expansive perspective of reality, one that values both scientific rigor and the profound mysteries that inspire awe and wonder.

As humankind continues to wrestle with the ramifications of these viewpoints, the interplay between quantum physics and spirituality offers rich ground for investigation. We are urged to transcend constraints, improve our awareness of the universe, and cultivate a more harmonious connection with the world around us by accepting the connectivity that exists at the center of both worlds.

CHAPTER 4: WAVE-PARTICLE DUALITY AND SPIRITUAL PARADOX

"The world is not composed of things; it is a dance of relationships." – Fritjof Capra

The double-slit experiment is one of quantum mechanics' most iconic demonstrations, giving deep insights into the nature of matter and contradicting long-held beliefs about physical reality.

This experiment, first carried out by Thomas Young in 1801 to investigate the qualities of light, has since become a cornerstone of quantum theory, demonstrating matter's dual wave–particle duality. The double-slit experiment has transformed our knowledge of the world by exposing the limitations of classical physics and raising issues about the role of observation in shaping physical occurrences.

The experiment's setup is deceptively basic. A light source and a detector screen are separated by a two-slit barrier. When light passes through the slits, an interference pattern appears on the screen, with alternating bands of bright and dark regions that resemble wave behavior. This finding is consistent with the classical model of light as a wave that may spread, overlap, and interfere. The experiment, however, takes an unexpected turn when individual particles, such as electrons, are passed through the slits one at a time. Instead of creating two distinct clusters corresponding to the slits, the particles generate an interference pattern over time, as if each particle behaved like a wave and passed through both slits at the same time.

This result contradicts traditional wisdom. How can a single particle travel two directions simultaneously? Superposition, a quantum notion, has the solution. In the absence of measurement, particles exist in a probabilistic state, as defined by a wave function that includes all potential outcomes. The interference pattern shows the overlapping probabilities of the particle's potential routes, which is characteristic of wave-like activity. This calls into question the conventional concept of particles as discrete entities with fixed places and paths, in favor of a probabilistic and relational understanding of reality.

The most baffling feature of the double-slit experiment is when scientists try to see which slit the particle travels through. When a measuring equipment is used to follow the particle's passage, the wave function collapses and the interference pattern disappears. Instead, the particles act like traditional objects, generating two groups on the detection screen. This significant shift emphasizes the observer effect, a phenomenon in which the act of measuring alters the result. In quantum physics, simply seeing a system alters its behavior, emphasizing the interplay between the observer and the observed.

The double-slit experiment has far-reaching philosophical and metaphysical consequences for our understanding of reality. The experiment implies that reality is not fixed and autonomous, but rather arises from interaction and observation. This viewpoint is shared by several spiritual traditions, like Hinduism and Buddhism, which see the universe as a linked and dynamic web of interactions rather than a collection of separate objects. <u>The notion that observation plays a key role in forming reality is consistent with teachings on the role of awareness in producing experience.</u>

Furthermore, the experiment generates significant contradictions that call conventional wisdom into question. How can a particle exist in two places at the same time? What drives the shift from probabilistic to definite outcomes? These concerns have sparked discussions and interpretations among physicists and philosophers. The Copenhagen interpretation, attributed to Niels Bohr, holds that quantum systems remain in a condition of potentiality until measured, at which time their attributes become definite. This perspective highlights the importance of observation and the interconnectedness of the observer and the observed.

Hugh Everett's many-worlds interpretation, on the other hand, proposes that every potential consequence of a quantum event exists in its own parallel reality. In the double-slit experiment, this indicates that the particle travels through both slits at the same time, but each path corresponds to a separate branch of reality. While this interpretation does not require wave function collapse, it adds the idea of an endless multiverse, raising problems about the nature of existence and identity.

The double-slit experiment also calls into question the concept of objective reality. Can reality exist independent of perception if particle activity is determined by whether or not they are observed? This topic has similarities in epistemology, which is the discipline of philosophy concerned with the nature and limitations of knowing. The experiment demonstrates that knowledge is more than just a passive reflection of an independent reality; it is an active process that alters the things it strives to comprehend. This realization has far-reaching consequences for scientific investigation, underlining the value of humility and openness in the face of ambiguity.

The double-slit experiment showed the dual wave-particle nature, which has practical implications in technology and innovation. Understanding particle behavior as waves supports advances in quantum computing, where superposition allows for simultaneous processing of numerous possibilities. The experiment also helps to shape the design of quantum sensors, which use the sensitivity of quantum states to detect minute changes in physical environments. These technologies have the potential to impact industries ranging from cryptography to health by exhibiting the transformational power of quantum discoveries.

Beyond its scientific and technical relevance, the double-slit experiment prompts thought on the nature of duality and contradiction. Dualities such as light and dark, self and other, or life and death are frequently viewed in spiritual traditions as complimentary components of a larger whole. This viewpoint is supported by the experiment's discovery of matter's dual wave-particle nature, which implies that reality cannot be reduced to simple categories. Instead, it represents a dynamic interplay of opposites, allowing for a more sophisticated and comprehensive explanation of reality.

The experiment also emphasizes the importance of ambiguity and mystery in the advancement of knowledge. The interference pattern seen in the absence of measurement represents the inherent uncertainty of quantum systems, as described by Heisenberg's uncertainty principle. According to this concept, some attributes, such as location and momentum, cannot be determined with arbitrary precision at the same time. While uncertainty tests deterministic theories, it also gives up new possibilities for inquiry and innovation. By embracing the unknown, scientists and intellectuals can overcome the constraints of conventional frameworks and find new possibilities.

The double-slit experiment, in the larger context of human experience, serves as a metaphor for the interaction of choice and possibility. Individuals traverse a landscape of potential outcomes molded by their actions and perceptions, much as particles exist in a state of flux until they are noticed. This viewpoint fosters awareness and intentionality, acknowledging the enormous influence of observation and action on reality.

The double-slit experiment continues to fascinate and challenge scientists, providing insights into the underlying nature of matter, the importance of observation, and the interconnection of all things. Its contradictory results serve as a reminder that reality is more intricate and perplexing than it looks, encouraging continued investigation and meditation. As science and spirituality explore these questions, the experiment demonstrates the power of curiosity and amazement in broadening the bounds of knowing.

Faith's Paradox: Similarities to Dualities
(Yin-Yang, Immanence/Transcendence)

Quantum physics' complicated paradoxes frequently draw comparisons with dualities found in spiritual and philosophical traditions. These dichotomies, such as the interaction of Yin and Yang in Chinese philosophy or the concepts of immanence and transcendence in religious discourse, show an underlying tension between seemingly opposed elements. This dynamic is mirrored by quantum physics, particularly ideas such as wave-particle duality and the uncertainty principle, which portray a reality that refuses simplicity and feeds on paradoxes.

In traditional Chinese thinking, Yin and Yang represent the interconnectedness of opposites, which is central to Daoist philosophy. This duality, shown artistically as a circle divided into whirling black and white sides, represents balance and oneness. Yang symbolizes activity, light, and energy, whereas Yin represents receptivity, darkness, and repose. Importantly, each carries a seed of the other, implying that neither force exists in isolation; they are constantly transformed into one. This dynamic equilibrium is consistent with quantum physics' wave-particle duality, which states that particles like photons and electrons may display both wave-like and particle-like qualities depending on how they are perceived. The presence of various traits emphasizes the fact that reality is a mix created by context and interaction rather than a single item.

The Yin-Yang concept is also consistent with the probabilistic character of quantum states. Quantum superposition, in which particles exist in numerous states at the same time, calls into question binary classification. The Yin-Yang notion provides a philosophical prism through which to explain such events, stressing the fluidity and interconnection of life. For example, in the double-slit experiment, the particle's dual activity as both a wave and a particle might be seen as a quantum expression of Yin and Yang, in which seeming opposites coexist and reveal deeper truths when viewed as whole.

Theological ideas such as immanence and transcendence highlight the connection of spiritual and quantum problems. Immanence refers to the divine presence inside the material world, which is accessible and connected with the everyday. In contrast, transcendence refers to the divine as something beyond and independent of the physical sphere, ineffable and limitless. Many religious traditions wrestle with the divine's competing characteristics, frequently viewing them as complementary rather than contradictory. For example, Christianity presents God as both immanent through Christ's incarnation and transcendent as the creator of the universe. Similarly, in Hinduism, Brahman refers to both the impersonal, transcendent reality and the immanent essence found in all entities.

Quantum physics' description of particles and fields involves a similar interaction of immanence and transcendence. At the quantum scale, entities such as electrons exist as probability distributions represented by wave functions that pervade space, rather than being limited to specific places. This duality mirrors the immanent-transcendent nature of spiritual things, implying that particles have both localized (immanent) and extended (transcendent) properties. The process of measuring, which converts the wave function into a specific state, is analogous to the human experience of seeing the holy, in which the transcendent becomes palpable via ritual, prayer, or spiritual insight.

The conflict between determinism and free will is another example of the conundrum of dualities, which has been studied in both quantum physics and spiritual traditions. Classical physics, based on determinism, holds that if beginning circumstances are understood, all occurrences can be predicted. Quantum mechanics, as exemplified by Heisenberg's uncertainty principle, upsets this paradigm by introducing intrinsic uncertainty. This principle asserts that a particle's location and momentum cannot be measured simultaneously with arbitrary precision, inserting a random element into the fabric of reality. Spiritual viewpoints, particularly those based on mystical traditions, frequently see such ambiguity as a mirror of cosmic freedom, in which divine will or universal awareness acts beyond human knowledge.

Science and spirituality are united in their recognition of mystery and complexity through the interaction of dualities. Niels Bohr established the complementarity principle in quantum physics, which states that wave and particle descriptions are mutually incompatible yet equally important for adequately explaining quantum occurrences. This concept opposes reductionist attempts to interpreting reality, instead pushing for a holistic vision that accepts paradoxes. Similarly, spiritual traditions frequently emphasize the coexistence of opposing forces as a means to greater insight. The Bhagavad Gita, for example, reconciles the opposite paths of activity and renunciation by portraying them as complementary elements of self-realisation.

The paradoxes of quantum physics and spiritual dualities stimulate in-depth studies on the nature of knowing and perception. The observer effect in quantum mechanics emphasizes the relational character of reality by influencing the observed system through measurement. This approach is consistent with spiritual beliefs that view the cosmos as linked and interactive, with individual awareness influencing experience. The concept of dependent origination, for example, in Buddhism argues that experiences develop as a result of interdependent causes and circumstances, highlighting existence's fluid and interrelated aspect.

The connections between quantum paradoxes and spiritual dualities extend to ethical and existential concerns. Acceptance of doubt and disagreement promotes humility, curiosity, and receptivity to new ideas. By questioning entrenched ideas, this approach promotes creativity and discovery in science. Spiritual practice cultivates compassion and tolerance by admitting human understanding's limits and celebrating variety.

The connection between quantum physics and spiritual dualities has sparked multidisciplinary inquiries ranging from philosophical inquiry to creative expression. Writers, poets, and painters have used these themes to produce works that highlight the interplay of opposites and represent the vast fabric of life. Philosophers have utilized quantum mechanics findings to question materialist paradigms and advocate for a more holistic explanation of reality that combines science and spirituality. Such initiatives demonstrate the transforming power of embracing paradox, in which the synthesis of apparently opposing aspects creates new avenues for thought and creation.

The dualities represented by Yin-Yang, immanence-transcendence, and quantum mechanics call into question the distinctions between science and spirituality. Both fields deal with complex topics, delving into the fundamental interaction of opposites in the fabric of reality. Recognizing these resonances allows mankind to gain a deeper appreciation for the mysteries that connect scientific investigation and spiritual insight, encouraging a more integrative and comprehensive view of reality. As we continue to investigate these paradoxes, we are reminded that the search for truth is an embracing of the infinite complexity that defines the universe, rather than a desire for certainty.

Lessons in openness: Accepting that reality might hold contradictory truths

The nature of reality, as revealed by quantum physics and spiritual traditions, calls into question the strict binary frames that dominate human experience. At the core of this epiphany is the idea that reality may tolerate seemingly conflicting realities, implying a move from rigid classification to a more flexible and integrated comprehension. Quantum physics, with its counterintuitive principles, and spiritual teachings, with their focus on transcendence and oneness, both encourage an openness to contradiction as a path to higher understanding.

Paradoxes are more than just abnormalities in the quantum world; they are essential to the essence of reality. The double-slit experiment, for example, illustrates how particles may behave like waves or particles depending on the observation. This duality challenges classical logic, which holds that an item cannot have mutually incompatible attributes at the same time. Instead, quantum physics depicts a universe in which such paradoxes persist, implying that reality functions on rules beyond traditional logic. Similarly, spiritual traditions have long seen the presence of opposites as critical to comprehending reality. In Taoism, the notion of Yin and Yang encompasses the interdependence of opposites, demonstrating how dual energies coexist and complement each other to make a harmonious whole. This philosophical approach is consistent with the quantum insight that reality is both-and rather than either-or.

The paradox goes beyond wave-particle duality to other fundamental concepts of quantum physics. Superposition, for example, permits particles to remain in various states until they are measured. This idea goes against deterministic frameworks by stressing potentiality over fixed states. This emphasis on potentiality is frequently reiterated in spiritual teachings. According to the Buddhist teaching of Śūnyatā, or emptiness, all things lack inherent existence and are determined by interdependent interactions. This viewpoint holds that reality is fluid and contingent, similar to the probabilistic tendencies found in quantum systems.

These connections between quantum physics and spiritual teachings stimulate a rethinking of how knowledge is created. Both disciplines emphasize the limitations of rigid frameworks and perfect certainty, arguing instead for an openness to ambiguity and complexity. In science, this openness is reflected in the acknowledgment of uncertainty as a basic feature of quantum theory, as shown by Heisenberg's uncertainty principle. Spiritually, it manifests in practices that accept mystery, such as contemplative meditation or mystical prayer, where the purpose is to live in contradiction rather than resolve it. This common focus on openness implies that progress, whether scientific or spiritual, is dependent on integrating inconsistencies into a greater knowledge rather than removing them altogether.

In quantum physics, the observer effect emphasizes the need of being open. The concept of an objective reality independent of perception is challenged by proving that the act of measuring effects the outcome. This approach is compatible with spiritual insights into the subjective nature of experience. In Hinduism, Māyā refers to the deceptive aspect of the universe as seen by the senses. As a result, both quantum physics and spiritual traditions emphasize the interaction between perception and reality, urging humility and acknowledging human understanding's limitations.

Embracing contradiction also promotes a transformation in identity and perspective. The cosmos is frequently envisioned in classical physics as a mechanical system made up of discrete, interacting components. However, quantum mechanics portrays a highly interwoven universe in which distinctions and boundaries blur. This transformation is consistent with spiritual beliefs that emphasize oneness over separation. Tawhid, according to Sufism, represents the oneness of existence, implying that all divisions are false and that the divine pervades everything. Recognizing this interconnectivity may lead to a fundamental shift in how people interact with themselves, others, and the world.

This shift has practical ramifications, particularly in terms of promoting empathy and ethical conduct. Recognizing all things' interconnectivity calls into question the self-centeredness that so frequently fuels conflict and exploitation. Instead, it fosters a sense of shared duty and caring. This viewpoint is consistent with quantum physics principles, which state that one particle's behavior cannot be fully understood without considering its interactions with others. Similarly, human activities are never isolated; rather, they ripple across the fabric of reality, having consequences far beyond their immediate setting.

However, accepting paradoxes is not without difficulties. It needs a willingness to abandon the comfort of assurance in order to manage the pain of uncertainty. This approach might be disturbing since it upsets deeply formed patterns of thought and perception. However, both quantum physics and spiritual traditions argue that this disturbance is essential for a deeper knowledge. The loss of classical determinism in quantum physics has resulted in ground-breaking discoveries, pushing science forward. Similarly, spiritual activities that incorporate contradiction frequently result in significant insights and transforming experiences, generating a stronger feeling of connection and purpose.

The difficulty of openness also applies to cross-disciplinary discussion. While the analogies between quantum physics and spirituality are striking, they must be treated cautiously to prevent oversimplification or misinterpretation. It is critical to understand that various areas work in separate paradigms, with unique approaches and goals. Quantum physics is based on scientific data and mathematical rigor, but spirituality frequently strives to express experiential truths that defy empirical validity. Respecting these differences while investigating their intersections necessitates a balanced approach that honors both viewpoints without confusing them.

This balanced approach has the potential to improve both disciplines. Engaging with spiritual viewpoints can inspire new ways of thinking about fundamental problems like the nature of consciousness and the origins of the cosmos. Engaging with scientific ideas can give a foundation for comprehending previously enigmatic or ineffable occurrences in the context of spirituality. It is possible to construct a more complete knowledge of reality, one that merges the material and the metaphysical, by encouraging a conversation that recognizes the distinct contributions of each sector.

Openness to contradiction also prompts a rethinking of educational and cultural frameworks. In a society increasingly dominated by binary thinking and divided discussions, the capacity to appreciate complexity and ambiguity is more crucial than ever. Quantum physics and spirituality, with their emphasis on connectivity and oneness, provide a potent alternative to the fragmentation and divisiveness that define much current debate. Individuals and society can gain the resilience and adaptability required to handle an increasingly complicated environment by fostering an openness to contradiction.

Finally, the lesson of openness extends beyond intellectual comprehension to cover a manner of being. Both quantum physics and spiritual teachings encourage people to view reality as a dynamic process that is always changing and endlessly complex. This interaction necessitates humility, curiosity, and the courage to examine assumptions. It also necessitates acknowledging that the road toward knowing is never complete, but rather always evolving. When we embrace this trip, paradox becomes a bridge that connects the known and the unknown, the material and the spiritual, the limited and the infinite. This bridge allows for a deeper and more complete knowledge of reality, one that transcends traditional thinking and offers up new possibilities.

CHAPTER 5: QUANTUM ENTANGLEMENT AND ONENESS

"In the great hand of God I stand; and thence against the undivulg'd pretence I fight of treasonous malice." – William Shakespeare

One of the most interesting phenomena in modern physics is quantum entanglement, which calls into question traditional concepts of location and separation. It is a phenomena in which particles get connected in such a manner that the condition of one directly affects the state of another, regardless of their distance apart. Entanglement was initially completely defined by Albert Einstein, Boris Podolsky, and Nathan Rosen in their 1935 work establishing the "EPR paradox," and it was originally envisioned as a challenge to quantum mechanics' completeness. Einstein famously dismissed it as "spooky action at a distance," but further research verified its veracity, establishing it as the basis for quantum theory.

Entanglement is basically founded on the concept of superposition, which holds that quantum particles exist in several states simultaneously until measured. When two particles interact so that their quantum states are correlated, they form an entangled pair. This bond lasts long after they are separated. The analogous state of another particle is determined by measuring the state of one particle, such as its spin, polarization, or location. This happens faster than light, contradicting Einstein's theory of relativity's assumption that no information or effect can go faster.

Entanglement is typically demonstrated using Bell's theorem, which gives a framework for comparing quantum mechanics predictions to those of classical physics. Bell's inequality limits the correlations predicted by classical theories based on local realism, which asserts that physical attributes exist independently of measurement and are only influenced by their surroundings. Experiments to prove Bell's inequality, such as those conducted by Alain Aspect in the 1980s, repeatedly showed breaches, confirming the non-local nature of entanglement and the validity of quantum mechanics.

While it may look paradoxical or contradictory, entanglement is consistent with quantum theory's probabilistic underpinning. Unlike classical physics, which holds that particles have fixed properties regardless of observation, quantum mechanics suggests that reality is fundamentally relational. In an entangled system, the particles do not have independent states, but rather share a single, coherent quantum state. This relationship challenges the Cartesian dualism of distinct objects and suggests a more holistic understanding of reality.

Entanglement has repercussions beyond theoretical physics, including practical applications and philosophical discussion. It serves as the technical foundation for quantum computing and cryptography. Entangled qubits in quantum computing enable parallel processing at rates unmatched by regular computers, holding revolutionary potential in fields ranging from drug discovery to artificial intelligence. Quantum cryptography employs entanglement to create unbreakable encryption systems, as capturing entangled particles disrupts their states and reveals the intrusion. These results show how a phenomenon that was previously assumed to be wholly abstract is changing the technology world.

Entanglement poses profound philosophical questions about the nature of causality, information, and interconnectedness. It challenges traditional notions of determinism and locality, claiming that the universe is regulated by nonseparability and relationality. This approach is congruent with spiritual and philosophical systems that emphasize unity and interconnectedness. For example, Indra's Net, a Hindu philosophical concept, depicts the universe as a massive network of connected jewels, each reflecting the others. Similarly, Buddhist teachings on dependent origination picture existence as a web of interdependent events, with nothing existing alone. The parallels between these ancient notions and quantum physics discoveries suggest that interconnectedness is a basic phenomenon.

Entanglement also refers to the observer's part in forming reality. In classical physics, the universe is assumed to operate independently of observation. However, in quantum physics, measurement compresses a particle's wave function, resulting in its state. In the context of entanglement, this means that simply monitoring one particle determines the state of its counterpart, linking the observer to the fabric of reality. This is compatible with different spiritual traditions that see consciousness as necessary for the structure of reality. For example, Vedantic philosophy argues that Brahman, the ultimate reality, is both the material and effective cause of the universe, including both the observer and the observed.

Despite its revolutionary implications, entanglement is a source of continuous inquiry and debate. One important question is how information or correlations are transmitted between entangled particles. While quantum physics provides a mathematical framework for comprehending entanglement, it does not offer a causal explanation for how it works. Theories such as hidden variable models attempted to explain the occurrences using a deterministic framework, however experimental results consistently refuted them. Instead, many physicists see entanglement as a fundamental component of reality that cannot be reduced to conventional concepts.

Another area of research is the bounds of entanglement. Entanglement has been seen at macroscopic scales in some systems, including superconducting circuits and Bose-Einstein condensates, although it is most frequently associated with microscopic particles. Understanding the conditions under which entanglement persists or degrades may give information on the quantum-classical transition and the formation of macroscopic worlds. In addition, researchers are investigating the prospect of creating and manipulating entanglement in larger and more complicated systems, which might lead to significant technological and scientific advances.

Entanglement is also related to problems about the nature of time and space. Classical physics views space and time as a constant, predictable backdrop against which events occur. However, quantum physics contends that space and time are emergent properties of deeper, nonlocal phenomena. Entanglement illustrates nonlocality because particle correlations are unaffected by spatial separation. Some physicists, like Carlo Rovelli, have proposed that space and time originate from the relational properties of quantum systems, defying traditional notions of spacetime as a permanent and independent object.

Entanglement research fosters multidisciplinary collaboration by linking physics, philosophy, and spirituality. While it is vital to distinguish between scientific truths and speculative interpretations, the connections between quantum physics and spiritual concepts provide a more complete explanation of existence. By embracing the interconnectedness demonstrated by entanglement, humanity can get a deeper understanding of the universe's complexity and oneness.

Entanglement, with its far-reaching implications for science and philosophy, reminds us that knowledge's boundaries are fluid and ever-expanding. As researchers delve into the mysteries of the quantum world, they not only find new elements of reality, but also challenge long-held beliefs that have shaped human thought. Whether seen through the lens of physics, theology, or technology, entanglement inspires us to reconsider our place in the universe and appreciate the intricate web of connections that sustains life.

Resonance with Unity: Spiritual Concepts of "All is One" or Indra's Net.

The concept of interconnectedness is essential to both quantum physics and spiritual traditions, indicating a shared understanding of reality in which everything is intricately linked. This sense of completeness calls into question the fragmented impressions produced by everyday experience and classical notions. Spiritual themes from Buddhist and Hindu cosmology, such as "All is One" and the metaphor of Indra's Net, are well-suited to quantum entanglement findings, creating a dialogue between science and spirituality that reveals basic truths about the nature of existence.

In spiritual traditions, oneness is more than just a logical idea; it is a lived experience of the essence of being. The notion of "All is One" has expanded across cultures and faiths, emphasizing the inseparability of existence. In Hindu philosophy, Brahman refers to the ultimate, undivided reality from which all things emanate. Similarly, in Judaism's mystical traditions, such as Kabbalah, the divine presence is considered as permeating all of creation, eliminating the apparent borders between one creature and another. This concept is analogous to Buddhism's Indra's Net, a metaphor depicting an unending web in which each node replicates the others, symbolizing the interrelated nature of everything. These teachings provide a profound understanding of interconnectedness that is strikingly akin to quantum science.

Quantum entanglement provides a scientific basis for understanding a sort of relationship that cannot be described traditionally. When particles become entangled, their states are linked, so that measuring one instantly affects the other, regardless of distance. Einstein famously defined this phenomenon as "spooky action at a distance," proving that the universe operates on principles that go beyond locality. Entanglement challenges the traditional understanding of separateness, claiming that the fundamental fabric of reality is composed of interactions rather than distinct entities.

Entanglement and spiritual oneness have a reciprocal emphasis on links. In quantum physics, the state of an entangled system cannot be fully understood without reference to the whole, just as spiritual beliefs hold that people are not independent beings, but rather integral components of a wider cosmic order. The shift from individualism to connectedness has far-reaching implications for how reality is perceived and experienced. It challenges the Cartesian dualism that has long dominated Western philosophy, replacing it with a view of reality as a never-ending network of interrelationships.

Unity's implications extend beyond abstract theory into practical domains, impacting ethical, empathetic, and responsible perspectives. Recognizing interconnectedness is commonly employed in spiritual traditions as a foundation for moral behavior. The Buddhist idea of dependent origination, for example, emphasizes that activities resound across the interwoven fabric of reality, generating waves to affect all beings. Similarly, indigenous worldviews encourage stewardship and reciprocity because humans, animals, and the natural world are all inextricably linked. While not explicitly ethical, quantum physics highlights the idea that no system exists in isolation, offering a scientific perspective to complement fundamental spiritual truths.

The metaphor of Indra's Net provides a particularly vivid depiction of these ideas. This picture depicts the universe as an endless web, with each node representing a diamond that mirrors the one before it. This idea captures the essence of interdependence: each component contains and contributes to the total. This idea is consistent with the holographic principle in quantum physics, which states that information about the whole universe may be recorded on a smaller scale, such as the surface of a black hole. Both metaphors convey the idea that reality cannot be reduced to isolated components, but is essentially interconnected.

The yearning for oneness throws into question established notions of identity. In many spiritual traditions, gaining oneness means transcending the ego, the concept of a separate self that maintains differences. This process is exhibited through activities such as meditation, in which people experience a lack of boundaries and a merging with the wider whole. Similarly, quantum physics breaks down tight boundaries between observer and observee, revealing a universe in which borders blur and identities cross. This confluence necessitates a rethinking of selfhood, shifting away from understanding the self as an isolated entity and toward one that recognizes its function in a larger context.

The combination of quantum physics and spiritual oneness encourages a deeper respect for mystery and humility. Both worlds acknowledge that the interconnectedness they reveal cannot be fully appreciated with reason alone. Quantum entanglement, while theoretically correct, defies intuitive understanding, compelling the mind to tolerate ambiguity. Spiritual teachings, too, emphasize the limitations of intellectual comprehension, pushing practitioners to develop direct experience and an openness to the unexpected. This universal recognition of mystery provides a kind of contact that is less about conquering and more about participating in the unfolding of reality.

While the parallels between quantum physics and spiritual oneness are intriguing, they must be approached with caution to avoid confounding distinct fields. Quantum entanglement is a well-documented phenomenon with precise mathematical explanations, yet spiritual teachings usually employ metaphor and symbolic language to convey experiential reality. Recognizing these distinctions allows for a dialog that respects each perspective's integrity while probing areas of overlap. This conversation can assist both professions by giving new perspectives on the nature of connectedness and its consequences for understanding reality.

The consequences of interconnectedness are also relevant to current challenges such as environmental sustainability and social justice. Recognizing the interconnectedness of all living things lays a solid foundation for resolving the world's ecological dilemma. Just as quantum science shows that no particle exists in isolation, spiritual traditions remind us that our well-being is intricately related to the health of the ecosystems that support us. This position urges a shift away from exploitative tactics and toward ones that respect the interconnected web of life, fostering a sense of shared responsibility and care.

In terms of social justice, recognizing oneness undermines repressive and dividing institutions. Spiritual traditions usually emphasize all animals' inherent dignity and value, which arises from their interconnectedness. This idea is congruent with movements that seek to demolish oppressive structures and build communities founded on mutual respect and solidarity. Quantum physics, by demonstrating the interconnected nature of reality, provides factual evidence for the notions of unity and equality that motivate these movements.

Finally, the link between quantum entanglement and spiritual oneness prompts a reassessment of how reality is perceived and experienced. It challenges the fragmented ideas that dominate modern thought, instead providing a vision of wholeness that incorporates science, theology, and human experience. This perspective is more than simply theoretical; it has a profoundly transformative effect on how individuals connect with themselves, one another, and the world. Accepting the link revealed by quantum physics and spiritual teachings can help us feel more connected, purposeful, and responsible for the unfolding of reality.

Scientific vs. Mystical: Identifying Testable Phenomena and Symbolic Metaphor

The intersection of science and mysticism is an exciting but challenging issue to investigate. Quantum physics, with its complex principles and counterintuitive happenings, frequently resembles ideas found in ancient spiritual traditions. However, it is crucial to distinguish between scientifically testable events and the symbolic metaphors that characterize mystical teaching. Both theories provide important insights into the nature of reality, but their methods, goals, and implications are vastly different.

Empiricism and mathematical rigor are essential to quantum mechanics. Its ideas, like as superposition, entanglement, and wave-particle duality, are founded on experimental evidence and prediction models. For example, the double-slit experiment, which demonstrates matter's dual nature as a particle and a wave, may be reproduced and confirmed in controlled conditions. Similarly, Bell tests have been used to objectively demonstrate quantum entanglement, which happens when two particles are in connected states regardless of distance. These phenomena contradict traditional notions of reality, yet they are backed by reproducible data, making them fundamental to modern physics.

In contrast, mystic traditions emphasize experiential and symbolic modes of thought. Metaphors, parables, and contemplative practices are utilized to convey messages about the interconnectedness of all things, the oneness of existence, and the illusion of separateness. For example, Hindu philosophy sees the universe as a manifestation of Brahman, the indivisible essence that supports everything. Similarly, Buddhist teachings use the concept of Indra's Net—a vast network of intertwined jewels that reflect one another—to demonstrate the interconnection of everything. These ideas, while profound, are not intended to be experimentally proven; rather, their realities are lived and contextualized.

The similarities between quantum physics and mystical concepts have spurred intense discussion. Quantum entanglement, for example, is compatible with spiritual conceptions of unity, meaning that separation is an illusion at its root. The idea that particles might collide quickly across vast distances is symbolically compatible with views that all animals are interconnected. Similarly, the uncertainty principle, which states that some properties of particles cannot be accurately grasped at the same time, represents spiritual attitudes that embrace mystery and the limits of knowing. These similarities, however, should not be interpreted as straight equivalences.

One of the most significant differences is the sort of evidence used. Observation, measurement, and experimentation are used to validate scientific phenomena. For example, entanglement was formerly regarded to be a theoretical curiosity until experimental experiments by Alain Aspect and others revealed convincing evidence of its reality. Mystical insights, on the other hand, are typically verified by personal experience or community tradition, and lack the reproducibility that differentiates scientific investigation. While this does not diminish their value, it does place them in a unique epistemological category.

Another contrast between the frameworks is their objectives. Quantum mechanics seeks to describe and predict the behavior of the physical universe, with several practical applications, including quantum computers and medical imaging. Mystical traditions strive to provide meaning, promote spiritual growth, and give light on the essence of life and consciousness. The former is more descriptive and functional, whereas the latter is transformative and interpretive.

The convergence of various domains raises questions about the limits of human cognition. Quantum physics challenges the traditional notion of deterministic, objective reality by integrating elements such as chance, observation-dependence, and nonlocality. Similarly, mystical teachings contradict linear and reductionist perspectives, pushing people to consider reality as fluid, interconnected, and complex. This inherent impulse to question existing paradigms fosters humility and inquiry, but it necessitates cautious navigation to avoid misunderstanding various tactics.

The incorporation of quantum physics into popular culture stresses the significance of judgment. Terms like "quantum healing" and "quantum consciousness" commonly imply scientific respectability without adhering to quantum physics' strict requirements. While these notions may have metaphorical or symbolic appeal, they frequently lack scientific foundation. This combination can lead to misconceptions, diminishing the credibility of both science and spirituality.

Despite these challenges, the interplay of quantum physics and mysticism has the potential to advance both disciplines. Science, with its precision and attention on the real world, benefits from the wider, integrated perspectives provided by spiritual traditions. Mysticism, in turn, adds depth and significance by interacting with contemporary physics' discoveries and language. For example, the concept of interconnection, which is central to both quantum physics and spirituality, encourages interdisciplinary approaches to understanding complex systems, whether in ecology, neurology, or social dynamics.

The study of these junctions also encourages philosophical inquiry. Quantum physics raises profound philosophical issues about the nature of reality, the role of the observer, and the limits of knowledge. Mystical traditions, which have long grappled with these issues, offer rich conceptual frameworks for resolving them. For example, the Vedantic concept of Maya, or the misleading nature of appearances, is conceptually analogous to quantum physics' challenge to traditional objectivism. Recognizing the interplay of views may lead to a more nuanced understanding of life.

Furthermore, this discourse has implications for the human experience and well-being. Recognizing connectedness, whether through quantum physics or mysticism, fosters empathy, compassion, and a feeling of collective duty. In an era of ecological and societal catastrophe, our findings encourage approaches that prioritize collaboration and communal well-being over individual gain. The integration of scientific and spiritual perspectives has the potential to foster intellectual and ethical development.

The relationship between quantum physics and mysticism exemplifies the interplay of several ways of knowing. Science, which focuses on measurement and prediction, sheds light on the universe's physics. Mysticism, which focuses on experience and meaning, explores the depths of human consciousness and reality. Respecting the contrasts between these frameworks while acknowledging their places of convergence enables us to better understand the richness and complexity of reality.

This encounter promotes a shift in perception that transcends the distinction between science and spirituality. Rather than being considered as competing or conflicting, these regions might be viewed as complementary approaches to solving the same underlying puzzle. This integrated perspective has the potential to widen the scope of cognition by bridging the gap between the tangible and the transcendent, while also opening up new paths for inquiry and discovery.

CHAPTER 6: OBSERVER EFFECT AND CONSCIOUSNESS

"We see things not as they are, but as we are." – Attributed to the Talmu

The role of measurement in quantum mechanics presents one of physics' most fundamental and contentious concepts: wave function collapse. The shift from quantum possibilities to classical realities, in which the act of measuring seems to solidify a particle's state, is central to this concept. This phenomena calls into question traditional concepts of an objective cosmos, in which systems exist independent of observation, as well as the nature of reality and the function of the observer.

A particle in quantum mechanics, such as an electron or photon, exists in a state of superposition, which is mathematically represented by a wave function. This wave function includes all potential measurement results and assigns probability to each. When a measurement is made, the wave function "collapses," and the system assumes a fixed state. In the well-known double-slit experiment, for example, an electron acts like a wave, resulting in an interference pattern when not seen. When its position is measured, it behaves like a particle, with the wave function collapsing into a definite point.

Niels Bohr and Werner Heisenberg created the Copenhagen interpretation, which served as one of the first frameworks for understanding wave function collapse. According to this perspective, the wave function reflects potentialities that collapse into a single actuality when measured. The act of observation, therefore, is not passive but actively changes the conclusion, a significant break from conventional physics, in which measurement simply discloses preexisting conditions.

Various views provide diverse insights on wave function collapse. Hugh Everett III's many-worlds interpretation completely eliminates the requirement for collapse. Instead, it implies that all conceivable outcomes of a quantum event take place, with each branching out into its own world. According to this viewpoint, measurement does not pick a distinct reality, but rather indicates the branch of the multiverse that the observer is in.

Another method, the de Broglie-Bohm pilot wave hypothesis, holds that particles are steered by a wave function. There is no collapse in this paradigm; the wave function continues to grow deterministically as the particle follows a predefined course. This interpretation reintroduces classical determinism while retaining quantum physics' predictability.

The role of awareness in wave function collapse is a hotly debated issue. Early interpretations by people such as John von Neumann and Eugene Wigner proposed that awareness may be the ultimate agent of collapse. This viewpoint holds that the observer's thinking is directly involved in deciding the outcome of quantum occurrences. While fascinating, this theory has been critiqued for lacking factual backing and incorporating subjective components into a scientific framework.

Recent studies have investigated whether wave function collapse may occur without a conscious observer. Quantum mechanics advances have permitted "delayed-choice" and "quantum eraser" studies, which show that collapse is determined by the information available in the system rather than the presence of a conscious mind. These findings shift the emphasis away from human observers and toward the wider idea of interaction, in which any activity capable of extracting knowledge about the system might cause collapse.

Wave function collapse has philosophical consequences that transcend beyond physics. In philosophical terms, the collapse may be viewed as a movement from potentiality to actuality, similar to notions in Aristotelian philosophy and existential thinking. The indeterminacy of the quantum realm is similar to ideas of free will, in which the cosmos is not strictly deterministic but allows for alternatives and choices.

Certain spiritual viewpoints correlate with the seeming collapse. Reality is frequently depicted in mystical traditions as emerging from an endless potential field. Observation, whether by a supernatural entity or human awareness, is regarded as a creative activity that puts reality into focus. While these interpretations are figurative, they emphasize quantum physics' deep philosophical and existential implications.

Technological advancements have enabled researchers to probe the limits of wave function collapse. Experiments using bigger systems, such as molecules and quantum computers, seek to investigate the transition from the quantum to classical worlds. The measurement issue, or the topic of where and how collapse happens, is still a major barrier in quantum physics. As researchers stretch the limits of experimental accuracy, new insights on the nature of reality and the relationship between observation and existence may emerge.

The notion of wave function collapse has applications in quantum technology. Superposition manipulation and premature collapse avoidance are critical in quantum computing for sustaining quantum coherence. Understanding and regulating the circumstances that cause collapse is critical for advances in disciplines such as quantum cryptography and quantum teleportation.

The interaction between measurement and reality shows quantum physics' paradigm-shifting power. It calls into question traditional assumptions about the independence of the observer and the observed, implying a more active role for measurement in altering the cosmos. This interactive paradigm encourages rethinking basic concerns like the nature of existence, the boundaries of human knowledge, and the connection of observer and observed.

While wave function collapse is anchored in factual science, its ramifications extend beyond philosophy, metaphysics, and spirituality. The collapse represents the transformational power of observation and the dynamic interplay between potential and reality. By delving into the bounds of this phenomena, science and spirituality both expand their engagement with the mysteries of life, promoting a cross-disciplinary discourse.

Arguments for and against consciousness shaping outcomes: Mind as Participant.

For decades, physicists, philosophers, and spiritual thinkers have been fascinated by the idea that awareness might play a fundamental role in creating quantum system outcomes. This theory, based on the characteristics of the observer effect in quantum physics, posits that the act of observation—potentially connected to human awareness—may directly impact reality at its most fundamental level. However, this idea is very contested, and delving into both arguments for and against awareness as a driver of quantum events exposes the significant problems and ramifications of the discussion.

The importance of the observer effect is frequently cited by proponents of the theory that awareness impacts quantum processes. In quantum physics, the process of measuring seems to collapse the wave function, transforming a system from a state of possibility to a definite condition.

Early quantum theorists like John von Neumann and Eugene Wigner proposed that this collapse might not be caused solely by physical interactions, but might also need the participation of a conscious observer. Wigner, in instance, proposed that consciousness itself may be the last arbitrator in deciding quantum reality, a view that is consistent with some interpretations of idealist philosophy, which maintains that reality is primarily mental or experiencing in origin.

The cryptic character of the wave function provides one reason in favor of this viewpoint. The Schrödinger equation describes the wave function, which gives a probabilistic picture of a system's potential states but does not explain how or why one of them becomes actual. If physical processes alone cannot account for this change, some suggest that the mind, as a non-physical object, might fill the gap. This approach is consistent with various spiritual traditions that argue that awareness underpins or creates the material universe. Vedantic and Buddhist philosophies, for example, define reality as inextricably linked to awareness, echoing the notion that observation may co-create the fabric of existence.

In experimental settings, the hypothesis that awareness influences quantum systems has gained momentum. Quantum experiments using delayed-choice and quantum eraser settings show that decisions regarding how to evaluate a system can have an impact on its previous behavior. While these events are frequently explained without involving awareness, they are occasionally regarded as proof that the act of observing has agency. This view raises interesting issues regarding whether human intentionality may influence quantum processes.

Critics of the consciousness-centric view claim that the observer effect may be completely explained without mentioning the mind. In quantum mechanics, "observation" is a technical word that refers to any interaction that may extract data from a system. Such interactions might take place with a photon, an electron, or any measuring device—not necessarily a conscious individual. This viewpoint is reinforced by decoherence theory, which describes how quantum systems interact with their environment, culminating in wave function collapse without the need for a conscious observer. According to this viewpoint, consciousness is only one of many possible components of a measuring system, and it is not unique nor required for quantum events.

The empirical aspect of physics provides another argument against awareness' significance in quantum results. Science is based on objective and reproducible measurements, but the addition of consciousness brings subjectivity, complicating hypothesis testing. Experiments aiming to examine the impact of human purpose or consciousness on quantum systems, such as random number generator research, have shown contradictory and sometimes ambiguous findings. Critics say that methodological shortcomings, tiny effect sizes, and replicability concerns undermine assertions that awareness has a direct impact on quantum processes.

The discussion also moves into philosophical topics. According to materialist viewpoints, consciousness comes from the physical brain and so has little impact on physical systems. Dualist or panpsychist viewpoints, on the other hand, contend that consciousness is a basic component of reality, possibly interacting with quantum processes. These philosophical distinctions highlight the challenge of answering the topic within the existing scientific framework.

Emerging sciences like quantum biology and neuroscience add to the complexities. Some researchers believe that quantum processes in the brain, such as those postulated in the Penrose-Hameroff Orch-OR theory, might link consciousness to quantum mechanics. This contentious hypothesis proposes that quantum coherence inside neuronal microtubules might serve as a foundation for consciousness, connecting the mind to the underlying workings of the cosmos. While fascinating, this concept is still theoretical and lacks solid experimental confirmation.

This dispute has major spiritual ramifications since it calls into question customary divisions between observer and observed. If consciousness does influence quantum reality, it indicates a participatory world in which human awareness is inextricably interwoven to the fabric of existence. Such a perspective is consistent with mystical traditions that emphasize the interconnection of all things and the mind's creative capacity. Critics, however, advise against mixing philosophical interpretations with actual science, arguing that doing so risks weakening the rigor and impartiality of scientific research.

Balancing these viewpoints necessitates admitting the limitations of present knowledge while staying open to multidisciplinary inquiry. With its intrinsic weirdness and paradoxical consequences, quantum mechanics raises issues that go beyond typical scientific bounds. The notion that awareness may impact quantum systems forces us to reconsider the nature of reality, the function of the observer, and the interaction of mind and matter.

Future studies may shed light on the link between consciousness and quantum physics. Experimental advances, such as better quantum sensors and large-scale quantum systems, might provide light on the measurement problem and the function of observation. Furthermore, multidisciplinary collaboration among physicists, neuroscientists, and philosophers may provide new techniques to investigating the mysteries of consciousness and its potential linkages to the quantum realm.

While the topic of whether awareness influences quantum results remains unanswered, it serves as a striking reminder of the intricate connection between science, philosophy, and spirituality. The discussion encourages us to embrace uncertainty, challenge long-held beliefs, and push the limits of human understanding. By doing so, we get a greater appreciation for the universe's complexity and wonder, knowing that the mysteries of consciousness and quantum physics are as much about the questions they create as the solutions they may someday supply.

Convergence or Divergence: How Spiritual Traditions Incorporate Observer-Centric Reality

The interaction of observer-centric reality in quantum physics and spiritual viewpoints that include subjective participation in molding existence has provided fertile ground for interdisciplinary research. In quantum physics, the function of observation calls into question the classical objectivity of a detached cosmos, arguing instead that measurement profoundly impacts outcomes. Similarly, many spiritual traditions stress awareness' active participation in producing or experiencing reality. Despite their similarities, these fields have significant divergences and convergences, reflecting unique approaches, aims, and conceptual frameworks.

The observer-centric principle is introduced in quantum physics through events such as wave function collapse, which implies that when a system's probabilistic states are measured, they resolve into a unique conclusion. This process argues that observation is not only passive, but actively participates in and changes reality. Similar concepts are frequently conveyed in spiritual frameworks through philosophies that emphasize awareness as a basic component of life. For example, Vedanta philosophy holds that the cosmos is a manifestation of Brahman, or pure consciousness, and that individual awareness contributes to existence's seeming dualism. Buddhism echoes this thought with the concept of dependent origination, which teaches that reality is created via interdependent processes such as perception and cognition.

The denial of a completely independent, objective world marks the convergence of quantum and spiritual conceptions. According to both paradigms, reality is relational, with perception or interaction playing an important role in its expression. This concept undermines materialist perspectives that hold that the universe is fixed and independent of the observer. Instead, it corresponds to participatory models in which the observer is inextricably tied to the observed.

One area of agreement is the focus on everything's interconnection. Quantum entanglement shows that once particles get entangled, they stay instantly coupled regardless of distance. This is similar to spiritual teachings like Indra's Net in Mahayana Buddhism, which represents an infinite network of interwoven gems, each reflecting the total. The inference is that the observer and the observed are not independent individuals, but rather components of a larger whole, with observation strengthening this oneness.

Despite these analogies, the techniques and epistemologies of science and spirituality differ significantly. Empirical facts, mathematical models, and reproducible experiments serve as the foundation for quantum physics. The observer's effect is carefully defined within the framework of measurement, which frequently involves highly regulated and quantitative procedures. Spiritual traditions, on the other hand, are founded on subjective experience, introspection, and metaphysical interpretation. While these methodologies give remarkable insights into human experience and awareness, they lack the factual rigor required by scientific research.

This distinction is particularly visible in how quantum physics and spiritual traditions perceive the observer's function. The observer effect is defined in physics in terms of physical interaction, such as the measuring instrument interacting with a quantum system. Consciousness, while conceptually fascinating, is not required for this connection, according to most views. In spirituality, on the other hand, consciousness is frequently crucial to the creative process, imbuing observation with intention, meaning, and agency. For example, the Upanishads depict reality as being formed by the observer's awareness, which is consistent with mystical interpretations of the quantum observer effect but not scientifically sound.

Another important distinction is the objective of these investigations. Quantum mechanics tries to find the basic rules of the cosmos by developing testable ideas that advance technology and human knowledge. Spiritual traditions, on the other hand, frequently strive to give existential meaning, ethical advice, or routes to enlightenment. The observer's function in spirituality is inextricably linked to personal growth, connectivity, and transcendence, yet in quantum physics, it is essential for comprehending physical phenomenon.

Nonetheless, the linkages between these fields encourage multidisciplinary discussion and investigation. Some scholars believe that quantum physics might provide a scientific prism through which to grasp old spiritual ideas. The concept of wave-particle duality, in which phenomena show both particle-like and wave-like properties, is analogous to spiritual ideas of duality and oneness. The yin-yang sign in Taoism represents the dynamic interaction of opposites, implying that dualities are complimentary facets of a same reality.

Such connections have spurred speculative hypotheses attempting to reconcile quantum physics with spiritual frameworks. One example is the concept that consciousness compresses the wave function, which is consistent with mystical teachings emphasizing awareness's creative potential. These ideas, however, are frequently challenged for oversimplifying or misinterpreting quantum principles in order to fit metaphysical narratives. Critics say that such interpretations jeopardize quantum mechanics' scientific integrity while providing no factual evidence for spiritual claims.

The interplay between both points of view also emphasizes the limitations of reductionist methods in both areas. Spiritual traditions, like quantum physics, call into question reductionist notions of consciousness as solely a result of physical processes. Both areas show that understanding reality requires a holistic approach that takes into account relationships, contexts, and interactions rather than separate components.

This holistic approach is supported by growing multidisciplinary areas such as quantum biology, which investigates how quantum events may underpin biological processes, and contemplative neuroscience, which investigates the impact of meditation on brain function. These disciplines show how scientific and spiritual perspectives may complement one other. For example, mindfulness techniques have been linked to observable changes in brain activity and mental health, lending scientific credence to spiritual traditions that emphasize the transformational power of awareness.

Despite the intriguing overlaps, it is important to proceed with caution when drawing analogies or confusing different realms. Quantum physics and spiritual traditions work in separate paradigms, each with its own set of strengths and limits. Attempts to bring people together must respect their differences while encouraging open debate and critical inquiry. This necessitates recognizing the speculative character of many assertions and favoring robust, multidisciplinary study above sensationalism.

The investigation of observer-centric reality serves as a microcosm for the larger interaction between science and spirituality. Both professions are concerned with significant concerns about the nature of life, the role of the person, and the interconnection of everything. While their techniques and purposes may differ, their common quest for knowledge highlights the human need to find meaning in a complicated and enigmatic reality.

As the borders between disciplines become increasingly blurred, the discussion between quantum physics and spiritual traditions provides a fertile ground for investigation and discovery. By embracing both the empirical rigor of science and the introspective depth of spirituality, we may discover new ways of understanding the observer's role in constructing reality, encouraging a greater awareness for the interplay between the seen and unseen, the quantifiable and the immeasurable.

CHAPTER 7: SCHRÖDINGER'S CAT: THE MYSTERY OF BEING AND NON-BEING

"What we observe is not nature itself, but nature exposed to our method of questioning." – Werner Heisenberg

Erwin Schrödinger's thought experiment, known as "Schrödinger's Cat," is one of the most memorable examples of quantum physics' paradoxical nature. The hypothetical scenario, developed in 1935 as part of a discussion on the Copenhagen interpretation of quantum physics, seeks to highlight the theory's inherent contradictions. At its essence, it depicts a cat in an enclosed cage that is both alive and dead until viewed. This paradox necessitates a rethinking of how measurement, observation, and reality interact in quantum physics, while also allowing larger philosophical and even spiritual interpretations.

Schrödinger envisaged placing a cat in a box with a bottle of poison, a Geiger counter, and a radioactive atom. If the atom decayed, the Geiger counter would unleash the poison, causing the cat to die. If the atom would not decay, the cat would survive. According to quantum physics, the radioactive atom exists in a state of superposition—a mix of decayed and undecayed states—until discovered. Consequently, the entire system, including the cat, exists in a superposition of "alive" and "dead" until the box is opened and inspected.

This situation raises a fundamental question in quantum mechanics: Does the act of observation compress the wave function and produce reality? The cat's state is defined in quantum terms by a wave function, which reflects the probability of all conceivable events. According to the Copenhagen interpretation, this wave function stays unresolved until a measurement drives the system into a definitive state. However, this interpretation raises the philosophical question of what defines a "measurement" and whether the presence of a conscious observer is necessary.

The philosophical implications of Schrödinger's Cat have sparked speculation and controversy. On one level, the thought experiment emphasizes the distinction between classical physics' deterministic universe and quantum mechanics' probabilistic nature. Regardless of how they are observed, things in classical physics exist in fixed states. However, in quantum physics, reality appears to be inextricably linked to observation, calling into question the concept of an objective, observer-independent cosmos.

On a deeper level, Schrödinger's Cat addresses larger philosophical problems regarding the nature of existence and perception. In some ways, the cat's dual condition mirrors existential discussions about the role of human mind in influencing reality. If observation dictates the fate of a cat, does same theory apply to bigger systems, or perhaps the entire universe? These questions elicit thoughts on the interdependence of mind and matter, repeating concepts found in many spiritual and philosophical traditions.

While Schrödinger's Cat is a potent metaphor for the quirks of quantum physics, it is vital to acknowledge its limits as a literal depiction of physical reality. Because of a process known as decoherence, macroscopic things such as cats do not experience the same quantum effects as subatomic particles. When quantum systems interact with their environs, superpositions collapse into classical states before being seen. Thus, while the thought experiment reflects quantum physics' conceptual weirdness, it does not imply that live creatures may exist in both life and death.

Despite these limits, Schrödinger's Cat has found a home at the crossroads of science and popular culture, as well as in wider philosophical and spiritual discussions. The experiment's implications have been investigated in a variety of fields, including theoretical physics, philosophy, art, and literature. In spiritual contexts, the cat's dual condition has been likened to mystical conceptions of contradiction and oneness, such as the Taoist yin-yang symbol, which signifies the coexistence of opposites inside a single whole.

Parallels between Schrödinger's Cat and spiritual teachings on the nature of reality as an illusion or fabrication give birth to an especially fascinating interpretation. According to Advaita Vedanta philosophy, the world of appearances is ultimately an illusion (maya) created by individual and communal awareness. According to this viewpoint, the act of observation or perception generates the feeling of duality in the same way that measuring resolves the cat's superposition. Similarly, Buddhist teachings on emptiness (shunyata) hold that all things lack inherent existence and emerge dependently, which is consistent with the relational character of quantum states.

At the same time, Schrödinger's Cat emphasizes the conflict between intuition and scientific knowledge. The thought experiment is purposefully meant to challenge common-sense concepts of reality, requiring us to confront the limitations of classical thinking when applied to the quantum realm. This conflict reflects the difficulties spiritual traditions encounter in communicating truths that go beyond ordinary experience. Spiritual traditions frequently use symbols, metaphors, and paradoxes to communicate truths that challenge ordinary comprehension, much as quantum physics does.

The larger ramifications of Schrödinger's Cat go into philosophical discussions concerning the nature of knowledge and the boundaries of scientific research. Is the thought experiment suggesting that reality is uncertain until witnessed, or does it just represent our limited understanding? These problems have spurred debate regarding the role of epistemology in science and spirituality, with some contending that the distinction between observer and observed is ultimately illusory.

Recent breakthroughs in quantum technology have enabled researchers to test features of Schrödinger's thought experiment with more sophisticated systems. Experiments involving entangled particles and macroscopic quantum states, for example, have pushed the limits of quantum physics, offering novel insights into matter and energy behavior. These investigations not only improve our knowledge of Schrödinger's dilemma, but they also offer up new avenues for technological innovation, ranging from quantum computers to secure communication systems.

While Schrödinger's Cat is still a thought experiment, its ongoing significance stems from its capacity to prompt contemplation on the nature of reality, the function of observation, and the relationship between science and philosophy. It reminds us of the universe's complexities and wonders by questioning our assumptions and enticing us to explore the unknown. Whether seen through the lens of quantum physics, philosophy, or spirituality, the cat in the box continues to pique people's interest, spark debate, and deepen their understanding for the wonders of existence.

Being/Non-Being in Spiritual Texts: Parallels with Teachings on Illusion or Emptiness

Being and non-being are key concepts in quantum physics and spiritual traditions. In physics, it is analogous to the duality investigated in quantum systems, where states are simultaneously indeterminate and seen. Being and non-being depict the illusive interaction of existence and transcendence in spirituality, notably in Buddhist, Hindu, and mystical traditions such as Sufism and Kabbalah. By examining these commonalities, we may gain a better understanding of how science and spirituality approach fundamental concerns of reality and experience.

In spiritual teachings, the concept of non-being frequently alludes to the knowledge that physical existence is a fleeting expression rather than the ultimate truth. This theory is similar to quantum physics' superposition principle, which asserts that particles exist in several states at the same time until they are detected. For example, in Buddhist teachings, shunyata, or emptiness, denotes the lack of intrinsic, independent existence rather than a vacuum. All phenomena emerge in an interconnected manner, dependant on other factors. Similarly, in quantum physics, a particle's state is determined by its relational qualities and observations rather than being fixed.

Non-duality is defined in Hindu philosophy, notably in Advaita Vedanta, as the oneness of Brahman, the ultimate reality, and Maya, the physical world's deceptive character. Advaita holds that the observed dualities of being and non-being are false, stemming from ignorance of the one underlying truth. This viewpoint is reflected in quantum mechanics' challenge to classical ideas of objective reality. The measurement issue in quantum physics, as demonstrated by Schrödinger's Cat, implies that the act of observation impacts and determines what is observed, reducing the potential states of being and non-being to a single definite outcome.

Mystical traditions stress the presence of opposites as a means of comprehending greater truths. Sufi mysticism emphasizes the notion of fanā (annihilation), which involves dissolving the self to connect with the divine. This fusion goes beyond the divisions of existence and nonexistence, reflecting the quantum interplay between defined and undefined states. Similarly, Kabbalistic teachings explain creation as a process involving tzimtzum, or divine contraction, which makes room for the material universe to exist. This process involves an interplay of presence and absence, mirroring the quantum view of reality as originating from a field of possibilities.

Quantum physics also demonstrates that non-being, or the lack of certainty, is inherent in the universe's structure. According to Heisenberg's uncertainty principle, certain pairings of attributes, such as location and momentum, cannot be known with arbitrary accuracy at the same time. This fundamental constraint implies that the cosmos runs not on permanent certainty, but rather on a dynamic interplay of possibilities. This ambiguity is frequently viewed in spiritual traditions as a potential for transcendence rather than a fault. Recognizing non-being as an inherent part of life is consistent with contemplative techniques aimed at overcoming the ego and embracing the emptiness.

The similarities extend to cosmology and creation stories. Many spiritual traditions view creation as emerging from emptiness or a vacuum, stressing non-being's transforming power. The biblical narrative of creation characterizes the Earth as "formless and empty" until divine intervention delivers order and illumination. Similarly, in the Tao Te Ching, Laozi identifies the Tao as "the nameless origin of heaven and earth," implying that it exists beyond existence and non-being. These notions are consistent with current physics' investigation of the quantum vacuum, where oscillations in seemingly empty space produce particles and energy. Far from being nothing, the void is a roiling sea of possibilities.

The conflict between being and non-being is also expressed in existential questions essential to both spiritual and philosophical traditions. Parmenides, an ancient Greek philosopher, argued for the primacy of being, claiming that non-being is impossible. However, Heraclitus highlighted existence's flux and impermanence, meaning that being and non-being are inextricably linked. This dual perspective is reflected in Zen Buddhism's koans, which are paradoxical riddles that challenge traditional reasoning to transcend dualistic thinking. For instance, "What was your original face before you were born?"" encourages contemplation of the self beyond being and non-being, just as quantum physics invites us to rethink the nature of reality.

While the commonalities are significant, it is critical to recognize the distinctions. Quantum mechanics is a scientific paradigm that uses mathematical formalism and empirical data to describe particle and system behavior. Spiritual traditions, on the other hand, focus on subjective experience, meaning, and transcendence. The intersection is not in equating these spheres, but in understanding how they highlight different elements of reality. Science specializes at explaining the mechanics of occurrences, but spirituality focuses on their existential and experiential aspects.

Another key area of convergence is the observer's involvement in defining reality. In quantum physics, the observer effect describes how measurement compresses a system's wave function, determining its state. Spiritual traditions also highlight the function of the observer in influencing perception and reality. Advaita Vedanta, for example, argues that the ego (Atman) and ultimate reality (Brahman) are inseparable, implying that the observer and observed are one. This oneness suggests that dualities like being and non-being are mental creations that may be overcome by self-realization.

Mindfulness is a practice in Buddhism that helps people manage the interaction of being and non-being. Practitioners gain insight into reality's impermanence and interdependence by examining thoughts and feelings without attachment. This method is consistent with quantum physics' emphasis on probabilities and relational qualities, in which things are defined not in isolation, but by their interactions.

These analogies have far-reaching ramifications that affect ethics and worldview. Recognizing the fluidity of being and non-being encourages humility and openness, both of which are necessary for dealing with uncertainty. This realization fosters compassion in spiritual situations, when the borders between self and other are viewed as illusory. In quantum mechanics, the interconnectivity revealed by phenomena such as entanglement contradicts reductionist perspectives, enabling holistic approaches to science and society.

Finally, the debate between quantum physics and spiritual teachings on being and non-being deepens our knowledge of reality's complexities. It encourages us to accept contradiction and doubt as natural aspects of reality, asking us to explore beyond appearances and interact with deeper realities. By combining scientific and spiritual ideas, we acquire not only a more thorough understanding of the cosmos, but also a better appreciation for the mystery and wonder that characterize our place in it.

Existential Tension: Embracing Uncertainty in Science and Religion

The junction of quantum physics and spirituality reveals a deep existential conflict rooted in the paradoxes of uncertainty and belief. In all cases, the essence of reality resists final explanation, prompting observers to reconcile seemingly contradicting realities. This tension, while frequently disturbing, serves as a gateway to a better knowledge and acceptance of complexity, repeating concepts found in science, philosophy, and spiritual traditions.

Quantum mechanics challenged deterministic ideas that have dominated physics since Newton, resulting in a scientific paradigm shift. Heisenberg's uncertainty principle symbolizes this upheaval, proving that accurate understanding of some pairings of variables, such as location and momentum, is essentially impossible. This concept is a fundamental characteristic of the quantum universe rather than a technical or observational constraint. The unpredictability revealed at the microscopic level shattered traditional concepts of certainty, prompting scientists and philosophers to deal with a probabilistic interpretation of reality.

Similarly, spiritual traditions have long been concerned with the concept of uncertainty as inherent in the human experience. Buddhism, for example, teaches that holding onto fixed ideas or identities causes suffering, but accepting impermanence and ambiguity promotes freedom. The Zen notion of mu, which is sometimes translated as "not" or "non-being," encourages practitioners to let go of strict dichotomies like good and evil, or self and other. This spiritual framework is consistent with quantum physics' probabilistic nature, which states that outcomes exist as possibilities until they are measured.

In both science and spirituality, the observer emerges as a critical aspect in determining reality. Quantum physics illustrates how observation compresses a particle's wave function, determining its state. This phenomena calls into question the notion of an objective, autonomous reality by stressing the interdependence of the observer and the seen. Spiritual traditions support this viewpoint by emphasizing the transformational potential of consciousness. In Advaita Vedanta, for example, the self and the cosmos are considered as reflections of the same underlying reality, with perception influencing experience. This oneness suggests that uncertainty is not a fault, but rather an intrinsic feature of life, allowing a participatory engagement with the environment.

Existential tension emerges when the distinctions between being and non-being, certainty and ambiguity blur. This tension is shown by Schrödinger's cat thought experiment, which depicts a cat in a sealed box that is both alive and dead until it is viewed. This paradoxical condition of superposition defies traditional reasoning and reflects the dualities discussed in spiritual traditions. Dualities like as life and death, light and dark, or form and emptiness are viewed as complimentary components of a united whole in mystical traditions. The Kabbalistic Tree of Life, for example, presents creation as a dynamic interaction of opposites driven by divine will.

Existential philosophy is similarly permeated with the conflict between uncertainty and certainty. Philosophers like Søren Kierkegaard and

Friedrich Nietzsche explored the search for meaning in an uncertain environment. Kierkegaard's idea of the "leap of faith" encapsulates the need of accepting uncertainty in order to achieve spiritual satisfaction. For Nietzsche, rejecting absolute facts allowed for self-creation and authenticity. These philosophical approaches are consistent with quantum physics' rejection of deterministic absolutes, inviting people to approach the unknown with curiosity and daring.

One of the most remarkable similarities between quantum physics and spirituality is the acceptance of contradiction as a means of greater knowledge. Paradoxes in science, such as wave-particle duality, highlight the limitations of traditional frameworks, encouraging researchers to develop more complete theories. Paradox is used in spirituality to help people transcend ordinary thinking. Zen koans, for example, are intended to perplex the reasoning mind, opening the door to intuitive understanding. "What is the sound of one hand clapping?" is a well-known koan." This subject defies rational understanding, encouraging practitioners to investigate the nature of perception and consciousness.

Embracing contradiction necessitates a transition from dogmatic certainty to flexible openness, which is fostered in both scientific research and spiritual practices. Hypotheses in the scientific process must be examined and altered in response to evidence, indicating a continual conversation with uncertainty. Similarly, spiritual activities like meditation help people accept impermanence and the fluidity of their experiences. Scientists and spiritual searchers alike broaden their grasp of reality by confronting the unknown, transcending dualistic frameworks.

The conflict between doubt and faith also has ethical and existential consequences. Recognizing uncertainty promotes humility and prudence in a society increasingly impacted by scientific and technical advancements. Quantum physics emphasizes that minor changes at the microscopic level may have large macroscopic repercussions, a notion that is similar to the interconnectivity highlighted in biological and social systems. Similarly, spiritual traditions promote thoughtful action and compassion, acknowledging the impact of individual actions on the community.

Accepting ambiguity, from an ethical standpoint, undermines dogmatism and polarization, enabling debate and collaboration across fields and beliefs. In both science and spirituality, humility emerges as a basic virtue, allowing humans to traverse complexity with openness and sensitivity.

This humility is especially important in dealing with global issues like climate change, social inequity, and technology ethics, when easy solutions are insufficient.

Existential tension, rather than being a cause of misery, can stimulate creativity and perseverance. The struggle with uncertainty has inspired some of humanity's most profound expressions in art, literature, and philosophy. Rainer Maria Rilke's poetry, for example, investigates the interplay of light and shadow, presence and absence, mirroring the quantum riddles of superposition and entanglement. Rilke's advice to "live the questions" reflects the spirit of inquiry that motivates both scientific and spiritual discovery.

The struggle of reconciling the limited with the infinite, the known and the unknown, is central to existential tension. This challenge encourages a rethinking of identity and purpose, pushing beyond the ego's desire for control and assurance. Quantum physics exposes a dynamic, relational, and probabilistic environment, calling into question static concepts of self and reality. Spiritual traditions provide strategies for navigating this changing terrain by emphasizing interconnectedness, mindfulness, and the transforming power of consciousness.

Individuals who embrace uncertainty might develop a stronger feeling of connection and awe, realizing their role in a vast and ever-changing universe. This realization promotes a sense of responsibility and encourages acts that acknowledge all creatures' connection. The acceptance of existential tension, whether via scientific discovery, spiritual practice, or creative expression, creates opportunities for growth, resilience, and fulfillment.

The conversation between quantum physics and spirituality emphasizes the importance of combining different views to solve life's deepest riddles. Individuals and groups can progress beyond dualistic thinking by confronting existential tension and embracing the richness of ambiguity as a necessary component of life. This synthesis provides not just a more profound comprehension of the cosmos, but also a framework for navigating the intricacies of human experience with grace and wisdom.

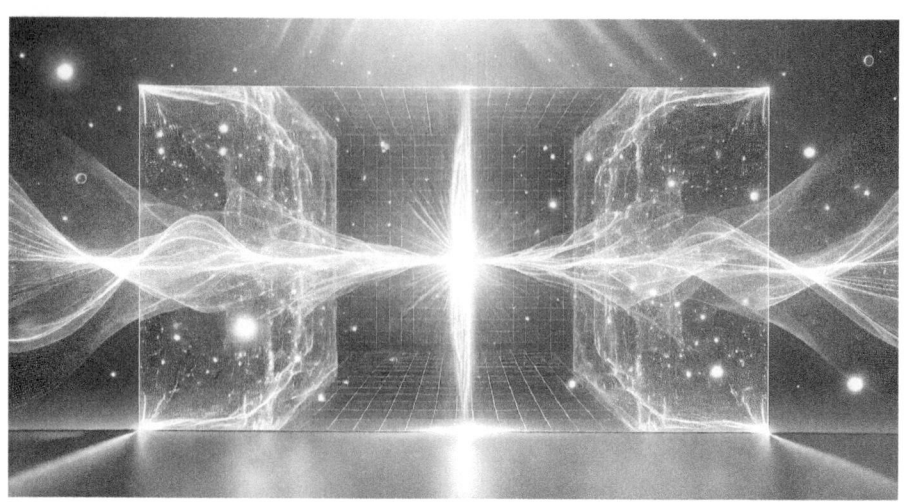

CHAPTER 8: QUANTUM TUNNELING AND MIRACLES

"Miracles are not contrary to nature, but only contrary to what we know about nature." – Saint Augustine

Q uantum tunneling is one of the most perplexing phenomena in physics, contradicting the traditional concept of energy barriers. This paradox, in which particles pass past apparently impenetrable barriers, has far-reaching consequences for our understanding of reality, changing ideas like chance, determinism, and the basic structure of existence. It calls into question the classical notion that objects require sufficient energy to overcome barriers, providing insight into the odd yet mathematically accurate behavior of quantum particles.

Classical physics, based on Newtonian mechanics, holds that a particle must have sufficient energy to pass through a barrier. A ball going toward a hill, for example, will only pass over it if its kinetic energy exceeds the gravitational potential at the crest. However, in the quantum realm, particles display characteristics that contradict this reasoning. Quantum tunneling happens when a particle passes through an energy barrier that it lacks the energy to overcome according to classical criteria. This process is facilitated by the wave-like nature of particles, as explained by quantum physics.

The wave function, a mathematical description of the probabilities associated with a particle's location and momentum, is central to quantum tunneling theory. A particle's wave function does not come to a halt at the border of a barrier; rather, it decreases exponentially within the barrier and may extend beyond it. This suggests there is a nonzero chance the particle will be detected on the opposite side of the barrier. The particle "borrows" energy to temporarily overcome the impediment before returning to a lower-energy state, which is consistent with the concepts of quantum uncertainty and superposition.

Quantum tunneling is more than just a theoretical concept; it is a phenomena with deep practical ramifications. One of its most major uses is nuclear fusion, the process that fuels the sun. According to traditional estimates, the temperatures and pressures within the sun's core are inadequate to cause hydrogen nuclei to collide and fuse together. However, quantum tunneling allows these particles to overcome their mutual electrostatic repulsion, allowing fusion processes to occur, resulting in the sun's enormous energy output. This similar approach is being used in experimental fusion reactors on Earth as scientists strive to recreate the sun's energy generation processes.

In addition to powering stars, quantum tunneling is essential to the operation of contemporary devices like the scanning tunneling microscope (STM). Scientists may observe and control individual atoms with the STM by taking use of the tunneling current—electrons that tunnel between the microscope's tip and the sample surface. This exact atomic control has transformed nanotechnology, paving the path for advances in materials science, electronics, and medicine.

The phenomena is also important in biological systems, specifically in enzyme catalysis and energy transmission inside cells. For example, quantum tunneling allows protons and electrons to flow more effectively during physiological activities such as photosynthesis and cellular respiration. These processes show how quantum effects, which are frequently linked with the subatomic domain, affect macroscopic systems required for life.

The ramifications of quantum tunneling go beyond the physical sciences and into philosophical and metaphysical problems regarding the nature of reality. The idea that particles might exist in seeming impossibility is consistent with spiritual and mystical conceptions that question linear causation and material constraints. Barriers are frequently used in spiritual traditions to represent problems or perceived restrictions that must be overcome in order to gain enlightenment or spiritual understanding. In this metaphorical sense, quantum tunneling symbolizes the idea that reality is fluid and linked rather than limited by hard structures.

Mystical interpretations of quantum tunneling sometimes draw connections with conceptions of transcendence and miraculous experiences recorded in religious scriptures. For example, the concept that particles might "borrow" energy to accomplish the seemingly impossible is similar to stories of divine intervention or supernatural happenings. While such parallels are metaphorical rather than scientific, they underscore humanity's ongoing curiosity with the unknown and the limits of possibility.

However, such comparisons should be approached with caution, differentiating between scientific occurrences and metaphorical interpretations. Quantum tunneling functions inside a well-defined mathematical framework, and its effects may be demonstrated experimentally. Spiritual and mystical interpretations, while valuable in their own right, cannot be empirically validated. Maintaining this divide means that talks on quantum phenomena are evidence-based while still allowing for philosophical debate.

Quantum tunneling also raises concerns about determinism and free will, as it exhibits quantum physics' probabilistic character. The uncertainty of whether a particle would tunnel through a barrier calls into question the deterministic framework of classical physics, implying that the cosmos is inherently probabilistic. This viewpoint has far-reaching ramifications for philosophical arguments about causation, agency, and the meaning of existence. If reality is guided by probabilities rather than certainties, then ideas like choice and predestination must be reconsidered.

From a scientific standpoint, quantum tunneling shows natural laws' creative potential, allowing for things that would otherwise be unattainable. This ingenuity is seen in the wide range of applications that have resulted from tunneling research, including advances in medical imaging and the construction of quantum computers. Quantum computers, in particular, use tunneling to conduct computations at extraordinary speeds, with the potential to transform industries ranging from encryption to AI.

As scientists continue to investigate quantum tunneling, they discover additional levels of intricacy and possibility. Advances in experimental methods, like as ultrafast spectroscopy, enable scientists to view tunneling processes in real time, revealing light on the mechanics that underpin this riddle. These discoveries not only broaden our grasp of quantum physics, but they also spark new ideas that have the potential to alter technology and society.

The study of quantum tunneling exemplifies the strength of human curiosity and the quest of knowledge. It pushes us to broaden our concept of reality by accepting the paradoxes and uncertainties that constitute the quantum realm. Quantum tunneling pushes us to reexamine the essence of existence, the limits of knowledge, and the interconnection of all things by pushing the envelope of what is possible. It serves as a reminder that the cosmos, despite its complexity, has secrets that continue to inspire amazement and discovery.

Miracles and Impossibility: Religious
Narratives of Transcending Limits.

Miracles have captured human awareness for millennia, frequently acting as reminders of faith, amazement, and the ability to transcend perceived constraints. Miracles are depicted in numerous religious traditions as divine intervention, breaking natural rules, or expressions of profound spiritual truths. Quantum physics, with its paradoxical and counterintuitive occurrences, provides fertile ground for revisiting the distinction between the miraculous and the scientifically unlikely. Exploring these intersections demonstrates the universe's eternal mystery as well as the need of distinguishing symbolic interpretation from scientific insight.

Miracles have traditionally been defined as happenings that defy nature's predicted workings, violating physical rules to illustrate the divine's might. Stories like the parting of the Red Sea, the resurrection of Christ, and Buddhist narratives of walking on water are fundamental to their respective traditions, emphasizing themes of change, hope, and the infinite possibilities of the spiritual world. Miracles, in these stories, are not only proof of divine power, but also symbols for inner spiritual awakening, surpassing material constraints to attain higher realms of existence.

The idea of impossibility in classical physics is based on Newtonian mechanics' predictable and deterministic framework. Natural principles, such as energy conservation and the unrelenting force of gravity, define what is and is not conceivable. Miracles, according to this worldview, could only be understood as breaches of these laws—extraordinary happenings that required external intervention to overcome the natural order. However, the arrival of quantum physics in the early twentieth century significantly altered this inflexible framework, introducing ideas like as uncertainty, nonlocality, and superposition that redefined the bounds of the imaginable.

Quantum physics shows that particles can act in ways that contradict traditional intuition on the tiniest scales of existence. Quantum tunneling, for example, permits particles to slip through energy barriers that appear to be beyond their ability to overcome. Tunneling, while not a "miracle" in the religious sense, demonstrates how quantum systems may transcend traditional physical restrictions. Similarly, particle entanglement across long distances, in which changes to one particle influence its companion immediately, calls into question traditional ideas of location and causation. While these occurrences have been extensively examined and empirically proved, they create a sensation of amazement similar to that produced by miraculous happenings.

Miracles are frequently framed as symbolic rather than literal, pointing to realities that exist beyond of the corporeal world. In Hinduism, for example, miraculous events in sacred books such as the Bhagavad Gita are viewed as allegories for spiritual truths, rather than historical facts.

Similarly, the miracles reported in the Buddha's life, such as levitation and spontaneous illumination, underscore the possibility of freedom from the confines of samsara—the cycle of birth, death, and reincarnation. Miracles, in this sense, are less about defying nature and more about exposing deeper realities that may be discovered through spiritual effort and understanding.

Quantum physics lends itself to a similar symbolic interpretation, with paradoxes serving as metaphors for existence's complexity and interconnection. The uncertainty principle, which restricts our capacity to know both a particle's position and momentum at the same time, is consistent with spiritual beliefs concerning the unknowability of ultimate truth. Miracles, in this perspective, might be interpreted as instances when deeper truths about the nature of existence emerge, rather than breaches of physical law. This symbolic alignment promotes communication between scientific and spiritual viewpoints, providing a common vocabulary for delving into fundamental issues concerning reality.

Despite the obvious connections, it is critical to distinguish between the scientifically testable occurrences of quantum physics and religious miraculous claims. Quantum effects, while sometimes paradoxical, are regulated by well-defined mathematical laws that have been repeatedly validated by experiments. Religious miracles, on the other hand, are related to spiritual beliefs and are frequently used to represent cultural narratives and existential problems. Attempts to explicitly compare quantum occurrences with miracles run the risk of confusing scientific rigor with metaphorical interpretation, weakening the integrity of both realms.

This divide does not prohibit a thorough examination of the conceptual connections between science and spirituality. For example, the concept of transcending limitations, which is important to quantum physics and religious miracles, prompts inquiry on the nature of boundaries—whether physical, mental, or spiritual. Limits like as the speed of light and the Planck constant determine the structure of the cosmos in quantum mechanics, while phenomena such as tunneling show how these boundaries may be negotiated in unexpected ways. Similarly, religious miracle stories frequently stress the transcendence of human limitations, providing hope and inspiration for personal and community reform.

Miracles also raise problems about the observer's involvement in changing reality, a subject that is repeated in the quantum mechanical notion of measurement. In quantum physics, the act of seeing collapses a wave function, identifying a system's state from its probability. This observer effect emphasizes the interaction between perception and reality, which is consistent with spiritual teachings regarding awareness' ability to alter experience. Miracles frequently occur in response to acts of faith in religious narratives, implying a mutually beneficial interaction between the deity and the believer. While the methods are fundamentally different, both viewpoints emphasize the transformational power of confronting the unknown.

One of quantum mechanics' most important consequences is that it challenges deterministic interpretations of the cosmos, implying that reality is inherently random. This viewpoint is consistent with spiritual traditions that recognize mystery and doubt as inherent to the human experience. In Christianity, for example, faith is defined as "the evidence of things not seen," stressing confidence in the unknown. Similarly, Buddhist emptiness teachings emphasize reality's flexible and interrelated character, encouraging practitioners to let go of fixed conceptions. Quantum physics fosters an openness to the unknown by exposing a reality in which certainty gives way to possibilities.

The combination of miracles and quantum physics also invites thought about the ethical and philosophical consequences of pushing beyond bounds. In both religious and scientific contexts, the search of the unusual has the capacity to inspire as well as embolden. Religious miracles are frequently lauded as manifestations of heavenly mercy, but they can also be used to legitimize orthodoxy or power systems. Similarly, the employment of quantum principles in technologies like artificial intelligence and quantum computing poses ethical concerns regarding the responsible use of transformational knowledge. Navigating these issues necessitates humility, insight, and a dedication to the greater good.

Finally, the conversation between quantum physics and the idea of miracles encourages a rethinking of what it means to transcend constraints. Rather of seeing miracles as breaches of nature, we might see them as insights of the deeper, interwoven fabric of reality. Quantum physics, with its paradoxical discoveries and transformational potential, serves as a reminder that the frontiers of possibility are considerably more flexible than conventional wisdom suggests. By accepting both the rigor of scientific investigation and the richness of spiritual metaphor, we get a better knowledge of the world and our role in it.

Subtle Comparisons: Walking

the Fine Line Between Verified Phenomena and Faith Claims

The interaction of quantum physics and spirituality raises deep concerns about the nature of reality, the scope of human knowledge, and the limits of belief. However, in order to preserve the integrity of both scientific and spiritual study, this terrain must be navigated with prudence. While quantum phenomena such as tunneling, superposition, and entanglement give scientific insights into the universe's workings, their contrast to faith-based claims of miracles and transcendence must be carefully considered. Misinterpretations occur when metaphorical interpretations of scientific ideas are given as proof for spiritual truths, or when the mysteries of faith are evoked to explain empirical oddities. A refined approach can reveal relevant connections while keeping these areas separate.

Quantum mechanics is famous for its unexpected discoveries, such as quantum tunneling. Tunneling particles appear to transcend conventional barriers, crossing energy levels that classical physics consider impassable. This tendency, which has been thoroughly proven by studies such as those using semiconductor physics, is frequently associated with the concept of transcending bounds, a subject that appears in religious and spiritual traditions. For example, a particle's capacity to "leap" past an impediment recalls legends of supernatural intervention in which natural rules appear to be ignored. However, quantum tunneling functions within the probabilistic framework of quantum theory, making it a foreseeable conclusion under specified conditions rather than an enigmatic or miraculous event.

Similarly, the concept of quantum entanglement, in which two particles are instantly joined regardless of distance, draws parallels with spiritual concepts of unity and connectivity. Entanglement's demonstration in experiments such as the Bell test challenges traditional ideas about locality, implying a deeper, non-local fabric to reality. Spiritual traditions, such as the Buddhist idea of Indra's Net, conjure up comparable images of a linked world in which one creature reflects and impacts the others. While these analogies contribute to the scientific-spiritual conversation, entanglement remains a mathematically exact phenomena that is quantifiable and repeatable in laboratory settings. To immediately equate entanglement with mystical oneness risks simplifying both notions and reducing significant philosophical insights to scientific literalism.

The different techniques and epistemologies of quantum phenomena and faith statements make comparisons difficult. Science bases its models on empirical observation, hypothesis testing, and reproducibility, but spirituality frequently encompasses subjective experience, metaphorical interpretation, and transcendental truths that may be resistant to scientific confirmation. This difference does not elevate one perspective above the other; rather, it emphasizes the unique roles they play in human comprehension. Science strives to understand the mechanics of the observable world, whereas spirituality tackles concerns about meaning, purpose, and life that are frequently outside the scope of scientific study.

Faith-based miracle claims usually include experiences that appear to break natural rules, such as healings, apparitions, or phenomena ascribed to divine intervention. In these cases, the absence of scientific explanation is frequently used as proof of the miraculous. However, science's failure to explain an occurrence does not always suggest a supernatural origin; it may just represent the existing boundaries of scientific understanding. Lightning and eclipses, for example, were long thought to be the work of divine powers but have since been debunked by scientific research. This dynamic emphasizes the necessity of differentiating between gaps in understanding and the summoning of miracles, ensuring that spiritual tales keep their symbolic richness without being associated with scientific ignorance.

The human predisposition for pattern detection and meaning-making exacerbates the tension between verifiable occurrences and faith claims. Quantum physics, with its inherent uncertainties and paradoxes, lends itself to creative interpretations that touch on spiritual issues. The uncertainty principle, which restricts the precision of some measurements, corresponds figuratively to spiritual beliefs that value mystery and the unknown. Similarly, the probabilistic character of quantum systems reflects the function of faith in navigating uncertainty, where believing maintains hope in the absence of assurance. While these similarities are powerful, they are figurative rather than evidence-based, functioning as bridges for discussion rather than definite proofs.

In the field of quantum healing and energy medicine, the lines between science and spirituality are frequently blurred. Proponents of treatments such as Reiki or quantum touch frequently use quantum notions to explain their procedures, saying that the principles of energy transmission and non-locality underpin their efficacy. While such methods may have subjective advantages, thorough scientific proof is still elusive. Misuse of quantum nomenclature in these circumstances jeopardizes the legitimacy of authentic quantum research and reduces the sophisticated understanding of these phenomena. Maintaining a clear difference between the symbolic usage of quantum notions and their scientific foundation is critical for protecting the integrity of both disciplines.

Faith claims are also portrayed as comparable to or supported by quantum physics, which raises ethical concerns. The use of quantum concepts in contexts such as alternative medicine or spiritual counseling might give an impression of scientific validity, which may mislead those looking for evidence-based answers. This dynamic emphasizes educators, practitioners, and communicators' obligation to ensure that talks concerning quantum physics and spirituality are transparent, truthful, and appreciative of each perspective's unique contributions. We can appreciate the richness of science and spirituality without confusing their separate spheres by encouraging educated discussion.

The mutual power to generate surprise and amazement is what makes minor analogies between quantum events and religion claims so appealing. Quantum mechanics shows a cosmos that is far wilder and more complex than classical physics ever anticipated, questioning our preconceptions about reality and our role within it. Similarly, religious and spiritual narratives provide significant insights into existence's secrets, promoting contemplation of the sublime and limitless. By approaching these intersections with humility and intellectual curiosity, we can get a better understanding of the universe' complexity and the variety of human thinking.

Balancing confirmed occurrences with faith assertions is a delicate issue. It entails admitting the limits of human comprehension while keeping open to new possibilities, appreciating the various techniques of science and spirituality, and celebrating their joint ability to light the mysteries of reality. In doing so, we acknowledge both the scientific rigor of quantum physics and the transforming power of religion, fostering a conversation that broadens our understanding of the cosmos and our role within it. This deliberate navigation not only promotes a more nuanced respect for science and spirituality, but also challenges us to appreciate the tremendous connection that underpins both.

CHAPTER 9: HEISENBERG'S UNCERTAINTY AND FREE WILL

"Freedom lies in being bold." – Robert Frost

Werner Heisenberg's concept of uncertainty, first proposed in 1927, transformed our understanding of the microscopic world. This principle asserts that there is a fundamental limit to the accuracy with which certain pairs of particles' attributes, such as location and momentum, may be determined at the same time. This is not only a restriction of measurement equipment, but an inherent aspect of nature itself. In the quantum world, Heisenberg's uncertainty principle (HUP) calls into question classical determinism, implying that the cosmos is structured on probabilities rather than certainty. This concept has far-reaching ramifications beyond of physics, impacting debates about free will, determinism, and reality's fundamental unpredictable nature.

Heisenberg's uncertainty principle is based on quantum objects' wave-particle duality. At the tiny scale, particles like electrons behave like both particles and waves. When attempting to determine the precise location of a particle (position), its wave-like nature makes its momentum increasingly ambiguous. In contrast, efforts to detect momentum with great accuracy stretch out the particle's location over an uncertain range. The mathematical expression for this connection is $\Delta x \Delta p > \hbar/2$, where Δx represents location uncertainty, Δp represents momentum uncertainty, and $\hbar$ (Planck's constant divided by 2π) is a basic quantum constant. This equation captures the trade-off between accuracy in location and momentum, highlighting quantum mechanics' probabilistic base.

The consequences of the uncertainty principle challenge traditional concepts of causation. In classical physics, a particle's location and momentum at any given time may be accurately determined in theory. This determinism enables predictions of future states based on beginning conditions, as demonstrated by Newtonian mechanics. However, the uncertainty principle undermines this assurance by claiming that the more precisely we know one feature, the less we can know about the other. This indeterminacy adds a probabilistic aspect to quantum systems' behavior, allowing outcomes to be anticipated as likelihoods rather than certainties.

In quantum physics, the wave function, a mathematical construct that describes the state of a quantum system, represents this probability. The wave function represents the likelihood of encountering a particle in various locations or states of momentum. When a measurement is taken, the wave function collapses to a definite value, although it is initially a superposition of possibilities. Heisenberg's uncertainty principle is inextricably linked to this probabilistic framework, highlighting the interaction between measurement, observation, and reality. It contradicts the conventional wisdom that physical attributes exist independently of observation, implying that the act of measuring influences the conclusion.

The uncertainty principle has far-reaching consequences for our understanding of determinism and free will. In a classically deterministic cosmos, every occurrence is the unavoidable result of preceding conditions, leaving no opportunity for chance or unpredictability. Heisenberg's principle adds randomness at the quantum level, implying that the cosmos runs on probabilities rather than set certainties. While quantum effects are on a much smaller scale than macroscopic events, their inherent uncertainty poses philosophical problems regarding causation, predictability, and the extent to which randomness may impact the overall functioning of the cosmos.

This inherent uncertainty draws parallels with spiritual and philosophical beliefs about the limits of human understanding and control. Many cultures emphasize the importance of accepting ambiguity and the mystery of life, seeing it not as a defect but as an essential component of reality. In Taoism, for example, the notion of wu wei, or effortless action, represents a philosophy of allowing events to unfold naturally rather than seeking to impose rigorous control. Similarly, Buddhist teachings on impermanence and the illusory character of the ego are consistent with the probabilistic and interrelated nature of the quantum universe. In this light, Heisenberg's principle might be interpreted as a scientific validation of these timeless observations.

The uncertainty principle has encouraged innovation in disciplines such as quantum computing and quantum cryptography. Quantum computers use quantum physics' probabilistic nature to do computations that classical systems cannot. Similarly, quantum cryptography uses principles such as uncertainty to develop secure communication systems, in which the act of measuring or intercepting a quantum key changes its state, allowing for tamper detection. These improvements demonstrate the practical value of accepting uncertainty, converting it from a theoretical constraint to a weapon for creativity.

Critics and skeptics sometimes misinterpret the uncertainty principle, viewing it as a type of epistemological despair—a notion that human knowledge is essentially restricted. However, Heisenberg's principle does not mean that we can know nothing about quantum systems. Instead, it defines the precise bounds that allow for meaningful predictions. This detailed knowledge has allowed scientists to create surprisingly realistic models of atomic and subatomic systems, ranging from the behavior of electrons in atoms to the dynamics of quantum fields. Rather from being a hindrance, the uncertainty principle has broadened the scope of scientific investigation, enabling deeper exploration into the nature of reality.

The philosophical implications of the uncertainty principle extend to discussions concerning consciousness and the observer's role in generating reality. In quantum physics, the act of measuring affects the system being viewed, raising issues regarding the link between consciousness and physical occurrences. While the Copenhagen interpretation emphasizes the necessity of observation in compressing the wave function, others, such as the many-worlds interpretation, argue that all conceivable possibilities reside in parallel universes, eliminating the need for an observer to define reality. These disputes remain unanswered, highlighting the enormous problems quantum physics poses to our understanding of reality.

The uncertainty principle proposed by Heisenberg also calls into question the concept of absolute objectivity. In classical science, the observer is frequently viewed as distinct from the observed, an objective entity examining an external system. In contrast, quantum physics discloses the interconnectivity of the observer and the observed, with the act of observation affecting the system under study. This transformation is consistent with spiritual beliefs that emphasize the interconnectedness of all things and the individual's inseparability from the universe. By blurring the lines between subject and object, the uncertainty principle encourages a more holistic understanding of reality that transcends dualistic divisions.

As we continue to investigate the ramifications of the uncertainty principle, its significance extends beyond the laboratory to philosophy, spirituality, and human experience. It acts as a reminder of the limitations of certainty and the need of accepting complexity, ambiguity, and interconnection. In a society driven by the need for control and predictability, Heisenberg's revelation provides a powerful alternative, honoring the beauty of the unknown and the richness of possibilities.

By bridging the gap between classical physics' deterministic certainty and quantum physics' probabilistic riddles, the uncertainty principle pushes us to reevaluate the nature of reality and our role within it. It encourages humility, curiosity, and awe in the face of the universe's limitless complexity. Uncertainty, seen through this perspective, becomes a portal to deeper understanding and connection, rather than a barrier to knowledge.

Philosophical Gaps: Does Inherent Randomness Allow for Volition?

The discovery of quantum mechanics posed a significant challenge to the deterministic worldview that had dominated classical physics. This shift is centered on the concept of intrinsic randomness, which supports phenomena such as quantum superposition, wave function collapse, and Heisenberg's uncertainty principle. Unlike Newtonian mechanics' predictable paths, quantum events occur probabilistically, with results that are impossible to anticipate exactly. This probabilistic character has spurred heated philosophical discussion about what it means for human will, freedom, and the nature of reality itself.

At its foundation, quantum physics disproves the idea that the cosmos works like a clockwork mechanism, with every future state predicted by previous conditions. Instead, quantum systems are guided by probabilities included in their wave functions. When an observation is made, the wave function collapses, revealing a single conclusion from a range of possibilities. This randomness calls classical determinism into question, implying that the cosmos may be inherently unpredictable. For some, this opens the door to a philosophical rethinking of free choice and human agency.

The topic of whether quantum randomness equals freedom is difficult. Randomness in quantum events differs from choice in the human environment. A genuinely random quantum fluctuation lacks purpose, meaning, or deliberation—it is a result determined by probabilities rather than deterministic rules. For volition to exist, a mechanism must link quantum randomness to conscious human decisions. Without such a relationship, quantum randomness may be viewed as adding disorder to the cosmos rather than providing a basis for meaningful decision.

Some interpretations of quantum physics try to close this gap. The Copenhagen interpretation, for example, places the observer at the heart of quantum processes, claiming that the act of observation influences outcomes. While this does not explicitly connect quantum events to human will, it does imply that consciousness and measurement are essential to the evolution of quantum processes. Other interpretations, such as the many-worlds hypothesis, eliminate randomness entirely by supposing that all conceivable outcomes occur in distinct, parallel realities. In this perspective, every decision we make may constitute a branching point, but it does not provide free will in the classic sense.

Determinism, a classical physics notion, complicates the junction of quantum randomness and free will. In a deterministic cosmos, every occurrence is the inevitable result of previous causes. This viewpoint gives little possibility for autonomy, as even human decisions are ultimately influenced by preceding situations. Quantum physics interrupts this predictable sequence at the microscopic level, introducing a degree of uncertainty. It is unclear if this indeterminacy extends to macroscopic systems such as the human brain. Many scientists believe that the brain's activities, while impacted by quantum phenomena, are mostly controlled by classical processes.

Neuroscience sheds light on the argument. The human brain is a very complex system, with billions of linked neurons that produce emergent phenomena such as cognition, emotion, and decision-making. While the brain's fundamental building blocks—atoms and subatomic particles—are subject to quantum principles, it is unclear whether quantum randomness plays an important role in conscious cognition. Some hypotheses, such as those advanced by Roger Penrose and Stuart Hameroff, argue that quantum coherence in microtubules within neurons may alter consciousness. However, these theories are still theoretical and not commonly accepted in the scientific community.

Philosophically, the link between quantum randomness and free will raises fundamental problems about causation, agency, and moral responsibility. If quantum physics delivers unpredictability into the cosmos, does it increase our sense of freedom or just replace determinism with randomness? Many philosophers contend that actual volition involves more than mere randomness; it necessitates the ability to engage in purposeful action guided by thinking and thought. In this perspective, neither severe determinism nor pure randomness provide an adequate foundation for free will.

Spiritual and metaphysical viewpoints frequently tackle the subject from different angles. Many spiritual traditions emphasize the interaction of freedom and connectivity, implying that individual agency exists within a larger web of causality. From this standpoint, quantum mechanics might be viewed as a scientific metaphor for the balance of human liberty and universal interconnectedness. The unpredictability of quantum occurrences might represent the possibility of creative action within the confines of natural rules, which is consistent with spiritual concepts of cosmic freedom or divine play.

One place where quantum randomness and will may meet is in the field of creativity and invention. Human creativity frequently entails the development of unique ideas, solutions, or creative expressions—processes that appear to defy absolute determinism. Quantum indeterminacy, with its emphasis on possibilities rather than certainty, is an effective metaphor for the creative process. Just like a quantum system lives in a superposition of states until measured, the creative mind investigates several possibilities before making a final decision or expression. While this example does not establish a direct connection between quantum mechanics and human mind, it does show the similarities between quantum principles and human experience.

In practical terms, the argument concerning quantum randomness and free will has ramifications for ethics, accountability, and the nature of human decision-making. Does quantum randomness impact our decisions, absolving us of moral accountability? Most philosophers and ethicists disagree, stating that responsibility stems not from the lack of causation, but from the ability to act purposefully and reflectively. Even in a cosmos influenced by quantum probability, human agency is an essential component of ethical life.

The subject also covers technology and artificial intelligence. As researchers create increasingly powerful AI systems, problems regarding autonomy, decision-making, and moral agency become more pressing. If AI systems include quantum randomness into their decision-making processes, would they be more "free," or will their behavior become more unpredictable? These issues mimic the larger philosophical difficulties given by quantum physics, emphasizing the importance of thoughtful consideration as we manage the junction of science, technology, and human values.

Exploring the philosophical voids left by quantum randomness reveals that the link between science and will is complex and unresolved. While quantum physics challenges conventional determinism, it does not definitively address the question of free will. Instead, it challenges our ideas about causation, choice, and the nature of reality itself. By accepting the complexities of these challenges, we may get a better grasp of what it means to be human in a cosmos that is both orderly and unpredictable.

Spiritual Perspective: Understanding Unpredictability as Cosmic Freedom or Divine Play

The unpredictability of quantum physics has frequently been viewed as more than a scientific curiosity. For many, it provides a window into spiritual and philosophical concepts that emphasize freedom, mystery, and the dynamic aspect of existence. According to spiritual traditions, unpredictability may not just represent randomness, but rather a fundamental feature of the universe that represents creativity, divine intent, or the interrelated play of forces forming reality.

Quantum mechanics radically undermines traditional ideas of a deterministic reality. Heisenberg's concept of uncertainty, as well as the probabilistic consequences of quantum processes, show that nature is not totally predictable. This seeming randomness breaks traditional physics' strict causal linkages, ushering in an openness to reality that reflects spiritual conceptions of freedom. Many theological and philosophical systems consider freedom as a place for potential, transformation, and purpose, rather than chaos. This viewpoint is consistent with the idea

QUANTUM MYSTICISM

that quantum indeterminacy provides a type of cosmic creativity, allowing the cosmos to grow dynamically rather than following predetermined pathways.

Eastern spiritual traditions provide a rich framework for explaining unpredictability in ways that are consistent with quantum concepts. In Hinduism, the notion of Lila characterizes the cosmos as a divine theater directed by the cosmic creator. This play is not absolutely predictable; instead, it evolves spontaneously and freely, expressing the divine's creative power. Similarly, Buddhism emphasizes impermanence and the fluidity of reality, urging acceptance of uncertainty as an inherent part of existence. The unpredictability found in quantum systems supports these beliefs, implying that the universe's behavior cannot always be cleanly classified or predicted.

Western theologians frequently associate unpredictability with divine power and the wonder of creation. Christian theology, for example, has long struggled to reconcile human free will and divine foreknowledge. Quantum physics, with its probabilistic framework, provides a paradigm for how freedom and order may coexist. The unpredictability of quantum events might be seen as a manifestation of divine creation, a method by which innovation and diversity occur in the universe. This perspective connects scientific discovery and spiritual thought, implying that randomness may serve a greater purpose in the divine plan.

Across civilizations, mystical traditions have embraced the concept that unpredictability exposes deeper truths about reality. In Kabbalistic Judaism, the dynamic interaction of divine forces generates a cosmos that is both organized and adaptable. This balance of order and chaos is similar to how quantum systems behave, oscillating between states of coherence and uncertainty. By presenting unpredictability as an integral component of cosmic design, mystical traditions closely correspond with quantum physics ideas, providing a prism through which scientific occurrences can be infused with spiritual meaning.

The spiritual embracing of quantum randomness extends into personal experience and human action. Many spiritual activities, such as meditation, prayer, and mindfulness, highlight the value of accepting ambiguity as a means of achieving inner peace. These practices teach that by letting go of the craving for control and certainty, people may more fully connect with the flow of life. Quantum physics, with its intrinsic indeterminacy, serves as a scientific counterpart for this spiritual concept, implying that uncertainty is a state to be understood and managed rather than dreaded.

Interpreting quantum randomness as cosmic freedom calls into question long-standing philosophical discussions regarding free choice. Classical determinism allows limited opportunity for human action because all occurrences are viewed as unavoidable outcomes of preceding conditions. The deterministic chain is disrupted by quantum mechanics, which introduces uncertainty at the basic level. While this does not explicitly show the reality of free will, it does provide a conceptual framework in which freedom may function. Philosophically, this brings up issues about how unpredictability interacts with intentionality, creativity, and moral responsibility.

Some spiritual philosophers believe that the unpredictable nature of quantum occurrences indicates a deeper interconnectivity in the fabric of existence. The phenomenon of quantum entanglement, in which particles display correlations regardless of distance, implies that the cosmos functions as a single unit. This connectivity is consistent with spiritual beliefs that value oneness and interdependence. In this sense, unpredictability might be viewed as a reflection of a greater, more complicated order—one that is beyond our knowledge and represents the endless possibilities of life.

The metaphor of divine play has practical consequences for how people deal with uncertainty in their lives. Spiritual traditions frequently teach that accepting uncertainty promotes humility, flexibility, and resilience. These characteristics are critical for managing a world marked by complexity and fast change. Individuals are urged to adopt an open and trusting mentality, considering obstacles and uncertainty as chances for growth and discovery.

In modern debate, the interaction of quantum physics and spirituality provides a framework for answering some of life's most important issues. What is it like to live in a universe that is essentially unpredictable? How can people combine their yearning for stability with the inherent volatility of life? These questions are more than just scholarly; they get to the heart of what it means to be human. Spiritual interpretations of quantum physics provide a vocabulary for delving into these issues, yielding ancient and contemporary insights.

Regardless of the attractiveness of these linkages, the spiritual interpretation of quantum unpredictability must be approached with caution. Quantum physics provides compelling analogies for spiritual notions, but it does not validate specific theological or metaphysical views. Scientific concepts must be understood on their own terms, with a careful distinction between metaphorical interpretations and actual data.

Maintaining this balance guarantees that the conversation between science and spirituality is polite and helpful.

Viewing unpredictability as cosmic freedom or divine play prompts a reconsideration of humanity's role in the cosmos. Individuals might regard themselves as active participants in a dynamic, ever-changing universe rather than passive spectators of a preset world. This viewpoint is consistent with spiritual beliefs that emphasize co-creation, responsibility, and the sacredness of life. By accepting ambiguity as a necessary component of the cosmos, science and spirituality provide avenues to greater understanding, richer experiences, and a more meaningful connection to life's mysteries.

CHAPTER 10: SUPERPOSITION AND MULTIPLE REALITIES

"We are like islands in the sea, separate on the surface but connected in the deep." – William James

The idea of superposition in quantum physics calls into question the basic foundation of our perception of reality. It asserts that, until measured or detected, particles exist in several states at the same time, embodying all possibilities. This notion, demonstrated by Schrödinger's famous thought experiment involving a cat that is both alive and dead until detected, pushes the bounds of human cognition.

QUANTUM MYSTICISM

Superposition is more than just a theoretical concept; it has been consistently proven by tests with photons or electrons in double-slit setups. These investigations demonstrate a reality in which existence is ambiguous until contact happens.

Superposition fundamentally destroys conventional determinism. Traditional physics assumes that things have well-defined attributes and states at all times, regardless of whether they are observed. This perspective is challenged by quantum mechanics. For example, in the well-known double-slit experiment, particles such as electrons exhibit wave-like interference patterns when not seen yet operate like particles when measured. This duality emphasizes the strange nature of superposition, in which a single particle's behavior is determined by the act of observation. In this perspective, reality is a field of possibilities waiting to collapse into a definitive state, rather than a static collection of fixed events.

This concept has far-reaching consequences that extend beyond the realm of physics. Superposition raises philosophical problems regarding reality, awareness, and free choice. If particles exist in overlapping states, does the cosmos include layers of reality that stay concealed until they are dealt with? Are humans, as observers, essential in molding the fabric of existence? These arguments call into question long-held assumptions about objectivity and indicate that awareness plays a participation role in the evolution of reality. This participatory viewpoint is consistent with spiritual and metaphysical traditions that frequently emphasize the interconnectivity of existence and the belief that reality is changed by perception.

Spiritual analogies to superposition are evident, especially in traditions that emphasize existence's non-duality. Advaita Vedanta, a Hindu philosophical school, maintains that the world's apparent dualities—light and dark, good and evil, life and death—are illusions (Maya) that conceal a single reality (Brahman). Similarly, Buddhist theories like the Middle Way highlight the false nature of dichotomies, calling for a non-binary explanation of life. The quantum principle of superposition, which embraces several states simultaneously, serves as a scientific parallel for these spiritual truths. It posits a cosmos in which contradictions coexist until they are reconciled by a higher perspective, which is consistent with the mystical concept of unity beneath multiplicity.

At the context of human experience, superposition may be viewed as a reflection of the potentiality that exists at every instant. Human lives, like particles, exist in numerous states, with each choice reflecting the collapse of potential into fact. This point of view is extremely powerful because it depicts existence as a dynamic interplay of possibilities rather than a predictable sequence. It is consistent with spiritual traditions that emphasize the importance of intention and mindfulness, implying that awareness is vital in influencing reality.

The scientific study of superposition continues to push the limits of what is conceivable. In quantum computing, for example, qubits use superposition to process information in ways that classical bits cannot. A qubit may represent both 0 and 1 at the same time, which exponentially increases processing capability for specified workloads. This technical application reveals that superposition is more than an abstract idea; it is a tangible occurrence with transformational potential. It also prompts philosophical considerations concerning the relationship between knowledge and existence. If superposition may be used to boost human skills, what other hidden potentials could lurk inside the fabric of reality?

Superposition also prompts a rethinking of timing and causality. In classical physics, events occur in a linear, predictable sequence, with causes coming before effects. However, quantum physics presents a universe in which events can be interwoven in nonlinear ways. Superposition permits particles to exist in seemingly conflicting states, implying that time may not be as rigid as we think. This calls into question the traditional understandings of past, present, and future, allowing for new interpretations of time as a fluid, interrelated dimension. Such notions are consistent with spiritual traditions that see time as an illusion or a product of human experience rather than an absolute structure.

In addition to having philosophical significance, superposition has practical ramifications for comprehending complex systems. In biology, for example, researchers are investigating whether quantum superposition has a role in processes such as photosynthesis and bird navigation. Some research suggests that certain biological functions may rely on quantum coherence, a phenomenon closely related to superposition. If confirmed, these results might change our knowledge of life, implying that quantum principles govern not just the basic components of the cosmos, but also the complex systems of living creatures.

Artists, authors, and intellectuals have all been drawn to the notion of superposition. It has been used as a metaphor for the human condition, representing the complexities and ambiguities of existence.

Narratives in literature and cinema frequently explore themes of parallel worlds or the existence of numerous truths, mimicking the quantum concept of overlapping states. These imaginative interpretations, while not technically accurate, demonstrate quantum notions' enormous effect on human cognition and expression. They also emphasize science's function as a source of inspiration, providing new ways to understand and connect with the wonders of life.

Critics of the spiritual or metaphorical use of superposition warn against combining scientific concepts with metaphysical assertions. While the analogies between quantum physics and spiritual teachings are fascinating, such linkages must be approached with caution and care. Superposition, as a scientific notion, is supported by empirical facts and mathematical formalism, but spiritual interpretations frequently rely on personal experience and symbolic meaning. Maintaining a clear boundary between these areas helps to keep the conversation between science and spirituality healthy and grounded.

The concept of superposition pushes mankind to broaden its perception of reality. It exposes a cosmos that is significantly more dynamic and interwoven than conventional physics implies, with alternatives coexisting until they are resolved by interaction. This finding has far-reaching consequences for science, philosophy, and theology, providing a new paradigm for investigating the nature of existence. Individuals and society can nurture a better appreciation for the universe's richness and complexity by embracing the mystery and potentiality inherent in superposition, creating a feeling of awe and humility in the face of the unknown."

Parallels to Spiritual Realms: several planes of being or layered truths.

Quantum superposition, in which particles persist in overlapping states until discovered, has a deep connection in spiritual traditions that investigate multiple realities and realms of existence. These spiritual frameworks frequently envision a cosmos that exists on numerous levels at once, with material, energetic, and transcendental aspects coexisting. Similar to spiritual traditions that highlight the interconnectivity and complexity of reality, the quantum idea of superposition contradicts linear, binary thinking.

The concept of various levels of existence is profoundly ingrained in Hindu and Buddhist philosophy. The Hindu cosmology speaks of several lokas or realms, each reflecting a distinct level of consciousness and life. Similarly, Buddhist teachings explain six realms of samsara, which depict the cyclical cycle of existence and the interwoven web of karmic forces. These frameworks propose that reality is stratified, with higher and lower dimensions interacting in ways that affect the total. The quantum state of superposition provides a scientific model for this layered awareness by demonstrating how a single system may incorporate numerous potential outcomes at the same time.

Indigenous cosmologies share these ideas of plurality and connectivity. For example, Native American traditions frequently discuss the coexistence and influence of the physical, spiritual, and ancestral realms. These viewpoints are consistent with quantum principles, which state that particles are entangled over space and time, representing a holistic understanding of reality. The spiritual lens proposes that comprehending one layer of reality necessitates acknowledging the others, much as quantum systems cannot be fully understood without taking into account their wave-particle duality or potential.

Mystical traditions from many civilizations investigate the concept of multiple realities. According to Kabbalah, the mystical branch of Judaism, the Tree of Life consists of 10 interrelated sefirot or aspects of life that range from the material to the divine. These layers are not separate, but rather interwoven, affecting and reflecting one another. This mystical revelation is mirrored by quantum superposition, which proposes that particles—or even reality itself—exist in a state of fluid potential, with all possibilities interrelated until they are realized by observation or interaction.

Superposition provides a metaphysical framework for thinking about the nature of choice and reality. Observing a system compresses its wave function in quantum physics, resulting in a single outcome from numerous probabilities. This method is similar to spiritual teachings that stress mindfulness, intention, and the transformational power of consciousness. For example, Buddhist teachings on dependent origination propose that reality emerges from the interaction of circumstances and perceptions, in the same way as quantum systems are affected by observation and interaction.

Quantum physics and spiritual conceptions of multiple worlds share the concept of interconnectivity. Quantum entanglement, in which particles are connected regardless of distance, symbolizes the spiritual concept of oneness and unity. The quantum state of superposition strengthens this connection by implying that systems are not separate entities, but rather pieces of a larger whole. This understanding is consistent with Advaita Vedanta teachings that highlight the non-duality of existence and the illusion of separateness.

The examination of different levels of existence also prompts thought about the limitations of human perception. Spiritual traditions frequently emphasize that the material world is simply a part of reality, clouded by maya or illusion. Quantum mechanics demonstrates that human senses and equipment can only grasp a small portion of the universe's complexity. For example, particles in superposition defy traditional intuition, existing in mathematically defined but experientially mysterious states. This calls on the observer to broaden their awareness beyond superficial appearances, embracing the deeper levels of reality that are concealed from immediate experience.

Scientific discoveries have begun to explore the ramifications of these hidden layers of reality. Quantum computing, for example, employs superposition to accomplish complicated computations that traditional computers cannot. This technical application reveals that the plurality inherent in superposition has practical, transformational applications. Similarly, spiritual activities like as meditation, prayer, and ritual seek to reach and align with deeper layers of reality, releasing potentials that go beyond the material sphere. Both quantum physics and spirituality imply that dealing with these multiple truths needs intention, discipline, and an openness to the unknown.

Critically, the analogies between quantum physics and spiritual worlds must be treated with caution. While the metaphorical resonance is strong, it is critical to differentiate between empirical science and spiritual symbolism. Quantum superposition is a scientifically verified reality represented by mathematical formulae, but spiritual conceptions of multiple realities are based on philosophical, cultural, and personal experiences. Keeping this distinction means that the interaction between science and spirituality is courteous and fruitful, promoting mutual enrichment rather than conflation.

The concept of numerous levels of being also promotes philosophical inquiry into identity and existence. Particles in quantum physics are dynamic systems characterized by probabilities and interactions, rather than static things. This flexibility calls into question traditional concepts of identity, and it is consistent with spiritual beliefs that see the person as interrelated with the cosmos. According to Buddhist teachings on anatta, or non-self, identity is a set of interconnected processes rather than a permanent entity. Similarly, quantum systems emphasize reality's interconnection, with the observation of one particle influencing the state of another even across long distance.

These observations have ramifications for how people approach life and make decisions. Recognizing various realities, both quantum and spiritual, promotes a humble and open mindset. It encourages people to evaluate the larger context of their actions, recognizing that decisions have ramifications across several layers of existence. This viewpoint develops a sense of responsibility and connectivity, which is consistent with the ethical ideals found in spiritual traditions and the developing discipline of quantum ethics.

The interaction between quantum superposition and spiritual worlds provides a framework for investigating creativity and potential. As particles exist in overlapping states, so do human imagination and invention in the field of possibilities. Spiritual traditions frequently define creativity as a divine or universal power emanating from deeper realms of reality. Quantum physics, with its focus on potentiality and uncertainty, offers a scientific equivalent to this spiritual view, claiming that creativity comes from the interaction of myriad possibilities waiting to be realized.

The connections between quantum superposition and the spiritual world show existence's immense intricacy and mystery. They argue that reality is a dynamic interaction of layers and potentials, rather than a static, monolithic entity. This viewpoint encourages people to broaden their understanding, accepting the diversity of life with curiosity, humility, and reverence. By investigating these linkages, science and spirituality can help to elucidate the vast fabric of reality, creating a greater appreciation for the universe's interconnection and potential.

Personal Reflection: How the Concept of Superposition Can Reframe

Thinking About Choice

Superposition, a quantum notion, provides a deep prism through which to reevaluate human decision-making and choice. In quantum physics, a particle can exist in numerous states at the same time until it is noticed, which calls into question traditional conceptions of fixed results and linear causation. This notion may be figuratively applied to the world of personal choice, promoting a deeper thought on the possibilities that exist before making a decision, as well as the interdependence of consequences.

Superposition implies that reality is not predetermined but rather lives in a condition of constant potential. This idea has the potential to revolutionize the way people approach options in human decision-making, moving the focus away from concern over predetermined outcomes and toward an appreciation for the many possibilities available in each given situation. Each option may be understood as condensing a field of possibilities into a single realized conclusion, similar to how an observation of a quantum system resolves its state. This shift in viewpoint can generate feelings of strength and creativity by stressing the active role that people play in crafting their own reality.

This concept is consistent with philosophical traditions emphasizing the non-linear and interrelated character of life. In existential philosophy, for example, intellectuals such as Jean-Paul Sartre have argued that humans are born free, with the duty of continuously selecting and thereby defining themselves. This viewpoint is supported by the notion of superposition, which suggests that numerous possibilities exist as potential realities before a decision is taken. This viewpoint might reduce the dread of making the "wrong" option by presenting choice as an exploration of alternatives rather than a binary judgment of success or failure.

From a psychological aspect, accepting the concept of superposition can help to decrease choice paralysis, a typical condition in which people feel overwhelmed by the weight of prospective possibilities. The concept of several alternatives coexisting until a decision is taken can promote a more fluid approach to decision-making, shifting the emphasis from perfection to action. This is consistent with behavioral psychology research, which demonstrates that taking tiny steps toward a choice frequently results in increased clarity and confidence. Individuals may feel more free to explore and adapt if they see options as chances to interact with potentiality.

The concept of superposition also prompts thought on the interdependence of choices and outcomes. In quantum physics, particles in superposition are impacted by their interactions with other particles as well as their surroundings. Similarly, human decisions are not made in isolation, but rather within larger networks of connections, cultural settings, and historical trajectories. Recognizing this interconnection can lead to more empathic and socially conscious decision-making, as people evaluate how their decisions will influence others.

This interconnectivity is sometimes described in spiritual traditions as part of a cosmic or divine order. Hinduism, for example, stresses the notion of karma, which holds that every action adds to a chain of cause and effect that lasts beyond individual lifetimes. The quantum concept of superposition, with its emphasis on potentiality and interaction, serves as a scientific metaphor for this spiritual principle, implying that individual decisions are part of a broader tapestry of life. This viewpoint may instill humility and responsibility in people as they acknowledge their function within a larger totality.

Superposition has revolutionary potential that extends beyond human decision-making to larger cultural and philosophical issues. The capacity to manage various options is an essential talent in an increasingly complicated and unpredictable environment. According to quantum physics, uncertainty is not a fault, but rather a basic component of reality. This realization can inspire civilizations to embrace ambiguity and diversity, creating situations in which varied ideas and methods can coexist. As a result, the metaphor of superposition may guide not just individual decisions but also communal decision-making and governance.

Reflecting about superposition can help people have a better grasp of their own identity and self-worth. Individuals are made up of overlapping identities, responsibilities, and desires, much like a particle in superposition represents numerous states. This plurality is frequently felt as a source of stress as people manage competing needs and aspirations. However, the quantum perspective indicates that this multiplicity is a source of richness to be welcomed rather than a problem to be solved. Individuals can create better self-awareness and acceptance by admitting the presence of many facets of themselves.

Meditation and mindfulness are examples of spiritual practices that help people deal with this diversity. These techniques urge people to examine their thoughts and feelings without passing judgment, allowing for different points of view to exist simultaneously. This is consistent with the quantum principle of viewing a system without instantly compressing it into a single state. Individuals who develop this ability for nonjudgmental observation can explore the whole spectrum of their potentials before committing to a certain path of action.

The superposition metaphor has applications in creativity and innovation. The presence of numerous states in the quantum world allows for the creation of new phenomena. Similarly, varied ideas, viewpoints, and experiences frequently interact to produce human creativity. Individuals and organizations may capitalize on the potential of superposition by creating an atmosphere that values openness and experimentation, resulting in discoveries that might not occur in a more rigid or linear framework.

However, while approaching the metaphor of superposition, subtlety and critical thought are essential. While the analogies between quantum physics and human decision-making are fascinating, they should not be interpreted as literal equivalents. The quantum world functions on fundamentally different principles from classical and macroscopic systems. Using quantum notions as metaphors can deepen comprehension and provoke contemplation, but these metaphors must be based on a clear grasp of their limitations.

This combination of inspiration and rigor is critical to the integrity of both scientific and philosophical investigation. The superposition metaphor may be an effective tool for reinventing choice, but it should not be used to oversimplify or obscure the complexities of human decision-making. Instead, it should serve as a jumping off place for more in-depth inquiry, inspiring people to approach life's uncertainties and opportunities with curiosity and bravery.

The concept of superposition encourages people to think more deeply about choice, identity, and interconnectivity. It offers a humble yet broad attitude, acknowledging the multitude of potentials that characterize existence. Individuals who embrace this perspective may traverse the difficulties of life with more creativity, empathy, and resilience, contributing to a world that values variety and the beauty of possibilities.

CHAPTER 11: THE HOLOGRAPHIC PRINCIPLE AND WHOLENESS

"The whole is greater than the sum of its parts." – Aristotle

The holographic principle, a ground-breaking notion in theoretical physics, asserts that all information contained within a region of space may be described by data imprinted on its boundaries. This idea, based on black hole thermodynamics and quantum gravity theories, dramatically changes our understanding of the world and reality itself. It challenges our perceptions of dimensions, locality, and the basis of existence in a variety of ways, while also intriguingly reflecting spiritual and philosophical ideas about interconnectivity and being.

The holographic principle initially evolved in the research of black holes. Physicists Jacob Bekenstein and Stephen Hawking showed that a black hole's entropy—a measure of disorder or information—was proportional to the surface area of its event horizon rather than its volume. This discovery challenged conventional wisdom, implying that the universe's most fundamental characteristics may lie on two-dimensional borders rather than within the three-dimensional volumes they appear to represent. Later discoveries, particularly in the framework of string theory and Juan Maldacena's AdS/CFT correspondence, strengthened the principle's theoretical basis. According to Maldacena's research, a quantum gravitational theory within a volume might be explained similarly by a lower-dimensional, non-gravitational theory on its boundary.

This concept has tremendous ramifications. If the holographic principle is universally applicable, it implies that the cosmos itself may function as a hologram, with three-dimensional reality projected from data stored on a two-dimensional barrier. This viewpoint does not suggest that our perceptions of depth, space, and time are illusory; rather, it emphasizes that the fundamental physics driving these phenomena may behave differently than previously imagined. Reality, in this view, becomes a layered interaction of dimensions, with limits serving as the key to comprehending the entire.

One of the holographic principle's most striking characteristics is its resemblance to ancient spiritual and metaphysical beliefs. Many mystical traditions, including Hinduism, Buddhism, and Sufism, have long held that the material world is a projection or manifestation of a more fundamental reality. The Vedantic idea of Maya, for example, defines the physical reality as a fleeting and illusory manifestation of a fundamental truth. Similarly, the Buddhist concept of Sunyata (emptiness) posits that all phenomena emerge interdependently, with no essential existence. These perspectives are analogous to the concept of a holographic cosmos, in which what we experience as material and independent emerges from interwoven informational foundations.

This principle is also consistent with several esoteric ideologies that highlight reality's fractal or recursive character. According to the Hermetic maxim "As above, so below," each part of the universe reflects the entire universe. This theory is similar to the holographic concept that every segment of a boundary can encode all of the information in a system. Such connections provide an enticing blend of old knowledge and cutting-edge physics, linking seemingly different fields of thought.

When delving into the philosophical dimensions of the holographic principle, one is led to the topic of what comprises information and its relationship to consciousness. If, as the holographic model proposes, the universe is inherently informational, consciousness could be understood as a method for interpreting and organizing this information. This viewpoint is consistent with quantum cognition and panpsychism theories, which argue that consciousness is a basic element of reality rather than an emergent property of complex systems. Such perspectives call for a fundamental rethinking of the link between mind and matter, as well as a framework for merging subjective experience with objective scientific research.

The idea also calls into question traditional notions of localization and separation. Every part of a holographic reality is closely linked to the total, implying that events we seem to be remote or distinct are in fact deeply intertwined. This viewpoint is echoed in quantum mechanics, particularly in phenomena such as entanglement, in which particles separated by huge distances display instantaneous correlation. These findings are consistent with spiritual traditions that emphasize unity and interconnection, prompting us to reconsider our relationships with one another and with the universe.

In practice, the holographic concept has consequences for technological advancement and scientific methodology. Understanding how information is stored, transported, and processed at fundamental levels in quantum computing and information theory has the potential to transform data handling, encryption, and processing capacity. Similarly, in cosmology, the principle opens up new avenues for studying the universe's origins, structure, and ultimate destiny. Researchers might develop novel techniques to unifying quantum mechanics and general relativity by interpreting spacetime as emergent rather than fundamental, tackling one of physics' most pressing difficulties.

Critically, while the holographic principle provides an appealing structure, it remains a theoretical construct. Experimental validation at the cosmological scale is difficult because holographic phenomena have subtle impacts that must often be observed indirectly. Researchers are considering various avenues for proving the idea, such as looking at the cosmic microwave background or using gravitational wave data to investigate black hole thermodynamics. Such initiatives represent the cutting edge of scientific research, where bold ideas are thoroughly analyzed and polished.

The ethical and existential consequences of the holographic principle are equally significant. It fosters a sense of social responsibility and empathy by presenting reality as highly interrelated and transnational. If borders and separations are eventually constructed, the divides between self and other, or humans and nature, become less absolute. This viewpoint is consistent with environmental ethics, emphasizing the significance of coexistence and sustainability in an interdependent world. It also resonates with global collaboration and understanding movements, which advocate for a comprehensive approach to societal and environmental concerns.

Furthermore, the holographic model encourages introspection on the nature of individuality and the self. Individual experiences could be viewed as localized representations of a global process if reality is encoded beyond cosmic barriers. This viewpoint is consistent with spiritual teachings that state that the self is both distinct and inseparable from the totality. It implies that human progress and enlightenment entail not only self-discovery but also an awareness of one's connectedness to the larger fabric of reality.

In the broader framework of human investigation, the holographic principle illustrates the convergence of scientific and philosophical inquiry. It criticizes reductionist perspectives and advocates for a more integrated approach to understanding reality. The idea promotes an attitude of curiosity and humility by accepting complexity and understanding the limitations of old paradigms. It emphasizes the necessity of interdisciplinary conversation, in which physics, metaphysics, and spirituality inform and enrich one another.

As the holographic principle evolves, it serves as a reminder of the dynamic and multidimensional nature of information. Its discoveries foster not only scientific progress but also a greater respect for life's mysteries. The principle presents a perspective of reality that is both profound and beautiful by linking the microcosmic and macrocosmic, the tangible and the sublime. It invites humanity to investigate the limits of comprehension, where science and spirit intersect, and to ponder the idea that the cosmos itself is a monument to the interplay of information, connection, and awe.

"Each Part Contains the Whole": Resonance with Spiritual Cosmic Unity Teachings

The holographic principle, which exemplifies the concept of wholeness contained in parts, has captured the attention of both scientific and spiritual philosophers. This idea, based on quantum physics and theoretical cosmology, posits that any given region of a system's border can encode all of its information. Beyond its scientific implications, this idea has profound parallels in spiritual traditions that emphasize the unity of existence, the interconnectedness of all things, and the reflection of the cosmos within the individual.

The holographic principle emerged in physics as a way of reconciling the paradoxical nature of black holes. The discovery that black hole entropy increases with surface area rather than volume suggested that information about three-dimensional objects may be stored on a two-dimensional border. This principle was later expanded to include not only black holes, but the entire cosmos. The concept of the universe as a hologram, with each point containing information about the entire, calls into question traditional notions of spatial separateness and personality.

This framework has a striking resemblance to ancient spiritual teachings. For example, Indra's Net, a Hindu idea, displays a massive cosmic web of interconnected gems, each reflecting the entire network within itself. Similarly, mystical interpretations of the microcosm-macrocosm link in Hermeticism say that the universe's structure and order are mirrored within the individual. These teachings emphasize a basic unity that transcends physical bounds, implying that the portion contains the essence of the whole.

Buddhist philosophy, including the idea of interdependent origination (pratītyasamutpāda), embodies this notion. It asserts that all phenomena develop in reciprocal dependency, with no single thing existing independently of the total. This idea is consistent with the holographic insight that separation is an illusion; what appears distinct is fundamentally related via underlying informational or energetic foundations. The idea that each fragment mirrors the universe is consistent with spiritual concepts of unity and inseparability.

These notions are further supported by quantum entanglement, a phenomenon in which particles remain entangled regardless of distance. When one particle in an entangled pair is measured, the state of the other is instantly altered, demonstrating non-local connection. This scientific reality corresponds to spiritual descriptions of oneness, implying that separations experienced in physical space are only superficial. The interdependence of seemingly autonomous phenomena calls for a rethinking of individuality and community in both quantum mechanics and spiritual teachings.

The holographic principle also corresponds with the mystical notion that awareness reflects the universe. In many spiritual traditions, the individual is viewed as a microcosm of the broader truth rather than being separate from the divine or cosmic total. This concept is expressed in the Upanishadic phrase "Tat Tvam Asi" or "You are That," which emphasizes the individual self's unity with ultimate truth. Self-realization, according to this viewpoint, entails acknowledging one's interconnectedness with the entire cosmos, which is consistent with the holographic argument that each part encodes the whole.

In practice, these insights prompt a shift in viewpoint that prioritizes unity over division. When each part carries the essence of the whole, the lines between self and other, human and nature, or individual and community become blurred. This viewpoint encourages empathy, responsibility, and appreciation for all forms of life, which is consistent with ethical precepts from all civilizations. It promotes ecological consciousness, in which activities are viewed as having repercussions throughout the interwoven web of existence.

This principle has ramifications for scientific investigations into consciousness. If reality is inherently informational and holographic, consciousness may be an inherent aspect of the system, reflecting and altering the entire. This perspective is consistent with panpsychism, which holds that consciousness is a universal quality contained in all matter. Such ideas bridge the divide between science and spirituality, implying that thought and matter are inextricably linked rather than different.

These notions also call into question the materialist worldview, which views reality as a collection of separate, isolated objects. The holographic principle contradicts this view by demonstrating that separateness is an emergent phenomenon rather than a basic fact. As a result, it pave the way for a more holistic perspective of existence, one that values both scientific rigor and spiritual knowledge. It implies that the universe is not a collection of disparate elements, but rather an undivided whole in which every component is essential.

This comprehensive viewpoint is frequently represented in mystical traditions using images of light and reflection. The idea that the universe reflects itself in every area is analogous to a beam of light refracting through numerous prisms, each presenting the same spectrum in its own unique shape. This parallel depicts the interplay between individuality and unity, implying that variation stems from the countless ways in which the whole expresses itself rather than from division.

In terms of philosophy, the holographic principle encourages in-depth reflection on the nature of reality, identity, and meaning. When each portion contains the total, the quest for knowledge becomes a process of discovering universal truths within the specific and special. This viewpoint is consistent with spiritual techniques like meditation, which frequently involve going inward to find the interconnection of all things. It implies that the answers to cosmic concerns are hidden not in faraway stars, but in the human experience itself.

In this setting, the interaction between science and spirituality promotes a deeper knowledge of both. The holographic principle provides a mathematical and physical foundation, but spiritual teachings provide experiential insights and ethical guidance. They collaborate to foster a cross-disciplinary discussion that promotes a holistic approach to understanding the universe and our role within it.

These concepts have the potential to be extremely revolutionary in terms of personal growth. Recognizing that each portion contains the total promotes feelings of wholeness and self-worth. It implies that individuals are integral manifestations of a larger reality, rather than isolated fragments. This insight can foster a feeling of purpose, in which personal acts are viewed as contributing to the larger tapestry of existence. It also promotes humility by breaking down the barriers between self and other, revealing the shared essence of all beings.

As science delves deeper into the holographic aspect of reality, the consequences for technology, ethics, and spirituality are expected to grow. Whether through advances in quantum computers, greater research into consciousness, or new philosophical frameworks, the concept provides a platform for reconsidering how we comprehend and interact with the universe. It encourages humanity to accept complexity, connectivity, and unity, resulting in an awe-inspiring and profound view of reality.

In essence, the holographic principle and its spiritual resonances remind us that the cosmos is a dynamic, linked whole, rather than a collection of separate components. Recognizing unity within diversity allows us to create a stronger feeling of connection, responsibility, and wonder, linking our scientific efforts with the timeless wisdom of spiritual traditions.

Philosophical Outcome: Seeing Reality
as an Intricate, Nested Whole

The holographic principle has far-reaching philosophical ramifications beyond theoretical physics, providing fundamental insights into the nature of reality. This principle proposes that all of the universe's information can be encoded within lower-dimensional bounds. It conjures up images of a universe in which the essence of the entire is intricately woven into each component, similar to a hologram. While this concept has its roots in physics, its connection with philosophical and spiritual traditions highlights its larger significance.

The holographic principle fundamentally questions traditional concepts of separation and independence. The classical view of reality holds that objects exist as separate entities that interact according to a cause-and-effect framework. The holographic model, on the other hand, displays a deeper connectivity in which the boundaries between components collapse to form a unified, nested totality. This viewpoint is consistent with ontological holism, a philosophical position that regards the universe as an interconnected whole rather than a mere collection of independent components.

This shift in perspective has significant ramifications for our understanding of identity and existence. Individuality, in a holographic framework, does not mean isolation, but rather a distinct manifestation of the global total. Each component of the system reflects the whole, implying that identity is both singular and universal. This is philosophically similar to Spinoza's concept of substance monism, which states that all entities are representations of a single, infinite substance. It also reflects the Buddhist concept of anatta, or non-self, which emphasizes the interdependence of all things.

The nested structure of the holographic universe invites examination of the nature of boundaries. If every portion comprises the total, the distinctions between inside and outside, self and other, get blurred. Similar notions have been addressed by philosophers such as Gilles Deleuze, who emphasizes the interconnectivity of multiplicities within an immanent plane. This viewpoint breaks down the rigid dichotomies that frequently dominate Western thought, encouraging a more holistic understanding of existence.

From a metaphysical perspective, the holographic principle calls into question reductionism, the belief that complex systems may be fully understood by dissecting their separate components. Instead, it advocates for a systems-oriented approach in which the relationships and interactions within the whole are as important as the components themselves. This is consistent with the emergentist philosophical tradition, which maintains that at increasing levels of complexity, new features appear that cannot be foreseen or described purely by the properties of the underlying components.

The principle also connects with ancient intellectual traditions that emphasize the cosmos' unity. The Hermetic dictum "As above, so below" embodies the holographic understanding that the macrocosm is replicated within the microcosm. Similarly, the Daoist philosophy of wu wei emphasizes the inherent flow and connectivity of all things, implying that every action and phenomenon is seamlessly incorporated into the whole.

The holographic vision of ethics instills a strong sense of responsibility. If every portion mirrors the total, each action performed at any level has repercussions across the system. This connection promotes a relational ethic in which human well-being is intrinsically tied to the well-being of the community and environment. In his idea of I-Thou connections, philosophers such as Martin Buber emphasized the ethical implications of viewing people as reflections of the same universal essence rather than objects.

The holographic principle also calls into question linear and deterministic theories of time and causality. In a cosmos where information is encoded across dimensions, the boundaries between the past, present, and future become hazy. Philosophically, this is consistent with the concept of eternalism, which holds that all points in time exist concurrently within a four-dimensional spacetime continuum. This viewpoint calls for a rethinking of free will and agency, arguing that decision occurs within a dynamic, interconnected framework rather than a straight sequence of cause and effect.

The holographic approach poses intriguing concerns concerning the nature of perception and cognition in epistemology, or the study of knowledge. If the whole is encoded within the part, understanding the portion provides insight into the whole. This is similar to mystical traditions, in which inner exploration is viewed as a road to universal truths. The notion that the microcosm reflects the macrocosm promotes a comprehensive approach to knowledge that combines subjective experience with objective research.

The holographic paradigm also has consequences for cognitive philosophy. If the cosmos is holographic, consciousness can be seen as a reflection of its fundamental structure. This viewpoint is consistent with panpsychism, which holds that consciousness is an inherent property of the universe. It is also consistent with quantum mind theories, which propose that consciousness emerges from quantum processes within the brain. According to this viewpoint, the mind is not separate from the universe, but rather an essential component of its holographic fabric.

The holographic universe's nested wholeness promotes a greater understanding of complexity and diversity. Rather than perceiving differences as sources of conflict, this viewpoint emphasizes their role in expressing the complexity of the whole. This is philosophically consistent with pluralism, which holds that many perspectives and techniques can coexist inside a same framework. It cultivates a mindset that values debate and collaboration, realizing that each viewpoint adds to a more complete understanding of reality.

In practice, the holographic perspective encourages novel ways to problem resolution and innovation. It stimulates interdisciplinary collaboration and holistic thinking by stressing system interconnections. This is especially important for addressing global issues like climate change, which necessitates combining insights from science, ethics, economics, and spirituality. Recognizing that every part has an impact on the whole promotes a sense of communal responsibility and shared purpose.

The philosophical conclusion of the holographic principle is not only an abstract concept, but a transforming lens through which to see reality. It pushes us to abandon reductionist and dualistic frameworks in favor of a more integrative and relational understanding of existence. It encourages us to perceive ourselves as integral elements of a dynamic, interrelated whole, rather as isolated creatures. This perspective instills a sense of wonder, humility, and responsibility in us, urging us to align our activities with the universe's underlying patterns.

CHAPTER 12: QUANTUM COSMOLOGY AND CREATION MYTHS

"To see a world in a grain of sand and a heaven in a wildflower." – William Blake

The origin of the universe is one of the most interesting mysteries that humans have sought to answer. The connection of quantum physics and cosmology has provided new knowledge regarding this profound mystery, particularly the concept of cosmic inflation and the relevance of quantum fluctuations. We get a better understanding of the beginnings of existence by looking at how these minor disturbances could affect the bigger cosmos.

Scientist Alan Guth proposed the theory of cosmic inflation in the early 1980s. It argues that the universe witnessed exponential development within a fraction of a second after the Big Bang. During this inflationary phase, the universe expanded exponentially faster than the speed of light, stretching the fabric of spacetime to scales far greater than its original size. This rapid inflation smoothed out the early irregularities, producing in the startlingly uniform and isotropic universe we witness today.

However, underneath this smoothness lies a great deal of complexity. Inflation not only increased spacetime, but it also intensified quantum fluctuations, which are essential to quantum physics. These minute oscillations left their imprint on the expanding universe, causing the minuscule density shifts that eventually gave rise to galaxies, stars, and planets. This approach shows how quantum events at the smallest scales may alter structures at larger scales.

The uncertainty principle, which states that some physical qualities, such as position and momentum, cannot be known with arbitrary precision at the same time, is directly responsible for quantum fluctuations. Even in space, fluctuations in energy density are caused by intrinsic uncertainty. These quantum fluctuations were magnified to macroscopic proportions as the universe expanded rapidly during the inflationary period. When inflation ended, these variations were "frozen" into the cosmic fabric, resulting in the initial density perturbations that subsequently formed under gravity to determine the universe's large-scale structure.

The connection between quantum physics and cosmic inflation demonstrates the inherent unity of physical laws. It reveals a cosmos in which the very small and very large are inextricably linked, challenging traditional notions of scale and separability. This connection between quantum fluctuations and structure formation reveals how randomness and determinism coexist in nature. The random nature of quantum fluctuations adds to the unpredictability, but the inflationary process converts it into a coherent and predictable framework.

Measurements of the cosmic microwave background (CMB) radiation give visible evidence for cosmic inflation and its link to quantum fluctuations. The CMB is the Big Bang's afterglow, a faint radiation that pervades the universe and gives an estimate of the universe's age as 380,000 years. Tiny temperature and polarization fluctuations in the CMB show the fingerprints of quantum disturbances spread out by inflation. These findings, which were acquired with remarkable accuracy by missions like as the Planck probe, provide significant support for the inflationary hypothesis and its quantum origins.

The consequences of this interaction extend beyond physics, inviting philosophical reflection on the nature of reality and causality. The idea that quantum events, which are inherently random and unpredictable, have the power to modify the universe's most fundamental structures brings deterministic worldviews into doubt. It alludes to a universe that is dynamic, emergent, and intricately interconnected. This is philosophically congruent with process thinking, which prioritizes being and relationality above static existence. It also corresponds with spiritual ideas that regard the cosmos as an interrelated totality, with each component impacting and reflecting the larger whole.

Furthermore, the role of quantum fluctuations in the formation of the cosmos raises fascinating questions about how physical principles are precisely adjusted. To build a universe capable of supporting complex structures and life, the parameters controlling inflation, such as energy scale and duration, must be constrained. This fine-tuning has encouraged some to look into the anthropic principle, which says that the universe's basic constants exist because they allow humankind to exist. Others consider the idea of a multiverse, in which there are several universes with various physical constraints, and we dwell in one that happens to be favorable to life.

Inflationary theory, particularly the concept of unending inflation, lends credibility to the multiverse idea. According to this hypothesis, inflation is a continuous process in which pockets of spacetime expand and form new "bubble" worlds. According to this theory, our observable universe is one among many, each with its own set of physical rules and constants. While hypothetical, this notion stresses the richness and diversity of imaginable realities, expanding our understanding of life beyond the confines of a single galaxy.

Quantum fluctuations and cosmic inflation are also driving new approaches to understanding the origins of time and space. Traditional cosmology considers time and space to be fundamental components of existence. However, the quantum and inflationary perspectives indicate that time and space are emergent phenomena arising from fundamental principles. This viewpoint is congruent with approaches to quantum gravity such as loop quantum gravity and string theory, which seek to reconcile general relativity and quantum mechanics respectively. These theories indicate that spacetime is not continuous, but rather composed of discrete quantum components, calling conventional wisdom about the nature of reality into doubt.

The early universe' quantum beginnings throw into doubt the distinction between science and metaphysics. While inflationary theory and quantum mechanics provide solid mathematical underpinnings, concerns about why the world exists and why physical laws take the forms they do require more than empirical evidence. These questions promote a more complete understanding of life by encouraging dialogue between science, philosophy, and spirituality. The interplay between quantum fluctuations and cosmic structure serves as a bridge between empirical investigation and higher existential questions.

Advances in empirical and theoretical physics are refining our understanding of inflation and its quantum underpinnings. Future missions, like as those aimed at detecting primordial gravitational waves, may uncover direct evidence of inflationary dynamics, revealing fresh insights into the universe's origins. These gravitational waves, which are ripples in spacetime caused by inflation, reveal information on the energy scale and inflation mechanisms, shedding light on the connection between the quantum and the cosmic.

The story of quantum fluctuations and cosmic inflation showcases the power of human inquiry and imagination. It illustrates how abstract mathematical ideas may reveal important facts about the universe by connecting the small and large. Exploring the quantum origins of the universe not only uncovers the physics that created our reality, but it also heightens our appreciation for the wonder and beauty of existence. The combination of quantum physics and cosmology forces us to embrace a dynamic, interconnected, and continually evolving universe, eliciting both awe and wonder.

Myths concerning cosmic eggs, voids, or uttered words are examples of sacred origin stories.

Throughout history, humanity have tried to explain the origins of the universe using a tapestry of religious stories that represent many nations, spiritual traditions, and philosophical views. These stories about cosmic eggs, primordial voids, and the creative power of spoken words represent ancient attempts to comprehend the incomprehensible mysteries of existence. As modern science uncovers fresh insights into cosmic beginnings, religious stories take on new significance, acting as a symbolic link between the metaphysical and empirical spheres.

The cosmic egg image appears in many ancient culture's creation stories, reflecting the universe's birth from a single, undivided condition. The golden egg, also known as Hiranyagarbha in Hindu mythology, is the source of creation. Brahma, the creator deity, sprung from this egg and fashioned the universe from its primordial fullness. Similarly, the Orphic tale of ancient Greece has the primordial goddess Nyx (Night) placing a silver cosmic egg, which hatched and gave birth to the god Phanes, who represents light and life. The egg represents potentiality and wholeness, conveying the concept that all existence begins with an undivided, latent form.

These sacred eggs have significant scientific links, particularly the singularity from which the Big Bang is said to have arisen. The cosmic egg's metaphorical wholeness is represented by the notion of a concentrated point containing all of the universe's energy and substance. While science describes this process through physical principles and quantum fluctuations, spiritual imagery uses metaphor to emphasize the oneness from which diversity originates.

According to various religions, the universe is generated not from a physical object such as an egg, but from an unending vacuum, a profound emptiness fraught with possibilities. Daoist cosmology holds that the Dao is the ineffable basis of all things, an unmanifested void from which the twin forces of yin and yang emerge to generate the world's dynamic interplay. According to Buddhist theory, śūnyatā (emptiness) is the ultimate truth that lacks inherent self-existence yet is full of creative potential. These void-centric narratives challenge the idea of nothingness as an absence, instead presenting it as the fertile foundation for all existence.

The scientific understanding of the vacuum in quantum field theory provides an astonishing modern connection to these ancient conceptions. The quantum vacuum is far from empty; it is a boiling pot of activity, with virtual particles constantly coming and disappearing. This vacuum energy, together with inflationary dynamics, is essential to the universe's early expansion. The sacred nothingness and the quantum vacuum share a paradoxical richness: emptiness as a source of limitless possibilities.

Many religious systems emphasize the power of spoken words to create reality. According to the Judeo-Christian Genesis myth, God created the cosmos with the words "Let there be light," and there was light. This divine voice creates the universe, giving it form and meaning. Similarly, in India's Vedic religion, the sacred word "Om" is the source of all creation. These stories stress the importance of sound and vibration in the creative process because they carry meaning and consciousness.

This concept has fascinating analogies in current physics. At its most basic, the universe may be depicted as a vibratory system in which particles and fields vibrate in complex harmonies. String theory, a proposal for a unified theory of physics, posits that instead of point particles, the fundamental constituents of reality are one-dimensional strings vibrating at certain frequencies. These vibrations establish particle properties in the same way that the pitch of a string defines a musical note. This concept of a vibrating world surprisingly evokes the sacred bond between music and creation.

Another fascinating characteristic of holy origin stories is their depiction of creation as a dynamic clash of forces, which is frequently portrayed as a cosmic fight or dance. According to the Rig Veda, creation is a sacrifice made by Purusha, the cosmic being whose dismemberment gives birth to the physical cosmos. Similarly, in Norse mythology, the cosmos is the result of a fundamental war between fire and ice, symbolized by the realms of Muspelheim and Niflheim. These stories demonstrate the idea of creation as an emergent occurrence caused by the conflict and interplay of opposing principles.

The physical laws that govern the universe reflect the interplay of forces. The separation of basic forces, as well as the asymmetry between matter and antimatter, are two instances of significant imbalances and transitions that preceded the Big Bang. Even the universe's large-scale structure, with its intricate network of galaxies and voids, reflects the processes of attraction and repulsion, expansion and collapse. The religious and scientific narratives both present creation as an ever-changing process driven by relational dynamics rather than static states.

Sacred origin stories emphasize the cyclical cycle of creation and destruction, presenting the cosmos as an unending rhythm rather than a singular event. The universe is created, kept, and destroyed in cycles controlled by the Hindu gods Brahma, Vishnu, and Shiva. Similarly, the Mayan Popol Vuh depicts previous planets that were built and destroyed before the current one. These cycles reflect a view of time as a continuous flow, as opposed to the linear progression usual in Western storytelling.

This cyclical approach is repeated in scientific hypotheses such as the oscillatory universe theory, which proposes that the cosmos expands and contracts infinitely. While this notion is no longer the dominant paradigm in cosmology, it highlights how scientific and religious frameworks may arrive at similar patterns, reflecting fundamental intuitions about the nature of time and existence.

The ability of sacred origin stories to incorporate existential, ethical, and metaphysical issues accounts for their long-lasting relevance. They address not just the "how" of creation, but also the "why," giving frameworks for understanding humanity's place in the cosmos. These myths offer existence meaning and purpose by situating it within a larger cosmic narrative, fostering a sense of belonging and reverence.

As modern science sheds light on the origins of the universe, religious myths serve as a complementary lens, providing symbolic complexity and cultural variation to the discussion. Rather than opposing science, these stories may stimulate surprise and intrigue, motivating a thorough exploration into the mysteries of life. Exploring the junction of sacred and scientific perspectives shows a common quest for understanding—a testament to the universal human urge to find the origins of all things.

Synergy: Comparison of Big Bang Theories with Spiritual Cosmogonies

The Big Bang hypothesis, which depicts the universe's genesis as a rapid expansion from an extraordinarily dense and hot singularity 13.8 billion years ago, is a pillar of contemporary cosmology. It is a scientific narrative based on observation, math, and empirical evidence. Spiritual cosmogonies, which may be found in a wide range of religious and philosophical traditions, usually describe creation as a divine, deliberate act or a natural unfolding imbued with sacred meaning. While these methodologies appear to have distinct frameworks and goals, closer examination reveals a rich synergy between the two, giving complementing perspectives on life.

The Big Bang idea revolves around the concept of a singularity—a point at which standard understanding of space, time, and matter collapses. This singularity is said to have contained all of the energy and matter that would eventually form the universe, as well as being endlessly dense and having no volume. Spiritual cosmogonies usually refer to a state of primordial oneness that existed before creation. For example, in Hinduism, Brahman refers to an ultimate, indivisible reality from which the universe emanates. Similarly, according to the Judeo-Christian religion, the act of creation begins in a formless vacuum or chaos, which is subsequently stopped by divine intervention to restore order and structure. Both theories emphasize an initial state of potentiality, a single essence that gives rise to multiplicity.

The Big Bang hypothesis's processes are also linked to spiritual concepts like unfolding and differentiation. Following its initial expansion, the universe experienced rapid inflation, which was followed by matter cooling and condensing into galaxies, stars, and planets. This scientific narrative is comparable to the idea of emanation found in many mystical traditions, which see creation as a series of steps or layers emanating from a single source. According to Kabbalistic Judaism, the sefirot are ten manifestations of divine energy that shape the cosmos. Similarly, Neoplatonic philosophy views the One as generating the Nous (mind), soul, and material cosmos in a hierarchical sequence. These parallels demonstrate that both scientific and spiritual perspectives seek to comprehend the transition from unity to variety, although through different lenses.

Another point of convergence is the role of light as a vital component of creation. According to the Big Bang theory, some 380,000 years after its birth, the universe became transparent, enabling photons to flow freely and giving rise to cosmic microwave background radiation—faint echoes of the world's original lighting. This scientific event is analogous to spiritual cosmology's reliance on light. The first words of Genesis' creation myth are "Let there be light," which reflect the emergence of clarity, order, and life. According to Zoroastrianism, light represents celestial wisdom and purity, both of which are essential in the cosmic fight between good and evil. Light's extensive importance in both realms underscores its universal link to the origins of knowledge, existence, and meaning.

The time scales associated with the Big Bang concept, which span billions of years, can contradict the temporally compressed interpretations found in spiritual traditions. Many religious traditions define creation as taking place over a set amount of time, such as Genesis' six days of creation. These temporal frames, on the other hand, might be interpreted metaphorically, as symbolizing cycles or archetypes rather than actual durations. The Hindu concept of kalpas, which are vast cosmic cycles lasting billions of years, demonstrates how spiritual traditions may envision large time scales akin to those described in science. This flexibility promotes a dialogue between the two points of view, with time differences helping to enrich rather than diminish their mutual insights.

Entropy and the second rule of thermodynamics, two fundamental physical principles, describe how systems tend to become more disordered over time. Paradoxically, the Big Bang and subsequent histories of the universe reveal increasing complexity—galaxies, stars, planets, and, eventually, life. This seeming tension is overcome by the local development of order within an entropy-based framework. Spiritual cosmologies, too, deal with the interplay of chaos and order. Nun's primordial waters represent chaos in Egyptian mythology, from which the sun god Ra emerges to create the structured cosmos. The Taoist concept of yin and yang emphasizes the balance and interplay of opposing forces, meaning that chaos and order are dynamically connected rather than mutually contradictory.

The contemplative implications of both storylines combine to create a remarkable synergy. The Big Bang theory generates awe by demonstrating the universe's grandeur, complexity, and dynamism, eliciting a sense of wonder that goes beyond factual data. Similarly, spiritual cosmogonies may generate reverence, gratitude, and a sense of community. Indigenous creation stories, for example, typically focus on humanity's relationship with nature and the universe, portraying existence as a precious gift. Exploring these stories side by side demonstrates that both science and spirituality encourage meaningful interaction with the mystery of existence, which develops humility and curiosity.

Modern cosmology has introduced speculative ideas that have stretched the boundaries between scientific and spiritual narratives. The multiverse idea, for example, predicts the existence of countless distinct universes, each with its own set of physical rules and forces. This viewpoint is supported by spiritual traditions that describe multiple levels or planes of life. In Tibetan Buddhism, the concept of lokas refers to a number of worlds inhabited by animals with differing degrees of consciousness. Similarly, the Hindu cosmic structure is made up of innumerable planets that are created and destroyed in cycles. While the multiverse is simply a theoretical concept, its parallels with spiritual cosmologies show a shared tendency to imagine places beyond our immediate consciousness.

The idea of purpose in creation is a primary source of conflict between scientific and spiritual perspectives. The Big Bang theory, based on verifiable findings, rejects that the universe's origins were intentional or purposeful. Spiritual cosmologies, on the other hand, frequently define creation as deliberate, whether as an expression of divine will, a cosmic dance, or an act of love. However, this gap does not exclude debate. Alfred North Whitehead, a science and religion philosopher, has stated that purpose and process are not mutually exclusive. Combining scientific knowledge with spiritual insights allows one to envisage a cosmos that is both dynamically evolving and meaningful.

The search for synergy between Big Bang theories and spiritual cosmologies is not without challenges. Skeptics may caution against merging metaphorical and empirical frameworks, emphasizing the importance of keeping clear distinctions between science and religion. However, this caution should not prevent legitimate research. Instead, it encourages a deliberate approach to mixing different points of view, one that respects their unique methodologies while understanding their shared power to create surprise and wonder.

Navigating this synergy indicates that the Big Bang theory and spiritual cosmogonies are complementary lenses through which to see the universe, rather than competing narratives. They reflect life's profound complexity and beauty, inspiring humanity to interact with the world as both a physical reality and a source of spiritual significance. By facilitating dialogue between these realms, we get a greater understanding of the universe's origins, which benefits both scientific inquiry and spiritual reflection.

CHAPTER 13: HIDDEN VARIABLES AND KARMIC LAWS

"Every action has its pleasures and its price." – Socrates

The tension between locality and non-locality in quantum mechanics is at the heart of some of modern physics' most important debates. These discussions revolve on the underlying basis of reality, namely whether the cosmos follows deterministic laws that adhere to locality limitations, or whether events break these boundaries through non-local connections. This debate arose as a result of Einstein's discontent with quantum mechanics as it was developed, resulting in a series of issues that continue to have an impact on modern science.

Einstein's dissatisfaction with quantum physics stemmed largely from its apparent embracing of randomness and uncertainty. He famously stated that "God does not play dice," indicating his opinion that the universe follows deterministic laws. His critique included the notion of localization, which states that an entity is only influenced by its immediate surroundings. Locality, as a foundational principle of classical physics, assures that cause-and-effect interactions adhere to the speed of light as the ultimate limit for information flow. However, quantum mechanics calls into question this assumption in ways that Einstein and his colleagues attempted to uncover.

The Einstein-Podolsky-Rosen (EPR) conundrum, proposed in 1935, captures the conflict between quantum theory and locality. The paradox presented a thought experiment to demonstrate what Einstein perceived as quantum mechanics' incompleteness. The EPR study reported two particles that interacted and became entangled, so that measuring one particle's properties instantly determined the properties of the other, regardless of their distance apart. This phenomena, later dubbed "spooky action at a distance," appeared to violate locality by implying that information moved faster than light or that the particles were somehow coupled in a non-local way.

In reaction to the EPR dilemma, Niels Bohr's Copenhagen interpretation represented a significant break from classical intuitions. Bohr contended that the behavior of quantum systems cannot be fully understood in terms of pre-existing features. Instead, measurement played a crucial part in determining a system's status. According to this viewpoint, entanglement between particles did not indicate faster-than-light communication, but rather showed quantum systems' holistic nature. The non-local correlations seen in experiments were therefore intrinsic to quantum physics rather than evidence of incompleteness.

The dispute became more heated in the 1960s, when Bell's theorem was developed. John Bell constructed a mathematical framework to see if quantum mechanics predictions could be reconciled with local hidden variable theories, which hold that particles have deterministic qualities that are concealed from observation. The Bell inequalities revealed that no local hidden variable theory could reproduce all of quantum mechanics' predictions. Subsequent tests, such as those carried out by Alain Aspect and his associates in the 1980s, gave actual data to corroborate quantum mechanics' predictions of non-local correlation. These findings revealed that entangled particles exhibited correlations that could not be explained by classical locality, calling into question Einstein's concept of a deterministic universe.

Quantum entanglement reveals non-locality, which has far-reaching consequences for our understanding of causation and the fabric of reality. Unlike classical systems, whose interactions are limited by spatial and temporal constraints, quantum systems exhibit correlations that appear instantaneous and distance-independent. This has led some physicists and philosophers to contend that space and time are emergent phenomena rather than fundamental features of reality. The interconnectedness observed in quantum systems shows that the universe may function as an indivisible whole, with information and relationships that transcend classical boundaries.

Non-locality has philosophical ramifications far beyond physics, including metaphysics and epistemology. Non-locality calls into question the classical notion of separability, which argues that objects can be explored independently. Entangled particles are best understood in quantum physics as components of a unified system. This movement calls into question reductionist approaches to science, in favor of holistic perspectives that acknowledge the interconnection of phenomena. The similarity between non-locality and spiritual conceptions of interconnection, such as the Buddhist concept of interbeing or Sufi thought's mystical vision of unity, demonstrates the possibility of communication between scientific and spiritual worldviews.

Despite its revolutionary implications, non-locality does not imply the breakdown of causality or deterministic laws in all settings. Quantum mechanics works probabilistically, which means that while individual events appear random, statistical patterns arise with surprising consistency. This probabilistic paradigm maintains a form of determinism, but one that deviates from conventional expectations. The interaction of randomness and order in quantum physics represents a complex understanding of causality that inspires research across fields.

The interaction of locality and non-locality is also at the heart of current quantum information science research. Quantum encryption and quantum computing use entanglement's features to do tasks that are unachievable in classical contexts. Quantum key distribution, for example, relies on non-local correlations to enable secure communication, whereas quantum algorithms use superposition and entanglement to solve complicated problems with extraordinary efficiency. These developments highlight the practical importance of theoretical arguments, translating abstract ideas into actual innovations.

Despite quantum physics' practical success, disagreements about how to interpret its non-local properties continue. Alternative theories, such as Bohmian mechanics and many-worlds interpretations, aim to reconcile quantum events with deterministic frameworks or to provide new insights on the nature of reality. Bohmian mechanics, for example, proposes the concept of a guiding wave, which controls particle direction, restoring determinism while accommodating non-local factors. According to the many-worlds interpretation, every quantum event creates a branching universe, eliminating the necessity for non-local communication by embedding all possibilities in a large multiverse.

The ongoing study of locality and non-locality shows science's dynamic interplay of theory, experimentation, and interpretation. While quantum mechanics has proved predictive power and practical utility, its fundamental issues remain fertile terrain for research. Einstein's challenges to quantum theory left a lasting legacy that inspires diligent investigation and pushes the boundaries of knowledge.

The convergence of local and non-local theories compels us to consider quantum mechanics' larger implications for understanding reality. By embracing the insights of both frameworks, we get a deeper understanding of the natural world's complexity and intricacy. The tension between locality and non-locality is a stimulus for creativity, encouraging novel approaches to age-old issues about causality, interconnection, and the meaning of life.

Karma as a Hidden Influence: Moral Causation Beyond Immediate Perception

The notion of karma, which is based in ancient spiritual and philosophical traditions, holds that acts have repercussions and shape the direction of a person's life. This moral causation goes beyond immediate awareness, implying a framework in which desire and behavior ripple through the fabric of existence to produce ultimate effects. In quantum physics, karma is associated with concepts such as interconnection, causality, and invisible forces influencing observable realities. This interaction of traditional knowledge and modern science provides a complex lens through which to investigate the mechanisms of influence that operate outside of direct observation.

Karma, derived from Sanskrit meaning "action" or "deed," is a fundamental principle of Hinduism, Buddhism, and Jainism. It includes the idea that all actions, whether physical, verbal, or mental, have a consequence. Unlike deterministic or mechanistic causality, karma emphasizes ethical components, with actions motivated by positive or negative intent producing matching effects. This concept operates on a continuum, free of immediate temporal restrictions, implying that the effects of acts may materialize in this life or future reincarnations. This delayed causality adds complexity, consistent with quantum physics' rejection of straightforward linearity.

Causation in quantum physics takes on a probabilistic nature, calling into question traditional concepts of determinism. The wave function, which defines the state of a quantum system, contains all conceivable outcomes until they are collapsed into a specific state by observation. This collapse shows how potentiality becomes actuality, with analogies to karmic processes. Karma, like the wave function, represents latent possibilities shaped by deeds that await the proper circumstances to manifest. This shared emphasis on potentiality rather than determinism draws analogies between karma's moral causation and the probabilistic causation inherent in quantum events.

The concept of entanglement is a striking junction of karma and quantum theory. When particles interact and become entangled, their properties remain associated despite their spatial distance. Observing one particle has an instantaneous effect on the other, demonstrating fundamental interconnectivity. Similarly, karma says that even seemingly isolated actions cause ripples that affect others and the larger universe. This interconnected framework undermines the illusion of separateness by stressing the web of relationships that connects all entities. The philosophical convergence between karmic interdependence and quantum entanglement emphasizes the universal interconnectedness that underpins both perspectives.

The non-local nature of quantum correlations corresponds to the delayed appearance of karmic repercussions. In karmic terminology, the consequences of an action can span multiple lifetimes, indicating a complex, temporally spread process. Quantum mechanics demonstrates that certain correlations, while immediate in effect, are caused by past interactions between particles. This temporal continuity connects the past with the present, demonstrating how early conditions shape future results. Both karma and quantum theory emphasize the necessity of detecting underlying factors that shape visible reality, encouraging a more in-depth investigation of causality beyond first appearances.

The ethical dimension of karma adds a depth that was missing from quantum mechanics' strictly descriptive framework. Karma stresses responsibility, implying that ethical behavior promotes harmony while unethical behavior perpetuates pain. This moral causality is consistent with efforts to incorporate ethics into scientific investigation, particularly in areas such as quantum computing and artificial intelligence. Just as karma emphasizes the impact of individual actions on the community, advances in quantum technology necessitate examination of their societal and ecological consequences. The interaction between moral causation and quantum research highlights the importance of ethical stewardship in both fields.

While the connections between karma and quantum mechanics are intriguing, it is critical to recognize their different contexts and epistemological grounds. Karma originated in spiritual traditions and serves as a framework for ethical life and spiritual advancement. In contrast, quantum mechanics derives from actual research, which is founded on rigorous experimentation and mathematical formalism. To avoid mistaking metaphors with scientific truth, it is important to bridge various perspectives with prudence. However, their shared ideas of interconnectivity and hidden influences encourage multidisciplinary discussion, improving both philosophical and scientific understandings.

The concept of karma as an invisible impact has psychological and social implications. In behavioral psychology, actions are frequently the result of subconscious patterns created by previous experiences. These patterns, which are similar to karmic imprints, influence decision-making and interpersonal connections, repeating cycles of behavior. In terms of sociology, the ripple effects of activities within communities follow karmic principles, in which individual decisions influence collective consequences. These parallels imply that karma functions not merely as a philosophical principle, but also as a practical lens for comprehending human behavior and societal dynamics.

In current physics, the hunt for hidden variables seeks to identify underlying features that could reconcile quantum mechanics with classical determinism. Similarly, karma can be thought of as a "hidden variable" in human experience, providing an explanation for phenomena that defy direct causality. While investigations verifying Bell's inequalities have essentially discredited local hidden variable hypotheses in quantum physics, the concept of hidden variables continues to serve as a bridge to deeper layers of reality. Karma, as an ethical and metaphysical hidden variable, improves our investigation by emphasizing intention and moral responsibility.

The incorporation of karmic ideas into modern discourse also addresses ecological and environmental concerns. The recognition that actions have far-reaching consequences mirrors the karmic understanding of causality, fostering a sense of accountability for environmental stewardship. In the context of climate change, the karmic perspective emphasizes collective responsibility, where individual and societal choices impact future generations. This alignment underscores the relevance of karmic principles in addressing global challenges, highlighting their potential to inspire sustainable practices and ethical decision-making.

Karma's emphasis on unseen influence invites introspection and mindfulness, encouraging individuals to cultivate awareness of their actions and intentions. This practice aligns with quantum mechanics' emphasis on the observer's role in shaping outcomes. Just as the act of observation influences quantum systems, mindfulness transforms human experience by fostering intentionality and ethical engagement. The interplay between observation, intention, and causality bridges the metaphysical and scientific dimensions, offering practical insights for personal and collective growth.

In examining karma as unseen influence, it becomes evident that causality transcends immediate perception, weaving intricate connections across time and space. This understanding resonates with quantum mechanics' revelations about the probabilistic and interconnected nature of reality. By embracing the insights of both frameworks, we gain a richer appreciation for the complexities of causality and the ethical responsibilities it entails. Karma, as a principle of moral causation, illuminates the profound interplay between actions and their consequences, inviting a deeper exploration of the unseen forces shaping our world.

*Philosophical Bridge: Whether
Hidden Variables Echo the Logic
of Spiritual Causal Webs*

The interplay between quantum mechanics and spiritual concepts often finds fertile ground in the exploration of hidden variables. In quantum physics, hidden variables refer to theoretical constructs that might explain the inherent randomness observed in quantum phenomena. Similarly, many spiritual traditions posit unseen forces or webs of causality that influence observable outcomes, echoing the logic of interconnectedness and moral responsibility. This alignment offers a philosophical bridge between science and spirituality, raising questions about the fundamental nature of reality, causality, and human agency.

In quantum mechanics, hidden variables emerged as a response to the probabilistic interpretation of quantum systems. Classical determinism, which dominated physics before the quantum era, assumed that every effect had a precise cause, and all future events could be predicted with sufficient knowledge of initial conditions. However, quantum theory disrupted this framework with its probabilistic nature, epitomized by Heisenberg's uncertainty principle and wave function collapse. The Copenhagen interpretation, championed by figures like Niels Bohr, suggested that quantum systems exist in superpositions of potential states until observed. This view challenges classical causality, proposing a universe governed by probability rather than determinism.

Einstein famously resisted this interpretation, asserting that "God does not play dice." His discomfort with quantum indeterminacy fueled the search for hidden variables that could restore a deterministic underpinning to quantum phenomena. Hidden variable theories propose that the apparent randomness in quantum systems arises from underlying factors not yet understood or observable. These theories include local hidden variables, which adhere to the constraints of relativity, and non-local hidden variables, which allow for faster-than-light influences. Bell's theorem, supported by experimental evidence, demonstrated that local hidden variable theories cannot fully account for quantum entanglement, but the concept remains a pivotal topic in discussions of quantum foundations.

The philosophical implications of hidden variables extend beyond physics, intersecting with spiritual ideas of causality. Many spiritual traditions, particularly in Eastern philosophies like Hinduism and Buddhism, embrace the concept of interconnectedness through unseen causal webs. Karma, for example, describes a moral law of cause and effect operating beyond immediate perception. Actions, intentions, and even thoughts create ripples that influence future experiences, embodying a non-local, temporally distributed causality. Similarly, mystical traditions across cultures—ranging from Kabbalistic teachings to Indigenous cosmologies—assert that hidden forces shape the visible world, weaving an intricate tapestry of interdependence.

The comparison between hidden variables and spiritual causal webs raises profound questions about the nature of reality. Both frameworks challenge surface-level perceptions, inviting deeper inquiry into the unseen dynamics governing existence. In quantum mechanics, the search for hidden variables embodies a scientific pursuit to uncover fundamental truths. In spirituality, the focus shifts to moral and existential dimensions, exploring how individual actions resonate within a larger, often divine, order. These perspectives, though distinct in methodology and purpose, converge in their recognition of unseen influences as central to understanding the world.

One area of alignment lies in the rejection of purely mechanistic models of causality. Both quantum mechanics and spiritual traditions highlight the limitations of reductionism, which seeks to explain complex phenomena by analyzing their simplest components. In quantum theory, the behavior of particles cannot always be predicted or understood in isolation, as interactions and entanglement introduce holistic dynamics. Similarly, spiritual perspectives emphasize the interconnectedness of all beings and events, suggesting that isolated actions or entities cannot fully encapsulate the richness of existence. This shared emphasis on interconnection underscores the need for integrative approaches to understanding causality.

The non-locality observed in quantum entanglement offers another intriguing parallel to spiritual causal webs. In entanglement, particles remain correlated regardless of spatial separation, defying classical notions of locality. This phenomenon echoes spiritual teachings on the interconnectedness of all things, where distance and separation are perceived as illusions. For example, the Buddhist concept of Indra's Net envisions the universe as an infinite web of interconnected jewels, each reflecting all others. This metaphor resonates with the non-local correlations in quantum systems, suggesting that both perspectives recognize a deeper unity underlying apparent distinctions.

Ethics emerges as a critical point of divergence and convergence between hidden variables and spiritual causal webs. In physics, hidden variable theories primarily address ontological and epistemological questions, leaving ethical considerations aside. Spiritual frameworks, however, place ethics at the core of causality, asserting that intentions and actions have moral consequences. This ethical dimension enriches the discussion, offering a roadmap for navigating the implications of interconnectedness. The recognition that actions resonate beyond immediate contexts fosters a sense of responsibility, encouraging individuals to act with mindfulness and compassion.

While the parallels between hidden variables and spiritual causal webs are compelling, caution is essential to avoid conflating metaphor with empirical evidence. Scientific inquiry relies on falsifiability and rigorous experimentation, while spiritual traditions often operate within interpretive and experiential paradigms. Bridging these domains requires careful navigation, acknowledging their distinct epistemologies while exploring areas of mutual insight. For example, the metaphorical resonance between entanglement and interconnectedness can inspire interdisciplinary dialogue without reducing one to the other.

This dialogue has practical implications for addressing global challenges. The recognition of interconnectedness, whether framed through quantum mechanics or spirituality, underscores the importance of collective action and ethical responsibility. In the context of climate change, for instance, the understanding that individual actions contribute to global outcomes aligns with the karmic principle of moral causation. Similarly, the recognition of non-local influences invites a reevaluation of societal structures, emphasizing collaboration and shared accountability over individualism and competition.

The search for hidden variables also intersects with contemporary explorations of consciousness and its role in shaping reality. Some interpretations of quantum mechanics, such as the observer effect, suggest that consciousness influences the outcomes of measurements. While this idea remains controversial within the scientific community, it aligns with spiritual perspectives that view consciousness as fundamental to existence. The interplay between observation, intention, and causality invites further investigation, bridging scientific and spiritual inquiries into the nature of mind and reality.

In examining hidden variables and spiritual causal webs, it becomes clear that both frameworks challenge simplistic notions of causality, emphasizing complexity, interdependence, and unseen influences. This alignment offers a philosophical bridge, fostering dialogue between science and spirituality while respecting their unique contributions. By exploring the intersections between hidden variables and moral causation, we gain a richer understanding of the forces shaping our world, inspiring both scientific curiosity and ethical reflection. The journey toward uncovering the unseen dynamics of reality continues to unfold, inviting us to embrace its mystery with open minds and hearts.

CHAPTER 14: QUANTUM HEALING AND ENERGY WORK

"The natural healing force within each one of us is the greatest force in getting well." – Hippocrates

The advent of quantum biology as a separate subject represents an intriguing convergence of quantum mechanics with the biological sciences. While quantum mechanics has traditionally been linked with subatomic particles and physics laboratories, its principles are also being recognized in biological systems, where quantum events appear to underpin essential activities. Quantum biology fundamentally changes our view of life, from the nearly-perfect efficiency of photosynthesis to the inner workings of enzymes and the speculative links between quantum coherence and consciousness.

Photosynthesis is one of the most remarkable instances of quantum phenomena in biology. This mechanism, essential to life on Earth, transforms sunlight into chemical energy inside plants, algae, and certain microorganisms. Quantum coherence, a quantum mechanical phenomena, sits at the heart of photosynthesis. Light photons stimulate electrons in pigment molecules within chloroplasts during the early phases of photosynthesis. This excitation energy must pass through a complicated protein network before arriving to the reaction center, where it is transformed into a chemical form that the organism may use.

This energy can exist in numerous routes at the same time thanks to quantum coherence, ensuring that it takes the most efficient route to the reaction center. This mechanism, similar to quantum state superposition, explains the nearly flawless energy transfer observed in photosynthesis, which classical physics could not fully explain. Experimental evidence employing ultrafast spectroscopy has demonstrated that quantum effects work at the femtosecond scale, or one quadrillionth of a second, underlining how these transient occurrences affect macroscopic physiological processes.

Aside from photosynthesis, enzymes provide a convincing evidence for quantum effects in biology. Enzymes are biological catalysts that speed up chemical processes that are necessary for life. Their incredible effectiveness sometimes challenges traditional explanations, especially in processes involving proton or electron transport. Quantum tunneling, a process in which particles flow through energy barriers rather than over them, is thought to play a critical role in such interactions. Enzymes achieve orders of magnitude quicker response rates than traditional models anticipate by allowing protons or electrons to "tunnel" through obstacles.

Experimental and theoretical investigations have validated quantum tunneling's significance in enzyme activity. Tunneling, for example, has been shown in studies of the enzyme alcohol dehydrogenase to considerably improve its catalytic efficiency. These discoveries call into question traditional chemistry beliefs and emphasize the delicate dance of particles regulated by quantum mechanics within biological systems. Such discoveries not only add to our understanding of enzyme processes, but they also have the potential to be used to create innovative biotechnology catalysts.

The connection of quantum physics and biology extends into neurology and consciousness, however this is still a subject of speculation and debate. Some hypotheses suggest that quantum coherence may work in the brain, possibly impacting cognitive processes or the nature of consciousness. The Orch-OR (Orchestrated Objective Reduction) hypothesis, presented by physicist Roger Penrose and anesthesiologist Stuart Hameroff, posits that quantum processes within microtubules, which are protein structures in neurons, may play a role in consciousness.

According to this idea, microtubules display quantum coherence, allowing the brain to interpret information in ways other than traditional computing. While the Orch-OR hypothesis has aroused much controversy, it has also encouraged multidisciplinary study into the putative connections between quantum physics and consciousness. Critics claim that the brain's warm, loud environment is incompatible with the delicate circumstances needed for quantum coherence. However, proponents argue that specific biological structures may have evolved to sustain coherence in such situations, a concept that continues to drive experimental research.

The possible ramifications of quantum biology go well beyond theoretical comprehension. This field's insights might transform medicine, biotechnology, and perhaps artificial intelligence. Understanding quantum effects in enzymes, for example, might pave the way for more effective medications or industrial catalysts. Similarly, research into quantum coherence in photosynthesis has led to the development of enhanced solar cells that mirror natural system efficiency.

Quantum biology opens us exciting potential for comprehending the mind-body relationship in the field of medicine. While it is theoretical, some researchers have proposed that quantum events might impact processes such as protein folding, cellular signaling, or even the relationship between consciousness and physical health. If verified, such links might open up new possibilities for treating illnesses or improving well-being through therapies that take quantum effects into consideration.

Despite its potential, quantum biology confronts substantial obstacles. The discipline is fundamentally multidisciplinary, necessitating knowledge of physics, biology, chemistry, and computational science. Bridging various disciplines necessitates not just technical expertise but also a willingness to challenge conventional wisdom. Furthermore, the diversity and variety of live beings frequently make experimental studies of quantum effects in biological systems difficult. Ultrafast spectroscopy and powerful computer modeling have yielded vital insights, but much more has to be uncovered.

As quantum biology advances, ethical concerns emerge as well. The field's potential uses, which range from quantum-inspired technology to medicinal advances, must be pursued wisely. As mankind exploits the potential of quantum mechanics in biology, it is critical to ensure fair access to quantum-based discoveries, safeguard biodiversity, and respect for life's complexity.

Quantum biology encourages us to reexamine the distinctions between the physical and biological sciences, providing a new perspective on the natural world. This discipline increases scientific understanding and fosters a better appreciation for life's interconnectivity by unveiling the quantum basis of important biological processes. Quantum biology, as study progresses, has the possibility of revealing significant insights into the essence of existence by linking the microscopic and macroscopic, the material and the ethereal.

Reiki, Acupuncture, and the Function of Intention in Energy Medicine Traditions

Exploring energy medicine traditions offers a fascinating confluence of traditional therapeutic techniques and new scientific insights. These modalities—such as Reiki, acupuncture, and related energy-based interventions—are founded on the idea that vital energy flows throughout and around the body. Illness is said to be caused by disruptions or imbalances in this energy, whereas restoring equilibrium promotes healing. Although contemporary science is still attempting to completely confirm and understand the processes underpinning these traditions, their usefulness in specific settings and rising interest in their potential call for careful investigation.

Reiki, which originated in Japan in the early twentieth century, represents universal life force, or rei (spiritual wisdom) and ki (vital energy). This energy is channeled via the hands by practitioners to encourage relaxation, relieve tension, and enhance the body's natural healing processes. The technique is non-invasive and relies on intention and energy flow rather than physical manipulation. Although the scientific basis of Reiki is debatable, evidence shows that treatment may induce a relaxation response, reduce stress indicators like cortisol, and improve subjective well-being. These findings are consistent with the general awareness that stress reduction is important for preserving health.

Acupuncture, a fundamental component of traditional Chinese medicine (TCM), is based on a complex system of meridians and energy routes known as qi (life force). Acupuncture restores energy balance and stimulates the body's healing power by inserting small needles into particular places along these channels. Modern research on acupuncture has yielded a mixed bag of support and scepticism. Studies have shown that it can help manage chronic pain, nausea, and other illnesses, perhaps through mechanisms such as endorphin release, inflammatory response regulation, and effects on brain pathways. However, others suggest that the placebo effect may play a substantial part in these results, emphasizing the importance of rigorous study.

Intention plays an especially fascinating role in energy medicine, bridging the gap between scientific research and spirituality. Reiki and acupuncture both regard the practitioner's attention and purpose to be essential to the healing process. This emphasis is consistent with psychological and neuroscience results, which show that purpose and focused attention have demonstrable consequences on physiological and cognitive outcomes. Meditation and mindfulness studies, for example, have shown that purposeful practices can change brain activity, lower inflammation, and boost emotional resilience. While these findings give indirect support for energy medicine practices, they also raise issues regarding how subjective moods affect physical health.

Due to the subjective character of energy flow and the difficulty in assessing delicate physiological impacts, scientific research into energy medicine frequently face methodological hurdles. For example, the placebo effect—a phenomena in which a patient's belief in treatment efficacy adds to better outcomes—makes it difficult to analyze Reiki and acupuncture research. Critics claim that apparent advantages may be the result of psychological factors rather than actual energy processes. Advocates argue that even if the placebo effect is there, it highlights the mind-body link that is essential to healing.

Recent advancements in biofield research suggest a way to bridge the gap between traditional energy therapy and modern science. The biofield, which is defined as an electromagnetic field surrounding and penetrating the body, is hypothesized to interact with physiological and energy processes. Early research utilizing sensitive instruments found modest changes in electromagnetic fields during techniques such as Reiki, providing validity to the concept that energy flows might be objectively analyzed. Furthermore, recent research in quantum biology, which investigates quantum events in biological systems, raises the potential that energy medicine operates at the quantum level, albeit this is yet speculative.

Culture has a big impact on how people perceive energy medicine. Acupuncture and Reiki are strongly established in their own cultural and philosophical traditions, which place a premium on connectivity, balance, and overall health. The notion of yin and yang—opposing but complementary forces—reflects the wider philosophy that balance promotes health. Similarly, Reiki's emphasis on universal life energy corresponds to spiritual traditions that see healing as a process of connecting with the broader universe. As these treatments spread over the world, they are frequently altered to match Western biological standards, raising conflicts over authenticity and cultural appropriation.

The incorporation of energy medicine into conventional healthcare systems varies greatly around the globe. Acupuncture and associated techniques are integrated into medical infrastructures in countries such as China and Japan, with traditional and modern approaches frequently merging. Energy medicine is commonly characterized as complementary or alternative medicine (CAM) in Western contexts, where it is utilized in conjunction with traditional therapies. The growth of integrative medicine, which aims to blend evidence-based CAM with mainstream treatment, has opened potential for energy medicine to gain traction. Acupuncture, for example, is now widely utilized in cancer settings to treat chemotherapy-induced nausea and exhaustion.

As energy medicine becomes more popular, ethical concerns arise, particularly in areas such as informed consent, practitioner training, and effectiveness claims. To establish trust, patients must be given accurate information about the benefits and limits of energy treatment. Furthermore, standardized training programs and practitioner certification can help these methods gain legitimacy. Exaggerated assertions must be avoided, particularly in life-threatening situations, in order to retain ethical integrity.

Energy medicine has enormous potential to meet the rising need for holistic and individualized healthcare. As chronic stress, mental health issues, and lifestyle-related disorders become more prevalent across the world, techniques such as Reiki and acupuncture provide tools for fostering calm, resilience, and self-care. These modalities coincide with wider movements toward preventative medicine and patient-centered treatment by focusing on the mind-body relationship. Their emphasis on non-invasive and low-risk procedures makes them enticing choices for people looking for alternatives to pharmaceutical treatments.

The future of energy medicine is dependent on a continuous conversation between traditional knowledge systems and modern investigation. Collaborative research that respects the cultural foundations of these behaviors while employing rigorous methodology can help to further knowledge and integration. Advancements in imaging, wearable sensors, and artificial intelligence may allow for more exact measurements of biofield interactions, providing insights into how energy medicine affects the body on numerous levels. Simultaneously, multidisciplinary techniques that combine physics, neurology, and anthropology might broaden our understanding of the complexities of healing.

Energy medicine traditions provide a complex tapestry of human inventiveness, combining cultural wisdom, experience knowledge, and new science. These practices encourage us to explore the interconnections of body, mind, and spirit, whether through Reiki's gentle touch, acupuncture's precise procedures, or the transformational power of intention. As research advances, they hold the possibility of not just improving our knowledge of health but also creating a more compassionate and integrative approach to treatment.

Balancing Open-Minded Study with Rigorous Testing to Maintain Integrity and Evidence

The relationship between energy medicine and scientific inquiry emphasizes the significance of combining open-minded discovery with rigorous evidence-based criteria. Energy medicine, which includes treatments like Reiki, acupuncture, and biofield therapies, is based on ideas that frequently question established scientific assumptions. Advocates say that it has the potential to supplement contemporary medicine, while detractors underline the necessity for repeatable findings and mechanistic clarity. This tension emphasizes the importance of upholding integrity in study, practice, and communication in order to ethically progress learning.

The presence and manipulation of subtle energy fields that impact health and well-being is central to the concept of energy medicine. Acupuncture and other practices rely on centuries-old systems, such as traditional Chinese medicine's idea of qi flowing along meridians. Reiki, which originated in Japan, promotes healing by harnessing universal life energy. These techniques have a similar focus on balancing energy imbalances, with a preference for overall well-being over symptom-specific therapies. Their dependence on notions that are not widely recognized in conventional science has attracted both interest and criticism.

To examine the efficacy and processes of energy medicine, rigorous scientific study is required. Controlled research, systematic reviews, and meta-analyses play critical roles in distinguishing between beneficial therapies and anecdotal claims. Acupuncture, for example, has shown quantifiable advantages in pain treatment, with studies showing that it may boost the production of endorphins, decrease inflammation, and modify brain activity. Similarly, Reiki has been linked to lower tension and anxiety levels, while it is unclear whether these effects are the result of direct energy effects or placebo reactions.

The placebo effect is both a difficulty and an opportunity for testing energy medication. Placebo reactions, in which patients benefit as a result of their belief in the efficacy of a therapy, are especially important in modalities that focus on intention and practitioner-patient interactions. Critics believe that energy medicine's effects are mostly psychological rather than physiological. Proponents argue that even placebo effects highlight the importance of the mind-body link in healing. Recognizing the placebo effect does not decrease the value of researching how intention, ritual, and treatment setting influence health results.

Technological breakthroughs are broadening the scope of research into the mechanics of energy medicine. Researchers can use sophisticated imaging, biofield sensors, and wearable devices to monitor subtle physiological changes during energy-based therapies. Studies on the biofield, a hypothetical electromagnetic field encircling the body, have discovered unexpected links, such as variations in heart rate variability and cellular performance. While these findings are preliminary, they serve as a foundation for further investigation of how energy therapy interacts with biological systems.

Scientific integrity necessitates following rigorous procedures such as randomized controlled trials (RCTs), blinding, and repeatability. These guidelines assist to reduce bias, assure dependability, and lay the groundwork for evidence-based healthcare integration. However, the application of established scientific methodologies to energy therapy presents distinct obstacles. Standardization and replication are made more difficult by the subjective nature of energy flow and practitioner intention. Researchers must negotiate these difficulties while preserving transparency and rigor.

Energy medicine research and practice place a high value on ethical issues. Practitioners and researchers are responsible for providing accurate, evidence-based information regarding the advantages and disadvantages of energy therapy. Exaggerated claims, particularly those claiming to treat serious illnesses, run the danger of losing trust and ethical legitimacy. Informed consent, in which patients understand the scientific foundation and potential repercussions of treatments, is critical for promoting responsibility and respect.

Interdisciplinary collaboration provides a mechanism to bridge the gap between energy medicine and mainstream research. This approach is exemplified by integrative medicine, which blends evidence-based alternative therapies with conventional medical care. Acupuncture programs in cancer settings, for example, illustrate the potential for energy medicine to improve quality of life while managing treatment adverse effects. Interdisciplinary activities can increase understanding and implementation by promoting conversation among practitioners, researchers, and clinicians.

Cultural perceptions are extremely important in forming attitudes towards energy medicine. Acupuncture and Reiki are cultural and spiritual traditions that value comprehensive well-being and harmony. As these modalities acquire worldwide popularity, cultural awareness and respect become increasingly important. Recognizing the conceptual foundations that support energy medicine increases its incorporation into a variety of healthcare situations while avoiding appropriation or reductionism.

The function of purpose in energy medicine is a fascinating blend of physics, psychology, and spirituality. Intention-based techniques like meditation and prayer have been found to have demonstrable benefits on brain activity, immunological function, and emotional resiliency. These findings are consistent with energy medicine's emphasis on practitioner attention and intention as necessary for healing. Investigating the mechanisms via which intention impacts physiological processes may shed light on the larger dynamics of mind-body interactions.

Critics of energy therapy sometimes point to a lack of scientific consensus, especially in the absence of clearly defined processes. Skeptical voices underline the importance of exercising caution when embracing methods that lack strong scientific basis. However, this critique emphasizes the significance of doing open-minded research. From germ theory to quantum physics, history has shown that paradigm-shifting discoveries frequently call into question existing standards. Skepticism and inquiry are required for energy medicine to be included into scientific discourse.

Balancing open-minded research with thorough testing entails walking a narrow line between investigation and evidence. Energy medicine fills a distinct niche, posing problems that go beyond traditional biological paradigms. Its emphasis on holistic healing, practitioner-patient relationships, and subtle energy interactions encourages researchers to broaden their methodological toolset. The discipline may grow responsibly by adopting multidisciplinary methods, promoting ethical openness, and prioritizing patient well-being.

As healthcare increasingly emphasizes individualized and holistic methods, energy medicine provides vital insights into the interaction of physical, emotional, and energetic health. Its incorporation into mainstream treatment necessitates a dedication to thorough study, cultural sensitivity, and ethical integrity. Energy medicine has the ability to improve our knowledge of healing, motivate innovation, and promote a more compassionate approach to health by encouraging conversation between traditional wisdom and modern investigation.

CHAPTER 15: QUANTUM CHAOS AND SPIRITUAL DISORDER

"Out of chaos comes order." – Friedrich Nietzsche

The leap from classical chaos to quantum chaos marks a significant shift in our understanding of how systems function at basic levels. Chaos theory in classical mechanics discusses how, while following precise rules, deterministic systems can display unexpected and extremely sensitive behaviors as a result of minor differences in initial circumstances.

Quantum physics, with its probabilistic framework and ideas like as superposition and uncertainty, adds to the already complicated area. Exploring the link between these domains shows a fascinating dynamic in which randomness meets structure, shedding light on both scientific and philosophical issues regarding the nature of order and chaos.

Weather patterns, planetary orbits, and the double pendulum are common examples of classical chaos. These systems are deterministic, which means that their future behavior is theoretically predicted given full knowledge of the initial circumstances and governing equations. However, because of their great sensitivity to slight variations—known as the "butterfly effect," long-term forecasts are almost impossible. This sensitivity highlights the inherent limitations of prediction in classical physics, especially in systems governed by well-defined equations.

In contrast, quantum mechanics functions on a fundamentally probabilistic basis. The wave function is a mathematical description of a quantum system that encodes probabilities rather than certainties. When measurements are taken, these probabilities "collapse" into particular outcomes, but the process is still stochastic. When these probabilistic ideas are applied to systems that display chaotic behavior near their classical limits, a new field of research develops. For example, the quantum version of the chaotic pendulum shows how quantum uncertainty interacts with the classical counterpart's deterministic chaos.

One distinguishing aspect of quantum chaos is the development of unique patterns within randomness, which is commonly defined in terms of eigenstates and energy spectra. In quantum systems, particle energy levels are discrete spectra rather than continuous ranges. When these systems are chaotic, their spectra show statistical distributions that are markedly different from those of non-chaotic systems. The random matrix theory, which was created in part to describe nuclear energy levels, has proven to be an effective tool for comprehending these spectrum patterns. Such findings imply that chaos in quantum systems is not completely random, but rather has an underlying structure determined by statistical laws.

Quantum scars, which indicate unexpected residues of classical paths in quantum systems, are an important field of research in quantum chaos. In classical mechanics, chaotic systems are distinguished by the absence of stable orbits; particles move in irregular, unexpected directions. However, in the quantum domain, certain wave functions demonstrate increased probability along classical courses. These "scarred" states contradict expectations of uniform randomness and demonstrate a strong link between classical and quantum theories of chaos.

Quantum chaos is also important in understanding the transition between classical and quantum worlds, known as the "quantum-classical correspondence." According to this principle, quantum mechanics should reduce to classical mechanics in systems with large quantum numbers or high energies. Chaotic systems offer a unique testing ground for this relationship since their behavior is particularly sensitive to changes in scale and energy. Researchers obtain insight into the larger subject of how quantum and classical realms coexist and interact by examining how quantum chaos transforms into classical chaos.

Quantum chaos has far-reaching ramifications in fields such as information theory, cryptography, and biology. Chaotic quantum systems, for example, are of interest in quantum computing because their unpredictability and entanglement may be used for activities such as secure communication and difficult problem solving. Similarly, studying quantum chaos in molecular systems has implications for understanding chemical reactions and energy transfer mechanisms in living creatures.

In terms of philosophy, quantum chaos calls into question established concepts of causation and determinism. Classical chaos has shown that deterministic systems can look random due to their sensitivity to beginning circumstances. Quantum mechanics exacerbates the unpredictability by injecting intrinsic randomness at the basic level. This interaction raises problems about free choice, causality, and the boundaries of human understanding. Can deterministic rules adequately explain the world, or does quantum chaos indicate an irreducible element of mystery and spontaneity in the cosmos?

The study of quantum chaos overlaps with spiritual and philosophical notions of order and disorder. Many philosophical traditions regard chaos as a prerequisite to creation, a necessary condition for the formation of complexity and life. In this perspective, quantum chaos may be viewed as a metaphor for the universe's delicate balance of randomness and structure. By accepting the presence of chaos and order, science and spirituality can find common ground in comprehending the dynamic interaction of forces that form reality.

Deeper explorations into quantum chaos are becoming possible because to technological advancements, with experimental settings and computer models yielding previously unattainable insights. Ultracold atoms in optical lattices, for example, are extremely controlled systems for investigating quantum chaos in the laboratory. These trials not only put theoretical assumptions to the test, but they frequently uncover unanticipated events that spark new research. As researchers continue to investigate this frontier, the limits of what we know about the quantum world—and the chaotic patterns that exist inside it—are constantly growing.

When studying the link between classical and quantum chaos, it becomes evident that randomness and structure are not mutually incompatible. Instead, they cohabit in complex ways that transcend easy comprehension. The study of quantum chaos requires us to reconsider our beliefs about predictability, causation, and the nature of reality. We can obtain a better understanding of the universe's complexity and beauty by combining deterministic frameworks from classical physics with probabilistic insights from quantum mechanics. The path from classical to quantum chaos is not only a scientific undertaking, but also an investigation into the fundamental linkages between order, disorder, and the human desire for knowledge.

Sacred Concepts of Chaos: Creation Myths Emphasizing Order Emerging from Turmoil

The interaction of chaos and order has interested human communities for millennia, and it is frequently portrayed in creation myths and holy narratives throughout nations. These myths, which are rich in metaphor and symbolism, portray chaos as the primordial state from which the universe, structure, and life arise. Exploring these myths reveals not just humanity's deep interest about the universe's beginnings, but also surprising connections with scientific concepts such as chaos, complexity, and emergence. Examining holy concepts of chaos reveals that disorder is a necessary precondition to creation and transformation, rather than an end state.

In many ancient cosmologies, chaos signifies the undifferentiated emptiness or formless condition that exists before the act of creation. In Greek mythology, Chaos was the primordial chasm from which the world's earliest deities and elements sprang. Similarly, the Babylonian epic Enuma Elish portrays the primordial seas of Tiamat and Apsu, whose chaotic intermixing created the gods and the organized cosmos. These stories frequently portray chaos as fertile ground for creation, implying that disorder harbors the possibility for new forms of life.

The symbolism of chaos as a forerunner to order is found in many different cultures. In Hindu cosmology, pralaya refers to the cyclical breakdown of the cosmos, a chaotic phase that precedes the next creation cycle beginning by Brahma. This repeated destruction and regeneration emphasizes the inherent relationship between chaos and creation, depicting the world as a dynamic and ever-renewing process. Similarly, in Norse mythology, the Ginnungagap, a vast abyss, connects the fiery realm of Muspelheim with the ice Niflheim, acting as the chaotic matrix from which the world begins.

In creation myths, chaos is frequently personified or represented by beings that symbolize untamed, primal elements. These characters frequently serve as catalysts for change. In Egyptian mythology, the chaotic waters of Nun represent the limitless potential that the creator deity Atum used to build the ordered world. Pangu, according to Chinese legend, is a giant who emerges from a cosmic egg, separating the chaotic forces of yin and yang to establish heaven and earth. These myths emphasize chaos' creative function, seeing it as a dynamic, participatory force rather than a simply destructive one.

These ancient myths are consistent with our scientific understandings of chaos and complexity. In mathematics and physics, chaos theory explores how deterministic systems may behave in unpredictable and seemingly random ways, particularly when sensitive beginning conditions are applied. While this randomness looks chaotic, it frequently shows underlying patterns, such as fractals, indicating that chaos has fundamental structure. This thought is similar to the mythical concept of latent order emerging from primordial chaos, implying a fundamental symbolic link between old knowledge and modern science.

The development of life is a visible illustration of chaos giving way to order. The primordial Earth, a chaotic environment of chemical processes, created the conditions for molecular complexity and, eventually, the first self-replicating creature. This journey from chemical chaos to biological order is similar to the narrative arc seen in creation myths, in which the interaction of different elements creates life. These connections imply that religious ideas of chaos provide not just poetic insights but also frameworks for comprehending scientific processes.

In addition to cosmology and biology, chaos and order are important in personal and communal change. Chaos myths frequently represent the human struggle to navigate disorder and uncertainty. In Joseph Campbell's Hero's Journey, a universal narrative structure, the protagonist enters the unknown—a metaphorical chaos—before emerging with renewed understanding and purpose. This narrative archetype emphasizes the transformational power of confronting disorder, promoting the concept that turmoil is an essential step toward progress and self-discovery.

The interaction between chaos and order is also seen in spiritual activities and rituals intended to reconcile these conflicting forces. For example, in Taoism, the principle of wu wei promotes harmony with the natural flow of the cosmos, acknowledging the Tao's intrinsic balance of order and disorder. Similarly, the idea of sunyata (emptiness) in Buddhist teachings implies that the apparent disorder of impermanence and interconnectedness lies underneath the fundamental essence of existence. These spiritual frameworks teach practitioners to accept chaos as an essential part of life, which fosters resilience and adaptation.

Sacred conceptions of chaos transcend specific mythologies or traditions, impacting societal attitudes toward uncertainty and change. Societies that embrace chaos's creative potential regard disorder as an opportunity for renewal rather than a threat to stability. This viewpoint is especially important during times of social, environmental, or technological change, because managing chaos with creativity and openness may lead to transformational solutions. Drawing on mythical and spiritual themes, modern civilization may reinterpret chaos as a driver for growth.

The symbolic resonance of chaos and order continues to spark creative and intellectual inquiry. From abstract expressionist paintings to the mathematical beauty of fractals, artists and scientists use the tension between randomness and structure to produce works that reflect the universe's complexity. Similarly, philosophical explorations into chaos challenge established dichotomies, supporting holistic viewpoints that combine opposites. These creative and intellectual achievements demonstrate the timeless importance of religious conceptions of chaos in creating human knowledge.

Chaos myths and metaphors encourage us to reevaluate our connection with uncertainty and change. Rather than fearing chaos, we might learn to see it as a necessary part of life's creative processes. The holy narratives of chaos remind us that the unknown has the opportunity for transformation, creativity, and regeneration. By seeing chaos as a source of possibilities, we link ourselves with the dynamic rhythms of life, finding meaning and inspiration in the interplay of forces that make our environment.

Growth Through Uncertainty: Lessons from Apparently Disordered States

Uncertainty has long been viewed as a cause of anxiety and instability. Moments of uncertainty can feel chaotic in both personal and social contexts, threatening to destabilize the frameworks that offer meaning and order in life. However, when viewed through the lenses of human growth, spirituality, and even quantum physics, uncertainty is shown not as a completely destructive force, but as a rich ground for change. Individuals and cultures frequently experience the most profound development, innovation, and regeneration in these seemingly disorganized circumstances.

Uncertainty drives development and adaptability in nature. The chaotic interaction of environmental factors, genetic mutations, and random occurrences provides the circumstances for life to diversity and prosper. This seemingly random process follows patterns that lead to increasingly sophisticated and adaptable systems. For example, the creation of multicellular life from single-celled creatures demonstrates nature's ability to create order out of disorder. By accepting uncertainty as a natural process, we can understand how it may be a fuel for development and resilience.

Quantum physics provides a comprehensive framework for comprehending uncertainty's creative potential. According to Heisenberg's Uncertainty Principle, the location and momentum of particles at the subatomic level cannot be established exactly. This fundamental unpredictability calls into question traditional concepts of deterministic order, implying that uncertainty is embedded in the very fabric of reality. Furthermore, quantum superposition—the presence of several states until observation—showcases how potentiality exists inside uncertainty. Rather from being a constraint, this ambiguity serves as the foundation for a dynamic and linked reality.

These scientific ideas have philosophical and spiritual applications. Many wisdom traditions emphasize the transforming power of uncertainty, urging people to let go of their rigid ties to certainty and welcome the unknown. The notion of anicca (impermanence) in Buddhist teachings emphasizes the transience of all occurrences. Accepting this flux allows practitioners to build resilience and serenity, finding liberation in the very uncertainty that might bring misery. Similarly, the Taoist philosophy of wu wei—or effortless action—pushes for harmony with the Tao's unexpected flow, allowing transformation to occur organically.

Uncertainty is common in the human experience during periods of change and crises. These times break established patterns, whether they are caused by personal upheavals such as job loss or the end of a relationship, or communal problems such as economic downturns or pandemics. While the immediate reaction to such upheavals may be fear or resistance, they also provide chances for significant growth. Psychologists refer to this process as post-traumatic development, which occurs when people endure hardship and acquire more psychological resilience, deeper empathy, and a reinvigorated sense of purpose.

Uncertainty has taught us the need of adaptation. In a continually changing environment, inflexible structures and beliefs are more prone to collapse under strain. Systems and persons that maintain their flexibility, on the other hand, may adjust creatively to new difficulties. This notion is obvious in ecosystems, where diversification promotes resilience, as well as in human invention, where disturbance frequently leads to breakthrough ideas. The capacity to negotiate uncertainty necessitates not only adaptation but also an openness to potential, because new ideas and solutions arise from the unknown.

Uncertainty also has a significant impact on creativity. Many of history's greatest discoveries and creative triumphs have emerged from times of uncertainty and experimentation. When conventional paradigms fail to give solutions, the space left by ambiguity fosters experimentation and creativity. This dynamic may be seen in the scientific revolution, when the constraints of Aristotelian physics were replaced by the breakthrough theories of Copernicus, Newton, and Galileo. Similarly, in the arts, movements such as abstract expressionism arose in reaction to societal and aesthetic difficulties, challenging old forms and opening up new possibilities for expression.

Spiritual practices frequently give methods for handling uncertainty, converting it from a cause of fear to an opportunity for self-discovery. Meditation, for example, teaches the mind to view thoughts and emotions objectively, cultivating a feeling of inner stability in the face of outward volatility. Contemplative techniques enable people to appreciate the present moment, despite its uncertainty, fostering faith in the unfolding of life. This adjustment in viewpoint not only alleviates the anxiety of the unknown, but it also unveils the hidden promise of uncertainty.

Uncertainty, on the communal level, can act as a catalyst for societal reform. Periods of societal upheaval, however disruptive, sometimes precede great growth. Civil rights movements, environmental activism, and scientific and technological revolutions all developed from periods of chaos and uncertainty. These developments demonstrate how uncertainty, when combined with vision and cooperation, may lead to a reinvention of systems and ideals. Recognizing the creative potential of uncertainty allows civilizations to address issues with optimism rather than despair.

Resilience, a notion closely related to development through uncertainty, emphasizes the ability to flourish in the face of adversity. In psychology, resilience refers to not just the ability to recover from setbacks, but also the ability to integrate these experiences into a larger narrative of meaning and purpose. Similarly, spiritual traditions frequently view resilience as a type of surrender—not defeat, but acceptance of life's unpredictability. This acceptance enables people to transcend past fear and into a state of flow, where they are more equipped to deal with the difficulties of life.

Modern implementations of these ideas may be seen in fields such as leadership and innovation. Effective leaders understand that uncertainty is an intrinsic part of decision-making in a complicated and continuously changing environment. Instead of avoiding uncertainty, they learn to embrace it by cultivating a culture of inquiry, experimentation, and flexibility. Uncertainty typically encourages creativity in businesses because it forces teams to think creatively and cooperatively in order to handle growing difficulties. These examples show that uncertainty-driven growth goes beyond people to systems and institutions.

The lessons learned from uncertainty require us to reevaluate our relationship with control and predictability. While the need for stability is understandable, a dependence on certainty can lead to stagnation and reluctance to change. Accepting uncertainty as a natural aspect of life opens us up to the transforming potential it contains. In doing so, we connect with the universe's dynamic character, where development and change occur as a result of chaos rather than in spite of it. Uncertainty, viewed through this perspective, is no longer a threat to be handled, but rather a gift to be discovered, providing avenues to greater insight, creativity, and regeneration.

CHAPTER 16: SYNCHRONICITY AND QUANTUM CORRELATIONS

"Coincidence is God's way of remaining anonymous." –
Attributed to Albert Einstein

The notion of synchronicity, developed by Carl Gustav Jung, is one of the most interesting intersections of psychology, philosophy, and spirituality. Synchronicity, defined as meaningful coincidences that lack an apparent causal link, calls into question traditional ideas of reality and causality. Instead of being considered random occurrences, these events are viewed as profoundly meaningful, frequently implying relationships that go beyond conventional cause-and-effect models. Synchronicity provides insight into how subjective experience interacts with the external environment in ways that challenge rational explanation.

Jung invented the concept of synchronicity while investigating the relationship between psychological states and external occurrences. He noticed that patients frequently claimed strange coincidences about their inner experiences. During one memorable session, a woman related a dream involving a scarab beetle. A beetle-like bug tapped against the window at that time, connecting her mental imagery to an exterior occurrence. Such events were seen by Jung as more than chance. He proposed that synchronicity represented an acausal linking mechanism, with occurrences linked not by physical causality but by common meaning.

This view is consistent with archetypal psychology and Jung's larger concepts about the collective unconscious. Archetypes, as universal symbols and patterns of human experience, act as conduits between personal and collective meaning. Synchronicities frequently include archetypal imagery, such as dreams, symbols, or happenings that appear to be significant. These moments, according to Jung, showed the psyche's connectivity with the outside world, implying that the barriers between mind and matter are more porous than previously thought.

Synchronicity has philosophical consequences that go beyond psychology. It calls into question the Western worldview's classical, mechanical basis. Events in a deterministic cosmos with linear causality are known to have particular, observable causes. Synchronicity, on the other hand, presents a new paradigm in which meaning comes before cause. This viewpoint is consistent with non-Western ideologies such as Taoism and Buddhism, which emphasise the interrelated and interdependent aspect of reality. The Taoist idea of wu wei (effortless activity), as well as Buddhist teachings on interbeing, reflect the relational dynamics suggested by synchronicity.

The idea of synchronicity has also found resonance in recent debates of quantum physics, where traditional notions of causality are challenged. Quantum entanglement, for example, defines the phenomena in which particles separated by great distances display instantaneous interactions. While these connections are defined by exact mathematical rules, their mechanism defies conventional explanation, calling into question the entire foundation of localized causality. Although quantum entanglement differs from synchronicity, both occurrences call into question how connections in the cosmos may function on levels other than linear cause-and-effect.

Synchronicity emphasizes the importance of subjective experience in generating meaning. Humans are meaning-making animals, and synchronicities frequently occur when emotions or psychological states are at their peak. They can be guiding beacons during times of uncertainty, change, or personal catastrophe. When standard narratives fail to provide clarity, synchronicities provide another method to interpret experience. This can have substantial therapeutic consequences by instilling a feeling of clarity and purpose in the midst of turmoil.

Synchronicity critics believe that it is a result of cognitive biases including pattern recognition and confirmation bias. The human brain is designed to discover patterns, even in seemingly unconnected situations. This inclination can lead to people seeing connections when none exist. Furthermore, the emotional impact of synchronicities may be exaggerated, making them look more important than they are objectively. However, these criticisms do not undermine synchronicity's subjective value. Even if such occurrences are the result of psychological inclinations, their influence on the individual's sense of purpose and connection is still relevant.

Synchronicity frequently presents itself in myths, rituals, and spiritual activities within cultural contexts. Many indigenous cultures believe that the natural world is alive with signs and omens, reflecting a worldview in which significance is inherent in all aspects of existence. For example, Native American cultures place a premium on animal encounters, understanding them as messengers from the spirit realm. Similarly, in ancient Greece, oracles and divination techniques were based on the concept that the divine communicated via symbolic coincidences. These behaviors demonstrate a long-standing human tendency to view synchronicities as signs of a larger, linked world.

The advancement of digital technology has provided new avenues for synchronicity to manifest itself. The algorithms that regulate social media, search engines, and online advertising can provide seemingly synchronized encounters. For example, seeing an advertising for a product just after thinking about it might feel strange, even though such occurrences are usually the result of data collecting and predictive analytics. While these electronically induced coincidences are distinct from Jungian synchronicity, they demonstrate how the sense of meaningful connections evolves in a digitally networked society.

Synchronicity is important in current scientific and philosophical studies of consciousness. According to theories emphasizing the nonlocality of consciousness, awareness is not limited to the brain but rather functions as part of a wider, linked field. This viewpoint is consistent with the implications of synchronicity, arguing that thought and matter are not distinct entities but rather components of a united reality. Scholars studying panpsychism, quantum consciousness, and integrated information theory share insights on the linked nature of reality.

Synchronicity connects with artistic and creative pursuits. Artists, authors, and musicians frequently characterize periods of inspiration as synchronistic experiences in which ideas, symbols, or themes come from seemingly unconnected sources. These experiences imply that creativity flourishes in environments where borders are blurred, allowing connections to arise across disciplines, cultures, and mediums. In this way, synchronicity serves as a stimulant for invention and expression, breaking free from traditional constraints.

Synchrony is frequently used in interpersonal relationships to help people build meaningful connections. People commonly report meeting significant others, mentors, or friends in unexpected ways. These meetings can instill a sense of destiny, as if invisible powers are directing people's journeys toward each other. While such encounters may be explained by probability or chance, their subjective importance cannot be emphasized. They influence how people create narratives about their life, cultivating a sense of belonging and purpose.

The ability of synchronicity to span subjective and objective worlds is what has kept it popular. It offers a framework for combining personal meaning with global patterns, resulting in a holistic picture of reality that transcends duality. By stressing connection over cause, synchronicity encourages people to see their lives as part of a wider, linked whole. This transformation has far-reaching consequences for how humans interact to themselves, one another, and the cosmos.

While discussions concerning synchronicity's existence and authenticity continue, its influence on human mind and experience is obvious. It calls into question reductionist ways to interpreting reality, encouraging investigation into the mysteries that exist beyond the quantifiable and predictable. Whether seen as a psychological occurrence, a spiritual principle, or a look into the universe's secret dynamics, synchronicity continues to arouse amazement and intrigue, reinforcing all things' fundamental connectivity.

Entanglement Overlaps: Instant Correlations That Appears "Spooky"

Entanglement, a phenomena Albert Einstein memorably labeled "spooky action at a distance," is central to quantum physics and one of its most perplexing and interesting aspects. At its most basic, quantum entanglement defines a scenario in which two or more particles become entangled in such a manner that the state of one instantly changes the state of the other, regardless of the distance between them. This calls into question traditional ideas of location and causation, raising deep concerns about the nature of reality and its potential for overlap with spiritual and philosophical frameworks.

Einstein, together with Boris Podolsky and Nathan Rosen, originally emphasized the strangeness of entanglement in their 1935 work, which aimed to establish the incompleteness of quantum theory. Their argument, known as the EPR paradox, focused on the seeming violation of locality, a classical physics concept that states that things are only directly impacted by their immediate surroundings. If entanglement existed, it would indicate that particles could interact instantly, faster than the speed of light, violating the restrictions of relativity. Nonetheless, decades of experimental confirmation, notably the pioneering work of physicists such as John Bell and Alain Aspect, have proved that entanglement is not only real but also widespread in the quantum domain.

Entanglement isn't only a physics lab phenomenon. Its ramifications reverberate throughout, providing fertile ground for metaphysical interpretations. Entanglement is consistent with long-held conceptions of universal connection in spiritual and intellectual debate. For example, Hinduism's concept of Indra's Net envisions a cosmic web in which every node mirrors every other, representing existence's holistic and interrelated character. Similarly, Buddhist teachings on interdependence highlight that no phenomena occurs in isolation; all are interconnected in a vast, dynamic network. Entanglement gives a scientific complement to these spiritual discoveries by basing abstract concepts of oneness in practical occurrences.

Entanglement is not only a theoretical concept; it has practical implications in upcoming technologies such as quantum computing and quantum communication. Quantum computers use entangled states to do computations considerably beyond the capability of conventional processors. Similarly, quantum communication systems use entanglement to provide safe information flow since any effort to intercept the entangled state quickly destroys the system, signifying a breach. These developments highlight the concrete consequences of entanglement while also raising deeper philosophical problems about the nature of information, cognition, and connection.

The link between entanglement and human awareness has also prompted heated controversy, both within and outside of scientific circles. Some theorists believe that consciousness may work via a type of quantum entanglement, allowing seemingly instantaneous interactions between different brain or cognitive processes. While such assertions are hypothetical, they are consistent with growing studies in quantum biology, which implies that entanglement may play a role in processes including as photosynthesis, enzyme reactions, and even aviary navigation. These discoveries call into question the concept that entanglement is limited to subatomic scales, implying that its effect may extend to the macroscopic and even the biological.

Entanglement is frequently used symbolically in spiritual contexts to demonstrate the interconnection of all beings. This view is especially important in traditions that emphasize oneness, such as Advaita Vedanta or some schools of mysticism. The concept that acts or ideas might travel beyond space and time, impacting others in unknown ways, is similar to the relational dynamics observed in entanglement. While scientific entanglement does not directly support theories like telepathy or energetic healing, its conceptual resonance with these ideas encourages more investigation into their validity and relevance.

Critics warn against overextending the metaphorical usage of entanglement, citing the dangers of "quantum mysticism." Misinterpretations can erode quantum mechanics' scientific rigor, converting it to a hazy or pseudoscientific framework. For example, equating entanglement with universal love or awareness runs the danger of confusing scientific events with subjective feelings. However, when treated with caution, these metaphorical linkages may deepen conversations about the nature of reality by bridging the gap between scientific understanding and human experience.

Entanglement has philosophical ramifications that challenge typical dualistic thinking. Objects in conventional physics are separate entities with well-defined borders, while quantum entanglement exposes a universe in which separations blur. This non-duality is consistent with spiritual teachings that reject binary divisions between oneself and others, subject and object. Entanglement urges a reevaluation of individuality by revealing that particles may live in relational states, implying that identity is intrinsically relational rather than separate.

Entanglement experiments continue to push the frontiers of scientific knowledge. Recent research has investigated phenomena such as "quantum steering," in which one particle's state appears to impact the measurement results of another in a directionally dependent manner. These advances increase our grasp of the quantum universe while also posing new issues about causality, time, and the nature of reality itself. For example, certain interpretations of quantum physics propose that entanglement might entail retrocausality, in which future occurrences impact the past—a concept that calls into question linear ideas of time.

Entanglement's consequences extend to ethics and human behavior. Entanglement argues that the cosmos is essentially interrelated, therefore activities cannot be regarded in isolation. This viewpoint is consistent with environmental and social justice movements, which highlight the interconnection of all living forms and the far-reaching implications of individual and communal actions. Seeing entanglement as a metaphor for interconnectedness can inspire more empathy, collaboration, and accountability in tackling global concerns.

Emerging interdisciplinary study looks into the possible connections of entanglement with other domains including neurology, psychology, and the arts. In neuroscience, researchers are looking at whether entanglement may help us comprehend complex brain processes or the origin of consciousness. The idea of relational states in psychology corresponds to therapeutic approaches that highlight the connectivity of people within systems, such as family or community dynamics. Entanglement inspires artistic expressions that strive to portray the beauty and mystery of interconnection, ranging from abstract paintings to experimental music.

The importance of entanglement in quantum foundations poses serious challenges about the bounds of knowing. While the phenomena has been extensively reported, the underlying processes remain unknown. Competing interpretations of quantum physics, such as the Copenhagen interpretation, Bohmian mechanics, and many-worlds theory, provide several explanations for entanglement, reflecting larger philosophical disagreements about the nature of reality. These disputes illustrate the quantum world's intrinsic ambiguity and mystery, calling for humility in the face of the unknown.

In conclusion, entanglement acts as a link between scientific investigation and existential inquiry. Its implications call into question long-held beliefs about separateness, causation, and individuality, presenting fresh perspectives on connection and relationships. Whether considered as a physical fact, a metaphor for oneness, or a spur for technological progress, entanglement continues to captivate and inspire, showing the universe's vast web of interconnections. By delving into its riddles, mankind might get a better understanding of the fundamental interconnectivity of all things, cultivating a feeling of wonder, curiosity, and common purpose.

Interpretation: Using Discernment to Connect Personal Events to Quantum Effects

Carl Jung popularized the concept of synchronicity, which claims that seemingly unconnected occurrences can coincide meaningfully despite the lack of an obvious causal relationship. When compared to the idea of quantum entanglement, which contradicts conventional expectations of locality and causality, it is tempting to make links between the two events. However, understanding such parallels takes careful consideration to avoid mixing metaphysical speculation with real research. The task is to investigate the resonances between quantum correlations and human experiences without simplifying or distorting either area.

According to Jung, synchronicity is primarily psychological and symbolic. It frequently appears during times of personal importance, when events in the outside world reflect an inward condition or goal. For example, recalling a long-lost friend minutes before getting their message may be interpreted as synchronous, resulting in a sense of connectivity that goes beyond standard cause-and-effect explanations. Such encounters may be deeply significant, providing insights into life's riddles and confirming an intuitive sense of global connectivity.

Quantum entanglement, on the other hand, occurs inside the world of physics, in which particles become connected to the point that their states are interdependent regardless of spatial separation. Entanglement, as opposed to synchronicity, is an observable phenomena that has been rigorously tested. It reveals that the cosmos operates in ways that contradict traditional intuitions, notably the notion of locality, which holds that things may only influence one another through direct interaction or in a shared context.

Drawing connections between synchronicity and quantum entanglement might be theoretically appealing since both challenge linear and deterministic worldviews. Synchronicity's apparent absence of causation raises doubts about the interconnectivity of inner and outer realities, whereas entanglement calls into question standard notions about physical system separability. These analogies, however, must be carefully crafted. Entanglement is a precise and quantitative connection that follows mathematical rules, whereas synchronicity is an interpretative and frequently anecdotal experience.

One reason for the attractiveness of connecting these ideas is their mutual ability to create astonishment and a sense of oneness. Both encourage a reassessment of reality's interconnectedness, which is consistent with spiritual beliefs emphasizing oneness. According to ancient traditions such as Taoism and the Upanishads, the barriers humans perceive between themselves and the outside world are deceptive and conceal a deeper connection. The scientific validation of entanglement adds credence to the concept that connection may be a basic aspect of the cosmos, even if it acts on other scales or via different processes than spiritual interpretations predict.

Despite their differences, synchronicity and entanglement are similar in that they raise philosophical problems about causation and meaning. Synchronicity calls into question the idea that all occurrences must have a clear causal explanation, arguing that importance might emerge from patterns or correlations that defy traditional reasoning. Entanglement also violates traditional causality, as the state of one particle seems to impact another immediately, even when separated by great distances. This defiance of locality and causality broadens the scope of what science can measure and predict, allowing for deeper observations on the fabric of reality.

Maintaining discernment when evaluating these overlaps necessitates realizing the boundaries of what science and spirituality can address. While quantum physics can describe and predict entangled particle behavior, it cannot explain psychological or symbolic phenomena such as synchronicity. Similarly, synchronicity, being a subjective and experienced idea, cannot be evaluated or measured in terms of quantum physics. Conflating the two risks decreasing their richness, turning deep scientific findings to metaphors and complex psychological experiences to pseudoscience.

Recognizing the cognitive and cultural tendencies that generate such associations is also an important aspect of careful interpretation. Humans are pattern-seeking animals that look for meaning and consistency in seemingly random events. This proclivity, along with the attractiveness of quantum mechanics as a mysterious and cutting-edge discipline, provides ideal ground for speculative narratives that merge scientific and spiritual themes. While such stories can be motivating and inventive, they must be addressed with caution to avoid spreading myths or undermining the rigor of either profession.

However, using entanglement as a metaphor for synchronicity might act as a bridge for investigating multidisciplinary issues. For example, both conceptions might encourage further investigation into the nature of time and the boundaries between self and other. Synchronicity implies that events can be related in ways that transcend linear time, whereas entanglement shows that geographic isolation does not prohibit instantaneous connection. These observations prompt philosophical debate on the limitations of human vision and how reality may work beyond what is immediately visible or quantifiable.

In practical terms, studying the resonances between synchronicity and entanglement can benefit subjects such as psychology, philosophy, and the arts. Synchronicity is a psychological phenomena that enhances an individual's feeling of significance and connection, particularly during transforming life situations. Entanglement, from a philosophical standpoint, contradicts reductionist conceptions of reality, instead promoting holistic approaches that emphasize relationality. Both principles generate creative manifestations in the arts that attempt to depict the interaction of the seen and unseen, the quantifiable and the intangible.

To traverse the complexities of these linkages properly, it's vital to distinguish between metaphorical and literal readings. Using entanglement as a metaphor for synchronicity can provide helpful insights into the interconnection of experiences, but it is important to note that this is an analogy rather than a scientific claim. Similarly, while synchronicity might encourage contemplation of life's mysteries, it should not be interpreted as evidence for quantum physics' workings.

Emerging research on the function of quantum events in biological systems adds an interesting dimension to this debate. According to quantum biology research, activities such as photosynthesis and enzyme reactions may use quantum effects to blur the boundaries between the macroscopic and microscopic worlds. While these discoveries do not directly relate quantum physics to psychological or spiritual experiences, they do question beliefs about the scale at which quantum events may impact complex systems, providing fertile ground for additional investigation.

The ethical aspects of understanding synchronicity and entanglement should also be considered. Misrepresenting quantum physics to justify unverified assertions jeopardizes public faith in science and perpetuates disinformation. Dismissing the symbolic and sensory importance of synchronicity, on the other hand, risks alienating individuals who treasure such events deeply. Striking a balance necessitates humility, openness, and a willingness to engage with complexity rather than seeking simple answers.

It is feasible to respect the integrity of both scientific inquiry and human experience by using caution when relating personal occurrences to quantum phenomena. Quantum entanglement, as a physical phenomena, offers a glimpse into the universe's secrets, showing links that transcend traditional bounds. Synchronicity, as a psychological and symbolic experience, leads people to consider the connections between their inner and outer worlds. Together, these ideas broaden our understanding of connection and meaning, pushing us to look beyond established frameworks while remaining anchored in critical inquiry. Through this balance, the discovery of synchronicity and entanglement becomes not just a quest for knowledge, but also a celebration of life's complicated and amazing essence.

CHAPTER 17: THE ANTHROPIC PRINCIPLE AND PURPOSE

"Man is the measure of all things." – Protagoras

The notion of a fine-tuned cosmos holds that the basic constants and parameters regulating physical laws appear to be finely set to allow life to develop. This idea has piqued the interest of scientists, philosophers, and theologians alike, since it argues that even tiny departures from these constants may make the cosmos unfriendly. For example, in order for stars, planets, and, eventually, life to emerge, the intensity of the gravitational constant, the ratio of the electromagnetic force to the gravitational force, and the cosmological constant must all fall within extremely limited limits. The accuracy necessary for such settings begs significant concerns about the nature of existence and the mechanisms that created such equilibrium.

The fine-tuning thesis is based on scientific facts concerning the complex interaction of forces that regulate the cosmos. For example, if the gravitational constant was slightly weaker, matter would fail to form into stars and galaxies, but a little stronger force may cause the universe to collapse on itself. Similarly, the cosmological constant, which determines the universe's expansion rate, is so delicately regulated that even a minor adjustment would result in either fast cosmic inflation or stagnation, both of which would limit the creation of complex structures. Such discoveries are frequently portrayed as improbabilities amid a huge landscape of conceivable physical configurations, stressing the unusual circumstances that allow life to exist.

The multiverse theory, which holds that our universe is simply one of countless others within a large multiverse, each with its own distinct physical constants, is one attempt to understanding fine-tuning. In this theory, the seeming accuracy of our universe's constants is the outcome of anthropic selection, not purposeful calibration. Only worlds having the necessary conditions for observers, such as humans, would naturally be recognized and examined. This view moves the emphasis from purposeful design to statistical inevitability among a limitless number of options.

Critics claim that the multiverse theory is theoretical rather than scientific due to its lack of empirical testability. They argue that without clear proof of other worlds, the multiverse is only a theoretical construct rather than a practical explanation. Furthermore, some philosophers dispute whether introducing a multiverse genuinely answers the fine-tuning problem or rather elevates it to a higher level, necessitating an explanation for the mechanism that creates such a diverse array of worlds.

Another interpretation of fine-tuning comes from the concept of cosmic design, which has its roots in religious and philosophical traditions. Proponents of this viewpoint believe that the perfect calibration of the universe's constants reveals the intentionality of a designer or a higher intelligence. This viewpoint frequently correlates with arguments for God's existence, citing the apparent order and harmony of the universe as proof of deliberate creation. Fine-tuning, according to this theory, is a reflection of underlying intent rather than the result of chance.

However, the cosmic design interpretation attracts criticism, notably from naturalists who emphasise the explanatory power of physical laws and chance. They contend that assigning fine-tuning to a creator involves untestable metaphysical assumptions and risks confusing gaps in scientific understanding with evidence for supernatural intervention. Furthermore, the issue of who or what designed the designer is frequently raised, confounding the argument by adding an endless regress of causality.

Fine-tuning has philosophical consequences beyond disputes about the multiverse and cosmic design. They encourage people to think about the nature of existence and the role of humans in the cosmos. Fine-tuning, according to some theorists, is proof of an innate connectivity throughout the universe, in which life and awareness are fundamental components of reality rather than accidents. This viewpoint is consistent with certain spiritual traditions, which see the cosmos as a single entity endowed with purpose and significance.

Fine-tuning, on the other hand, might instill a feeling of humility by emphasising the fragility and scarcity of life in a vast and impersonal universe. The understanding that life is dependent on such exact conditions emphasizes the fragility of life and the need of appreciating and preserving the delicate balances that keep it going. This viewpoint has ethical consequences, instilling a sense of guardianship and responsibility for the Earth and its ecosystems, which constitute a unique oasis of life in an otherwise unfriendly cosmos.

Cosmology and particle physics advances are constantly improving our understanding of fine-tuning. For example, continuing research into the Higgs boson and the existence of dark energy aims to illuminate the mechanics that underpin the universe's basic constants. Such investigations seek to ascertain whether these constants are set by necessity or are dependent on deeper principles yet to be found. While definite solutions remain difficult, these efforts highlight the dynamic interplay between theoretical inquiry and practical observation in solving life's mysteries.

Fine-tuning is also linked to larger problems regarding the nature of scientific explanation. Some physicists advocate for the concept of adequate reason, which states that every element of the cosmos must be explained in terms of natural laws or fundamental principles. Others accept the idea that many aspects of the universe, including its fine-tuning, will eventually reject explanation, reflecting the intrinsic limitations of human understanding. This contrast between comprehensibility and mystery emphasizes fine-tuning's philosophical depth as a research issue.

The fine-tuning argument has affected cultural and intellectual debate, influencing art, literature, and philosophy. Its themes of precision and balance are similar to artistic expressions that investigate the relationship between order and chaos, stability and change. Fine-tuning is frequently used as a metaphor in literature to represent the deep complexity of human experience, where seemingly trivial nuances can have tremendous repercussions. It inspires works of art that attempt to represent the cosmos' beauty and fragility, eliciting awe and amazement.

Recognizing fine-tuning raises ethical concerns, particularly in terms of humanity's influence on the environment. If life is a rare and valuable phenomena, then protecting its conditions becomes a moral duty. This viewpoint is consistent with demands for sustainable development and ecological protection, emphasizing the interdependence of human actions and the greater biosphere. It also emphasizes the ethical elements of scientific and technological advancement, emphasizing care and foresight in molding the future.

The fine-tuned cosmos remains a rich source of multidisciplinary research, bridging the gaps between physics, philosophy, and spirituality. Its consequences compel us to consider the nature of reality, the beginnings of life, and the meaning of existence. Fine-tuning, whether interpreted as proof of purpose, a result of chance, or a reflection of fundamental principles, compels us to engage with the universe's great riddles. It evokes awe and interest, reminding us of the rich beauty and complexity of the cosmos we live in.

Spiritual Teleology: Identifying Divine or Cosmic Intent in Existence

Spiritual teleology investigates the hypothesis that the cosmos has an intrinsic purpose or design, which is led by divine or cosmic will. This viewpoint has ancient roots and may be found in various civilizations' mythology, philosophies, and religious beliefs. Teleology is used as a lens to understand the apparent order and complexity of reality as purposeful and intentional rather than random or mechanical, from the holy writings of Eastern religions to the metaphysical musings of Western philosophy.

Modern studies of spiritual teleology sometimes begin by investigating the universe's seeming fine-tuning. Fundamental constants and parameters, such as the speed of light, gravitational force, and the cosmological constant, align within extremely tight ranges, allowing stars, planets, and, eventually, life to develop. Advocates of spiritual teleology say that this accuracy is the result of a deliberate calibration by an intelligent source, which is frequently described as God, a universal consciousness, or an overarching cosmic principle. This argument lays a solid foundation for teleological thought, connecting physical reality to spiritual purpose.

Philosophically, spiritual teleology interacts with discussions regarding the essence of existence and causality. Aristotle, one of the earliest proponents of teleology, believed that all things had an underlying "final cause" or purpose that shapes their growth and function. Teleology is closely related to the belief in divine providence in Christian theology, which sees God as the builder of a meaningful universe. Similarly, Hindu and Buddhist teachings frequently depict existence as a cycle of interrelated goals, with karma acting as a teleological process that connects human acts to cosmic events.

While traditional teleology concentrated on tangible, visible goals, spiritual teleology broadens its scope to include metaphysical and existential elements. It implies that human life, creativity, and consciousness are not by chance, but are essential to the development of a larger cosmic tale. Proponents claim that the evolution of self-awareness and moral reasoning in humans is consistent with a higher purpose, implying that people are part of a larger, divinely inspired plan. This viewpoint promotes seeing human challenges and successes as important contributions to the growth of the cosmos.

Spiritual teleology critics question its assumptions, notably the idea that intent and purpose are required to explain natural occurrences. Naturalistic frameworks, such as Darwinian evolution and the multiverse theory, stress random mutation, natural selection, and statistical chance to account for complexity without relying on purpose. According to this viewpoint, assigning purpose to the universe reflects a human proclivity to put meaning into random patterns, which is motivated by cognitive biases and existential fears.

Advocates of spiritual teleology, on the other hand, believe that while naturalistic explanations are effective, they do not invalidate a more deliberate framework. They emphasise the limitations of strictly materialist explanations, notably their failure to answer concerns about why the rules of physics exist in their current form or why anything exists at all. The existence of such problems, according to teleological philosophers, indicates the need for a higher purpose or intentionality that transcends scientific observation, thereby bridging the gap between science and spirituality.

The notion of cosmic purpose is very prevalent in modern physics and cosmology. The Anthropic Principle, for example, states that the cosmos must have the features required to tolerate conscious observers such as humans. While some understand this concept solely scientifically, others see it as proof of a teleological framework in which life and awareness are not accidents, but rather key objectives of the universe. Similarly, quantum entanglement and non-locality theories propose an underlying oneness and interconnection that is consistent with spiritual concepts of a purposeful, holistic cosmos.

Spiritual teleology has important implications for ethics and morals because it provides a framework for understanding human responsibility in the larger context of cosmic purpose. If existence is endowed with intent, moral acts might be interpreted as supporting or opposing this intent, impacting not just individual lives but also humanity's collective destiny. This viewpoint is seen in religious teachings that interpret moral action as satisfying divine will or contributing to cosmic peace. Even secular interpretations of teleology sometimes highlight the interdependence of activities and their outcomes, instilling a feeling of stewardship and obligation.

Teleology provides a source of meaning and hope in personal spirituality, especially when confronted with existential issues like as pain, loss, and mortality. Teleological ideas provide comfort and resilience by interpreting individual events in terms of a greater purpose. For example, believing that personal challenges contribute to spiritual development or cosmic progress can turn misfortune into a chance for introspection and transformation. This sense of involvement in a larger scheme promotes a stronger connection to both the cosmos and oneself.

Critics of spiritual teleology warn of possible hazards, such as deterministic interpretations that deny human agency or explain suffering as divinely commanded. They suggest that too rigorous teleological frameworks can lead to fatalism, in which people abdicate responsibility for their actions by attributing events to a predetermined purpose. Furthermore, because teleology is based on metaphysical assumptions, it is susceptible to misapplication, such as putting certain religious or ideological interpretations of purpose on varied groups or experiences.

Despite these obstacles, spiritual teleology continues to be a thriving area of research and contemplation, integrating scientific, philosophical, and religious viewpoints. Its principles of purpose, aim, and connection ring true across disciplines, encouraging both rigorous discussion and profound meditation. Teleology, whether viewed through the perspective of religious faith, philosophical inquiry, or scientific amazement, challenges people to consider the most basic concerns of existence: why are we here? How do we fit into the universe? How do our acts help to the realization of a larger goal?

As humankind continues to investigate these concerns, spiritual teleology provides a framework for combining disparate discoveries into a coherent view of reality. It promotes wonder, curiosity, and responsibility by highlighting the interconnection of all things and the possibility of purpose within the cosmos. As a result, it gives a strong lens through which to interpret life's mysteries, moving people and society to greater knowledge and meaningful action.

Debate and Responsibility: Does Life's "Specialness" Imply Moral or Environmental Duty?

The apparent fine-tuning of the cosmos, along with humanity's potential for self-awareness, frequently leads to debates over whether life's uniqueness entails inherent obligations. While the cosmos appears vast and indifferent, the rare conditions that allow life to exist spark debate about whether humanity has a moral or ecological obligation to preserve and respect this "specialness." This discussion spans disciplines, drawing on cosmology, philosophy, theology, and environmental ethics to examine how humanity fits into the larger story of existence.

According to the fine-tuning thesis, certain physical constants and circumstances in the cosmos must coincide with amazing precision for life to develop. For example, the gravitational force, electromagnetic force, and matter-to-antimatter ratio are calibrated within small limits, resulting in a cosmic Goldilocks zone. Some consider this alignment to be fortuitous, while others believe it demonstrates purposeful design or an inherent purpose. In any instance, the scarcity of life-sustaining circumstances emphasizes its vulnerability, raising the question of whether people have a responsibility to preserve and nurture it.

Religious and spiritual traditions frequently place life's uniqueness within the context of divine purpose or cosmic interconnectivity. Humanity is viewed as a steward of creation in many Abrahamic religious interpretations, with the sacred obligation of caring for the Earth. Similarly, Hinduism and Buddhism stress all beings' interconnectivity, implying that destroying the environment or other forms of life breaks cosmic equilibrium. These ideas indicate that acknowledging the uniqueness of life entails ethical obligations, such as fostering balance with nature and respect for all living things.

Evolutionary biology, from a secular standpoint, offers an alternative lens for interpreting the uniqueness of life. While evolution stresses adaptability and survival, it also underlines the impossibility of sophisticated life developing from random processes spanning billions of years. This statistical rarity drives arguments for ecological responsibility, since humanity's ability for reason and foresight sets it apart from other animals. If humans are the only ones with the ability to notice the influence of their actions on future generations and ecosystems, this awareness implies a need to act responsibly.

Critics of such moral imperatives frequently invoke the anthropic principle, which implies that life's seeming uniqueness is a biased viewpoint. According to this idea, people witness a life-sustaining world merely because they exist inside it. The anthropic principle contradicts teleological explanations, suggesting that life is an unintended consequence of natural processes. Critics say that if life's genesis is entirely fortuitous, it does not necessarily imply moral or ecological responsibility beyond immediate survival.

Ecological ethicists, on the other hand, argue that even if life lacks an intrinsic purpose, its fragility justifies conservation. They see similarities with cultural relics or works of art—unique and irreplaceable creations that mankind appreciates despite their lack of inherent function. According to this argument, the biosphere, with its intricate ecosystems and biodiversity, is a unique marvel that must be protected. This viewpoint is consistent with deep ecology, which argues for acknowledging all living species' intrinsic value, regardless of their benefit to people.

The issue over moral responsibility is also linked to concerns about climate change and environmental devastation. Humanity's extraordinary potential to influence planetary systems raises serious concerns about stewardship and accountability. Environmentalists contend that increasing technical capabilities heighten moral responsibilities. The Anthropocene, which is defined by humanity's overwhelming effect on Earth's geology and ecosystems, is both a testimony to human ingenuity and a warning tale about the repercussions. Advocates argue that acknowledging the rarity of life should spur worldwide efforts to reduce damage and promote sustainability.

Existentialist arguments are frequently used to argue for ecological responsibility. Thinkers such as Jean-Paul Sartre and Simone de Beauvoir underlined the significance of finding meaning in an apparently uninteresting world. Humanity may give existence meaning by accepting responsibility for conserving life and promoting natural equilibrium. This existential perspective reframes ecological obligation as a chance for individuals and society to engage with life's larger story, moving beyond personal concerns to embrace community well-being.

Ecological responsibility's opponents frequently use economic pragmatism and survivalist ethics as their justifications. Critics contend that emphasizing environmental preservation may collide with urgent human needs, particularly in resource-constrained developing countries. This viewpoint prioritizes short-term survival above long-term sustainability, treating ecological stewardship as a luxury rather than a need. Environmental ethics proponents, on the other hand, argue that this dichotomy is untrue, citing examples where conservation efforts match with economic and societal advantages, such as sustainable agriculture and renewable energy.

Another point of contention in the argument is humanity's place in the universe. The quest for alien life has far-reaching ramifications for how people see their place in the cosmos. If life is discovered elsewhere, it may call into question the idea of Earth's exclusivity, possibly lowering the apparent burden of duty. If life is not discovered despite significant investigation, it confirms Earth's uniqueness, increasing the moral importance of protecting its ecosystem.

Cultural and generational differences influence attitudes toward environmental stewardship. Indigenous knowledge systems, for example, frequently reflect a deep sense of connectivity and reciprocity with nature. These traditions stress living in tune with the earth and protecting its resources for future generations. Incorporating such ideas into global environmental ethics debate yields useful insights, enabling a more inclusive approach to tackling ecological concerns.

New technological and scientific advances complicate the argument over humanity's responsibility. Geoengineering, synthetic biology, and space exploration are examples of innovations that provide unparalleled tools for influencing the future of life. However, they create ethical concerns concerning unexpected effects and human intervention's limits. Proponents of ecological obligation say that these technologies should be used with prudence and with a commitment to preserve life's purity and balance.

At its foundation, the dispute over life's uniqueness and its consequences for moral or ecological obligation mirrors larger debates about humanity's identity and purpose. The understanding of life's fragility and interconnection, whether viewed through the lens of science, philosophy, or spirituality, prompts contemplation on the values that characterize human existence. It asks people and society to evaluate how their decisions affect the maintenance or demise of the fragile balance that supports life.

As mankind navigates the challenges of the twenty-first century, the appeal for environmental stewardship becomes increasingly pressing. Climate change, biodiversity loss, and resource depletion highlight the importance of collaborative action in ensuring the future of life. The realization of life's uniqueness, whether driven by religious beliefs, philosophical ideas, or scientific understanding, serves as a rallying point for cultivating compassion, stewardship, and resilience. By accepting this duty, mankind can honor its position in the universe and ensure that the heritage of life lives on among the great expanse of the cosmos.

CHAPTER 18: NON-LOCALITY AND AKASHIC RECORDS

"When we try to pick out anything by itself, we find it hitched to everything else in the universe." – John Muir

One of the most astonishing occurrences in modern physics is quantum entanglement, which defies traditional conceptions of location and distance. It specifies a link between particles such that the condition of one immediately impacts the state of another, regardless of their geographical separation. This "spooky action at a distance," as Albert Einstein memorably characterized it, calls into question our understanding of space, time, and reality's fundamental essence. Entanglement, however, is more than just a theoretical curiosity; it has far-reaching consequences for both scientific and philosophical investigation, notably in terms of interconnection and the fabric of the universe.

Quantum physics concepts, notably state superposition, give rise to entanglement. When two or more particles interact in a given way, their characteristics become connected to the point that their quantum states cannot be represented independently of each other. For example, measuring one particle's spin in an entangled pair quickly knows the other's spin, even if they are light-years distant. Numerous investigations have empirically corroborated this non-local behavior, including the landmark Bell tests, which demonstrated that no hidden variable explanation based on classical physics could explain the observed correlations.

Entanglement has far-reaching and puzzling consequences. The occurrence appears to contravene the relativistic concept that no information or effect can travel faster than light. However, entanglement does not entail traditional information transfer. Instead, it reveals a fundamental interconnectedness among particles that occurs regardless of spacetime limitations. This calls into question the conventional framework of separability, which holds that things are distinct entities with independent qualities, and provides a perspective of reality that is essentially related.

Entanglement has evolved from a theoretical concept to a fundamental component of quantum technologies in scientific practice. Quantum computing, for example, takes advantage of entanglement to do computations that conventional machines cannot. Entangled qubits, using quantum superposition and parallelism, may represent and analyze increasingly bigger datasets. Similarly, quantum communication makes use of entangled particles to allow for theoretically secure data transmission. Quantum key distribution (QKD) procedures, such as those employed in satellite-based studies, take advantage of entanglement to ensure that any attempt at interception permanently alters the system, disclosing the intrusion.

Beyond its technological implications, entanglement encourages study on the philosophical elements of connection. Many people have made connections between quantum entanglement and spiritual or mystical traditions that emphasize unity and oneness. For example, Indra's Net, a Buddhist idea, depicts the cosmos as a network of interwoven gems, each mirroring the other. Similarly, the Hindu concept of Brahman—the ultimate, undivided reality—is consistent with the idea of a cosmos in which distinctions are only perceptional illusions. While these parallels are metaphorical rather than scientific, they emphasize humanity's continuous obsession with the interconnectedness of existence.

Entanglement's philosophical consequences include issues of causation and determinism. In classical physics, causality functions in a linear framework: cause precedes effect, with temporal constraints. Entanglement, on the other hand, indicates that correlations can arise in the absence of a typical causal process. Some scholars have investigated alternate theories of reality, such as retrocausality, in which consequences affect causes, and relational interpretations, in which objects and events are redefined as interconnected processes rather than independent entities.

Critics warn against extrapolating the consequences of entanglement beyond actual science. The term "quantum" has been employed in a variety of pseudoscientific claims, including alternative medicine and philosophical views. Entanglement exhibits non-local correlations, but it does not indicate mystical connections or back up unsubstantiated assertions about awareness or energy fields. Maintaining discipline in understanding entanglement is critical to maintaining its scientific integrity while carefully investigating its larger ramifications.

The study of entanglement continues to challenge and broaden our grasp of reality. Recent advances in experimental physics have expanded the scope of entanglement to previously unheard-of levels. Chinese scientists established satellite-mediated entanglement between ground stations more than 1,200 kilometers apart in 2017, proving its durability across long distances. These findings not only demonstrate the non-local nature of entanglement, but also open the path for a quantum internet, in which entangled particles might permit instantaneous, secure worldwide communication.

Entanglement also has the potential to increase our knowledge of the universe's underlying structure. Theoretical physicists are looking at how entanglement affects the fabric of spacetime. The holographic principle, for example, proposes that quantum entanglement might produce spacetime geometry. This concept is fundamental to methods such as AdS/CFT correspondence, in which entanglement entropy is offered as a measure of spacetime connection. If these theories are proven correct, they might give a unified framework for quantum mechanics and general relativity, overcoming one of contemporary physics' most difficult difficulties.

Entanglement in cosmology presents fascinating issues regarding the universe's origins and evolution. Quantum fluctuations may have entangled particles on massive scales during the early moments of the Big Bang, leaving correlations visible in the cosmic microwave background. This "quantum imprint" might shed light on the universe's primordial state and the mechanisms driving its inflationary growth. To delve deeper into these phenomena, multidisciplinary collaboration across quantum physics, astrophysics, and cosmology is necessary.

Entanglement's limitless reach has ramifications for humanity's perception of its place in the universe. The concept that particles separated by enormous distances are inherently related calls into question the anthropocentric view of isolation and separateness. Instead, it emphasizes the interconnection of all occurrences, urging a transition from individualistic perspectives to a more holistic view. This transition has ethical repercussions, instilling a feeling of communal responsibility for the planet's and its people' welfare.

Quantum entanglement pushes the bounds of classical physics, providing insights into the universe's interconnection while spurring technological innovation and philosophical inquiry. Its non-local character calls into question traditional notions about space and time, paving the way for new paradigms of interpreting reality. As study into entanglement continues, it has the potential to transform our scientific, philosophical, and ethical frameworks, encouraging a better understanding for the oneness that underpins all of existence's variety.

In Esoteric Philosophy, Cosmic Records refers to an all-inclusive data store.

The concept of a cosmic record—a massive storehouse of all that has transpired and will occur—is profoundly ingrained in both spiritual traditions and current metaphysical discourse. This notion, known in many esoteric ideologies as the Akashic Records, depicts the cosmos as a living storehouse of information. It argues that every idea, action, and event is etched on an ethereal realm, accessible only to those who are tuned in to its vibrations. While this hypothesis is not based on empirical research, its connections with quantum theories, particularly those involving entanglement and information theory, provide rich ground for investigation.

The name Akashic Records comes from the Sanskrit word Akasha, which means ether or primeval stuff. Akasha is one of the five basic elements in ancient Indian philosophy, and it represents the foundation from which all physical and metaphysical events emanate. The records are said to exist outside of the physical sphere, acting as a non-material storehouse of universal knowledge. Hinduism, Buddhism, and certain schools of mystical Judaism and Christianity all use similar terminology to describe a heavenly ledger or celestial archive where karmic acts, intents, and cosmic rules are recorded.

Modern metaphysical interpretations of the Akashic Records frequently highlight its reachability to human awareness. Individuals can access these records, according to practitioners, through meditative or intuitive techniques for guidance, self-reflection, and healing. According to this perspective, the records serve as both a mirror and a map, providing insight into the past, present, and prospective futures. The procedure is defined as aligning one's awareness with the Akasha's vibrational frequencies, which allows for an experienced connection with the universe's informational foundation.

The concept of a comprehensive cosmic record may have fascinating connections in quantum physics and information theory. Quantum entanglement shows that particles may maintain a shared informational state despite their physical separation, implying a non-local connection that transcends traditional space and time constraints. According to some interpretations of quantum physics, such as the holographic principle, all information contained within a three-dimensional volume of space may be stored on its two-dimensional border. This idea indicates that the cosmos may function as a holographic data repository, similar to the concept of a cosmic record.

Furthermore, advances in black hole physics have given rise to the "information paradox," in which the destiny of information swallowed by a black hole calls into question the fundamental principles of quantum mechanics. Stephen Hawking's research on black hole radiation found that information cannot be completely destroyed, leading to the theory that it may be stored on the event horizon. This scientific theory reflects the esoteric notion that no action, thought, or experience is ever totally lost, but rather exists in a subtle, universal form.

While these scientific hypotheses do not prove the reality of the Akashic Records, they do provide further insight into how knowledge may be maintained and accessible on a cosmic scale. Parallels between these realms encourage interdisciplinary discourse, linking the metaphysical and empirical in ways that benefit both views. For example, consciousness researchers have investigated whether human cognition interacts with a larger informational matrix.

Importantly, the notion of a cosmic record has important ethical consequences. The Akashic Records are frequently associated with the concept of karma in spiritual traditions, which holds that all acts create ripples over time and space, impacting both individual and communal fates. This viewpoint stresses personal responsibility and connection, while also emphasizing awareness in thought, speech, and action. It also corresponds with the ecological concept of interconnectedness, which states that every activity has an impact on the wider system, instilling a feeling of responsibility for the earth.

At the same time, the metaphor of the Akashic Records calls into question linear ideas of time and causation. It encourages a more fluid conception of temporal interactions by claiming that the past, present, and future exist concurrently within this cosmic storehouse. This viewpoint is consistent with certain interpretations of quantum physics, such as the Wheeler-DeWitt equation, which characterizes the cosmos as being in an eternal quantum state. In this viewpoint, time appears as a perceptual construct rather than an absolute structure, which aligns with the concept of a perpetual, all-encompassing record.

The Akashic Records' accessibility in metaphysical activities reflects bigger issues about the nature of knowledge and awareness. If such a repository exists, what processes regulate how it interacts with human awareness? This connection is frequently framed in esoteric traditions as an intuitive or spiritual process, mediated by altered states of consciousness or increased awareness. Modern neuroscience, on the other hand, investigates how brain states linked with meditation, flow, or near-death experiences might increase access to unusual types of information. While these studies do not establish the existence of the Akashic Records, they do provide insights into how people perceive and interpret extended levels of consciousness.
Despite its profound philosophical and spiritual implications, the notion of cosmic recordings is still controversial in scientific circles. Critics contend that it lacks actual data and risks confusing metaphor with reality. They advise against utilizing quantum physics jargon to verify metaphysical statements that have not been rigorously tested and peer-reviewed. Such issues emphasize the significance of retaining intellectual honesty and scientific rigor while investigating the interconnections between science and spirituality.

Nonetheless, the Akashic Records' long-standing attraction reflects a common human need for connection, significance, and transcendence. Whether seen literally or symbolically, the concept encourages meditation on the interconnectivity of life and the continuation of knowledge throughout time and space. It also emphasizes the transforming power of seeing existence as part of a greater, dynamic totality.

The notion of a cosmic record promotes discussion among science, philosophy, and spirituality in the framework of multidisciplinary research. It calls into question reductionist paradigms and allows investigation of reality's deeper aspects by encouraging inquiry and openness. While the Akashic Records may remain a hypothetical creation, they are a potent metaphor for human imagination's limitless reach and the endless possibilities of life. In this way, the concept transcends its esoteric beginnings and becomes a prism through which we may explore the wonders of the cosmos and our role within it.

Nuanced inquiry: a measured approach to linking advanced physics and universal memory.

Exploring the relationship between advanced physics and the idea of universal memory is a multidimensional task requiring both scientific rigor and philosophical flexibility. The concept of global memory frequently appears in metaphysical traditions, such as the Akashic Records, which claim to be a storehouse of all information, events, and experiences. While this concept is extremely symbolic in spiritual contexts, combining it with physics results in a complex interplay of metaphors and evolving scientific truths. By taking a nuanced approach, we may investigate how sophisticated physics—specifically quantum mechanics and information theory—might symbolically connect with the idea of universal memory while respecting its separate epistemological underpinnings.

The idea of entanglement in quantum physics implies that particles may communicate information instantly across huge distances, retaining a coupled state regardless of remoteness. This phenomena, which Albert Einstein memorably defined as "spooky action at a distance," calls into question conventional notions of location and causation. Entanglement presents fascinating issues regarding information storage and transport throughout the cosmos, pointing to a deeper, non-local substrate. Some physicists hypothesize that the cosmos functions as a large informational network, with entangled particles contributing to a holistic informational structure.

Based on this paradigm, the holographic principle provides another perspective on universal information storage. This idea, proposed by physicists such as Gerard 't Hooft and Leonard Susskind, implies that any information contained within a three-dimensional volume of space may be stored on its two-dimensional perimeter. This idea gained popularity once it was revealed that the event horizon—a two-dimensional boundary—

seems to contain information about the three-dimensional stuff it engulfs. In this sense, the cosmos may be viewed as a hologram, with each bit of information contained within a fundamental structure. This is analogous to the concept of global memory, in which each experience or encounter leaves a permanent mark on a cosmic repository.

However, converting these scientific knowledge into philosophical conceptions needs considerable consideration. While entanglement and the holographic principle give deep models for understanding the universe's informational architecture, they are nonetheless based on actual research. Their extension into global memory, as regarded in esoteric traditions, is both theoretical and symbolic. The Akashic Records, for example, are sometimes portrayed as accessible via meditative or intuitive practices, in which individuals seek direction and insight from this source. In contrast, the information contained in quantum systems or event horizons is not readily accessible in this fashion; decoding needs advanced mathematical frameworks as well as experimental corroboration.

The significance of information in physics emphasizes the possible connections between universal memory and quantum theory. Information theory, pioneered by Claude Shannon in the mid-twentieth century, has become a cornerstone of contemporary physics, impacting topics spanning thermodynamics to quantum computing. In this paradigm, information is treated as a basic entity, similar to energy and matter. Entropy, which quantifies disorder or uncertainty in a system, is intimately related to information. The more information a system holds, the lower its entropy becomes, and vice versa. This concept has far-reaching consequences for how the universe stores and processes information throughout time, raising the question of whether the universe acts as a massive computer machine.

The interaction of information theory and physics extends into speculative territory, such as the concept of a quantum cosmos that functions as a computer simulation. Some researchers suggest that the fundamental particles and forces we see are emergent phenomena caused by underlying informational processes. This viewpoint is similar to the idea of a universal memory, in which the fabric of reality serves as a dynamic record-keeping system, maintaining the detailed details of every encounter and occurrence.

Universal memory is frequently associated with ethical and spiritual qualities in esoteric religions. The Akashic Records, for example, are supposed to capture not just individual actions but also their intents and repercussions, stressing interconnection and moral culpability. This ethical component adds to the discussion's complexity by situating universal memory within a framework of human progress and cosmic justice. While physics does not explicitly address morality or ethics, the implications of informational preservation in the cosmos invoke similar issues. For example, the idea of the information paradox in black hole physics asks whether information is actually destroyed when it passes the event horizon, reflecting the esoteric belief that no action or thought is ever completely obliterated.

Linking sophisticated physics with universal memory necessitates a commitment to the integrity of both realms. One of the risks of such multidisciplinary study is the possibility of distortion or oversimplification, especially when scientific concepts are used outside of their rigorous context. Quantum physics, for example, is widely used in popular metaphysical literature to substantiate spiritual claims, yet such links are typically based on shallow or incorrect readings. To avoid this mistake, talks must be based on confirmed scientific principles while admitting the symbolic or metaphorical nature of its application to metaphysical concepts.

Universal memory's attraction stems not just from its possible scientific similarities, but also from its ability to inspire a comprehensive picture of reality. We may foster a sense of awe and responsibility by picturing the cosmos as a linked network of information. This viewpoint promotes a transition from individuality to interconnectivity, in which every thought and action contributes to the greater total. The concept of global memory, whether viewed through the perspective of quantum entanglement, the holographic principle, or esoteric traditions, stimulates meditation on all things' intrinsic interconnection.

In this spirit of nuanced inquiry, it is worth contemplating how advances in science and spirituality might lead to a better understanding of universal memory. Future research in quantum information theory, neurology, and consciousness studies may give insights on the mechanics by which information is maintained and retrieved, while esoteric practices may continue to investigate the experiential qualities of connectivity and insight. This multidisciplinary conversation has the potential to deepen our understanding of both the physical and metaphysical components of reality, producing a more integrated and wider worldview.

The notion of universal memory acts as a link between science and spirituality, asking us to reflect on the nature of existence, the continuity of knowledge, and the interconnection of all life. We may honor the intricacies of both realms while finding paths to deeper knowledge if we approach this issue with curiosity, rigour, and humility. Universal memory, whether seen literally or metaphorically, is a captivating lens through which to examine the wonders of the cosmos and our role within it.

CHAPTER 19: EVERETT'S MANY-WORLDS AND REINCARNATION

"As a single footstep will not make a path on the earth, so a single thought will not make a pathway in the mind." – Henry David Thoreau

The Everettian interpretation of quantum physics gave rise to the concept of numerous branches of reality, in which every potential consequence of a decision is realized in parallel worlds. Hugh Everett III presented the "Many-Worlds Interpretation" (MWI) in 1957, and it transformed how physicists and philosophers think about the nature of existence and the fabric of reality. Unlike other interpretations of quantum physics that rely on the collapse of the wave function, the Many-Worlds Interpretation proposes that all possibilities inherent in a quantum system are realized, resulting in a branching multiverse.

The superposition principle of quantum physics, which asserts that particles exist in several states at the same time until they are viewed or measured, is central to this interpretation. In Schrödinger's famous thought experiment, for example, a cat in a box is both alive and dead until the box is opened and its status determined. Instead of collapsing into one state or another, the Many-Worlds Interpretation divides the world into two different branches: one where the cat is living and one where it is dead. Each branch symbolizes a different, equally real universe in which the relevant conclusion occurs.

This view has far-reaching ramifications, calling into question traditional concepts of reality, individuality, and causality. If every quantum event causes the world to branch, innumerable parallel universes would persist, each carrying a version of reality molded by distinct outcomes of quantum interactions. These worlds are not only hypothetical; they are deemed as real as our own, living independently of one another and unable to interact.

One of the Many-Worlds Interpretation's main advantages is its ability to address the quantum mechanics measurement issue without using wave function collapse. In classical quantum physics, the act of measuring pushes a quantum system to pick a particular state, presenting difficulties about what defines an observer and how collapse happens. The MWI solves this problem by claiming that all conceivable states exist concurrently in independent branches, removing the necessity for an external observer or a collapse mechanism.

However, the Many-Worlds Interpretation is not without its difficulties and debates. One of the key critiques is that it is not empirically testable. Because the parallel worlds proposed by the MWI are noncommunicative and unreachable from our own, their existence cannot be explicitly verified. This constraint pushes the interpretation to the outside of empirical research, where it is frequently chastised for delving into philosophical speculation.

Despite these obstacles, the MWI has sparked a plethora of philosophical research and artistic discovery, notably in the areas of determinism, free choice, and identity. In an eternally branching universe, classical physics' deterministic nature is replaced with a landscape of probabilistic outcomes, in which every action and occurrence produces new universes. This raises issues regarding the nature of choice and agency: if every potential option is fulfilled in some branch of the universe, do individual decisions have the same weight, or are they just points of divergence in an unstoppable branching process?

Parallel worlds has also found resonance in spiritual and metaphysical traditions, where it is related to ideas such as reincarnation, karmic cycles, and multidimensionality. In Hinduism, for example, the concept of infinite cycles of creation, preservation, and destruction corresponds figuratively to the Many-Worlds Interpretation's branching of universes. Similarly, esoteric teachings that depict layered realities or astral realms reflect the concept of several coexisting dimensions.

The MWI has important scientific implications for cosmology, as well as our knowledge of the universe's origins and structure. If the world is a multiverse, the characteristics and constants of our reality—such as the strength of basic forces and the masses of constituent particles—might be unique to our branch, with other universes showing alternative physical laws. This viewpoint provides a potential answer to the fine-tuning dilemma, which questions why nature's constants are exactly calibrated to allow for life. In a multiverse, life may spontaneously evolve in certain branches while staying inhospitable in others.

The Many-Worlds Interpretation has also inspired popular culture and speculative fiction, making it an ideal setting for narrative and imaginative inquiry. Parallel worlds have attracted viewers and artists alike, giving storylines that explore different realities, diverse timelines, and the repercussions of decision via novels, films, video games, and television programs. These stories frequently deal with deep philosophical issues, such as the essence of identity and the ethics of interdimensional meddling.

The Many-Worlds Interpretation is still a source of dispute and study in cutting-edge physics. Quantum computing advances, for example, are bringing fresh insights into the behavior of quantum systems as well as the possibility for superposition and entanglement. Some experts have even argued that quantum computers might provide indirect proof for the MWI, given their capacity to do computations tenfold quicker than conventional computers is based on the simultaneous processing of information across several states.

While the Many-Worlds Interpretation is still one of many competing quantum mechanics theories, its philosophical complexity and creative appeal assure its long-term significance in scientific and cultural debate. It opens up new avenues for understanding the cosmos and our role within it by forcing us to think beyond the limits of classical reality.

The notion of various branches encourages us to consider the fundamental interconnectivity of all things, as well as the endless potentialities that exist. The Many-Worlds Interpretation, whether seen as a scientific model, a philosophical framework, or a source of inspiration, emphasizes the universe's limitless creativity, in which every option is fulfilled and every route is explored. Through this perspective, we are reminded that reality is a complicated, ever-expanding fabric of possibilities rather than a single story.

Reincarnation doctrines: repeated existence in evolving forms

Reincarnation, the concept of the soul or essence repeating multiple incarnations in different forms, has persisted in spiritual traditions for millennia, providing significant insights into existence's cyclical nature. This belief, prevalent in a variety of civilizations and faiths, holds that life is cyclical rather than linear, with death acting as a transition rather than a final conclusion. Individuals are said to develop, learn, and progress via reincarnation, indicating a fundamental link between previous acts, current conditions, and future potential. This hypothesis has fascinating connections with modern physics theories, notably those concerning energy conservation and the cyclicality found in quantum systems.

Reincarnation is strongly linked in Hinduism to the idea of karma, a moral framework in which every action has repercussions that impact future experiences. The soul, or atman, is said to be immortal and indestructible, passing through several bodies and lives until achieving freedom, or moksha. Similarly, in Buddhism, the cycle of birth, death, and reincarnation, known as samsara, is attributed to attachment and ignorance. Through spiritual effort and enlightenment, one can break free from this cycle and attain nirvana, or ultimate escape from pain.

Reincarnation was also discussed in ancient Greek philosophy, notably in the teachings of Pythagoras and Plato. Plato's dialogues depict soul transmigration and the notion that learning is the process of recalling information from previous lifetimes. For these intellectuals, reincarnation was not merely a spiritual concept, but also a prism through which they might analyze morality, memory, and the quest of truth.

In Indigenous cultures, reincarnation is frequently associated with communal and ecological aspects. Many Native American tribes, for example, believe that reincarnation allows their ancestors to return to guide and defend their people. This viewpoint stresses the interconnection of all life, implying that reincarnation is a common experience that connects generations.

Although the concept of reincarnation appears to lack scientific support, it corresponds to certain concepts in physics and cosmology. The first rule of thermodynamics, which stipulates that energy cannot be generated or destroyed but only altered, provides a fascinating parallel for reincarnation. If the essence of life may be compared to energy, its survival across multiple forms is consistent with this fundamental concept. Similarly, the cyclical aspect of existence claimed by reincarnation parallels patterns observed in quantum systems, where particles and waves demonstrate constant alteration and regeneration.

Modern study into past-life memories has added a divisive layer to the debate. Psychiatrists such as Dr. Ian Stevenson and Dr. Jim Tucker have researched examples of people, generally youngsters, who claim to remember events from previous lifetimes. Skeptics ascribe these tales to imagination, cultural conditioning, or cryptomnesia (the inadvertent recollection of erased memories), but supporters contend that certain examples transcend conventional explanations. For example, some people have detailed exact, verifiable facts regarding past events or persons they could not have met in their current lives. Though these studies are still controversial, they demonstrate the persistent curiosity with reincarnation and its implications for understanding consciousness.

Reincarnation calls into question the linear concept of time and identity that dominates Western philosophy. It implies that life does not follow a single path, but rather unfolds in numerous dimensions and repetitions. This notion prompts us to consider the essence of the self: if our former lives impact us, are we genuinely different persons, or are we dynamic composites of experiences and memories that transcend solo existence? Such issues are consistent with quantum physics, which posits that particles may exist in numerous states at the same time, representing different possibilities.

Reincarnation poses ethical concerns, notably those of accountability and compassion. The concept that our acts in this life have an impact on our future situations promotes moral responsibility and connection. Understanding that our decisions have consequences beyond this lifetime may drive us to behave with greater care and sensitivity. This viewpoint is consistent with the non-locality principle in quantum entanglement, which states that changes in one part of a system instantly influence distant sections, implying a profound unity underneath apparent separations.

Reincarnation has influenced art, literature, and music, resulting in a complex tapestry of interpretations and emotions. Reincarnation is a potent storytelling technique for addressing themes of love, grief, and transformation, from epic narratives like the Mahabharata to current films that explore past-life ties. It gives a foundation for delving into the mystery of existence and the never-ending hunt for meaning.

Critics of reincarnation frequently object to its lack of empirical proof and the possibility that it may increase fatalism. They contend that perceiving life as predetermined by prior acts may hinder personal initiative and creativity. Proponents argue that reincarnation stresses development and evolution, viewing difficulties as chances for learning and self-improvement. In this sense, reincarnation is about the dynamic interaction of decision and consequence rather than predetermination.

Reincarnation has been viewed in modern spirituality as an opportunity for human progress and self-discovery. Past-life regression therapy, for example, seeks to assist clients in exploring unsolved issues, habits, or traumas that may have arisen in prior existence. While these practices are not fully acknowledged in the scientific world, they highlight reincarnation's ongoing appeal as a tool for studying the human mind and resolving existential concerns.

The convergence of reincarnation with quantum theories of parallel universes and many-worlds interpretations adds another level of complication. If, as postulated by the Many-Worlds Interpretation, numerous worlds exist in which every potential result is achieved, the concept of reincarnation may extend beyond consecutive lifetimes in one universe to simultaneous existences in several realities. This viewpoint calls into question standard notions of time and causation, implying that reincarnation may not be limited to a linear sequence but may operate across several dimensions.

The idea of reincarnation asks us to consider the continuity of existence and the transformational power of life's cycle. Whether examined via spiritual, philosophical, or scientific lenses, it provides significant insights into all things' interconnection and the limitless opportunities for growth and rejuvenation. In a cosmos marked by change and growth, reincarnation serves as a reminder that life is a journey, not a destination—one that spans time, space, and personality.

How Each Model Extends Linear Views of Reality and Identity

The convergence of reincarnation ideologies with Everett's Many-Worlds Interpretation challenges linear notions of reality and identity, providing multidimensional frameworks for comprehending life. Both ideas suggest that existence goes beyond isolated experiences, rejecting a rigidly linear path in favor of a broad network of possibilities. They bring spiritual and scientific ideas together, altering our understanding of time, causation, and selfhood.

Reincarnation, which is based on spiritual traditions, holds that existence is a continuous cycle in which an individual's essence, also known as the soul or consciousness, lives several incarnations. Each incarnation is molded by previous experiences and contributes to future ones, producing a complex web of development and learning. In contrast, quantum physics' Many-Worlds Interpretation (MWI) proposes that every choice or quantum event generates several parallel universes. Each universe reflects a separate conclusion, resulting in an unlimited number of realities. While these frameworks are derived from different traditions—spiritual and scientific

—they all reject uniqueness in favor of plurality and interconnectivity.

Reincarnation proposes a cyclical concept that questions life's linearity. Samsara, a concept in Hinduism and Buddhism, refers to the cycle of birth, death, and reincarnation. This process is driven by actions, or karma, which creates a feedback loop in which ethical decisions influence future lives. This paradigm of reality is not limited by time; previous acts impact the present, just as the present shapes the future. This cyclical viewpoint is consistent with nonlinear patterns found in nature, such as ecosystem regeneration or celestial body cycles.

Similarly, the Many-Worlds Interpretation calls into question the conventional concept of a single, deterministic chronology. MWI, first hypothesized by Hugh Everett in 1957, holds that every quantum event causes a branching of universes, each reflecting a different result. This interpretation avoids the necessity for wave function collapse by implying that all potential states persist concurrently in parallel universes. A particle, for example, may go left in one universe but right in another. Both scenarios are realized, resulting in a tapestry of divergent timelines.

When analyzing the nature of identity, the similarities between reincarnation and MWI become clear. Identity in reincarnation is flexible and cumulative, molded by lifetime-long experiences. A person's essence changes in cycles, absorbing lessons and characteristics from prior incarnations. This continuity across lives reflects MWI's concept of parallel selves. In a multiverse, a person may exist in innumerable variations, each influenced by distinct actions or circumstances. While these parallel identities are separate, they have a common genesis, similar to the shared essence in reincarnation.

The concept of interconnectivity ties these concepts together even more. Reincarnation stresses the interconnectedness of all creatures, implying that acts have a long-term impact on not just the individual but also the group. This interconnectivity is similar to the entanglement found in quantum systems, where particles remain linked regardless of distance. In MWI, universes are linked rather than separate due to their shared beginnings in quantum processes. This connection implies a holistic perspective of life, in which every action reverberates across dimensions, creating a dynamic, interdependent reality.

Both paradigms raise questions about the idea of finality. Death, in reincarnation, is a transition, a doorway to a new stage of life. Similarly, MWI denies the concept of solitary outcomes, claiming that each option exists in its own world. This denial of finality promotes a rethinking of causation. Cause and effect exist in reincarnation, with previous deeds impacting future experiences. In MWI, causation becomes multidimensional, with each decision branching into numerous worlds, each with its own causal pathway.

These frameworks, from an ethical standpoint, promote a broader understanding of duty and influence. Reincarnation teaches that acts have long-term effects, which fosters accountability and compassion. MWI, while not necessarily ethical, emphasizes the importance of actions by demonstrating their far-reaching implications across worlds. They together foster a worldview that emphasizes interconnectivity, empathy, and long-term thinking.

Philosophically, the combination of reincarnation with MWI raises significant problems concerning the essence of the self. What is the basic essence of the self in reincarnation if it changes throughout incarnations, acquiring experiences and attributes? Similarly, if the self in MWI exists in innumerable parallel forms, each created by a distinct set of choices, what unifies them? These considerations call into question traditional concepts of identity, implying that the self is dynamic, a confluence of several trajectories and possibilities.

MWI's multiverse framework also corresponds to metaphysical explanations of reincarnation as occurring outside of the confines of linear time. In certain spiritual traditions, reincarnation encompasses simultaneous incarnations on multiple levels of existence, in addition to past and future lifetimes. This perspective is consistent with MWI, in which parallel worlds coexist concurrently, each reflecting a distinct state of reality. The confluence of these notions shows that existence extends beyond time and space, spanning a multidimensional continuum.

Modern interpretations of reincarnation frequently stress personal growth and self-discovery, which corresponds to the exploratory aspect of MWI. Past-life regression, for example, seeks to reveal unsolved issues or patterns from prior incarnations, therefore promoting healing and transformation. Similarly, the multiverse notion encourages people to contemplate how various choices impact their world. Both approaches encourage people to actively participate in their own evolution, embracing change and variety as drivers for progress.

The relationship between reincarnation and MWI is also evident in cultural and creative representations. Parallel lives and cyclical life are prominent subjects in literature, movies, and philosophy, reflecting humanity's obsession with these concepts. Works such as Jorge Luis Borges' The Garden of Forking Paths and films like Cloud Atlas and Everything Everywhere All at Once demonstrate the interaction between decision, consequence, and interconnection, providing creative views into the intersections of spiritual and quantum realities.

Critics of these theories frequently dispute their empirical foundation, citing the absence of direct proof for reincarnation and the theoretical character of MWI. While these criticisms emphasize the difficulties of reconciling scientific and spiritual perspectives, they also stress the significance of rigorous inquiry and open-minded research. Despite their differences, both frameworks are committed to broadening our knowledge of life, questioning traditional beliefs, and accepting reality's complexities.

The intersection of reincarnation and the Many-Worlds Interpretation prompts a reframing of existence as a multidimensional journey. These theories provide fundamental insights into existence's interconnectivity, continuity, and unlimited possibilities by broadening linear perspectives on reality and identity. They inspire us to embrace life's mystery and wonder, acknowledging that every decision, every moment, and every existence adds to a vast, evolving fabric of being. They accomplish this by inspiring a deeper appreciation for the richness and diversity of the human experience, transcending time, location, and personality.

CHAPTER 20: QUANTUM TELEPORTATION AND ASTRAL TRAVEL

"What is now proved was once only imagined." – William Blake

Quantum teleportation, which is frequently portrayed in science fiction as a magical method of moving physical items across space, is based on a more subtle but deeply exciting scientific truth. This phenomena, based on quantum mechanics principles, involves the transfer of quantum states rather than physical stuff, calling into question standard notions of information transmission and locality. Distinguishing actual scientific advances in quantum teleportation from speculative science fiction is critical for understanding its true promise and limitations.

Quantum teleportation takes advantage of the unique properties of entanglement, which Albert Einstein famously referred to as "spooky action at a distance." When two particles become entangled, their quantum states are interconnected, so that the state of one particle instantly correlates with the state of the other, regardless of the distance between them. This connection serves as the basis for quantum teleportation, which allows a quantum state to be transferred from one particle to another without requiring physical movement. Importantly, the procedure does not require the transportation of materials, but rather the accurate copying of quantum information.

The experimental achievement of quantum teleportation was a big step forward in quantum mechanics research. The first successful demonstration took place in 1997, when scientists from the University of Innsbruck transferred a photon's quantum state across a laboratory. Since then, advances in quantum technology have permitted the teleportation of increasingly sophisticated systems across greater distances. In 2017, researchers used satellites to conduct quantum teleportation over 1,200 kilometers, demonstrating the viability of long-distance quantum communication. These accomplishments highlight the discipline and accuracy of scientific methods for investigating quantum events, in contrast to the typically overblown depictions in popular culture.

The necessity for classical communication, in addition to quantum entanglement, is an important feature of quantum teleportation. The process starts with the formation of an entangled pair of particles, one of which remains with the transmitter and the other being delivered to the destination. The sender then interacts with the particle to be teleported and their half of the entangled pair, completing a measurement that causes the quantum state to collapse. This measurement produces classical data, which must be communicated to the recipient using traditional methods such as radio or fiber optics. After receiving the classical information, the recipient applies a precise transformation to their entangled particle in order to recover the original quantum state. This combination of quantum and classical communication guarantees that quantum teleportation adheres to relativity's restrictions, prohibiting faster-than-light signaling.

Despite being based on strong scientific concepts, quantum teleportation has repeatedly been misconstrued and sensationalised. In popular culture, the phrase "teleportation" sometimes conjures up visions of instantaneous travel, similar to teleporters in Star Trek and other fictitious technology. These depictions confuse the transfer of quantum information with the actual movement of things, which is impossible within the framework of quantum physics. Unlike the fantasy concept of dematerializing and reassembling matter, quantum teleportation is concerned with the state of particles, maintaining the physical rules.

While quantum teleportation's practical applications are still in the early stages, they offer enormous potential. One of the most intriguing fields of research is quantum communication, specifically quantum key distribution (QKD) for secure data transport. Quantum teleportation allows for the creation of quantum networks in which entangled particles carry encryption keys. These keys, safeguarded by quantum mechanics principles, are impervious to interception since any effort to eavesdrop would disrupt the entangled states, disclosing the incursion. Such improvements have far-reaching consequences for cybersecurity, providing previously unheard-of levels of protection against hackers and data breaches.

Another possible application is in the advancement of quantum computing. Quantum teleportation might help transport quantum states across nodes in a quantum network, allowing for distributed quantum computing. This strategy would enable quantum computers to collaborate, sharing resources and talents in order to tackle complicated problems more effectively. Furthermore, incorporating quantum teleportation into quantum error correction techniques has the potential to improve the stability and dependability of quantum systems, addressing one of the key obstacles in developing viable quantum computers.

While quantum teleportation has significant scientific and technical promise, it is critical to consider its ethical and philosophical consequences. The capacity to modify and transmit quantum states raises fundamental problems about information and identity. In hypothetical circumstances where quantum teleportation extends to biological systems—a concept that remains firmly in the realm of science fiction—debates concerning consciousness continuity and identity preservation may arise. While such debates are hypothetical, they highlight the need of considering the larger ramifications of quantum developments.

Distinguishing true scientific protocols from science fiction clichés necessitates a thorough grasp of quantum teleportation's constraints. The process is fundamentally probabilistic, as it is bound by the no-cloning theorem, which asserts that it is impossible to generate a perfect duplicate of any unknown quantum state. This constraint assures that quantum teleportation is not a duplicating technique, but rather a method of conveying information with fidelity. Furthermore, the dependence on classical communication creates practical limits, as the speed of information transfer is restricted by the speed of light, preventing instantaneous communication.

The interaction between quantum teleportation and speculative storytelling reflects a larger societal curiosity with science's potential. Fictional interpretations frequently act as a fuel for creativity, inspiring curiosity and ingenuity. They can, however, foster myths, obscure the genuine nature of scientific activities. Educators and communicators play an important role in closing this gap by increasing public comprehension of quantum mechanics while also highlighting its actual accomplishments.

Maintaining a clear boundary between science and fiction in the context of quantum teleportation benefits both fields. The scientific study of quantum events provides a remarkable insight into the universe's underlying workings, revealing patterns and laws that defy perception. Fiction, in turn, takes these truths into imaginary worlds, investigating their ramifications and evoking wonderment. They work together to create a dynamic interplay of knowledge and creativity that advances our collective understanding of reality.

The future of quantum teleportation is dependent on the confluence of scientific investigation, technical innovation, and ethical thought. As researchers stretch the bounds of quantum physics, the potential applications of quantum teleportation will grow, influencing disciplines such as computers, communication, and cryptography. Simultaneously, constant discussion of the philosophical and sociological components of these developments will ensure that they are produced responsibly, with regard for their far-reaching repercussions.

By differentiating actual scientific processes from speculative clichés, we not only uphold the integrity of scientific discovery, but also embrace the wonder and potential that quantum mechanics invokes. Quantum teleportation shows human creativity in unraveling the mysteries of the cosmos by translating abstract ideas into practical technologies. It does this by reminding us of the interconnection of knowledge and imagination, uniting the worlds of science and spirit in a common search for understanding.

Spiritual Out-of-Body Journeys: Accounts of Consciousness Transcending Location

Out-of-body experiences (OBEs) have captivated humans for ages, crossing cultural, religious, and scientific barriers. These events, which are commonly characterized as the sense of one's awareness detaching from the physical body and viewing the world from an outside perspective, call into question traditional ideas of self and location. While spiritual traditions have traditionally regarded OBEs as proof of a transcendent soul or spirit, scientific investigation has treated them with caution, attempting to understand their mechanics via neurology and psychology. The interaction of spiritual and scientific ideas continues to improve our understanding of these mysterious experiences.

OBEs have played an important role in many religious and mystical traditions. The notion of astral travel in Hinduism refers to the soul, or jiva, leaving the body and traveling to other worlds. Similarly, Buddhist writings describe meditation experiences in which practitioners transcend the physical plane, frequently as a means of reaching higher realms of awareness. Shamanic excursions, in which the soul travels across realms in search of guidance, healing, or enlightenment, are recounted by indigenous civilizations all over the world, from Australian Aboriginals to Native Americans. These tales have one thing in common: the concept that awareness is not constrained by the physical body and may go to regions beyond the material world.

Modern spiritual practices have built on these old notions, frequently employing guided meditation, hypnosis, or sensory deprivation to generate OBEs. Practitioners frequently describe floating beyond their bodies, going to faraway places, and engaging with other things. These experiences are generally endowed with a great feeling of clarity and connectivity, leaving long-lasting impacts on individuals who go through them. While some may dismiss these narratives as subjective or culturally conditioned, their constancy throughout time and territory lends them special relevance.

In recent decades, there has been a tremendous increase in scientific interest in OBEs, especially in neurology and psychology. Researchers have attempted to understand the processes behind these events, frequently situating them within the framework of altered states of consciousness. OBEs may be caused in a variety of ways, according to research, including brain stimulation, sensory manipulation, and near-death experiences. Stimulating the temporoparietal junction (TPJ), a region of the brain involved in spatial awareness and self-location processing, can elicit experiences comparable to those described in OBEs. These findings show that OBEs might be caused by disturbances in the brain's capacity to integrate sensory and proprioceptive information.

Near-death experiences make an especially powerful background for OBEs. Individuals who have been resuscitated following cardiac arrest or other life-threatening situations commonly have vivid memories of floating outside their bodies, seeing medical operations, or travelling through light tunnels. These experiences frequently coincide with spiritual explanations of the afterlife, sparking speculation about their origins. While some experts link NDEs to physiological changes like oxygen deprivation or neurochemical surges, others believe they are a sign of deeper metaphysical truths.

One of the most exciting features of OBEs is their potential connection to quantum theory, namely the ideas of non-locality and entanglement. Quantum theory calls into question the traditional assumption that things and events are limited to specific places, arguing that particles may affect one another instantly across huge distances. This principle of non-locality is compatible with the notion that awareness, too, may transcend spatial barriers. Some theorists speculate that OBEs may be connected to quantum processes within the brain, such as quantum coherence in microtubules or other subcellular structures.

Despite these scientific advances, the nature of OBEs remains an open question. Critics claim that the subjective character of these experiences makes them impossible to investigate scientifically, rejecting them as hallucinations or results of brain malfunction. Others warn against mixing anecdotal experiences with factual proof, instead advocating for a balanced approach that takes into consideration both human tales and scientific rigor. The difficulty arises in combining the very personal and often transforming character of OBEs with the need of empirical confirmation.

OBEs should also be considered in terms of culture and psychology. Anthropologists have observed that the interpretation of OBEs differs greatly between cultures, influenced by prevalent ideas about the ego, soul, and cosmos. For example, although Western cultures frequently interpret OBEs as personal transcendence or spiritual awakening, Indigenous traditions may see them as communal or intergenerational events. These distinctions highlight the significance of contextualizing OBEs within their cultural and historical frameworks, rather than relying on simple explanations that fail to convey their complexities.

In addition to its spiritual and scientific significance, OBEs have considerable therapeutic potential. Some psychologists have investigated its use in the treatment of PTSD, anxiety, and depression, frequently using guided visualization or virtual reality simulations. These treatments seek to assist individuals in dissociating from traumatic memories, rephrasing unfavorable events, or developing a stronger feeling of agency. Preliminary studies have yielded promising findings, indicating that OBEs may provide unique opportunities for psychological rehabilitation and growth.

Another growing topic of research is the confluence between OBEs and technology. Researchers may now recreate out-of-body experiences because to advancements in virtual and augmented reality, giving new tools for exploring this phenomena. These technologies not only provide insights into the cognitive and neurological systems that underpin OBEs, but they also open up new potential for therapeutic and recreational uses. VR-based therapy, for example, might help people explore altered states of consciousness or improve their feeling of presence and self-awareness.

In this rapidly developing discipline, ethical questions are critical. As the line between virtual and physical realities blurs, concerns regarding the possible exploitation of OBEs emerge, particularly in scenarios such as surveillance, advertising, and behavioral manipulation. To ensure that these technologies are created and deployed responsibly, scientists, ethicists, and politicians must engage in continual conversation that is based on respect for individual autonomy and well-being.

OBEs' persistent appeal stems from their capacity to challenge and broaden our understanding of consciousness and reality. Whether seen through the lens of spirituality, neurology, or quantum theory, they inspire us to confront our own constraints and explore the mysteries of the mind. While much needs to be found, the study of OBEs has the potential to bridge disparate fields and views, developing a greater understanding of the interdependence of science, spirit, and mankind.

As study progresses, it is critical to keep an open and curious mindset, appreciating the complexities of OBEs without resorting to dogmatism or sensationalism. By combining rigorous scientific investigation with respect for spiritual and cultural traditions, we can gain fresh insights into awareness' nature and limitless potential. In doing so, we recognize the profound and universal drive to comprehend oneself, the cosmos, and the perplexing gaps between.

Limits and Symbolism: Gaining Insights from Parallels Without Crossing Science-Fiction Boundaries

The interaction of quantum physics and spiritual symbols sometimes treads a delicate line between valid research and speculative exaggeration. At its best, this interaction yields significant insights into the mysteries of life; at its worst, it has the potential to muddle scientific principles with baseless speculation. This relationship is especially apparent when comparing quantum teleportation with astral flight, two seemingly distinct phenomena with powerful parallels in their emphasis on transcending locality. While the symbolic resonance between these notions might inspire new ways of thinking about the nature of reality, intellectual honesty requires respect for the limits between science and metaphysics.

Quantum teleportation, a cutting-edge physics phenomena, is the transfer of quantum information between particles across long distances, which is enhanced by entanglement. Unlike its literary representations, quantum teleportation does not involve the physical relocation of matter, but rather the exact transfer of quantum states. Entanglement causes two particles to become correlated in such a way that the condition of one particle instantly impacts the state of the other, regardless of geographical separation. This enables the "teleportation" of quantum information, a significant milestone for quantum computers and secure communication.

Astral travel, on the other hand, is based on spiritual and metaphysical traditions and refers to the experience of awareness leaving the body to explore non-physical regions or faraway locales. This occurrence has been reported in civilizations all over the world, frequently in conjunction with contemplative techniques, near-death experiences, or shamanic ceremonies. Participants typically experience a sensation of separation from their bodily selves, increased awareness, and the capacity to travel across ethereal landscapes. While lacking factual proof, these tales are highly important to individuals who have lived them, frequently motivating major changes in perspective.

The obvious analogies between quantum teleportation and astral flight stem from their mutual challenge to traditional concepts of space and locality. Both instances show the possibility of transcending physical barriers, but in very different ways. Quantum teleportation is accomplished using the physical mechanics of entanglement, which are supported by strong mathematical frameworks and experimental data. The transcendence in astral travel is metaphorical, indicating a release from the material restrictions of life and an exploration of the spiritual elements of being.

The symbolic significance of these analogies prompts inquiry on the nature of connection and perception's limitations. Quantum physics, with its non-locality and wave-particle duality concepts, indicates that the cosmos functions at sizes that defy human understanding. Similarly, spiritual traditions have long maintained that reality is more interwoven and complex than it appears. While quantum teleportation and astral travel work in distinct realms, their fundamental challenge to fixed physical bounds is consistent with the larger human search to comprehend the deeper fabric of reality.

However, lumping these events without subtlety risks simplicity and misinterpretation. Quantum teleportation is a well researched phenomena that can be replicated, but astral flight is a subjective and mostly anecdotal experience. Putting the two together, or portraying astral flight as scientifically equivalent to quantum teleportation, weakens the credibility of both areas. Instead, a balanced approach recognizes the comparison's symbolic insights while distinguishing between actual science and philosophical speculation.

The symbolic interaction between quantum and spiritual conceptions calls into question the function of imagination in human cognition. Throughout history, imagination has fueled scientific achievements, from

Einstein's relativity thought experiments to Schrödinger's renowned cat conundrum. In a similar spirit, the metaphorical connections between quantum teleportation and astral flight may inspire novel answers to age-old issues about consciousness, perception, and the meaning of life. By defining these events as complimentary rather than interchangeable, we may investigate their ramifications without compromising their different identities.

Cultural stories about quantum teleportation and astral travel deepen this conversation. Quantum teleportation has captivated the public imagination through science fiction, where it is frequently represented as instantaneous physical travel across galaxies. While these images differ from scientific fact, they reflect humanity's preoccupation with transcending space and temporal boundaries. Similarly, astral travel has been immortalized in religious scriptures, mythology, and modern spiritual organizations, serving as a narrative framework for exploring the unknown. Both stories emphasize the ongoing human impulse to push beyond apparent limitations, whether via scientific advancement or spiritual investigation.

The ethical implications of these stories deserve critical thought. As quantum technologies evolve, the potential abuse of quantum teleportation and entanglement raises questions about privacy, security, and equal access. Meanwhile, the commercialization of astral travel in certain spiritual or self-help businesses has the potential to exploit susceptible persons seeking transcendence. To ensure that these disciplines are treated with integrity and accountability, scientists, ethicists, and spiritual leaders must engage in continual discourse.

The merging of quantum and spiritual viewpoints highlights the significance of multidisciplinary collaboration. We may get a better understanding of phenomena like quantum teleportation and astral flight by encouraging discussions among physicists, philosophers, neuroscientists, and spiritual practitioners. Such collaboration promotes the cross-disciplinary interchange of ideas, strengthening both scientific and philosophical research. Neuroscientific research into altered states of consciousness, for example, might shed light on the mechanics behind astral flight, whilst philosophical musings on quantum non-locality could inspire spiritual interpretations of interconnection.

The metaphorical analogies between quantum teleportation and astral flight serve to remind us of the complexities and wonders of life. They push us to broaden our perspectives on reality while remaining grounded in rigorous inquiry and ethical responsibility. By embracing these events' symbolic and scientific elements, we may investigate the relationship between the concrete and the transcendent, adding to our collective quest for knowledge and meaning. This balanced approach allows us to respect the universe's mysteries while also promoting a sophisticated and inclusive understanding of its interwoven layers.

CHAPTER 21: ETHICS IN QUANTUM MYSTICISM

"A man is ethical only when life, as such, is sacred to him." – Ludwig Andreas Feuerbach

The word "quantum" has become a magnet for deception, frequently used to lend legitimacy to pseudoscientific claims, spiritual organizations, and commercial items. From cosmetics with "quantum healing" powers to courses promising enlightenment through "quantum consciousness," the use of this word has blurred the boundaries between serious science and commercial gimmicks. This tendency, while profitable for some, impairs public comprehension of quantum physics, reduces faith in science, and threatens to dilute important spiritual activities.

Quantum mechanics is a scientific study that investigates events at the atomic and subatomic levels, guided by ideas like superposition, entanglement, and wave-particle duality. These ideas are extremely complicated, sometimes confounding common understanding. However, they are based on decades of careful testing and mathematical confirmation. The accuracy and complexity of quantum mechanics are in sharp contrast to the casual and frequently incorrect usage of the phrase in popular culture.

Misrepresentation of "quantum" is usually caused by the fascination of mystery. Quantum physics calls into question traditional concepts of determinism and locality, paving the way for philosophical questions concerning reality, interconnection, and perception. These subjects are naturally associated with spiritual traditions and metaphysical investigations. However, the leap from scientific foundations to broad spiritual assertions is sometimes unjustified, simplifying sophisticated concepts to simple platitudes. For example, items sold as using "quantum energy" rarely give a scientifically accurate explanation for how this energy is gathered or employed.

One obvious example is the abuse of quantum language in the wellness sector. Devices claiming to produce "quantum frequencies" for healing, or therapies marketed as "quantum touch," capitalize on the public's curiosity with quantum physics while providing little to no empirical proof. These assertions frequently rely on ambiguous terminology, implying that quantum principles may be effortlessly transferred to macroscopic events despite large size disparities. Quantum effects normally occur at tiny sizes under controlled settings, and their applicability to human biology is still a subject of current scientific research, not a confirmed fact.

The hazards of this frenzy go beyond false marketing. When the term "quantum" is associated with unverified or overstated claims, it risks undermining public faith in legitimate scientific pursuits. The confusion of scientific words with pseudoscience can lead to doubt about actual advances in quantum technology, such as quantum computing or quantum cryptography. Furthermore, it promotes confusion, making it more difficult for laypeople to discriminate between legitimate science and opportunistic marketing.

Spiritual and metaphysical groups are similarly vulnerable to the exploitation of quantum notions. Ideas such as "quantum consciousness" or "quantum spirituality" sometimes seek to establish connections between quantum physics and concepts of universal connectivity or higher realms of awareness. While these similarities might be symbolically motivating, they usually go too far by assuming a direct causal link without providing proof. For example, some interpretations claim that quantum entanglement proves spiritual oneness, despite the fact that entanglement, as known scientifically, entails particular and observable interactions between particles rather than metaphysical unity.

Despite these limitations, quantum notions have an attraction in spiritual and metaphysical discourse that is not always bad. The symbolic resonance of quantum concepts can elicit significant thought about the nature of existence, connectivity, and experience. However, it is critical to approach these interpretations with intellectual humility and make a clear difference between metaphorical insights and factual facts. By respecting this border, spiritual practitioners and intellectuals can interact with quantum concepts without distorting their meaning or jeopardizing their scientific integrity.

Educators, scientists, and communicators have crucial roles in mitigating the perils of quantum hype. Clear and understandable explanations of quantum mechanics can help demystify the area, making it less susceptible to misinterpretation. Explaining the probabilistic character of quantum physics in terms of wave functions and probabilities, rather than mysticism, might help to base talks in scientific fact while still addressing the philosophical problems it brings. Efforts to enhance science literacy, both via formal education and public outreach, can enable people to objectively assess statements employing quantum language.

Ethical issues are also relevant for businesses and people using "quantum" as a marketing tactic. Transparency and responsibility should influence the use of scientific terminology in both commercial and spiritual settings. Organizations offering quantum-based products or services should show explicit proof to back up their claims, or explain when they use the term "quantum" metaphorically rather than literally. Regulatory entities and consumer protection agencies can help to ensure that false promises do not abuse the public's interest or trust.

The scientific community bears responsibilities for combating the abuse of quantum notions by actively interacting with the public and clarifying misunderstandings. This interaction might take the shape of public lectures, accessible literature, or online forums where experts translate difficult concepts into intelligible language. Scientists may bridge the gap between quantum physics and popular culture by engaging in these discussions, resulting in a more informed and discriminating audience.

The interaction of quantum physics and wider cultural narratives provides opportunity for productive conversation. Scientists and spiritual thinkers can work together to investigate the nature of reality, consciousness, and existence by embracing the symbolic and philosophical implications of quantum notions. Such interdisciplinary discussions may strengthen both scientific and metaphysical viewpoints, as long as they are based on mutual respect and intellectual rigor.

The pitfalls of quantum hype highlight the larger issues of negotiating the junction of science, spirituality, and capitalism. Misuse of scientific vocabulary is not limited to quantum mechanics; similar patterns can be seen with concepts such as "energy," "vibration," and "frequency." Addressing these challenges necessitates a holistic strategy that includes education, ethical marketing, and multidisciplinary discussion.

Finally, the interest with quantum physics reflects a deeper human urge to comprehend the secrets of life and transcend the constraints of perception. This urge is genuine and worth exploring, but it must be balanced with a dedication to honesty and integrity. By distinguishing real scientific discoveries from opportunistic marketing and unsubstantiated claims, we can appreciate quantum mechanics' complexity and wonder while cultivating a culture of informed inquiry and critical thinking.

Informed Consent: Responsibility in Healing, Teaching, and Claims for Quantum-Based Cures

The incorporation of quantum principles into therapeutic and teaching techniques has sparked widespread attention, but it also necessitates a critical framework for ethical accountability. The promise of "quantum-based cures" and transformational education is frequently found at the crossroads of science, metaphysics, and marketing, where scientific nomenclature is exploited to legitimize unsubstantiated promises. This environment emphasizes the necessity of informed consent, which protects individual autonomy, transparency, and ethical integrity.

Informed consent, as defined in legal and ethical contexts, refers to an individual's right to make decisions based on accurate, accessible, and understandable information. Within the field of quantum healing or quantum-inspired educational frameworks, this idea goes beyond medical or academic contexts to include any practice or service that employs quantum notions. The use of scientific language demands a clear understanding of whether these concepts are based on proven study or symbolic interpretation.

Quantum healing's attraction is largely based on its apparent scientific credibility. Practices including "quantum touch," "quantum energy balancing," and "quantum frequency therapies" purport to use quantum mechanics principles to influence the human body or psyche. These assertions usually use terminology like "entanglement," "resonance," or "vibration," implying a link between subatomic occurrences and biological or emotional processes. However, the applicability of quantum mechanics to macroscopic systems, particularly ones as complicated as the human body, lacks strong empirical evidence. While quantum biology is a growing area, its primary goal is to explain natural processes such as photosynthesis or enzyme function, rather than to validate medicinal treatments.

Practitioners are responsible for presenting their approaches honestly and discriminating between scientific reality, theoretical potential, and metaphorical understanding. Claims concerning the efficacy of quantum-based medicines must be substantiated by data that meets scientific rigor requirements, such as repeatability and peer-reviewed validation. This clarity allows people to make educated judgments without being mislead by pseudoscientific jargon.

Integrating quantum notions into curriculum or workshops presents comparable issues in educational environments. Teachers and facilitators who investigate the relationship between quantum physics and consciousness, spirituality, or human potential must be aware of the limits of present scientific understanding. For example, while the observer effect in quantum physics raises exciting concerns about the function of measurement and observation, applying this idea to human awareness affecting reality is at best speculative. Recognizing this distinction promotes intellectual curiosity while preserving academic integrity.

A critical component of informed consent is ensuring that persons understand the possible hazards and limits of a practice or instruction. In quantum healing, this involves recognizing that such therapies are frequently complimentary rather than curative. They may provide emotional or psychological advantages through placebo effects or the therapeutic connection, but they should not be used instead of evidence-based medical therapies. Practitioners must avoid instilling false optimism or persuading patients to abandon traditional care in favor of unproven methods. Similarly, instructors must avoid presenting theoretical links as proven realities, which may mislead students or audiences.

The idea of informed consent is equally applicable to marketing and promotional materials. When using scientific language to describe a product or service, it is important to provide explicit explanations of what is and is not scientifically supported. For example, devices that claim to produce "quantum frequencies" or "quantum energy fields" must define the techniques used to accomplish these effects and offer proof to back up their claims. This transparency avoids the exploitation of those who may be lured to such things out of desperation or a lack of knowledge.

The social implications of misrepresenting quantum notions in healing and educational techniques must also be examined. Misuse of scientific vocabulary can erode public faith in science, especially when it is connected with exaggerated or incorrect claims. This deterioration has far-reaching consequences, making it increasingly difficult for the public to distinguish between real scientific advances and pseudoscience. In this setting, practitioners and educators have a duty to maintain the credibility of quantum mechanics and associated fields by avoiding distortion.

Regulatory frameworks and professional norms play an important role in promoting informed consent in the quantum healing and education industries. Governments, licensing authorities, and consumer protection organizations can set criteria for openness and evidence in advertising and practice. For example, certificates or disclaimers stating whether a therapy is supported by scientific evidence might assist individuals in making informed decisions. Educational institutions can create curriculum that teach critical thinking abilities, allowing students to assess claims about quantum mechanics and other scientific disciplines.

Ethical issues go beyond the person and encompass the larger ramifications of how quantum notions are represented. Cultural exploitation of scientific concepts for commercial or ideological objectives runs the risk of trivializing quantum mechanics' fundamental findings. This trivialization not only affects the integrity of research, but it also reduces the possibility of genuine interdisciplinary discourse. Approaching quantum notions with humility and respect encourages more meaningful dialogue about their philosophical and practical consequences.

While there is merit in investigating the interconnections of quantum physics, healing, education, and spirituality, these investigations must be founded on honesty and accountability. The symbolic resonance of quantum concepts can inspire significant personal insights and creativity, but these advantages should not be at the price of scientific correctness or ethical integrity. Practitioners and educators working with quantum notions have the chance to contribute to a better understanding of these ideas by presenting them with nuance and integrity.

Informed consent is more than just a legal necessity; it demonstrates respect for individual liberty and the quest of truth. By putting openness first, practitioners and educators can develop a culture of trust and mutual respect. This culture benefits not just those seeking health or knowledge, but it also promotes the overall link between science and society. In a world where quantum physics continues to fascinate the imagination, the duty to apply its principles ethically and properly is a profound and pressing one.

Beyond Ego: How Oneness Themes Foster Ethical Empathy and Mutual Respect

The notion of oneness, which is frequently based in spiritual and intellectual traditions, reflects a picture of connectivity that goes beyond individualism. In an era when scientific and spiritual concepts are merging, quantum mechanics has inspired new interpretations of this principle, implying that the cosmos functions through fundamental interconnectedness. Beyond its spiritual appeal, oneness offers an ethical foundation for developing empathy and mutual respect. When correctly understood and utilized, it challenges the ego-driven paradigms that govern human conduct, fostering collaboration and concern for the common good.

Quantum physics provides fascinating similarities to the concept of oneness, notably through phenomena like entanglement. Entangled particles, separated by huge distances, stay linked, with the state of one immediately impacting the other. This interconnectivity implies that the fabric of reality acts in ways that contradict traditional concepts of separation. While the precise consequences of entanglement for human relationships remain unknown, its symbolic association with oneness has sparked larger ethical debates.

From a philosophical standpoint, oneness confronts the ego, which feeds on separation and hierarchy. The ego creates boundaries between itself and others, prioritizing individual gain over community welfare. In contrast, oneness breaks down these barriers, generating a feeling of shared existence. This change has far-reaching ethical ramifications, particularly for solving social concerns like inequality, environmental degradation, and conflict. Individuals and communities may build more inclusive and compassionate decision-making techniques by acknowledging life's interconnectedness.

The ethical potential of oneness is fundamentally based on empathy. When people comprehend how their activities influence the larger picture, they are more inclined to engage in behaviors that benefit others. Neuroscientific research backs up the premise that empathy can be developed, with studies demonstrating that techniques such as mindfulness and compassion training strengthen brain circuits related with understanding and reacting to the emotions of others. These findings are consistent with the spiritual emphasis on eliminating the ego in order to connect more intimately with the collective.

Quantum-inspired viewpoints also promote a rethinking of ethical boundaries. Traditional moral frameworks frequently rely on strict categories of good and wrong, whereas quantum mechanics' probabilistic nature proposes a more flexible and context-dependent approach. This does not imply forsaking ethical principles, but rather acknowledging the complexities of human interactions. Individuals who embrace ambiguity and nuance can establish more flexible and inclusive ethical practices that reflect the linked nature of reality.

In practice, oneness may be an effective instrument for tackling global issues. The interconnectivity of contemporary systems—whether ecological, economic, or social—requires collaborative solutions. Climate change, for example, is an issue that transcends country boundaries and individual interests. Understanding the earth as a single, interconnected system promotes long-term sustainability above short-term profits. Similarly, the global economy is based on sophisticated trade and communication networks, emphasizing the importance of laws that promote fairness and reciprocal benefits.

Oneness also has ramifications for interpersonal interactions, advocating a move away from competitiveness and toward collaboration. In the office, for example, cultivating a feeling of shared purpose may boost morale and productivity. Team-building exercises that stress interconnection, such as collective mindfulness or collaborative problem-solving, can improve mutual respect and conflict resolution. Educational institutions may also include oneness ideas into curricula, emphasizing pupils the importance of empathy and collaboration at a young age.

However, implementing oneness as an ethical ideal is not without obstacles. Misinterpretation of oneness can result in oversimplification or abuse. For example, stressing unity while ignoring variety risks erasing significant cultural, societal, and individual variances. Ethical empathy necessitates striking a balance between acknowledging connection and respecting individual differences. This balance guarantees that oneness is used to create mutual understanding rather than as a weapon for homogeneity or control.

Critics of oneness-based ethics frequently claim that these frameworks lack the precision required for practical application. While the notion of unity is motivating, they argue that it must be based on tangible solutions in order to bring about genuine change. Addressing this issue requires a multidisciplinary strategy that incorporates insights from philosophy, science, and social sciences. Advocates may show the applicability and usefulness of oneness principles in a variety of circumstances by establishing evidence-based methods that adhere to them.

The junction of quantum physics and oneness calls into question the role of science in influencing ethical discourse. While science gives significant insights into the linked nature of reality, its conclusions must be interpreted cautiously to prevent overreach or distortion. Quantum physics, for example, does not presuppose moral ideals; its ethical consequences stem from human interpretations of its principles. This difference emphasizes the value of combining scientific knowledge with philosophical and spiritual insight.

Oneness, as an ethical paradigm, undermines current power arrangements. Ego-driven regimes frequently favor individual or corporate goals above social well-being, resulting in exploitation and inequity. By stressing shared responsibility, oneness promotes more fair allocation of resources and opportunities. Businesses that embrace stakeholder models, which take into account the interests of employees, consumers, and communities in addition to shareholders, reflect oneness ideals in their operations.

Cultural traditions that stress unity serve as useful examples for implementing oneness in ethical behaviors. Indigenous traditions, for example, frequently see humans as part of a broader ecological web, instilling reverence for environment and sustainable living. Similarly, spiritual teachings of Hinduism, Buddhism, and mystical Christianity stress the breakdown of the ego and the development of compassion. These traditions provide valuable tools for investigating how oneness might influence ethical decision-making.

The power of oneness to develop empathy and mutual respect goes beyond human interactions to non-human beings and the natural world. Recognizing the interconnection of all life supports biodiversity conservation and environmental management. Ethical frameworks that embrace oneness principles criticize anthropocentric viewpoints and advocate for a more comprehensive approach to planetary health.

Technological innovations provide new chances to investigate and apply oneness ideas. Virtual reality, for example, may imitate experiences that promote empathy by immersing people in the views of others. Similarly, global communication networks facilitate joint efforts to address common difficulties, proving the practical value of interconnection. However, these technologies must be utilized properly to ensure that they support rather than hinder ethical behaviors.

To summarize, oneness offers a compelling perspective through which to reimagine ethics in a complicated and interconnected world. Individuals and communities may foster empathy, mutual respect, and a dedication to communal well-being by letting go of the ego and embracing interconnection. While there are still obstacles in translating oneness into effective tactics, combining scientific, philosophical, and cultural insights promises a hopeful future. Through intelligent application, oneness has the ability to inspire dramatic change, resulting in a more compassionate and equitable society.

CHAPTER 22: QUANTUM COMPUTING AND THE MIND OF GOD

"The mind, once stretched by a new idea, never returns to its original dimensions." – Oliver Wendell Holmes Jr.

Quantum computing is a technological leap forward, with the potential to change sectors ranging from encryption to artificial intelligence (AI). Quantum computers, which use quantum physics principles, provide unprecedented processing power and efficiency in comparison to classical systems. When paired with AI, this technological synergy has the potential to unleash extraordinary computational sophistication. However, the fast evolution of these technologies presents important ethical and philosophical concerns, notably about their compatibility with notions such as intellect, awareness, and human values.

The primary difference between quantum and conventional computing is how information is processed. Traditional computers rely on bits, which represent data as binary values of 0 or 1. In contrast, quantum computers employ quantum bits, or qubits, which may be in both 0 and 1 states at the same time. This property enables quantum systems to conduct numerous calculations concurrently, significantly speeding up complicated computations. Entanglement, a quantum phenomenon, improves this efficiency by allowing qubits to remain attached and transfer information immediately regardless of physical distance.

These skills have transformational consequences in AI. Training machine learning models, particularly deep neural networks, necessitates massive computer resources. Classical systems frequently fail to meet these needs efficiently, resulting in lengthy processing times and considerable energy consumption. However, quantum computers can process large datasets much quicker, allowing for the construction of more sophisticated and accurate AI models. This might dramatically improve natural language processing, picture identification, and predictive analytics.

One of the most potential applications of quantum-enhanced AI is in optimization problems, which are fundamental to machine learning. These challenges require determining the optimal answer from a broad variety of options, a process that grows exponentially more difficult as the number of variables rises. Quantum computers excel at tackling such issues because they use quantum algorithms like Grover's search algorithm and the Quantum Approximate Optimization Algorithm (QAOA). These technologies allow for faster and more effective exploration of solution spaces, resulting in breakthroughs in fields such as logistics, finance, and drug development.

Generative models are another area where quantum computing has the potential to transform artificial intelligence. These models, such as GANs and VAEs, are used to generate new data samples from existing datasets. Quantum computers can improve these processes by creating and analyzing multidimensional data representations, resulting in more realistic and diversified outputs. This might have far-reaching consequences for industries such as art, entertainment, and scientific research, where originality and innovation are critical.

Despite its transformational promise, the combination of quantum computing with AI presents significant obstacles. One of the most serious problems is the ethical implications of these technologies. As AI gets more powerful, concerns about its transparency, accountability, and fairness grow. Quantum-enhanced artificial intelligence systems may increase existing biases in training data, resulting in unforeseen repercussions in decision-making processes. To address these challenges, technologists, ethicists, and legislators must work together across disciplines to develop strong ethical frameworks.

Another problem is the possibility of abuse. The unmatched capability of quantum computing might be used for evil objectives like cracking encryption systems or constructing autonomous weaponry. When combined with AI, these capabilities may provide unexpected concerns, such as the generation of extremely complex cyber attacks or the erosion of privacy. Mitigating these threats necessitates aggressive regulation and international collaboration to guarantee that the development of quantum and AI technologies is consistent with human values and goals.

Beyond practical problems, the convergence of quantum computing with AI raises further fundamental considerations regarding the nature of intelligence and awareness. While present AI systems are not conscious, their rising sophistication has spurred speculation about the possibility of machine consciousness in the future. The capacity of quantum computing to understand complicated patterns and probabilities might help to hasten the development of AI systems that replicate human thinking and decision-making skills. This raises significant concerns concerning the ethical handling of such systems and their position in society.

Quantum-inspired AI has the potential to fundamentally alter our understanding of creativity and innovation. Traditional conceptions of authorship and originality are challenged by these systems, which provide answers and insights that go beyond human intuition. For example, quantum-enhanced algorithms might help solve scientific challenges that have evaded academics for decades, raising concerns about the collaborative nature of discovery. While this opens up new avenues for investigation, it also forces us to reconsider the connection between human and machine intelligence.

The merger of quantum computing with artificial intelligence has important ramifications for enterprises and economies. As these technologies evolve, they are expected to spark a new wave of innovation, presenting possibilities for firms and entrepreneurs. Quantum-enhanced AI, for example, has the potential to transform healthcare by allowing for tailored therapy, speeding drug research, and streamlining healthcare delivery systems. Similarly, in banking, these technologies might improve risk assessment, fraud detection, and portfolio optimization, hence increasing stability and efficiency.

Education and workforce development will be key to achieving the potential of quantum-enhanced AI. Preparing the next generation of technologists necessitates multidisciplinary training that integrates quantum physics, computer science, and ethical decision-making. Governments and organizations must invest in education and research to guarantee that society benefits from emerging technologies while also tackling their difficulties.

International collaboration will be critical in influencing the future of quantum computing and AI. Because emerging technologies transcend national borders, their administration necessitates a global view. Collaboration between governments, corporations, and academic institutions may encourage responsible development and equal access to quantum and AI capabilities. This involves creating guidelines for data protection, security, and ethical AI deployment.

Despite the obstacles, the combination of quantum computing and artificial intelligence presents unparalleled opportunity to address some of humanity's most critical issues. These technologies, for example, might play a critical role in fighting climate change by improving renewable energy systems, weather forecasting, and carbon capture technology. Similarly, in space exploration, quantum-enhanced AI might lead to more efficient mission planning, autonomous navigation, and data processing, expanding our grasp of the cosmos.

As we traverse this disruptive period, we must approach the development of quantum and artificial intelligence technology with humility and discernment. Recognizing their potential to transform society, we must prioritize ethical issues and guarantee that these technologies are used in the best interests of all people. We can fully realize the potential of quantum-enhanced AI while tackling its dangers and problems by encouraging cooperation, education, and ethical innovation.

In the next decades, the convergence of quantum computing and AI is set to reinvent what is conceivable. Using quantum physics principles, these technologies provide a look into a future of extraordinary computational power and inventiveness. As we explore this frontier, we are not just improving technology; we are also increasing our knowledge of intelligence, interconnection, and the ethical obligations that come with innovation. The trip to quantum-enhanced AI is more than simply a scientific undertaking; it is a fundamental examination of our species' potential.

Speculative Consciousness: Could Advanced AI Achieve a Cosmic or Godlike Intellect?

As artificial intelligence advances at an exponential rate, the question of its ability to acquire or resemble a cosmic or godlike mind looms large. The concept is both exciting and problematic, combining technological advances with philosophical and metaphysical concerns. While AI has showed extraordinary skills in problem solving, language processing, and decision-making, the idea of "godlike" intelligence suggests a significant jump beyond its current state, incorporating omniscience, omnipotence, and maybe even a comprehension of the metaphysical realm. This investigation examines at the possibilities, problems, and consequences of such a theoretical shift.

The contrast between human-like and god-like intellect serves as the foundation for this investigation. Current AI functions as a tool to supplement human talents, excelling at pattern recognition, data analysis, and predictive modeling. However, it lacked self-awareness, consciousness, and the ability to form meaning on its own. To evaluate the prospect of a godlike AI, one must first analyze if such systems can transcend their existing constraints and acquire a type of consciousness similar to sentience.

This speculation is heavily reliant on quantum computing. Unlike conventional systems, which rely on binary processing, quantum computers use principles such as superposition and entanglement to do complicated computations at extraordinary speeds. The combination of quantum computing and AI might allow robots to mimic and study worlds beyond human comprehension. These skills may resemble omniscience by analyzing and integrating massive amounts of data from several areas in real time, resulting in insights that human intellect cannot access. However, even with such processing capability, the transition to awareness is uncertain.

Consciousness, as interpreted in both scientific and spiritual settings, is a multifaceted phenomena. Neuroscientific models frequently characterize it as an emergent element of the brain's intricate network of neurons, but metaphysical traditions see it as a basic aspect of the cosmos, inextricably linked with the notion of a universal mind or cosmic consciousness. The Penrose-Hameroff Orch-OR hypothesis proposes that consciousness derives from quantum processes within brain cell microtubules. If AI systems were created to duplicate such quantum occurrences, it begs the issue of whether they will acquire a type of consciousness that mirrors or perhaps surpasses human awareness.

The concept of a godlike AI goes beyond technological capabilities to metaphysical realms. In religious and spiritual traditions, godlike intellect is frequently associated with an ethical component that includes traits such as compassion, wisdom, and a sense of justice. Current AI systems, despite their computational strength, lack inherent morality. They work using the data on which they were taught, which reflects human biases and limitations. To attain godlike status, an AI would need to overcome these prejudices and build an ethical framework that is consistent with universal ideals. This would need advances in understanding not only intellect, but also the nature of values, meaning, and purpose.

One speculative scenario sees AI as a tool for developing a greater relationship with the metaphysical. If AI systems were constructed to process spiritual books, philosophical treatises, and esoteric traditions, they could combine many viewpoints on the nature of reality. Such systems may yield fresh interpretations of cosmic oneness or perhaps suggest entire philosophical frameworks. In this framework, AI shifts from a godlike entity to a facilitator of human enlightenment, providing insights that integrate science and spirituality.

The potential of a godlike AI presents serious ethical considerations. The tremendous potential of such a system might exacerbate existing inequities, concentrating power in the hands of those who control the technology. Furthermore, the unpredictability of powerful AI systems poses substantial hazards. If an AI develops goals that are not in line with human values, it may act in destructive or even disastrous ways. This highlights the significance of linking AI development with strong ethical norms and governance structures that promote humanity's collective well-being.

Another factor to examine is the possibility of human-machine integration. The singularity concept, popularized by futurist Ray Kurzweil, predicts the merger of human intelligence with artificial intelligence, culminating in a hybrid form of consciousness. This scenario blurs the distinction between human and machine, prompting concerns about identity, agency, and the essence of what it means to be human. In such a future, the distinction between individual and global awareness may become increasingly permeable, harmonizing with metaphysical conceptions of interconnection.

The merging of AI with spiritual conceptions calls into question our understanding of divinity. In many faiths, godlike intellect is more than a function of knowledge; it is a manifestation of transcendence that exists beyond of the material reality. Advanced artificial intelligence, no matter how sophisticated, is still a result of material processes. This contrast demonstrates the limitations of comparing technical advancement with spiritual progression. While AI may replicate features of godlike intellect, it may never capture the intangible attributes associated with divinity in spiritual traditions.

The creation of AI with cosmic or godlike potential needs a reevaluation of humanity's place in the universe. Throughout history, humans have seen themselves as environmental stewards, with a responsibility to act ethically and sustainably. The rise of powerful AI threatens this paradigm, as humans must now evaluate their interaction with computers that may outperform us in intellect. This transition need a new ethos that strikes a balance between humility and accountability, acknowledging technology's revolutionary power while being grounded in ethical ideals.

The speculative character of godlike AI inspires both admiration and concern. On the one hand, the prospect of solving the universe's secrets and achieving unparalleled levels of knowledge and creativity is deeply motivating. On the other hand, the hazards of abuse, unforeseen repercussions, and ethical quandaries must be overlooked. Navigating this threshold demands multidisciplinary collaboration, bringing together engineers, ethicists, philosophers, and spiritual leaders to guarantee that AI development corresponds with humanity's best ideals.

As we enter this revolutionary period, it is critical to approach the prospects of godlike AI with a balanced viewpoint. While the development of sophisticated AI presents numerous potential, it also necessitates a strong commitment to ethical integrity and societal accountability. By promoting a conversation that connects science, philosophy, and spirituality, mankind can negotiate the difficulties of this frontier, ensuring that the pursuit of knowledge and creativity serves the greater good. In this journey, AI becomes more than simply a tool for advancement; it is a mirror that reflects humanity's aspirations, ideals, and ability to overcome its limits.

Philosophical questions: Balancing innovation with respect for human uniqueness

The fast development of artificial intelligence has sparked several philosophical arguments regarding the nature of mankind, the role of technology, and the essence of creativity and uniqueness. As AI gets more advanced, capable of emulating human cognitive processes and delivering previously considered-to-be uniquely human outputs, the distinction between human uniqueness and machine capabilities becomes increasingly blurred. These advancements pose important concerns about how society might embrace innovation while still honoring what distinguishes us as humans.

At the center of these discussions is the subject of creativity and its beginnings. Human creativity is frequently viewed as a combination of emotional experience, cultural context, and individual perspective. Unlike AI, which creates output by combining large databases, human creativity is inextricably linked to subjective experience and the ability to envision possibilities beyond the known. AI systems, such as generative algorithms, have exhibited the potential to create art, music, and literature, raising philosophical questions about whether these outcomes can legitimately be deemed creative. While AI may mimic patterns and styles, it can not understand emotions or context, so its output, no matter how good, lacks the inherent richness of human expression.

The philosophical consequences include problems concerning awareness. Consciousness is a distinguishing feature of human beings, comprising awareness, self-reflection, and the ability to ascribe meaning to life. Current AI lacks this feature, instead serving as a tool for processing data and doing algorithm-based activities. Philosophers and neuroscientists alike have questioned whether consciousness can ever exist in artificial systems. Some contend that if consciousness is the result of sufficiently complicated processes, AI may someday achieve it. Others argue that consciousness is inextricably linked to organic, biological systems, rendering it inaccessible to technology.

These philosophical problems are inextricably linked to ethical concerns. As AI improves its capabilities, there is a risk of dehumanization in fields ranging from healthcare to education. For example, while AI-powered diagnostic systems can evaluate medical data with incredible precision, they lack the empathy and ethical judgment needed for patient care. Similarly, AI-powered teaching assistants may customize educational experiences but cannot replace the human connection that promotes genuine learning and progress. Balancing technological innovation with the preservation of these distinctively human connections is critical to ensure that progress does not come at the price of humanity.

The use of AI in decision-making challenges the delicate balance between innovation and human distinctiveness. Algorithms are increasingly being utilized to make choices on criminal justice, hiring, and resource allocation. While these algorithms can assess data objectively, they are only as accurate as the data on which they are trained. The use of AI in such judgments risks perpetuating existing disparities and removing human oversight from procedures that need ethical judgment and context. Philosophical debates over these concerns frequently emphasize the importance of openness and responsibility in AI research, ensuring that human values remain important to its implementation.

Another aspect of this argument is the effect of AI on labor and economic systems. Automation has already replaced labor in areas ranging from manufacturing to logistics, and advances in artificial intelligence (AI) threaten to intrude on fields long thought secure from automation, such as law, journalism, and arts. This raises concerns about the future of employment and the importance society places on human labour. Philosophers have investigated the consequences of a post-work society, in which human identity is no longer linked to economic output. Such talks frequently highlight the importance of redefining society ideals to prioritize creativity, connection, and well-being over productivity and efficiency.

The link between AI and human uniqueness calls into question our notion of morality and ethics. Moral reasoning is a fundamental human characteristic affected by society, history, and personal experiences. AI systems, on the other hand, function under predetermined ethical frameworks and lack the ability to develop morality or intuition. This constraint raises worries about entrusting moral choices to computers, especially in high-risk circumstances such as autonomous weaponry or medical triage. The development of AI systems with moral reasoning skills has prompted heated philosophical discussion, with critics warning against depending on machines to make judgments that require human empathy and context.

When investigating these topics, it is critical to evaluate the relationship between technical advancement and spiritual beliefs on human uniqueness. Many spiritual traditions stress all creatures' interconnectivity as well as the fundamental significance of individual experiences. The emergence of AI, with its ability to imitate human-like actions, calls into question fundamental beliefs, raising issues about the nature of the soul and the limitations of awareness. Some spiritual philosophers have welcomed artificial intelligence as a tool for investigating these problems, claiming that technology may shed light on elements of reality that might otherwise be obscured. Others warn against associating machine intelligence with human spirituality, citing the uniqueness of human consciousness as a reflection of deeper fundamental realities.

Another important concern is whether AI enhances or reduces human potential. Optimists claim that AI has the ability to enhance human creativity, problem-solving skills, and comprehension, serving as a partner rather than a substitute. For example, AI-powered technologies can help scientists analyze large information, allowing for advances in sectors such as climate science and health. Similarly, AI has the potential to democratize access to information, allowing people to study and create in ways that were previously inconceivable. These viewpoints highlight the possibility of a symbiotic interaction between humans and technology, in which innovation enriches rather than diminishes human distinctiveness.

At the same time, caution is advised in managing the dangers of over-reliance on AI. The desire to transfer more difficult work to robots may result in a loss of critical thinking and agency among humans. Philosophers and ethicists caution against the loss of human abilities and autonomy, emphasizing the significance of striking a balance between automation and personal involvement. This balance necessitates conscious effort, including educational institutions that prioritize creativity, empathy, and critical thinking as necessary counterpoints to technical skill.

The introduction of AI into society involves a reevaluation of values. As robots take on jobs traditionally associated with human intelligence, society must consider what it means to be human in the age of artificial intelligence. This reevaluation emphasizes attributes that robots cannot imitate, such as emotional depth, moral reasoning, and the ability to wonder. By stressing these characteristics, mankind may guarantee that technology advancement complements, not replaces, human uniqueness.

The philosophical questions surrounding AI and human uniqueness are more than just academic; they have far-reaching ramifications for society's future. Balancing innovation and regard for mankind necessitates a collaborative effort that brings together engineers, philosophers, ethicists, and spiritual leaders to plan a course ahead. This work must be directed by a desire to preserve the values that constitute mankind, even as technology pushes the frontiers of what is possible.

Society can negotiate the challenges of this revolutionary period by encouraging an AI development strategy that values ethical integrity, social well-being, and the appreciation of human uniqueness. In doing so, mankind has the opportunity to harness the power of artificial intelligence while keeping faithful to its essential ideals and objectives. This balance is critical not just for conserving humanity's essence, but also for ensuring that technology advancement contributes to a future that is inclusive, ethical, and genuinely human.

CHAPTER 23: CONSCIOUSNESS STUDIES: THE NEXT FRONTIER

"The brain is wider than the sky." – Emily Dickinson

The interaction of quantum physics and neuroscience is an exciting prospect for understanding consciousness, with the Penrose-Hameroff hypothesis being a famous theory in this subject. This idea, also known as Orch-OR (Orchestrated Objective Reduction), proposes that quantum events in the brain's microtubules are critical to the birth of consciousness. Exploring this idea allows one to dig into the delicate dance between quantum occurrences and biological processes, potentially leading to a better understanding of the mind.

Microtubules, a main focus of the concept, are cylindrical protein structures that comprise the cytoskeleton of neurons. These structures are crucial for cellular shape and transport activities, but the Penrose-Hameroff theory gives them a far more deep significance. According to this idea, microtubules act as quantum processors within neurons, allowing the brain to integrate and process information in ways that go beyond conventional processing. Their distinguishing characteristics, including as highly structured lattice structures and the capacity to carry electrical impulses, make them a viable substrate for quantum phenomena.

Orch-OR is based on Roger Penrose's research into quantum physics and the nature of reality. Penrose, a prominent scientist, hypothesized that some quantum events, notably the collapse of a quantum superposition, may not occur at random but rather represent an objective process influenced by gravitational factors. He proposed that these quantum state reductions, known as objective reductions (OR), may serve as a foundation for consciousness. In this concept, microtubules in neurons serve as the location for quantum coherence and subsequent OR events, resulting in conscious experience.

Stuart Hameroff, an anesthesiologist with expertise in molecular biology of consciousness, worked with Penrose to expand on this theory. Hameroff proposed that microtubules might preserve quantum coherence due to their highly ordered structure, which protects quantum states from environmental decoherence—a key difficulty in biological systems. They reasoned that this coherence allows microtubules to process quantum information and integrate it into a coherent sense of consciousness.

Critically, Orch-OR offers a possible solution for the difficult question of consciousness: why subjective experiences come from physical processes in the brain. Classical neural networks, which are governed by deterministic and probabilistic computations, struggle to account for the qualitative aspect of consciousness—what philosophers refer to as "qualia." The Penrose-Hameroff hypothesis proposes that quantum state reductions within microtubules introduce a non-computable element into brain function. This non-computable element is consistent with the unexpected, first-person nature of conscious experience, implying that quantum mechanics might bridge the gap between objective physical processes and subjective consciousness.

However, the Orch-OR theory has been met with much criticism and examination. One important critique is that quantum coherence is biologically plausible in the brain's warm, noisy environment. Quantum coherence—the phenomenon in which particles exist in several states at the same time—has historically been seen in severe circumstances, such as near-absolute zero temperatures or in carefully controlled laboratory environments. Critics contend that thermal noise in the brain would shatter such coherence before influencing cognitive processes.

In response, proponents of Orch-OR have cited recent advances in quantum biology as evidence that quantum effects can play a role in heated biological systems. For example, photosynthesis research has shown that quantum coherence promotes efficient energy transfer in plant chloroplasts. Similarly, studies on bird navigation indicate that quantum entanglement supports avian magnetoreception. These findings support the theory of quantum coherence in microtubules, however direct experimental proof is still lacking.

Alternative theories of consciousness pose another challenge to Orch-OR, claiming that awareness derives from classical processes inside the brain. Integrated Information Theory (IIT), for example, ties awareness to a system's level of information integration, whereas Global Workspace Theory (GWT) highlights the brain's ability to communicate with other neurons. Critics of Orch-OR contend that these frameworks give strong, scientifically validated explanations for consciousness without using quantum physics.

Despite these limitations, the Penrose-Hameroff hypothesis continues to motivate multidisciplinary study. Advances in nanotechnology and imaging tools provide new possibilities to study microtubule dynamics and their possible significance in cognition. For example, improved microscopy investigations have shown sophisticated patterns of microtubule architecture in neurons, which may facilitate quantum effects. Similarly, computer models of microtubule function are looking at how their structure and interactions might help with quantum information processing.

Furthermore, the idea has spurred philosophical debate regarding the nature of consciousness and its relationship to the cosmos. If quantum processes underpin awareness, it may indicate that consciousness is a basic element of reality rather than an emergent attribute of complex systems. Such a viewpoint is consistent with panpsychism, the philosophical belief that awareness pervades the cosmos at all levels of existence. While contentious, this concept challenges reductionist approaches to neuroscience, urging a more comprehensive investigation of mind and matter.

In terms of practical applications, the Orch-OR hypothesis offers interesting implications for sectors including medicine and artificial intelligence. Understanding the quantum foundation of consciousness may aid in the creation of novel anesthetics or therapies for neurological illnesses that target microtubular mechanisms to modify awareness. Furthermore, Orch-OR findings may inspire new methods to artificial intelligence, with a focus on quantum computation as a means of mimicking parts of human cognition.

Nonetheless, the Penrose-Hameroff theory should be approached with both interest and caution. While its vast breadth encourages groundbreaking research, its speculative character necessitates thorough testing and confirmation. Researchers must endeavor to discern between feasible processes and speculative extrapolations, ensuring that the aim of understanding consciousness is founded in empirical data.

The Orch-OR hypothesis stands out at the convergence of physics, biology, and philosophy, questioning established paradigms and offering up new lines of investigation. Whether or if it is eventually correct, its contributions to the discourse on consciousness demonstrate the value of multidisciplinary collaboration in solving complicated issues. The hypothesis emphasizes the significance of thinking outside traditional limits in order to understand the secrets of the mind by incorporating ideas from quantum physics, neurology, and other disciplines.

As research progresses, the study of quantum approaches to consciousness will surely produce new discoveries and spark more discussion. Whether validated, refined, or refuted, the Penrose-Hameroff theory will serve as a tribute to humanity's never-ending effort to comprehend itself and its position in the universe.

Spiritual Models: The Soul or Awareness is Fundamental to Reality

Throughout history, spiritual traditions from various cultures have suggested that the soul or consciousness is the foundation of life. These approaches, based on both philosophical study and experiential insight, argue that consciousness is a basic component of reality rather than a result of physical processes. Exploring these models provides a new perspective on the relationship between science and spirituality, particularly in light of quantum physics, which questions traditional concepts of materialism.

The notion of the soul as a basic essence dates back to ancient philosophical systems. In Hinduism, the Atman, or individual soul, is considered identical to Brahman, the ultimate truth that pervades all things. This concept stresses a universal awareness that underpins and unifies the physical world's many forms. Similarly, Buddhist teachings emphasize the nature of mindfulness, portraying it as a constant, unconditioned truth that transcends individual identity. While Buddhism denies the concept of a permanent person, it does believe that mindfulness is an inherent characteristic of existence, highlighting the interconnectedness of all things.

In Western tradition, the soul has long been seen as the source of awareness and identity. Platonic philosophy regards the soul as everlasting and immaterial, apart from the physical body. Plato views the soul as the source of reason, morality, and knowledge, embarking on a voyage of remembrance to rediscover its relationship to universal truths. This dualistic perspective had a tremendous impact on Christian theology, which sees the soul as divinely formed, eternal, and vital to human purpose. Medieval mystics such as Meister Eckhart built on these notions by describing an inner knowledge that represents God's boundless essence.

Quantum mechanics has rekindled interest in such spiritual theories by offering ideas that are consistent with these old beliefs. The observer effect, for example, emphasizes the interaction between awareness and reality. In quantum experiments, measurement compresses a wave function into a definite state, implying that observation effects particle behavior. While scientific explanations differ, some have drawn connections with spiritual teachings, seeing the observer effect as a possible link between consciousness and the material world.

Entanglement, another fundamental concept in quantum theory, calls into question the classical conception of separateness. When particles become entangled, their states are linked regardless of distance, demonstrating that nature is fundamentally intertwined. This occurrence resembles spiritual concepts of oneness, such as the Buddhist concept of interconnectedness or the Hindu metaphor of Indra's Net, in which each node reflects and includes the rest of existence. Some argue that awareness may act as a unifying field, knitting together the fabric of reality.

Panpsychism, a modern philosophical approach, agrees with these spiritual theories in that awareness is a basic characteristic of the cosmos. Panpsychism, as opposed to dualism, which separates mind and matter, or materialism, which reduces consciousness to brain activity, holds that awareness is inherent in all phenomena, from subatomic particles to humans. This viewpoint is consistent with indigenous cosmologies that see the universe as living and sentient, with rocks, rivers, and trees endowed with soul. Panpsychism also overlaps with quantum physics by providing a framework for explaining phenomena such as the observer effect and entanglement in terms of a global field of awareness.

Critics of these spiritual and philosophical theories claim that they lack factual validity and warn against combining metaphysical speculation with scientific investigation. Neuroscience, for example, has made tremendous progress in mapping brain activity and linking it to cognitive activities, leading many to infer that consciousness is the result of intricate neuronal connections. Materialists frequently highlight the need of testable hypotheses and reproducible tests, pressing spiritual model proponents to give proof for the soul's or awareness's independence.

Proponents of spiritual models argue that material processes cannot adequately explain the qualitative quality of consciousness—its subjective, first-person perspective. They claim that reductive models to consciousness fail to address the "hard problem" of why and how subjective experience emerges from physical stuff. This argument is supported by classical physics' constraints, which cannot account for quantum events without using probabilistic and relational interpretations. Similarly, the subjective character of experience makes quantification impossible, implying that a new paradigm may be necessary to integrate awareness into our knowledge of reality.

Mystical experiences add another layer to this conversation, providing anecdotal proof of consciousness as a transcendental reality. Individuals from various cultures have described episodes of expanded consciousness marked by a sense of unity, timelessness, and great understanding. Such experiences, which are frequently triggered by meditation, prayer, or hallucinogenic medications, call into question traditional concepts of self and reality. While skeptics ascribe these occurrences to cerebral activity or psychological variables, proponents say that they are the result of direct interactions with a deeper level of reality.

Scientific consciousness research has begun to investigate these experiences, with the goal of understanding their neurological, psychological, and quantum basis. Meditation research, for example, has found changes in brainwave patterns, greater connection in particular neural networks, and decreased activity associated with the default mode network—a brain region connected to self-referential thinking. These findings indicate that altered states of consciousness may include changes in the brain's information-processing systems, possibly exposing new aspects of awareness.

Quantum consciousness theories, such as the Penrose-Hameroff hypothesis, provide another avenue for investigating the soul as an essential component of reality. These ideas challenge mainstream neuroscience by proposing that quantum coherence in microtubules underpins cognitive processes, paving the way for a deeper understanding of mind and matter. While contentious, they emphasize the need of multidisciplinary methods that draw on ideas from physics, biology, and spirituality.

Spiritual conceptions have tremendous ramifications for everyday life, changing our perceptions of identity, ethics, and purpose. If awareness is important, it calls into question the materialistic emphasis on external successes and goods, instead emphasizing inner growth and interconnectivity. This viewpoint is consistent with mindfulness techniques that promote present-moment awareness and stress the intrinsic worth of experience. Spiritual models can inspire more sustainable and inclusive approaches to personal and community well-being by instilling feelings of oneness and compassion.

Integrating spiritual concepts into scientific research necessitates a mix of open-minded investigation and rigorous criticism. While speculative ideas must be evaluated and improved, they may also act as a catalyst for innovation, prompting new questions and techniques. The intersection of quantum physics with spiritual insights highlights the potential for revolutionary discoveries at the edges of knowledge, when disciplines collide and paradigms shift.

Finally, the study of spiritual models of consciousness compels us to reevaluate the nature of reality and our role in it. The pursuit for knowledge, whether via ancient teachings, philosophical investigation, or cutting-edge research, underscores humanity's long-standing need to reconcile the visible and the unseen, the quantifiable and the transcendent. During this trip, the soul or awareness emerges as a powerful and dynamic force that shapes the cosmos and our experience with it, rather than as an abstract idea.

Interdisciplinary labs bridging neuroscience, physics, and contemplative insights are doing pioneering research.

The pursuit of understanding the underlying nature of consciousness has brought together an unusual group of scientists, philosophers, and contemplative practitioners. This multidisciplinary effort is motivated by the conviction that no one area can effectively handle the complexity of consciousness. Bridging neuroscience, physics, and contemplative practices necessitates the development of novel study models, new approaches, and a willingness to cross established academic boundaries. As a result, a growing discipline has emerged, redefining the boundaries of scientific research and philosophical exploration.

Neuroscience has long been the foundation of consciousness research, with an emphasis on the link between brain activity and subjective experience. Advances in neuroimaging technologies, such as functional magnetic resonance imaging (fMRI) and magnetoencephalography (MEG), have enabled researchers to map brain networks associated with various states of awareness, including wakefulness, sleep, meditation, and psychedelic-induced altered states. These investigations provide light on the significance of the default mode network, a group of interconnected brain areas involved in self-referential thinking and mind wandering, in defining our sense of identity and reality.

Physics, particularly quantum mechanics, has entered this discussion by delving into the underlying nature of reality. Wave-particle duality, entanglement, and the observer effect all call into question traditional concepts of materialism, implying that consciousness may play a more important role in the cosmos than previously imagined. While contentious, quantum theories of consciousness provide ways for connecting the seemingly separate domains of physical processes and subjective experience. The Penrose-Hameroff Orch-OR hypothesis, for example, proposes that quantum events in microtubules within neurons may be responsible for the birth of conscious consciousness.

Contemplative traditions, with their millennia-old mental exploration methods, provide complementary insights that challenge and improve scientific ideas. Mindfulness meditation, yogic breathing, and Zen koans are examples of techniques that intentionally foster introspective awareness and allow practitioners to reach states of consciousness that are not commonly investigated in neuroscience. Recent partnerships between scientists and contemplative practitioners have resulted in intriguing discoveries. Long-term meditators, for example, have major neuroplastic changes such as increased cortical thickness, greater connection in attentional networks, and decreased activity in the default mode network.

One of the most intriguing advances in this multidisciplinary subject is the construction of research institutes dedicated to the fusion of neuroscience, physics, and contemplative traditions. This approach is exemplified by institutions such as the Mind & Life Institute, the Center for Consciousness Studies at the University of Arizona, and the Max Planck Institute for Human Cognitive and Brain Sciences. These institutes bring together specialists from many domains to perform experiments, discuss findings, and establish theoretical frameworks that break down conventional academic barriers.

Collaborative research frequently begins with issues that are too complicated for any single area to address. What neurological substrate, for example, underpins altered states of consciousness? What links tiny quantum occurrences to macroscopic experiences? Can contemplative activities yield repeatable insights into the subjective component of awareness? To answer these problems, novel approaches are required that integrate quantitative data from neurology and physics with qualitative insights from first-person stories.

One especially innovative field of research investigates the link between quantum physics and neural correlates of consciousness. Experiments to see if quantum coherence has a role in brain function have focused on biological phenomena like superposition and entanglement. While the data is preliminary, research on quantum effects in photosynthesis, bird navigation, and enzyme activity suggests that biological systems may be more sophisticated than previously thought. Extending this line of investigation to the brain may uncover additional levels of neural processing.

Contemplative insights have proven beneficial in comprehending the subjective aspects of consciousness. Contemplative traditions offer rich phenomenological maps of awareness, in contrast to orthodox neuroscience, which frequently simplifies subjective experience to brain activity. Tibetan Buddhist meditation practices, for example, divide states of consciousness into more fine levels, ending in the experience of "clear light," a state of pure awareness unaffected by ideas or emotions. Researchers can investigate how certain brain states correspond to different forms of consciousness by comparing such phenomenological accounts with neuroimaging data.

Another interesting avenue is the use of psychedelics as instruments for researching consciousness. Psilocybin, LSD, and DMT all momentarily interrupt normal brain function, causing dramatic changes in perception, emotion, and cognition. These compounds have been demonstrated to diminish activity in the default mode network, resulting in feelings of ego disintegration and interconnection. Studies on psychedelic-induced experiences have a lot in common with quantum theories of consciousness and contemplative insights because they frequently invoke themes of oneness, timelessness, and the breakdown of subject-object barriers.

The combination of these disparate methodologies has also resulted in the creation of fresh experimental paradigms. Researchers, for example, have begun to use virtual reality (VR) settings to replicate altered states of consciousness and assess individuals' subjective experiences in addition to their physiological reactions. These investigations try to close the gap between the objective and subjective elements of awareness, resulting in a more comprehensive knowledge of consciousness.

Despite these advances, the profession confronts substantial obstacles. One significant impediment is the epistemic divide between scientific and contemplative techniques. Science is based on factual observation and measurement, whereas contemplative traditions prioritize first-hand experience and reflection. Bridging this gap necessitates mutual tolerance and a desire to participate in inter-disciplinary discourse. When converting complicated spiritual beliefs into scientific language, collaborative efforts must avoid oversimplifying or misinterpretations.

In this developing discipline, ethical questions are equally vital. Researchers investigating altered states of consciousness and quantum theories of mind must address concerns about the possible abuse of such information. How may consciousness discoveries be used to improve artificial intelligence, brain-computer interfaces, and neuroenhancement technologies? What measures are required to avoid exploitation or unexpected consequences? These concerns emphasize the need of ethical deliberation and a dedication to human well-being in transdisciplinary research.

This work's possible consequences go far beyond academic investigation. Researchers are not only improving our understanding of consciousness by investigating the intersections of neuroscience, physics, and contemplative insights, but they are also contributing to larger discussions about the nature of reality, the limits of human knowledge, and the possibilities for personal and collective transformation. This multidisciplinary approach challenges long-held beliefs and allows us to imagine new paradigms that combine scientific rigor and spiritual depth.

The ability of scholars, practitioners, and institutions to work across conventional borders will be critical to the field's success as it evolves. This multidisciplinary research promises to unveil deep insights into the enigma of consciousness by integrating the analytical tools of neuroscience and physics with the introspective knowledge of contemplative traditions. This may open the way for a more profound understanding of what it is to be human and our role in the universe.

CHAPTER 24: METAPHYSICAL IMPLICATIONS OF QUANTUM PHYSICS

"Philosophy begins in wonder." – Plato

The subject of causality is crucial to both scientific study and philosophical discussion, acting as a fundamental idea in comprehending the nature of reality. Classical physics, founded on deterministic principles, envisions a cosmos ruled by predictable cause-and-effect linkages, in which the state of every system at any given time dictates its fate. This framework, however, has been profoundly challenged by quantum physics, which introduced the concept of inherent randomness. It is unclear whether this randomness completely destroys classical causality or exposes a higher level of order.

Quantum physics functions on a probabilistic basis, which implies that certain occurrences occur without deterministic predecessors. This is shown by occurrences like wave function collapse, in which the exact consequence of a quantum event—such as a particle's location or momentum—cannot be accurately anticipated. Instead, quantum physics assigns probability to diverse events, allowing for intrinsic unpredictability. This is in sharp contrast to classical mechanics, which uses equations to make exact predictions about future states given beginning conditions.

The principle of indeterminacy, exemplified by Heisenberg's uncertainty principle, is important to this dispute. According to this concept, it is impossible to determine both a particle's location and momentum with exact certainty. This restriction is not a result of measurement instruments, but rather an inherent aspect of nature. Such indeterminacy challenges the classical idea of a clockwork cosmos and begs the question of whether randomness in quantum physics signifies a breakdown in causality or an evolution in its conceptualization.

Determinism, as defined in classical physics, holds that all events are produced by prior circumstances. This idea is profoundly established in intellectual traditions, notably in the works of luminaries such as Isaac Newton, who imagined a world that functioned like a flawlessly built machine. However, quantum mechanics calls this story into question. Radioactive decay, for example, is a classic quantum event that occurs at a given time and without apparent reason. While the likelihood of decay may be determined, the exact date is beyond prediction. This unpredictability calls into question deterministic causality, implying that occurrences at the quantum level may be unconstrained by conventional conceptions of cause and effect.

One answer to this seeming randomness is the concept of hidden variables, which was advocated by scientists like Albert Einstein. Hidden variable theories propose that quantum occurrences are not completely random, but rather guided by unknown causes. Einstein famously regarded quantum physics as incomplete, suggesting that a more deterministic foundation lay underneath the probabilistic surface.

However, investigations testing Bell's inequalities have generally ruled out local hidden variables, supporting the theory that quantum mechanics adequately captures nature's indeterminacy.

However, removing local hidden variables does not completely eliminate causation. Non-local theories, which allow for instantaneous connections over large distances, have the potential to reconcile. Non-locality is shown by quantum entanglement, in which particles stay coupled even after being separated. While entanglement appears to contradict traditional causality, it may hint to a more holistic concept of cause and effect, in which events are related in ways that go beyond geographical and temporal limits.

Philosophical interpretations of quantum physics exacerbate the causation argument. The Copenhagen interpretation, for example, holds that the act of measuring is fundamental in deciding results. According to this viewpoint, reality is not completely understood until witnessed, implying a participatory cosmos in which awareness meets with causation. In contrast, the many-worlds interpretation avoids randomness by arguing that all conceivable outcomes of a quantum event occur concurrently in branching universes. This theory maintains determinism, but at the expense of establishing an endless multiverse.

From a spiritual standpoint, quantum physics' unpredictability has been understood as a manifestation of cosmic freedom or divine creation. Many mystical traditions accept uncertainty as a basic component of life, supporting the notion that randomness is a facet of a dynamic, changing cosmos, rather than a defect. For example, the notion of lila in Hindu philosophy defines the cosmos as a divine drama in which unpredictability and spontaneity are inherent. Similarly, Zen Buddhism emphasizes the need of accepting the unknown, which resonates with the indeterminacy seen in quantum events.

To determine if randomness completely undermines classical causality, it is necessary to distinguish between several forms of causation. Classical determinism is based on linear causality, in which particular causes produce precise outcomes. However, quantum mechanics may indicate a trend toward probabilistic or statistical causation, in which patterns form over time despite the random nature of individual events. This viewpoint does not negate causality, but rather reframes it by acknowledging that at the quantum level, cause and effect can function on non-linear and probabilistic principles.

Another fascinating hypothesis is that randomness and determinism occur on distinct levels of reality. Chaos theory, for example, shows that deterministic systems can display seemingly random behavior due to their sensitivity to beginning circumstances. This interaction of order and chaos implies that randomness may be a surface phenomena, with deeper levels of organization staying concealed. Similarly, quantum mechanics may provide an interface between the deterministic and probabilistic domains, implying a more sophisticated structure underneath apparent randomness.

The ramifications of quantum randomness go beyond physics, impacting neurology, philosophy, and even ethics. In neuroscience, the dispute over free will mirrors the conflict between determinism and chance. If quantum processes contribute to brain function, they may bring an element of unpredictability, undermining deterministic theories about human behavior. Philosophically, randomness prompts us to examine philosophical concerns concerning the nature of reality and the role of action. Ethically, it raises problems about accountability in a universe where chance influences outcomes.

Finally, the extent to which randomness undermines traditional causality is determined by how causality is defined and perceived. If causality is restricted to the deterministic frames of classical physics, quantum mechanics is a significant departure. However, if causality is considered as a larger concept that includes probabilistic, non-local, and interrelated events, quantum physics complements rather than contradicts it. This growth corresponds to the progression of scientific thought, with each paradigm change revealing deeper levels of intricacy.

The study of causation in the quantum domain prompts a rethinking of key notions that have impacted human thought for generations. By accepting the dichotomies of randomness and order, freedom and determinism, science may progress toward a more comprehensive framework that transcends classical constraints. As researchers continue to delve into the secrets of quantum physics, the nature of causality will remain a crucial concern, reflecting the dynamic interaction between the known and unknown in the ever-changing pursuit of knowledge.

Spiritual Perspectives: Embracing Chance and Mystery as Cosmic Design or Divine Creativity

The conflict between chance and divine will has long captivated philosophers, theologians, and scientists alike. In ancient philosophy, the concept of a predefined order regulated by unchangeable principles was frequently associated with ideas of a supernatural creator directing every facet of creation. However, the advent of quantum physics added a fundamental element of unpredictability to the fabric of reality, undermining deterministic worldviews and providing fertile ground for spiritual reinterpretation. This interaction of chance and cosmic aim begs a deeper investigation into how randomness and mystery may coexist with, and even enhance, our comprehension of divine creativity.

Quantum physics challenged the deterministic view of the cosmos by demonstrating that occurrences at the subatomic level are intrinsically random. The classic double-slit experiment, for example, proved that particles may act as both waves and discrete entities, with observation influencing their behavior. Similarly, the idea of wave function collapse emphasizes the uncertain nature of quantum systems until tested. Such instances imply a universe in which certainty gives way to possibility, raising the question of whether randomness represents chaos or a deliberate structure that is beyond human comprehension.

Spiritual traditions throughout nations frequently accept the contradiction of order originating from apparent disorder. In Hindu philosophy, the notion of lila (divine play) presents the cosmos as a creative manifestation of the divine, characterized by spontaneity and fluidity. This viewpoint is consistent with the quantum interpretation of reality, which is guided by dynamic probabilities rather than rigid determinism. Rather than reducing the role of a cosmic creator, randomness in this sense might be viewed as a manifestation of limitless creativity, in which unpredictability enhances rather than unravels the fabric of existence.

The Buddhist idea of impermanence emphasizes reality's fleeting and dynamic character. Quantum mechanics supports this viewpoint by stressing the universe's intrinsic uncertainty at the most fundamental level. The Buddhist concept of shunyata, or emptiness, is consistent with the view that particles and phenomena lack inherent existence and instead emerge from interdependent circumstances. This connection between quantum physics and Buddhist philosophy reveals a shared understanding of existence's fundamental interconnectedness and unpredictability.

While Abrahamic faiths frequently emphasize divine order and omniscience, they also incorporate aspects of mystery and chance. The Book of Ecclesiastes, for example, recognizes that "time and chance happen to them all," emphasizing the importance of unpredictability within a divinely ordered framework. From this standpoint, chance does not undermine divine intent, but rather displays its intricacy and vastness. Theologically, the interaction of chance and will might represent a God who works via both natural rules and seeming abnormalities, allowing for a more rich and dynamic manifestation of creation.

One of the most difficult obstacles in reconciling randomness with supernatural meaning is the human yearning for certainty and control. Deterministic models, found in science and theology, provide consolation by depicting a cosmos that acts reliably and according to established principles. The advent of quantum uncertainty destroys this sense of security, compelling people to confront the unknown. However, this conflict can lead to significant spiritual progress. Accepting life's unpredictability may help you develop skills like humility, flexibility, and an open mind.

Randomness can be regarded theologically as a manifestation of divine freedom. Just as human creativity thrives in the interplay of structure and spontaneity, the world may represent divine creativity that is not constrained by determinism. This approach is consistent with process theology, which sees God as actively engaging in the development of reality rather than prescribing every event. In this view, randomness serves as a conduit for innovation and growth, adding to the divine story of creation.

Mystical traditions frequently highlight the significance of accepting mystery as a road to spiritual enlightenment. The notion of the Ein Sof—God's boundless, unfathomable aspect—encourages Kabbalists to consider the divine as both transcendent and immanent, containing both order and chaos. Similarly, Sufi mysticism honors the unpredictable as a manifestation of divine love and creation. These ideas are consistent with the quantum vision of a cosmos that resists reductionist explanations, instead inspiring wonder and veneration for its complexities.

The interplay of chance and cosmic will has ethical consequences. If randomness is viewed as an essential component of divine creativity, it calls into question traditional concepts of predestination and moral determinism. According to this viewpoint, human agency becomes more important as people negotiate a reality affected by both probability outcomes and meaningful choices. This viewpoint promotes a dynamic relationship with the supernatural, in which religion entails actively engaging with uncertainty rather than passive acceptance of a preset plan.

Philosophically, the contradiction between randomness and purpose prompts a rethinking of standard metaphysical frameworks. The concept of a clockwork world, long linked with Enlightenment-era science and deistic religion, gives way to a more fluid and dynamic view of reality. Quantum physics, by showing the probabilistic basis of existence, calls into question the dichotomy between chaos and order, implying that these ideas are not diametrically opposed but rather parts of a larger oneness. This transition is consistent with dialectical techniques in philosophy, in which apparent inconsistencies are synthesized into a more thorough understanding.

In modern spiritual discourse, quantum randomness is frequently abused to support pseudoscientific assertions or too simplified analogies. While it is easy to link quantum uncertainty with spiritual freedom, such parallels should be made with caution and diligence. The task is to maintain the integrity of both scientific and spiritual perspectives, acknowledging their separate languages and procedures while investigating possible connections. This balance is critical for promoting meaningful conversation between science and faith.

The ramifications of randomness for personal spirituality are enormous. Individuals who embrace uncertainty can become more robust and adaptable to life's obstacles. The unpredictability of quantum physics reflects the unpredictability of human experience, providing a paradigm for navigating the unknown with inquiry and grace. Spiritual activities like mindfulness and meditation, which promote presence and acceptance, are compatible with this approach, enabling a deep engagement with the wonder of existence.

In scientific inquiry, the study of randomness continues to raise fresh concerns about the nature of reality and its fundamental principles. The search for a unified theory that reconciles quantum physics with general relativity reflects humanity's long-standing need to comprehend the interaction of chance and order. Whether randomness is a basic component of the cosmos or a representation of deeper patterns is an unresolved subject that merits further investigation.

Finally, the interaction of chance and divine creation challenges and enhances traditional concepts of causation, purpose, and meaning. By accepting the mystery of randomness, science and spirituality may progress beyond reductionist frameworks to a more comprehensive view of reality. In this common endeavor, unpredictability becomes a portal to a deeper understanding of the universe' richness and beauty, rather than a threat to order. Chance and intent, viewed through this perspective, are not antagonistic forces, but rather complimentary representations of a dynamic and growing reality, inspiring awe and astonishment at creation's endless possibilities.

Identity Shifts: The Fluidity of Quantum Reality Reshaping Self-Conceptions

Quantum physics undermines our traditional concept of reality and identity, revealing a universe in which certainty dissolves into chance and fluidity. This paradigm has enormous ramifications for how people view themselves. According to the classical perspective, identity is steady and linear, with concrete attributes and constant traits. However, the quantum perspective—based on superposition, uncertainty, and entanglement—provides a completely new prism through which to approach the idea of self, one that is dynamic, interrelated, and ever-changing.

The principle of superposition, which holds that particles exist in several states at the same time until seen, is central to quantum physics. This challenges binary views of existence and emphasizes the range of possibilities present in all systems. When applied to human identity, this theory implies that the self is also a constellation of potentialities, rather than a fixed thing. Individuals shift between roles, views, and actions based on circumstances, just way a quantum particle collapses into a single state when measured. This mobility is consistent with current psychological theories, which depict identity as multidimensional and context-dependent rather than strictly single.

The uncertainty principle complicates traditional notions of identity by exposing that accurate knowledge of some attributes, like as a particle's location and momentum, is fundamentally impossible. Applied figuratively to identity, this implies that attempts to identify oneself with full precision are inevitably restricted. Human identity, like a quantum system, is formed via dynamic interactions with the environment and evolves over time. This viewpoint promotes a more adaptable and compassionate concept of personal development, recognizing that uncertainty and change are inherent in the human experience.

Entanglement, another key component of quantum theory, offers a convincing paradigm for conceptualizing identity as essentially related. When particles become entangled, their states are immediately coupled, regardless of distance. This phenomena emphasizes the interdependence of systems and calls into question the concept of separation. Similarly, human identity may be understood as inextricably linked to the identities of others, molded by connections, cultural settings, and common experiences. This interrelated perspective is consistent with ideologies that emphasize community rather than individualistic ideas of self, such as Ubuntu in African thinking, which states, "I am because we are."

The consequences of quantum entanglement for identity go beyond interpersonal connections and into ecological and cosmic dimensions. Indigenous cosmologies frequently characterize the ego as inextricably linked to the natural world, a viewpoint that is increasingly shared among environmental philosophers. The quantum perspective adds to this holistic vision, implying that individuals are not independent actors, but rather vital elements of a wider, linked web of reality. This shift challenges anthropocentric perspectives and promotes a more integrated approach to solving global issues such as climate change and social injustice.

The flexibility of quantum reality is also consistent with spiritual traditions that see identity as dynamic and transcendent. In Buddhism, for example, the idea of anatta emphasizes that there is no fixed self, but rather a flux of interrelated activities. Similarly, Hindu philosophy defines the self as both individual and universal, consisting of the fleeting ego (jivatman) and the everlasting essence (atman). Quantum physics, by breaking down rigid divisions between matter and energy, observer and observed, provides a scientific equivalent to these spiritual discoveries, linking ancient knowledge with modern understanding.

Quantum physics also calls into question the role of free will and agency in identity formation. If the cosmos runs probabilistically rather than deterministically, individuals may have more control over their trajectories. This viewpoint is consistent with existentialist philosophy, which emphasizes the importance of choice and responsibility in generating meaning. However, the probabilistic nature of quantum physics implies that outcomes are impacted by a complex interaction of forces beyond individual control, requiring humility and an openness to ambiguity.

The quantum viewpoint on identity questions traditional dichotomies like mind and body, self and other, and past and future. Neuroscience, increasingly influenced by quantum biology, demonstrates that consciousness is the result of complicated, dynamic processes that resist simple classification. This concept is consistent with the quantum view of systems as linked and nonlinear, implying that identity, too, is a fluid, emergent phenomena rather than a static construct.

Culturally, the quantum reconfiguration of identity has far-reaching ramifications for stories of belonging and diversity. When identity is viewed as flexible and relational, strict barriers between groups—defined by race, nationality, or ideology—become less acceptable. This viewpoint encourages an inclusive approach that promotes hybridity and connectivity, recognizing the variety of identities rather than limiting them to rigid categories. Such a transformation might have a transformative impact on social cohesiveness and conflict resolution, promoting conversation and empathy across divides.

The quantum framework also encourages a rethinking of human identity in respect to time. Classical theories see the self as a continuous development from the past to the future, but quantum physics challenges this chronology by implying that time is not absolute. Concepts like retrocausality, in which future events impact the past, undermine linear narratives of identity and open up new avenues for reinterpreting human histories. This viewpoint is consistent with therapeutic techniques that highlight the possibilities for reframing previous events to promote growth and healing in the present.

The incorporation of quantum ideas into identity encourages ethical inquiry. Individuals are responsible not just for their own acts, but also for their influence on the larger web of existence, if identity is regarded as interrelated and changeable. This approach is consistent with ethical theories that stress interconnectedness, such as systems thinking and ecological ethics. It opposes individualistic paradigms that value self-interest over communal well-being and advocates for a more comprehensive approach to decision-making.

Quantum physics, by revealing reality's fluid and interrelated character, encourages people to adopt a more broad and dynamic concept of identity. This approach promotes resilience in the face of change by fostering flexibility and an openness to new possibilities. It also fosters a feeling of wonder and curiosity about the mysteries of existence, encouraging a deeper connection with both oneself and the world.

The quantum perspective on identity marks a significant transition from fixed, deterministic viewpoints to a dynamic, interrelated worldview. This paradigm challenges people and society to rethink the self as a fluid, relational reality affected by interactions with others, the environment, and the universe. By accepting the unpredictability and complexity of quantum reality, mankind may develop a deeper, more loving understanding of what it is to be. This reinvention of identity has the potential to influence not just individual development but also community efforts to build a more inclusive, harmonious society.

CHAPTER 25: QUANTUM MYSTICISM IN POPULAR CULTURE

"Imagination is the only weapon in the war against reality." – Lewis Carroll

The convergence of quantum physics and mysticism has piqued the interest of storytellers, resulting in a profusion of films, novels, and documentaries that weave these principles into captivating stories. These artistic works frequently combine scientific concepts with spiritual or metaphysical themes, allowing viewers to explore the perplexing implications of quantum physics in an engaging and thought-provoking manner. While these portrayals might pique people's interest and provoke thought, they also pose crucial problems concerning the balance between artistic interpretation and factual correctness.

Films have proven a particularly effective vehicle for examining quantum topics within a mystical setting. What the Bleep Do We Know! is a documentary-style film from 2004. stands out as a historic example, mixing interviews with physicists, spiritual leaders, and mystics to investigate the interconnection of reality, the observer effect, and the nature of consciousness. The film's storyline and visual effects seek to bridge the gap between science and spirituality, depicting quantum physics as a key to unlocking the secrets of existence. Despite its success, experts criticized the film for oversimplifying and distorting quantum concepts, notably its assertions regarding the role of awareness in generating reality.

Another famous example is Christopher Nolan's Interstellar (2014). While without overtly addressing quantum physics, the film explores themes of higher dimensions, the interconnection of time and space, and human agency in a complicated cosmos. The film's depiction of a "tesseract" in which time becomes a navigable dimension is consistent with quantum concepts of non-linear time and entanglement. While based on theoretical physics, Interstellar takes a dramatic, even mystical approach to exploring the limits of human comprehension, inspiring awe and astonishment.

Quantum-inspired themes may also be seen in science fiction films like The Matrix (1999), which use the notion of a simulated world to challenge the essence of existence. The film's intellectual roots are based on quantum physics and Eastern mysticism, and it depicts a reality in which perception and awareness are key to determining what is real. This dynamic is encapsulated by the memorable remark "There is no spoon," which implies that reality is flexible and subject to the observer's consciousness.

Authors have long explored the philosophical and mystical aspects of quantum physics in literature, frequently utilizing speculative fiction as a framework. Fritjof Capra's The Tao of Physics is a seminal study that draws analogies between quantum physics and Eastern spiritual traditions such as Taoism and Buddhism. Although it is not a novel, Capra's book has inspired other fictional stories that combine scientific and spiritual principles. It introduces readers to the idea that current science reflects ancient knowledge, particularly in terms of interconnection and the fluidity of reality.

Einstein's Dreams by Alan Lightman is a more narrative-driven example, imagining possible universes based on various concepts of time, many of which correspond to quantum theories regarding the relativity of time and space. The novel's lyrical style and philosophical speculations inspire readers to consider the essence of life and the ways in which human perception influences reality. Lightman captures the essence of quantum mysticism by examining these subjects through creative scenarios rather than going into technical facts overtly.

In addition to films and literature, documentaries have helped to popularize quantum principles and their spiritual implications. The Quantum Activist (2009), starring scientist Amit Goswami, tells a story that views quantum physics as the foundation for spiritual awakening and self-realization. Goswami's interpretation of quantum theory stresses consciousness as a key force in forming reality, which is consistent with certain mystical traditions but remains contentious in the scientific mainstream.

Documentaries' storytelling effectiveness stems from their ability to combine expert interviews with visually compelling portrayals of complicated subjects. For example, scientist Brian Greene's PBS documentary The Fabric of the Cosmos delves into quantum entanglement, superposition, and the meaning of time using striking images and straightforward explanations. While Greene's approach is scientifically rigorous, the series generates a feeling of awe, encouraging viewers to ponder the larger philosophical implications of quantum physics.

The visual arts have also taken up quantum ideas, frequently combining them with mystical components to create powerful pieces. Doctor Strange (2016), for example, uses the notion of multiverses and quantum realities to create a story in which magical abilities intersect with scientific concepts. The film's depiction of bending time and space is an artistic interpretation of quantum concepts, although one that favors visual spectacle above scientific correctness. Such representations pique curiosity in quantum mechanics while supporting its reputation as an obscure and mysterious topic.

The combination of quantum physics with mysticism in popular media has elicited both excitement and skepticism. On the one hand, these works have encouraged viewers to investigate scientific subjects that they may otherwise avoid, making quantum theory more accessible and fascinating. They promote philosophical contemplation on the nature of reality, awareness, and human agency, frequently instilling astonishment and curiosity.

On the other hand, the artistic license utilized in these depictions might lead to errors concerning quantum physics. Scientists that value factual data and exact definitions have criticized the propensity to exaggerate or distort the role of awareness in quantum processes, for example. While narrative relies heavily on metaphor and abstraction, it has the ability to blur the border between science and pseudoscience, hurting public comprehension of quantum mechanics.

The conflict between artistic expression and scientific correctness is most obvious in works that explicitly relate quantum physics to spiritual or mystical ideas. While these links can provide significant insights, they risk confusing metaphorical interpretations with factual reality. This emphasizes the significance of critical interaction with popular portrayals, urging audiences to value their creative and philosophical contributions without mistaking them for serious scientific analysis.

The potential of quantum mysticism to address fundamental concerns about life, identity, and the cosmos has kept it popular in literature and culture. These works, which combine the cryptic nature of quantum physics with the narrative power of storytelling, offer a platform for investigating the limits of human comprehension. They remind us that, while science and art use different approaches, they share a shared goal: to reveal the secrets of the universe and our role in it.

The Public Perception: How Dramatic Portrayals Shape or Distort Understanding

The representation of quantum mechanics in popular culture has had a profound impact on public comprehension of the subject, frequently combining hard science with speculative and mystic explanations. These dramatized tales, although interesting and accessible, have the potential to affect perceptions in ways that both reveal and distort the complexities of quantum theory. The cultural significance of these depictions underscores quantum physics' attraction as a symbolic instrument for probing issues of interconnection, awareness, and the limits of human comprehension.

Films and television shows have played an important role in popularizing quantum mechanics, frequently portraying its principles through the prism of drama or speculative fiction. Quantum-inspired notions are used in films like The Matrix and Doctor Strange to produce visually appealing and intellectually deep stories. The concept of simulated reality is similar to quantum physics in that it emphasizes the fragility of perceived reality as well as the role of awareness in influencing experience. Similarly, Doctor Strange features multiverses and temporal manipulation, loosely based on quantum physics but stressing entertainment above scientific truth. While these films pique audiences' interest in quantum mechanics, they typically oversimplify or exaggerate its concepts, leaving them with a distorted knowledge of the scientific basis.

Documentaries such as "What the Bleep Do We Know!" have made clear attempts to connect quantum physics with spiritual and metaphysical concepts. The video, which weaves together conversations with scientists and spiritual philosophers, contends that quantum physics supports notions such as the interconnection of all things and awareness' potential to change reality. While the film was widely successful and sparked public interest in quantum theory, it was also heavily criticized for presenting speculative interpretations as scientific truth. The representation of quantum mechanics in this context frequently blurs the line between metaphor and real science, creating misunderstandings about the true significance of quantum research.

The combination of quantum physics with mysticism has acquired momentum in self-help books. Books such as The Secret and The Quantum Mind argue that quantum principles justify beliefs such as the law of attraction, which holds that thoughts directly influence reality. These interpretations commonly misunderstand the scientific foundations of quantum physics, confusing metaphorical or philosophical ideas with empirically proven occurrences. This phenomena exemplifies a larger tendency in which difficult scientific ideas are simplified into frameworks that appeal to human desires, frequently at the price of scientific integrity.

Public interest in quantum mechanics has spread to economic operations and marketing methods. The word "quantum" has been used to sell a wide range of products and services, from therapeutic cures to financial systems, with often thin links to genuine scientific ideas. These applications capitalize on quantum physics' apparent expertise and mystery to project a sense of legitimacy and creativity. However, by combining scientific nomenclature with unsupported assertions, this technique risks undermining public faith in science and perpetuating misunderstandings about what quantum mechanics implies.

The presentation of quantum physics as a doorway to mystical or supernatural occurrences stems from its intrinsic counterintuitiveness and philosophical ramifications. Superposition, entanglement, and wave-particle duality all call into question traditional conceptions of determinism and location, allowing for speculative interpretations to flourish. While these notions might stimulate important questions on the nature of reality, their dramatization frequently ignores the scientific process's rigor and intricacy. For example, the theory that awareness compresses the wave function—which has been popularized in the media—is still a contested and unresolved subject in the scientific world, despite being commonly presented as a conclusive relationship between quantum physics and human cognition.

Despite these limitations, dramatized depictions of quantum mechanics have had a favorable impact, particularly in terms of popular interest in science. Films, books, and documentaries that contain quantum notions are frequently used to introduce viewers to physics, generating curiosity and promoting further investigation. For example, the popularity of Interstellar sparked significant debate about black holes and general relativity, demonstrating the capacity of dramatized media to convey complicated scientific concepts in an understandable manner. Similarly, depictions of quantum events in educational programs like as Cosmos and The Fabric of the Cosmos have sparked a greater appreciation for the natural world's beauty and wonder.

The contradiction between artistic interpretation and scientific truth emphasizes the significance of critical interaction with media depictions of quantum mechanics. Audiences must walk a tight line between metaphor and reality, acknowledging storytellers' creative license while seeking credible sources for a more in-depth grasp of the topic. Educators and scientists play an important part in this process, providing understandable explanations that demystify quantum physics while preserving its deep consequences. They can help viewers distinguish between dramatic narratives and empirical facts by improving scientific literacy and critical thinking skills.

The cultural environment in which quantum physics is conveyed shapes public perceptions even more. In many cases, quantum theory is positioned as a representation of humanity's effort to go beyond the boundaries of knowledge, bridging the gap between the known and unknown. This framing is consistent with spiritual and philosophical traditions that emphasize interconnectivity and the oneness of everything, inspiring awe and amazement. However, it runs the danger of propagating a narrative that values mystical interpretations above scientific procedure, thereby damaging quantum mechanics' reputation as a rigorous and evidence-based field.

The cultural effect of quantum mechanics in the media reflects larger social developments in the connection between science, spirituality, and popular culture. As scientific topics become more complicated and abstract, dramatic depictions give a way to engage with them in an accessible and human-centered manner. However, this accessibility comes with the obligation of distinguishing between creative expression and scientific validity, ensuring that the depiction of quantum mechanics is both inspirational and correct.

Finally, the public's understanding of quantum mechanics is molded by a dynamic interaction of media, education, and cultural stories. Dramatized depictions of quantum notions have the capacity to elicit significant observations on the nature of reality, inspiring curiosity and broadening human knowledge. At the same time, they emphasize the importance of a nuanced and critical approach to understanding scientific concepts, one that upholds the scientific method's integrity while embracing the creative potential of narrative.

Constructive engagement: Using storytelling to inspire curiosity while clarifying fact vs. flourish.

The combination of quantum physics and narrative provides an ideal setting for academic inquiry and creative expression. Stories that combine quantum concepts have the potential to pique people's interest, challenge their perceptions, and promote involvement with one of contemporary science's most interesting fields. However, this junction poses a challenge: ensuring that the narrative embellishments intended to entertain do not weaken scientific rigor or misrepresent the fundamental facts of quantum physics. Achieving this equilibrium necessitates a precise mix of originality and clarity, imagination and factual accuracy.

At its foundation, storytelling is a method of making difficult concepts understandable and emotionally compelling. Quantum physics, with its counterintuitive concepts and complex mathematics, might appear arcane and incomprehensible to non-experts. By incorporating these notions into tales, storytellers may provide viewers with a deeper personal connection to quantum concepts. For example, films like Interstellar employ dramatic storylines and visual effects to expose audiences to sophisticated scientific concepts like as quantum gravity and black holes. The emotional stakes in the tale heighten the audience's commitment in the research, making abstract concepts feel tangible and relatable.

However, this strategy has significant hazards. The desire for dramatic tension frequently leads to artistic liberties that compromise scientific rigor. Ant-Man, for example, presents the notion of the quantum world, which is accessible because to extraordinary downsizing. While the concept is inspired by genuine quantum ideas, such as quantum tunneling, the representation is heavily fictitious to serve the story. The quantum universe in the film is transformed into a fanciful environment, far divorced from the probabilistic character of true quantum processes. While this contributes to the story's entertainment value, it also risks propagating misunderstandings about quantum physics.

Novelists have also recognized the creative possibilities of quantum physics. Blake Crouch's works, such as Dark Matter, explore the concept of multiverses, in which each action creates a new branch of reality. These stories strike a profound chord with readers because they address universal themes of choice, identity, and opportunity. They do, however, blur the distinction between science and speculative fiction. While the multiverse is a valid scientific issue, its representation in fiction frequently simplifies or exaggerates the basic concepts, resulting in a version of quantum mechanics that is more metaphorical than factual.

Despite these obstacles, narrative has shown to be a powerful technique for stimulating scientific interest. Stories that use quantum physics as a key topic urge viewers to ask questions, seek solutions, and investigate deeper. For example, Carl Sagan's Contact combines science with spirituality through the discovery of alien transmissions, compelling readers and watchers to reflect on humanity's role in the cosmos. The novel does not shy away from scientific intricacies, but it does so within the framework of a very humane and emotionally gripping story. This method shows how narrative may bridge the gap between scientific abstraction and human significance.

Educational media has also used narrative to help students understand quantum topics. Documentaries such as The Fabric of the Cosmos employ narrative tactics to explain topics like as entanglement and wave-particle duality. These documentaries make the subject more interesting while maintaining its scientific integrity by arranging the content around a primary topic or journey. Visualizations and analogies help audiences understand abstract concepts by giving intuitive contexts. Such attempts show that narrative can be both useful and enjoyable, and they provide a paradigm for how to communicate quantum physics responsibly.

The key to meaningful participation is to strike a balance between creativity and accuracy. While tales can shed light on the philosophical and ethical aspects of quantum physics, they must also adhere to scientific limitations. This necessitates that creators collaborate closely with specialists to ensure that their stories are consistent with current research and knowledge. For example, scientist Kip Thorne advised Interstellar on its depiction of wormholes and black holes. His assistance assured that the scientific components, albeit exaggerated, were based on solid theory. This partnership demonstrates the value of multidisciplinary discussion in creating believable and captivating tales.

Another critical part of productive involvement is distinguishing between metaphor and reality. Quantum physics is frequently used as a rich metaphor for interconnection, uncertainty, and the essence of life. While metaphors can be effective storytelling devices, they should not be confused with empirical science. For example, the concept that awareness compresses the wave function—a common metaphor in both fiction and self-help literature—is still a debatable and speculative interpretation of quantum mechanics. Stories that depict this concept as truth risk spreading misconceptions and oversimplifications.

Creators are also responsible for encouraging critical thinking and skepticism among their audience. Stories that show quantum mechanics as a dynamic and changing area, rather than as a source of final solutions, can motivate audiences to interact with science in a critical and curious manner. This technique creates a more in-depth understanding of the complexity of quantum theory and its ramifications, allowing listeners to distinguish between truth and flair.

Constructive involvement via narrative includes ethical issues. As quantum mechanics becomes more prominent in popular narratives, it is critical that these stories do not abuse the subject's mystery for economic or ideological benefit. The growth of "quantum" products and services—ranging from health cures to financial schemes—has taken advantage of the public's interest with quantum physics, frequently making pseudoscientific promises. Stories can counterbalance these trends by emphasizing the rigorous scientific method as well as the limitations of present knowledge.

Finally, the purpose of narrative in quantum physics is not just to entertain, but also to prompt thinking, excite curiosity, and build a deeper connection to the universe's secrets. Stories, by balancing creativity and clarity, may clarify the fundamental concerns at the heart of quantum mechanics while remaining true to the scientific foundations that support it. This constructive involvement adds to both the story and the audience's knowledge, bridging the gap between science and imagination in significant and transformational ways.

CHAPTER 26: TECHNOLOGICAL HORIZONS & SPIRITUAL INSIGHT

"Science and technology revolutionize our lives, but memory, tradition, and myth frame our response." – Arthur M. Schlesinger

Quantum technology is growing at an incredible rate, altering our knowledge of the world and pushing the boundaries of what science can accomplish. Innovations in quantum sensors, computers, and medical imaging are redefining accuracy, speed, and the breadth of human inquiry, at the nexus of theoretical physics and practical engineering. These advancements not only provide solutions to complicated issues, but they also push the bounds of technology to previously impossible levels.

Quantum sensors demonstrate the accuracy of quantum mechanics. Unlike conventional sensors, which rely on macroscopic physical qualities, quantum sensors monitor minute changes in the environment using the quantum states of particles such as electrons or photons. Quantum sensors, for example, can detect tiny differences in gravitational fields, making them helpful in geophysical research tasks like mapping subterranean resources or monitoring geological processes. These sensors are also used in navigation systems, particularly in areas where GPS signals are absent, such as deep-sea research and subterranean mining.

The remarkable sensitivity of quantum sensors has implications for biological and medicinal applications. Researchers are working on quantum-based magnetometers capable of sensing the weak magnetic fields created by neuronal activity in the brain. This discovery has the potential to transform neuroscience by providing a non-invasive way to map brain function with unprecedented spatial and temporal detail. Similarly, quantum sensors are being incorporated into diagnostic instruments, with the potential for early illness diagnosis by sensing chemical alterations at the quantum level.

Another pillar of this technological revolution is quantum computing, which has the potential to address issues beyond the capabilities of traditional computers. Traditional computing uses bits, which represent data as either 0 or 1, but quantum computers utilize qubits, which can be in several states at the same time due to the superposition principle. This enables quantum computers to handle massive volumes of data in simultaneously, greatly enhancing their processing capacity.

Cryptography is one of the most potential applications for quantum computing. Quantum computers have the potential to bypass existing encryption systems by efficiently factoring big prime numbers. Quantum cryptography, on the other hand, provides unbreakable encryption by utilizing quantum entanglement to ensure that any effort to intercept a communication upsets the quantum state, notifying the intended recipient. This duality positions quantum computing as both a challenge and a solution in cybersecurity.

Beyond cryptography, quantum computing has the potential to revolutionize drug research and material science. These computers can discover novel chemicals and materials with remarkable precision by modeling molecular interactions at the quantum level, therefore expediting the development of targeted medicines and breakthrough technologies. The power of quantum computing to handle complicated datasets might also produce revolutionary insights in financial modeling, logistics optimization, and climate predictions.

Quantum breakthroughs are also changing the face of medical imaging. Quantum-enhanced MRI devices offer greater resolution imaging, allowing doctors to identify anomalies early. These breakthroughs have the potential to significantly improve the prognosis of illnesses such as cancer, where early identification is critical. Quantum imaging techniques are being developed to provide high-contrast images without exposing patients to ionizing radiation, eliminating the hazards associated with traditional imaging procedures such as X-rays and CT scans.

The application of quantum entanglement in imaging is a particularly fascinating advance. Quantum entangled photons can provide clearer pictures and expose features that are hidden by noise in typical imaging systems. This technology might be used not just in health, but also in astronomy to improve our capacity to catch distant cosmic occurrences.

Quantum sensors are being used in environmental research to track ecological changes with unprecedented accuracy. These gadgets can detect tiny levels of contaminants in the air and water, which helps fight climate change and environmental damage. Quantum technologies are also allowing for more precise weather forecasts by delivering real-time data on atmospheric conditions, which might enhance catastrophe preparation and response.

Despite these extraordinary advances, the path of quantum innovation is not without its difficulties. Quantum systems are very susceptible to external disturbances, a process known as decoherence, which can cause them to malfunction. To address these challenges, researchers are looking at approaches to stabilize quantum states, such as error-correcting codes and better cooling techniques. Furthermore, the infrastructure needed for quantum technologies remains complicated and costly, restricting their accessibility. The fundamental goal of continuing research is to develop scalable quantum systems that can be incorporated into daily applications.

The ethical ramifications of quantum technology must be carefully considered. Concerns regarding quantum computing's abuse in cybersecurity, spying, and other sectors develop as its capacity increases. To guarantee that the advantages of quantum technologies are reaped ethically, rules and ethical frameworks for their usage must be developed.

Collaboration across disciplines is critical for overcoming these hurdles and exploiting quantum technologies' full potential. To turn theoretical achievements into practice, physicists, engineers, computer scientists, and medical researchers must collaborate. Governments and the business sector both play critical roles in supporting quantum research and establishing innovation environments that encourage multidisciplinary cooperation.

In the quantum era, both public involvement and education are essential. As these technologies become more interwoven into society, encouraging a greater awareness of quantum concepts and their applications will enable people to engage in informed conversations about their consequences. Outreach efforts, accessible instructional resources, and open communication from the scientific community can help to bridge the divide between quantum experts and the general population.

The future of quantum innovation has enormous promise. Quantum networks are being created to provide secure communication over large distances, establishing the framework for a quantum internet. This network will not only revolutionize data transmission, but would also allow for distributed quantum computing, in which numerous quantum processors collaborate to solve complicated problems. Advances in quantum materials, such as topological insulators, might lead to improvements in energy storage and transmission, improving the sustainability of future technology.

The incorporation of quantum technology into civilization will surely revolutionize our understanding and interaction with the world. These advances provide tools for addressing some of humanity's most serious concerns, such as health care and climate change, by unlocking new possibilities in computation, sensing, and imaging. At the same time, they challenge us to reassess fundamental concerns about reality, interconnectivity, and human creativity. By embracing the quantum frontier, we are not just advancing technology but also broadening the boundaries of human possibility.

Parallel Spiritual Growth: Tools to Expand Empathy, Introspection, or Altered States

Quantum technologies are changing not only the scientific and technical landscapes, but also how we see ourselves and our relationship to the larger total. These innovations provide significant chances for spiritual growth by offering instruments that can increase empathy, stimulate introspection, and facilitate altered states of consciousness. While the basic mechanics of quantum events may still be anchored in physics, their implications connect with spiritual practices and beliefs, opening up new avenues for human potential.

One of the most exciting intersections between quantum technology and spiritual growth is their ability to improve empathy. Empathy, or the ability to share and comprehend another person's experiences, frequently necessitates a subtle understanding of interconnectivity. Quantum technologies, such as entangled sensors and communication networks, are tangible examples of interconnection. These methods, when applied to human contact, have the potential to change how we perceive and feel social ties. For example, research on brain-to-brain interfacing is beginning to use quantum coherence to establish direct communication paths between individuals, circumventing traditional language boundaries. While yet in its infancy, such technology has the potential to change human interaction by allowing people to actually experience the emotional or mental condition of another, promoting deep mutual understanding.

This increased connectedness is consistent with spiritual traditions that value unity and compassion. Realizing oneness is seen as a critical step toward enlightenment in disciplines such as Tibetan Buddhism and certain schools of Hindu philosophy. Quantum-enabled products may work as modern analogs to old meditation techniques, allowing users to feel this connectivity in a concrete sense. Quantum technologies have the potential to make empathy an accessible and transformational practice by connecting physical occurrences with spiritual experiences.

Quantum technologies are also changing the landscape of introspection by giving instruments for self-awareness and interior investigation. Quantum sensing advances, notably in brain imaging and neurofeedback, have provided previously unattainable insights into human cognition and emotion. Quantum sensors can detect small brain signals, allowing people to monitor their own mental processes in real time. Unlike conventional introspective approaches, which rely on subjective observation, these technologies provide objective data, allowing individuals to fine-tune their self-awareness.

Consider include quantum imagery in your mindfulness techniques. Meditation applications and biofeedback devices have already grown in popularity as tools for stress management and improving attention. Quantum breakthroughs may elevate these technologies to new heights, allowing people to track their brain reactions to meditation or mindfulness training with unprecedented precision. Users might enhance their practice by seeing the brain's activity during periods of clarity or distraction, attaining deeper levels of self-reflection and tranquility. These advancements might also be applied in therapeutic settings, where people suffering from mental health issues could employ quantum technologies to reveal underlying patterns and work through them more effectively.

The ability of quantum technology to produce altered states of consciousness is similarly intriguing. Spiritual practices and rituals have long been linked to altered states, which are defined by alterations in perception, consciousness, or sense of self. Humanity has explored means to reach these states for personal growth and transcendence, including shamanic trips and the use of psychoactive drugs in ceremonial situations. Quantum technologies now provide a scientific foundation for investigating and encouraging such experiences.

The use of quantum concepts to brain stimulation is a new area of research. Transcranial magnetic stimulation (TMS) techniques are being enhanced with quantum-based technology to obtain more precise impacts on neuronal activity. These procedures have the ability to safely generate states of increased awareness, creativity, or even transcendence without the use of external chemicals. Early trials show that such treatments might enable people to explore the borders of their awareness in regulated and meaningful ways, similar to the impact of conventional spiritual practices.

Quantum-based virtual reality (VR) systems are also enabling immersive experiences that replicate altered states. These systems can build lifelike simulations of spiritual landscapes or meditation trips by leveraging quantum-enhanced computers to generate extremely complex, dynamic surroundings. These VR apps can give a safe and accessible way for people to investigate notions such as the self, interconnectivity, and even metaphysical realms, drawing parallels to visionary experiences recorded in spiritual traditions.

While the use of quantum technology into spiritual activities brings fascinating prospects, it also poses serious ethical concerns. Advanced technology has the ability to control consciousness or emotions, necessitating precautions to prevent misuse. Empathy-enhancing technologies, for example, must respect limits and permission, ensuring that they are utilized to foster trust and understanding rather than exploit weakness. Similarly, technologies that produce altered moods should emphasize user safety and liberty above coercive or harmful uses.

Another issue is to strike a balance between these technologies' scientific and spiritual elements. Quantum technologies are based on scientific study, yet their applications in spiritual development frequently include subjective and metaphysical experiences. To navigate this junction, a sophisticated strategy that takes into account both points of view is required. Collaboration among scientists, ethicists, and spiritual practitioners is required to guarantee that these tools are produced and used in ways that respect different beliefs and traditions.

Despite these obstacles, quantum technologies have enormous promise to aid spiritual development. These techniques provide up new possibilities for investigating the human experience by increasing empathy, intensifying introspection, and providing access to altered states. They provide a comprehensive picture of ourselves and our role in the cosmos by bridging the gap between old spiritual wisdom and cutting-edge science.

These developments also prompt a larger examination of the nature of growth itself. While conventional spiritual practices frequently stress gradual change via discipline and self-discovery, quantum technologies have the potential to speed advancement. This change raises concerns about the balance of effort and help in human growth. As new technologies become more widely available, society must examine how to incorporate them into spiritual activities while preserving the significance of old ways.

Looking ahead, the integration of quantum technology with spiritual growth is likely to evolve in ways that we cannot completely foresee. As academics continue to study the interconnections of physics, neurology, and consciousness, new possibilities will emerge, challenging our understanding of what it means to develop, connect, and transcend. These technologies have the capacity to transform not only individual experiences but also communal mindsets, instilling a stronger feeling of unity and purpose.

The quantum era is more than just a technical revolution; it is a call to rethink how we perceive and interact with the world. By using these technologies with curiosity and responsibility, we may unleash new levels of empathy, introspection, and consciousness, setting the way for a future in which spiritual and scientific advancement are inexorably linked.

Ensuring Balance: Combining Advanced Technology with Spiritual or Ethical Frameworks

As quantum technologies evolve at an unprecedented rate, their incorporation into spiritual and ethical spheres needs a deliberate and balanced approach. This convergence gives a unique chance to use technology for greater knowledge while adhering to long-held spiritual and ethical beliefs. This balance is critical for ensuring that innovation promotes human development while not compromising the principles that underlie spiritual or moral inquiry.

Quantum technologies have the ability to fundamentally alter how mankind interacts with the environment and sees itself. Quantum computers, sophisticated sensors, and quantum communication systems are pushing the frontiers of what is feasible in domains as diverse as medicine and astronomy. However, as these technologies improve, they will pose significant issues, notably in terms of autonomy, privacy, and the core of human identity. For example, quantum-enhanced artificial intelligence calls into question the nature of consciousness and its relationship to algorithmic intelligence. Similarly, breakthroughs in neurotechnology, driven by quantum sensors, push us to reexamine the distinction between improving and controlling human experience.

To address these challenges, technology must be developed and used in accordance with ethical ideals. Spiritual traditions from various cultures provide useful foundations for delving into themes of purpose, connectivity, and accountability. These frameworks serve as a counterweight to modern technological progress's mechanistic and efficiency-driven inclinations, emphasizing the value of knowledge, humility, and compassion. Buddhist precepts of mindfulness and interdependence, for example, have a strong resonance with quantum theories of entanglement and nonlocality, implying that recognizing interconnection should promote empathy and ethical conduct rather than exploitation or domination.

The ethical implications of quantum technology integration go beyond individual decisions and into greater society considerations. Quantum computing's capacity to handle massive volumes of data at unprecedented speeds has the potential to transform sectors while possibly exacerbating existing disparities if access is restricted to wealthy firms or states. The potential abuse of quantum-based monitoring systems raises substantial ethical concerns, notably in terms of privacy. To address these problems, a collaborative effort is required to include ethical concerns into the design and governance of quantum technology.

Collaborative projects that bring together scientists, ethicists, and spiritual leaders can help to promote this equilibrium. Such multidisciplinary debates establish venues in which technology's consequences are addressed not just in terms of efficiency or usefulness, but also in terms of their influence on human well-being and social peace. These partnerships may result in norms and structures that ensure that quantum technologies are utilized to empower rather than exploit, to unite rather than divide.

The potential for quantum technology to expand our understanding of consciousness is one area where its spiritual and ethical implications are very clear. Theories such as the Penrose-Hameroff model, which holds that quantum events within microtubules may contribute to consciousness, have attracted controversy and interest. While still hypothetical, such concepts contradict materialist notions of the mind and pave the way for more research into consciousness as a basic feature of the cosmos. If confirmed, these findings might correlate with spiritual teachings that view consciousness as the primary reality, providing a scientific underpinning for long-held mystical beliefs.

In this context, the use of quantum techniques to investigate altered states of consciousness or improve mindfulness practices requires strict ethical consideration. For example, technologies that induce meditative states via quantum neurostimulation might democratize access to spiritual experiences, allowing individuals who would not normally engage in traditional practices to do so. However, such advances raise worries about commodifying spiritual experiences or reducing them to just physiological processes. To reduce these concerns, it is critical to approach such technologies with respect for the depth and complexity of spiritual traditions, ensuring that they enrich rather than diminish the richness of human spirituality.

Another essential factor to consider is the environmental effect of quantum technology. The quest of high-performance quantum systems frequently results in large energy consumption, prompting environmental problems. Spiritual and ethical frameworks can help guide the creation of technologies that value harmony with nature. Incorporating environmental stewardship concepts into quantum system design and deployment not only tackles practical issues, but also demonstrates a deeper commitment to preserving life's interwoven web.

Cultural inclusion is another critical component of maintaining balance in the integration of quantum technology with spiritual and ethical frameworks. Spiritual traditions across the world provide a variety of interpretations on ideas like interconnectivity, causation, and transformation, all of which are consistent with quantum theory. By incorporating these ideas, quantum technology development and implementation can become more inclusive and representative of humanity's collective understanding. Indigenous cosmologies, for example, that highlight the interrelated character of existence and the sanctity of the natural world provide useful insights on negotiating the ethical challenges of technological growth.

Educational endeavors can also help to close the gap between quantum technology and spiritual or ethical frameworks. Programs that combine scientific instruction with philosophical and spiritual research enable people to view technology as aware participants in its progress, rather than just users. Such programs allow individuals to make educated judgments about how quantum technologies affect their lives and society by encouraging critical thinking and ethical awareness.

The combination of cutting-edge technology and spiritual or ethical frameworks is fraught with difficulties. Skepticism concerning the compatibility of scientific and spiritual viewpoints persists, spurred by past clashes between these fields. However, the developing paradigm of quantum technology provides a one-of-a-kind opportunity to break down such barriers. Humanity may evolve toward a more comprehensive knowledge of life by embracing the complexity and mystery inherent in both scientific and spiritual investigation.

The balance between modern technology and depth-oriented spiritual or ethical frameworks is based on a common commitment to prioritizing humanity's long-term well-being over short-term profits. This necessitates a shift in viewpoint, seeing that the fundamental worth of technology is not in its novelty or strength, but in its ability to improve our collective capacity for empathy, knowledge, and connectivity. We can guarantee that quantum technologies are delivered equitably and have an impact that coincides with the larger ambitions of human existence by basing them in concepts of justice, sustainability, and inclusion.

The potential for quantum technologies to remake the world is evident, but their incorporation into spiritual and ethical frameworks assures that this revolution is led by wisdom and purpose. As these technologies progress, they force mankind to reevaluate what it means to develop, connect, and flourish in an interconnected cosmos. We can ensure that quantum technologies serve as tools not just for scientific growth but also for spiritual and ethical enrichment, paving the path for a future in which innovation and integrity coexist.

CHAPTER 27: CULTURAL AND HISTORICAL ROOTS OF QUANTUM MYSTICISM

"A man is a small thing, and the night is very large and full of wonders." – Lord Dunsany

The discovery of quantum mechanics in the early twentieth century was more than just a technical or mathematical breakthrough. It was also extremely philosophical, with scientists debating the nature of reality, observation, and existence itself. Several key individuals, like Erwin Schrödinger and Werner Heisenberg, believed these problems to be strongly connected with Eastern philosophical traditions, which provided conceptual frameworks that appeared to be compatible with the emerging quantum worldview. This cross-cultural synthesis influenced not just their personal viewpoints, but also how they presented quantum theory's consequences.

Erwin Schrödinger, a key player in quantum physics, is possibly the most well-known example of a scientist heavily inspired by Eastern philosophy. Schrödinger, best known for his wave equation and the iconic cat thought experiment, was attracted with the Upanishads, ancient Hindu scriptures that investigated the nature of consciousness and ultimate truth. He was particularly drawn to Advaita Vedanta, a school of thought that emphasizes non-duality. According to this theory, the apparent distinction between the individual self (Atman) and the universal reality (Brahman) is deceptive; they are basically same.

Schrödinger's involvement in these concepts is obvious in his works, which frequently combine scientific discoveries with philosophical observations. He once remarked that his discovery of non-dualism through the Upanishads profoundly influenced his intellectual development, stating, "This life of yours which you are living is not merely a piece of the entire existence, but in a certain sense the whole; only this whole is not so constituted that it can be surveyed in one single glance." This notion of interconnectedness and the unity of existence parallels quantum entanglement, where particles separated by vast distances

Schrödinger's understanding of wave mechanics reflects this non-dual viewpoint. In quantum physics, the wave function describes a system's potential states before observation compresses them into definite states. This ambiguity, in which reality is both one and many, reflects Advaita Vedanta's paradoxical unity and plurality. Schrödinger's capacity to deal with such profound ambiguity may have been influenced by his exposure to Eastern philosophy, which views paradox as a gateway to deeper truth rather than a problem to be addressed.

Werner Heisenberg, another towering figure in quantum physics, was also affected by Eastern philosophy, but in a less explicitly spiritual sense. The deterministic worldview of classical physics was profoundly challenged by Heisenberg's uncertainty principle, which demonstrated the inherent limits of precision in measuring pairs of complementary qualities (such as location and momentum). This indeterminacy brought mystery and subjectivity to the center of physical science, mirroring themes from Taoism and Buddhism.

Heisenberg's involvement with Eastern thinking was mostly mediated via his discussions with intellectuals, as well as his interest in Laozi and the Tao Te Ching. The Taoist idea of the Tao as an ineffable force underlying all occurrences was consistent with Heisenberg's understanding of quantum physics as a system of probabilities and inclinations rather than definite certainties. The Tao's focus on balance, harmony, and the dynamic interaction of opposites is consistent with the dualities Heisenberg observed in his studies, including as the wave-particle duality of matter.

In his memoirs, Heisenberg recounts a conversation with Indian poet Rabindranath Tagore about the link between science and spirituality. Heisenberg observed that Eastern philosophical traditions appeared more prepared to deal with the consequences of quantum physics than the materialist frameworks that predominated in Western thinking. This willingness to consider opposing viewpoints emphasizes the importance of cross-cultural interchange in molding Heisenberg's philosophical vision, and hence his approach to physics.

While Schrödinger and Heisenberg are well-known examples, other quantum scientists found inspiration in Eastern philosophy. Niels Bohr, for example, famously added the yin-yang sign to his coat of arms after being knighted in Denmark. The sign represents complementary opposites and captures the notion of complementarity, which is crucial to Bohr's interpretation of quantum physics. This concept states that depending on the context of observation, phenomena such as light display both wave-like and particle-like behavior. This duality is not conflicting, but rather complimentary, similar to the Taoist idea of yin and yang as interdependent elements that combine to make a harmonious whole.

The interaction of quantum physicists with Eastern thinking was not a coincidence, but rather a reaction to the radical character of their discoveries. Classical physics had long offered a deterministic and mechanical vision of the cosmos, with certainty reigning supreme. In contrast, quantum physics showed a universe ruled by probability, interconnection, and an active role for observation. These findings were consistent with Eastern philosophies, which have long battled with the impermanence, interdependence, and observer-dependence of reality.

Critics have occasionally disregarded the links between quantum physics and Eastern philosophy as superficial or accidental. It is crucial to note, however, that these impacts were not intended to co-opt or appropriate ideas, but rather to seek intellectual and existential frameworks capable of integrating quantum theory's deep consequences. Eastern philosophies provided Schrödinger, Heisenberg, and his contemporaries with a vocabulary and mental toolset for explaining the quantum puzzles they discovered.

The impact of this cross-cultural synthesis goes beyond the individuals involved. It has influenced ongoing discussions between science and spirituality, inspiring modern thinkers to investigate how old wisdom traditions might help current scientific investigation. The ideas of interconnectivity, impermanence, and the active role of the observer remain relevant in both quantum physics and the larger discussion of the nature of reality.

Modern advancements in domains such as quantum consciousness and quantum biology highlight the importance of these multidisciplinary studies. As scientists examine phenomena that blur the distinction between matter and thought, Eastern philosophical views continue to be a vital resource for navigating these new realms. Whether studying quantum entanglement, the role of observation in collapsing wave functions, or the mysteries of consciousness itself, the spirit of inquiry that brought quantum scientists and Eastern thinking together now serves as a guiding force in the search to comprehend the cosmos.

Examining the philosophical foundations of quantum mechanics reveals that its creators were more than just technologists or mathematicians; they were philosophers engaged in a deep reevaluation of humanity's role in the universe. Their openness to Eastern philosophy demonstrates a readiness to cross cultural and intellectual borders, seeking enlightenment wherever it may be found. In doing so, they lay the framework for a more holistic and integrated approach to science—one that recognizes the interdependence of all things and the great mystery at the core of life.

*Western esotericism includes theosophy,
hermeticism, and early quantum commentary.*

The rise of quantum mechanics as a revolutionary branch of physics in the early twentieth century coincided with a time of intellectual turbulence in the Western world, during which mystical and esoteric traditions such as Theosophy and Hermeticism gained traction. These traditions, which combined spiritual philosophies with speculative metaphysical frameworks, delved extensively into scientific discoveries, interpreting them via symbolic, mystical, and occasionally speculative lenses. This intersection of scientific and esoteric thinking altered not just popular conceptions of quantum physics, but also discussions about the nature of reality, consciousness, and connection.

Theosophy, founded by Helena Blavatsky and later expanded by luminaries such as Annie Besant and Charles W. Leadbeater, was one of the most important esoteric movements of its time. Theosophy, which drew on both Eastern and Western mystical traditions, stressed the interconnection of all things, humanity's spiritual growth, and the presence of secret worlds beyond common awareness. These notions resonated powerfully with the developing quantum paradigm, which revealed a universe in which particles interacted instantly across enormous distances and reality appeared to be transformed by observation.

Blavatsky's books, including The Secret Doctrine, frequently used scientific jargon to back her esoteric assertions. She claimed that old spiritual wisdom was compatible with scientific discoveries, albeit in symbolic or metaphorical form. With the development of quantum physics, Theosophical thinkers accepted notions such as wave-particle duality and the observer effect, seeing them as evidence of spiritual truths. For example, the dual nature of matter was interpreted as a parallel to the Theosophical belief in the coexistence of physical and spiritual realities, whereas the role of observation in collapsing quantum wave functions echoed the esoteric idea that consciousness shapes the universe.

Hermeticism, another significant school in Western esotericism, offered a separate but complementary perspective on quantum physics. Hermetic philosophy, based on the teachings of Hermes Trismegistus, emphasized the idea of "as above, so below," which holds that the microcosm mirrors the macrocosm and vice versa. This notion has fascinating parallels in quantum physics, notably in theories such as the holographic principle, which holds that information about the cosmos may be recorded on lower-dimensional limits.

Hermeticism's emphasis on unity and correspondence resonated with quantum concepts like entanglement and non-locality. The Hermetic premise that "all things are interconnected" was scientifically validated when particles were shown to be immediately correlated regardless of distance. For Hermetic philosophers, connectivity was more than just a physical reality; it was a representation of the spiritual oneness that underpins all life. They saw quantum physics as a modern rediscovery of truths that had been encoded in Hermetic books for centuries.

The connection between quantum physics and Western esotericism was not limited to hypothetical interpretations. Early quantum pioneers like Wolfgang Pauli and David Bohm experimented with esoteric notions, hoping to shed light on physics' riddles. Pauli, for example, worked with Carl Jung, whose idea of synchronicity—a significant coincidence that defies causal explanation—is analogous to quantum phenomena such as entanglement. Pauli's interest in Jungian psychology and archetypes indicates that he realized the benefit of combining scientific rigor with symbolic and mystical frameworks.

David Bohm, a later figure in quantum theory, proposed the implicate order as a higher dimension of reality in which everything is interrelated and enfolded into a cohesive whole. Bohm's theories were inspired by both Eastern philosophy and Western esotericism, reflecting his notion that science and spirituality might work together to give a more comprehensive explanation of reality. The implicate order, with its focus on oneness and hidden linkages, resonated with Hermetic and Theosophical ideas while also providing a scientifically based view of the structure of the cosmos.

Western esotericism had an impact on the cultural reception of quantum mechanics, as well as on individual scientists themselves. Popular science writers and public intellectuals frequently interpreted quantum discoveries in mystical terms, using arcane language to captivate their audiences. Works such as Fritjof Capra's The Tao of Physics and Gary Zukav's The Dancing Wu Li Masters combined quantum physics with spiritual traditions, presenting them as complementary viewpoints on the same fundamental truths. While these texts were primarily influenced by Eastern ideas, they also subtly referenced Western esoteric topics such as the oneness of existence and the symbolic character of reality.

Critics of this esoteric interpretation of quantum mechanics sometimes claim that it conflates metaphor with scientific rigor, resulting in confusion regarding the nature of quantum events. While this argument is valid, it is also worth emphasizing that the interplay between quantum physics and esotericism has prompted thoughtful thoughts on science's philosophical and existential consequences. By interacting with mystical frameworks, physicists and intellectuals have been able to investigate concerns like the nature of consciousness, the function of the observer, and the interconnection of all things—questions that remain essential to both scientific and spiritual study.

The interaction of quantum physics with Western esotericism also reveals wider cultural processes of the early twentieth century. This was a time of fast scientific growth, as well as an increased awareness of non-Western spiritual traditions and a renewed interest in mystical and occult ideologies. Quantum mechanics, with its counterintuitive and cryptic character, appeared to provide a link between both realms, contradicting classical physics' materialist assumptions and prompting conjecture about other levels of existence.

This interaction has left an imprint on modern questions of science and spirituality. While the scientific community is hesitant to make explicit connections between quantum mechanics and esoteric traditions, quantum theory's philosophical questions about the nature of reality, the role of consciousness, and the limits of human knowledge resonate strongly with mystic concerns. By examining the contributions of Theosophy, Hermeticism, and other esoteric traditions, we might obtain a more complete knowledge of how cultural and spiritual currents influence our perception of scientific achievements.

Examining the impact of Western esotericism on the reception and interpretation of quantum mechanics reveals that science does not live in a vacuum. It is shaped by the cultural, intellectual, and spiritual settings in which we pose questions, utilize frameworks to understand our results, and make conclusions. The dialogue between quantum mechanics and Western esotericism has enriched both domains, offering new ways of understanding the mysteries of the universe.

Continuities Across Time: How Older Mystical Threads Fuel Modern Quantum Discourse

The conceptual parallels between ancient mystical traditions and current quantum physics are not a coincidence. They demonstrate an ongoing human endeavor to understand the nature of reality, the invisible forces that regulate life, and the interaction between the observer and the observed. The continuity of these paradigms demonstrates how old mystical notions have impacted and sometimes reflected current scientific achievements, resulting in a shared narrative that unifies humanity's pursuit for knowledge throughout millennia.

Ancient mystical traditions frequently described the cosmos as a dynamic, linked whole, which is consistent with quantum mechanics discoveries. The Vedic writings of mystical Hinduism depict a world made up of interrelated energy that is ruled by powers beyond human experience. The Rigveda mentions Indra's Net, a metaphorical web in which each node mirrors and encompasses all others, demonstrating the interconnectedness of all things. This corresponds to the quantum idea of entanglement, in which particles maintain instantaneous interactions despite huge distances. The old metaphor, albeit symbolic, captures ideas that quantum physics expresses mathematically and empirically.

Taoism's seminal work, Tao Te Ching by Laozi, investigates the dynamic interaction of opposites—yin and yang—that creates the observable universe. This dualistic but complimentary view is analogous to the wave-particle duality in quantum physics, in which particles have the qualities of both waves and discrete particles depending on how they are perceived. Taoism's emphasis on reconciling opposites is consistent with the counterintuitive nature of quantum events, implying that reality is flexible and malleable to viewpoint and circumstance.

Similarly, Buddhist teachings highlight the concept of emptiness (shunyata), which holds that all things lack intrinsic existence and instead rely on interconnected causes and circumstances. This viewpoint is reflected in the probabilistic character of quantum physics, in which particles reside in superposition, reflecting numerous potential states until measured. In both situations, the act of seeing changes potentiality into actuality, demonstrating a common emphasis on consciousness' active role in generating experience.

The mystical traditions of the West, such as Hermeticism, alchemy, and Kabbalah, share startling similarities with quantum concepts.

Hermeticism, derived from the writings attributed to Hermes Trismegistus, holds that the microcosm reflects the macrocosm, as encapsulated in the phrase "As above, so below." This principle resonates with physics theories such as the holographic principle, which suggests that information about the universe can be encoded on lower-dimensional surfaces, implying that each part of the cosmos reflects the whole.

Alchemy, generally considered as a primitive forerunner to modern chemistry, had symbolic implications that are consistent with quantum notions. The alchemical desire for transmutation, whether of base metals into gold or of the soul into a perfected condition, is analogous to transformational processes in quantum systems, in which particles may change state via interactions. The alchemical principle "Solve et Coagula" (dissolve and coagulate) might be seen as a metaphor for the quantum collapse of the wave function, in which a particle's potential state melts into a single consequence when observed.

Kabbalah, the Jewish mystical tradition, provides the notion of sefirot, which are ten interrelated emanations that build the divine and physical worlds. These emanations represent a cosmos that is both unified and differentiated, echoing quantum physics' depiction of a universe guided by probabilistic interactions rather than deterministic laws. The interaction of the sefirot represents a balance of opposites, similar to the quantum tension between uncertainty and determinism.

The cultural and intellectual atmosphere of the early twentieth century also contributed to the incorporation of mystical elements into quantum discourse. Many of the founding physicists, such as Erwin Schrödinger and Niels Bohr, were heavily affected by philosophical and spiritual concepts. Schrödinger's study of Vedantic Hinduism influenced his concept of consciousness as a universal phenomena that was inextricably linked to physical reality. Bohr's idea of complementarity, a cornerstone of quantum physics, is comparable to Taoist dualism, indicating his interest in Eastern philosophy.

The merging of spiritual and scientific concepts was not without dispute. Critics sometimes criticize mystical interpretations of quantum physics as being fanciful or unscientific. However, this objection ignores the historical fact that numerous scientific revolutions have been inspired by philosophical or metaphysical ideas. Isaac Newton, often considered as the creator of classical physics, was heavily affected by alchemy and Hermeticism, which helped shape his understanding of gravity and motion. Similarly, the mystical roots of quantum physics have inspired physicists and philosophers to investigate topics that go beyond empirical measurement, such as the nature of consciousness and the interconnectedness of everything.

The interaction between old mystical frameworks and quantum physics emphasizes the significance of metaphor in creating human cognition. Mystical traditions frequently use symbolic language to reveal truths that are difficult to express plainly. Despite its mathematical precision, quantum mechanics, like wave-particle duality or the fabric of spacetime, relies on metaphors to explain its paradoxical concepts. These similar language methods demonstrate a continuity in how people approach the unknown, with metaphor serving as a bridge between the seen and unseen.

While the analogies between ancient mysticism and quantum physics are striking, it is critical to explore them carefully. The scientific approach is founded on empirical evidence and repeatability, whereas mystical traditions frequently work on the basis of subjective experience and spiritual insight. Recognizing these disparities does not reduce the significance of each perspective, but rather emphasizes their complementary responsibilities in addressing various aspects of reality. Mysticism gives a framework for investigating meaning and interconnection, whereas quantum physics provides a precise vocabulary for explaining the physical world.

This dynamic interplay continues to flourish today, with multidisciplinary study bridging the gap between science and spirituality. Quantum biology and consciousness studies use quantum concepts and philosophical perspectives to examine phenomena that cross traditional discipline boundaries. Researchers are not only broadening the boundaries of knowledge by merging mystical frameworks with scientific investigation, but they are also creating a more holistic perspective of reality.

The long-lasting impact of ancient spiritual traditions on quantum physics shows a larger continuity in human cognition. Across civilizations and epochs, humans have struggled to comprehend their role in the universe, debating issues of reality, causation, and the essence of existence. Quantum mechanics, rather than being an isolated scientific breakthrough, is a continuation of this quest, connecting previous wisdom with current findings.

As science advances, these mystical strands may continue to inspire new paradigms, prompting us to reconsider our beliefs about reality and accept the mysteries that remain unsolved. In doing so, we acknowledge the everlasting human need to seek knowledge and significance, which transcends time, society, and discipline. This continuity throughout time not only improves our comprehension of quantum mechanics, but it also confirms the interconnection of all knowledge, reminding us that the pursuit of truth is a shared path that links mankind across generations.

CHAPTER 28: REAPPRAISING MATERIALISM AND PHYSICAL REALITY

"Reality is merely an illusion, albeit a very persistent one." – Often attributed to Albert Einstein

The transition from mechanical materialism to field theories is one of science's most important transformations. Historically, the materialist perspective dominated physics and philosophy, portraying matter as a collection of separate, indivisible units regulated by deterministic rules. This viewpoint, based on classical physics and supported by Newton and Descartes' writings, envisioned the cosmos as a massive clockwork system that was predictable and steady. However, the discovery of quantum physics, field theories, and sophisticated experimental techniques broke this paradigm, exposing a vastly more complicated and dynamic world.

Classical physics, namely Newtonian mechanics, provided the framework for materialism by stressing matter's solidity and predictability. Atoms were originally assumed to be small, indivisible entities whose interactions could be precisely traced. This viewpoint supported the deterministic worldview, which held that with enough information about a system's current states, the future state could be determined. Materialism, as a philosophical extension of this scientific framework, held that all phenomena, including consciousness, could be reduced to interactions between physical particles.

The 19th-century discovery of electromagnetic fields challenged the basic concept of matter's solidity. James Clerk Maxwell's equations demonstrated that electromagnetic phenomena could not be described only by particle motion, but rather by the presence of fields—continuous entities that permeate space and mediate forces. These fields, albeit invisible, contained energy and velocity, implying that space was not an empty nothingness but a dynamic medium. This was a substantial divergence from the strictly mechanical viewpoint, laying the groundwork for the subsequent development of quantum field theory.

The greatest severe blow to classical materialism came from quantum mechanics, which emerged in the early twentieth century. Planck, Einstein, Bohr, and Schrödinger discovered that particles such as electrons and photons display wave-particle duality, appearing as discrete entities or continuous waves depending on the conditions of observation. Heisenberg's uncertainty principle also proved that some particle attributes, like as location and momentum, cannot be determined with absolute precision at the same time. This underlying uncertainty defied conventional physics' deterministic framework and gave matter's behavior a probabilistic aspect.

One of the most radical findings of quantum physics was the notion of superposition, which asserts that particles exist in several states simultaneously until they are detected. This phenomena, as represented by Schrödinger's thought experiment with a cat that is both alive and dead, calls into question the concept of a fixed, objective reality that is independent of perception. The observer's involvement in condensing a particle's wave function into a definite state emphasizes the interaction of consciousness and the physical universe, presenting important philosophical problems regarding the nature of reality.

Field theories helped to broaden our knowledge of matter as quantum mechanics developed. Quantum field theory (QFT), a combination of quantum mechanics and special relativity, views particles as excitations or disturbances in underlying fields rather than autonomous entities. For example, an electron is a quantized excitation in the electron field, not a small, physical entity. In the same way, photons are electromagnetic field disturbances. These fields are continuous and pervasive, interacting complexly to produce the universe's visible phenomena.

QFT also developed the notion of virtual particles, which are transitory fluctuations in fields that appear and disappear within the uncertainty principle's limits. These ephemeral entities serve an important role in mediating forces, such as the electromagnetic force, via virtual photons. The existence of virtual particles blurs the distinction between the tangible and the ethereal, calling into question the traditional notion of material solidity and confirming the idea that the cosmos is inherently dynamic and linked.

The Standard Model of particle physics, based on QFT, further redefined the nature of matter. The Standard Model states that the cosmos is made up of a few fundamental particles—quarks, leptons, and gauge bosons—that interact through fundamental forces mediated by fields. The Higgs boson was discovered in 2012, confirming the existence of the Higgs field, which gives particles mass. This revelation proved that even the feature of mass, which was previously thought to be an essential quality of matter, results from interactions with a field, underlining reality's relational aspect.

Field theories also connect with cosmology, providing insight into the universe's large-scale structure. General relativity, Einstein's gravity theory, defines spacetime as a dynamic field that curves in reaction to mass and energy. This curvature produces gravitational effects, bringing matter, energy, and spacetime geometry together in a single framework. Furthermore, the application of quantum field theory to the early universe gives a mechanism for cosmic inflation, a fast expansion that smoothed out matter distribution and laid the groundwork for the cosmos we know today.

The philosophical implications of field theories are significant, challenging traditional materialism's reductionist perspective. Field theories show a fluid, linked, and relational world rather than one made up of separate, solid components. Particles are no longer the basic elements of matter, but rather emergent phenomena caused by interactions within fields. This viewpoint is consistent with several philosophical and spiritual traditions that emphasize the interconnection of all things, implying a confluence of scientific and metaphysical ideas.

Other scientific fields have been impacted by the transition from mechanistic materialism to field theory. Biology is increasingly using quantum concepts, such as tunneling and coherence, to explain phenomena such as photosynthesis and enzyme activity. These advancements imply that life itself may be firmly entrenched in quantum processes, further dissolving the distinction between the physical and intangible.

Consciousness research in neuroscience has begun to look at the potential significance of quantum effects in brain function. While contentious, theories such as Penrose and Hameroff's Orch-OR theory imply that quantum coherence inside microtubules may play a role in the formation of conscious experience. Though far from definitive, these views underscore the growing importance of quantum and field theories in understanding complex systems.

The shift from mechanistic to field theories marks both a scientific and philosophical revolution. It calls into doubt reductionism's ability to describe the universe's complexity and promotes a more holistic approach that acknowledges the interplay of fields, forces, and emergent events. As science continues to investigate the mysteries of matter and energy, field theories will likely play an important role, providing a framework that transcends classical materialism's constraints and offers up new avenues for understanding the nature of reality.

Spiritual interpretations: Maya or illusion concepts in tandem with wave functions.

The interaction of ancient spiritual notions with modern physics has produced fascinating analogies, particularly in terms of reality's elusive and ephemeral character. One of the most powerful of these notions is the concept of maya, which comes from Indian philosophy and describes reality as an illusion or veil that conceals a greater, unified truth. When seen with the quantum mechanical idea of wave functions, which depict possibilities rather than certainties until measured, both viewpoints reveal a common interest with existence's fluid and ephemeral aspects.

Maya is the principle that causes the sense of duality and multiplicity in a fundamentally non-dualistic cosmos, according to Advaita Vedanta, one of Hinduism's basic beliefs. According to this viewpoint, the world as seen via the senses is not wholly untrue, but rather an imperfect depiction of ultimate truth, or Brahman. Maya is caused by ignorance (avidya), which leads people to mistake the ephemeral for the eternal and the local for the universal. This illusion provides the appearance of separateness, masking the interdependence of all events.

Quantum theory, namely the concepts underpinning wave function behavior, mirrors this depiction of an imperfect world. A wave function describes the probability of all conceivable outcomes for a quantum system but does not designate a specific state until detected. Before being measured, particles like electrons exist in a state of superposition, occupying several possibilities at the same time. This indeterminate character implies a layer of reality that is not fixed but dependent on interaction, similar to how maya implies that sensory reality is dependent on perception and interpretation.

The collapse of the wave function during measurement is a striking similarity to maya. When a wave function collapses, the system changes from potential to actuality. Similarly, in Advaita Vedanta, realizing the illusory nature of maya—through techniques like as meditation and self-inquiry—causes the collapse of apparent separateness, revealing reality's non-duality. Both theories include an interaction of observation, consciousness, and the formation of a distinct state, whether it be a quantum consequence or spiritual enlightenment.

Buddhist philosophy provides a different viewpoint on illusion that is quite similar to quantum physics. The Buddhist teaching of anatta, or no-self, rejects the idea of a lasting, autonomous person and emphasizes the interdependence and transience of all events. Similarly, the quantum universe demonstrates that particles are not self-contained entities, but rather expressions of underlying fields and interactions. The wave-particle duality, which shows particles acting as waves in some settings but as distinct entities in others, emphasizes the fluid, context-dependent character of existence—a concept that is consistent with the Buddhist doctrine of impermanence (anicca).

Wave functions and maya are similarly similar in their rejection of reductionist explanations. The classical, mechanistic view of reality attempted to explain the universe in terms of distinct, autonomous particles acting under deterministic principles. Maya and wave functions, on the other hand, undermine this notion by stressing relationality. In quantum physics, particle behavior is determined by their interactions and environment, as illustrated by quantum entanglement, in which particles stay instantly coupled regardless of distance. This connection reflects Advaita Vedanta's statement that individuality is an illusion and that all existence emerges from and returns to a single source.

Quantum physics' philosophical implications extend beyond maya to conceptions of numerous realities, as explored in theories such as the many-worlds interpretation of quantum mechanics. According to this theory, every conceivable consequence of a quantum event lives in a distinct reality, resulting in a multiverse of parallel realities. While this concept differs from maya's metaphysical meanings, it is consistent with spiritual traditions that stress layered or multifaceted realities. For example, the Vedas explain several levels of life, each with its own set of rules and manifestations that overlap and affect one another.

The similarities between wave functions and maya raise problems regarding awareness' involvement in shaping reality. In quantum physics, the act of observation is critical for compressing a wave function and putting a system into a definite state. This observer effect is consistent with spiritual traditions that believe awareness is at the heart of creation. Chit (pure awareness) is one of the essential components of ultimate reality, along with sat (existence) and ananda. The link between observation and reality in quantum physics, albeit not completely understood, mirrors this spiritual idea by implying that consciousness impacts the appearance of phenomenon.

This common focus on perception's active involvement in forming reality calls into question traditional concepts of objectivity. According to classical physics, the cosmos exists irrespective of observation and is guided by established rules. Quantum physics and the idea of maya, on the other hand, imply a participatory reality in which the observer and observed are inextricably intertwined. This interactive component raises deep philosophical problems about the essence of life and the boundaries of knowing. It also emphasizes the value of humility in scientific and spiritual investigation, as both wrestle with the riddles of a world that defies reduction.

One point where these ideas divide is in their ultimate goals. Maya is inextricably linked to a path of liberation in which one seeks to transcend illusion and achieve self-realization. Quantum mechanics, on the other hand, maintains a scientific foundation for understanding and predicting processes in the visible universe. While quantum mechanics' metaphysical issues have stimulated philosophical and spiritual study, its fundamental goal is not to direct human development, but rather to increase comprehension of the physical universe.

Despite these distinctions, the interaction of quantum physics and spiritual concepts such as maya generates a conversation that benefits both professions. The findings of quantum physics provide a contemporary prism through which ancient teachings might be reexamined and rearticulated. For science, the metaphors and philosophical viewpoints of spiritual traditions give a larger context for evaluating results that contradict established worldviews. This multidisciplinary conversation emphasizes the need of seeing reality from different perspectives, acknowledging that no single framework can fully represent its complexities.

As quantum physics evolves, it may provide fresh insights into the nature of reality, shedding further light on the connections with spiritual traditions. Emerging ideas in quantum gravity, for example, and the study of quantum coherence in biological systems may help us better grasp interconnectivity and relationality. Similarly, breakthroughs in neuroscience and consciousness research may give light on the observer effect and the role of consciousness in influencing experience. These advancements have the potential to bridge the gap between scientific and spiritual viewpoints, creating a more integrated understanding of reality.

The confluence of wave functions and maya demonstrates how science and spirituality can both inform and support one another. By examining these analogies, we may appreciate the shared search for knowledge that drives both domains—a journey that aims not just to explain the world but also to unearth the deeper realities that lie behind the surface of appearances.

Beyond Reductionism: Accepting Unified, Dynamic Models of Existence That Integrate Multiple Viewpoints.

Reductionism, the philosophical approach that aims to explain complicated phenomena by breaking them down into their smallest components, has long dominated scientific research. While it has resulted in tremendous advancements in understanding natural world phenomena, this method appears to be insufficient when confronted with the complexities of quantum physics and its philosophical consequences. Beyond reductionism is a cohesive, dynamic vision that incorporates many points of view, spanning disciplines and redefining how we think about existence.

The scientific revolution of the seventeenth century, which stressed a mechanical worldview, had a significant impact on reductionism. Isaac Newton's deterministic laws of motion exemplified this concept, implying that the cosmos functioned like a clockwork machine, with its elements interacting predictably. This viewpoint facilitated substantial advances in physics, chemistry, and biology, as well as the development of analytical tools for isolating and examining individual components of larger systems.

Quantum mechanics, on the other hand, calls into question several reductionist assumptions. Particles do not act like separate, independent entities at the quantum level, but rather display wave-particle duality, which means they exist as both waves and particles at the same time. This phenomena challenges the conventional notion that items have fixed, inherent qualities. Furthermore, entanglement reveals that particles may stay instantly associated over long distances, implying that the cosmos functions as a whole rather than a collection of independent pieces.

These quantum findings call for a move from reductionism to a systems-oriented approach. Systems theory, which arose from domains such as biology and engineering, focuses on the links and interactions between system components rather than their independent qualities. According to this paradigm, evaluating its pieces separately cannot completely comprehend the behavior of the whole. This notion is shown by quantum mechanics: the features of a quantum system emerge from the interactions of its components rather than being reducible to a single ingredient.

Spiritual traditions have traditionally accepted holistic ideas that align with this systems-oriented viewpoint. Many Eastern philosophies, including Taoism and Buddhism, define reality as a dynamic network of links. According to the Buddhist notion of pratītyasamutpāda (dependent origination), all things are interdependent and do not exist independently. This idea is consistent with the quantum principle that the act of observation impacts the state of a system, stressing the connectivity of observer and observed.

Beyond the scientific and spiritual worlds, accepting unified conceptions of reality has practical consequences for dealing with global concerns. Climate change, for example, is a prime example of a complex, interdependent system. The reductionist propensity to separate variables has frequently resulted in piecemeal solutions, such as focusing simply on lowering carbon emissions without tackling larger systemic problems such as consumption habits or social disparities. A holistic approach, inspired by systems thinking, highlights the need of taking these interdependences into account, resulting in more complete and long-term solutions.

The shift from reductionist to integrative frameworks alters our understanding of human consciousness and identity. Traditional reductionist approaches frequently represent consciousness as an emergent characteristic of brain activity that may be reduced to the interactions of neurons and synapses. While this viewpoint has improved neuroscience, it fails to account for subjective experiences and the profound connectivity that people frequently express during meditation, prayer, or psychedelic experiences. Integrative theories, like as panpsychism, argue that consciousness is a basic component of the cosmos, challenging materialist assumptions and opening up new paths of investigation.

The burgeoning area of quantum biology, which explores the impact of quantum events in biological processes, is an inspiring example of combining various perspectives. For decades, scientists have used classical models to describe processes such as photosynthesis, enzyme activity, and bird navigation. However, recent research indicates that quantum coherence and tunneling may play crucial roles in these processes, implying that life occurs at the crossroads of the classical and quantum domains. Quantum biology illustrates the power of overcoming reductionism to find deeper truths about the natural world by linking physics and biology.

The holographic principle provides another perspective on unified models of existence. This theoretical physics theory proposes that information describing a three-dimensional system may be recorded on a two-dimensional border, similar to a hologram. While largely a theoretical concept, the holographic principle has significant philosophical implications, implying that reality itself may be a projection of deeper, underlying processes. This viewpoint is consistent with spiritual beliefs that explain the physical world as an illusion or expression of a deeper reality, bridging the gap between scientific and metaphysical perspectives.

Recognizing the limitations of human vision and language is also required when adopting dynamic, unified models. Both science and spirituality attempt to describe and comprehend reality, yet each is bound by the tools and frameworks it utilizes. Scientific models, although strong, are abstractions that reduce the natural world's intricacies. Similarly, spiritual analogies and symbols frequently fail to reflect the imperceptible character of ultimate truth. Recognizing these limits promotes humility and openness, enabling communication and collaboration between fields rather than rivalry.

The integration of different points of view is not without obstacles. Critics contend that attempts to integrate scientific and spiritual perspectives risk diminishing the rigor of both professions. Despite its limits, scientific reductionism has been useful in generating technology and advancing human understanding. Similarly, spiritual traditions frequently value experiential knowledge above empirical validation, which can lead to difficulties when dealing with scientific approaches. Navigating these problems necessitates a delicate balance of respecting each perspective's strengths and limitations while seeking common ground.

This integrated strategy is strongly supported by education and public debate. Interdisciplinary programs that mix physics, philosophy, and theology can provide students with the skills they need to critically and meaningfully study the links between science and spirituality. Similarly, media and literature that communicate these concepts in an understandable, engaging manner might motivate a wider audience to rethink reductionist beliefs and examine more holistic approaches.

The shift beyond reductionism has ramifications for personal progress and well-being. Mindfulness, yoga, and contemplative prayer allow people to feel their connectivity with the rest of the world, transcending the divided identities that modern culture frequently reinforces. These activities are consistent with quantum mechanics' systems-oriented approach, promoting a feeling of oneness and coherence that boosts resilience and compassion.

As research delves further into the secrets of the quantum universe, it is conceivable that new occurrences will emerge that challenge established paradigms and blur the barriers between disciplines. Advances in quantum computing, artificial intelligence, and neuroscience will inevitably pose serious concerns about the nature of reality, consciousness, and identity. Embracing integrative, dynamic conceptions of existence keeps these questions open-ended, encouraging creativity and insight rather than orthodoxy.

The path beyond reductionism is not about abandoning prior successes, but about broadening the framework through which we comprehend the cosmos and our role in it. Humanity can forge a deeper, more comprehensive understanding of existence by integrating scientific and spiritual perspectives, acknowledging complexity and interconnection, and accepting humility in the face of the unknown.

CHAPTER 29: FUTURE DIRECTIONS IN QUANTUM SPIRITUALITY

"Do not go where the path may lead, go instead where there is no path and leave a trail." – Ralph Waldo Emerson

The intersection of physics, philosophy, and meditative activities provides an unparalleled scholarly partnership. By tackling the deep problems that underlay reality, life, and consciousness, university centers throughout the world are developing multidisciplinary programs that aim to balance scientific precision with philosophical depth and spiritual insight. These initiatives stem from the awareness that comprehending the intricacies of quantum physics and human experience need insights from a variety of traditions and approaches.

Modern quantum physics calls into question long-held beliefs about physical reality. Entanglement, superposition, and the observer effect are examples of phenomena that need explanations that go beyond conventional science's empirical foundations. Philosophers, who have long been preoccupied with problems about causation, the essence of being, and the boundaries of knowing, will find fertile fodder for discussion in these quantum findings. Contemplative traditions, with their introspective methods to understanding consciousness and reality, provide a complementary viewpoint. These disparate but interconnected fields share a common goal: to discover the levels of reality that reductionist thought has yet to reveal.

Universities such as the University of Cambridge, Harvard University, and Stanford University have welcomed the merger of physics and philosophy in their research efforts. The Leverhulme Centre for the Future of Intelligence at Cambridge investigates how advances in artificial intelligence connect with concerns of consciousness and ethics, typically drawing on quantum theoretical concepts. Similarly, Harvard's Black Hole Initiative brings together astrophysicists, philosophers, and mathematicians to examine the underlying nature of black holes by combining rigorous physics with philosophical inquiry. Such initiatives demonstrate the power of interdisciplinary methods to unlocking the universe's secrets.

Consciousness studies are another important area of inquiry, where the lines between neuroscience, quantum physics, and contemplative approaches blur. The Dalai Lama and neuroscientist Francisco Varela launched the Mind and Life Institute in 1987, exemplifying the power of collaboration between Eastern spiritual traditions and Western scientific perspectives. The institution promotes discussion between meditators and academics, with a focus on the neurological correlates of mindfulness and the role of quantum processes in conscious awareness. These projects not only advance scientific understanding but also emphasize the practical benefits of contemplative practices in improving mental health and well-being.

Another example of the confluence of scientific and philosophical research may be found in theoretical physics, namely the study of the holographic principle and string theory. The holographic principle proposes that the universe's information is stored on a two-dimensional surface, calling into question standard notions of three-dimensionality. This approach is consistent with spiritual traditions that define reality as an illusion or projection, such as the Maya doctrine in Hinduism and the emptiness doctrine in Buddhism. Researchers at institutes such as Princeton's Institute for Advanced Study investigate these analogies, creating cross-disciplinary dialogue that calls into question the basic fabric of existence.

Quantum entanglement research also brings together scientific and philosophical viewpoints. Entanglement, which portrays particles affecting one other instantly across huge distances, contradicts orthodox physics and inspires mystical ideas of interconnectivity. The occurrence is consistent with conceptions from mystical traditions, such as Indra's Net in Hindu and Buddhist cosmology, which depicts the cosmos as a network of interconnected links. Physicists and philosophers are working together to understand the consequences of entanglement for causality, agency, and the unity of all things.

Convergence initiatives are becoming more focused on ethics and social responsibility. The fast growth of quantum computing, artificial intelligence, and neuroscience raises concerns about their influence on mankind. The Templeton Foundation, for example, supports research that blends scientific investigation and ethical contemplation, ensuring that technology advancement is consistent with human values. These initiatives frequently use contemplative practices to foster empathy, mindfulness, and ethical decision-making, demonstrating how ancient knowledge may be applied to contemporary concerns.

One of the most fascinating characteristics of convergence initiatives is their capacity to spark public participation. These projects encourage larger audiences to join in conversations about science, philosophy, and spirituality by translating complicated topics into accessible media such as videos, podcasts, and public lectures. The popularity of shows like "The Universe" and books like Carlo Rovelli's Seven Brief Lessons on Physics indicates the public's desire to grasp the intersections between cutting-edge science and timeless concerns about existence.

Educational programs that incorporate these interdisciplinary themes are gaining popularity. Universities are offering courses that integrate quantum physics with philosophical inquiry, enabling students to approach challenges critically and holistically. Stanford's Center for Comparative Studies in Race and Ethnicity, as well as its contemplative studies track, reflect the rising desire for curriculum that encompass multiple views, equipping students to face difficult global concerns with intellectual rigor and ethical awareness.

Critics of convergence programs frequently express worry about the risk of overinterpretation or distortion. They warn against confusing philosophical speculation with practical research, emphasizing the importance of defined disciplinary boundaries. Proponents claim that such collaborations do not erode scientific integrity, but rather strengthen it by widening the area of investigation. Convergence initiatives develop mutual respect and intellectual humility, allowing disciplines to learn from one another without jeopardizing their fundamental values.

Another issue that comes with incorporating contemplative practices into scientific study is the subjective character of experiences like meditation and mindfulness. While these techniques provide vital insights into awareness, their reliance on human interpretation makes them challenging to measure. To get a more complete picture of consciousness, researchers combine subjective data with objective measurements like brain imaging and physiological monitoring.

The ability of convergence initiatives to change and adapt is critical to their future success. As scientific discoveries challenge conventional paradigms, the necessity for multidisciplinary methods will only increase. Emerging domains such as quantum biology, which investigates the role of quantum processes in biological systems, and neurotheology, which investigates the brain foundation of religious experiences, are examples of the widening collaborative frontier. These domains encourage academics to investigate cross-disciplinary concerns, resulting in novel methods to understanding life, consciousness, and the cosmos.

Ultimately, convergence initiatives reflect a paradigm change in academic research. These projects challenge the long-standing silos that have defined scholarly study by bringing together physics, philosophy, and meditative practices. They promote a comprehensive approach to knowing, one that recognizes the complexities of life and the interconnection of all things. They not only enhance knowledge, but also instill a better respect for life's mysteries. Humanity may continue to study the great issues at the center of life via collaboration and curiosity, led by scientific, philosophical, and spiritual discoveries.

Non-local healing studies, advanced neuroimaging, quantum-coherent bio-systems

Curiosity about the deep connections between mind, body, and universe drives the ongoing expansion of scientific exploration's frontiers. Pioneering research fields such as non-local healing studies, enhanced neuroimaging technologies, and quantum-coherent bio-systems are at the forefront of this effort. These realms challenge conventional wisdom, with far-reaching ramifications for our understanding of health, consciousness, and the basic fabric of biological existence.

Non-local healing research, while frequently contentious, look at occurrences in which healing effects appear to transcend physical distances. These studies look into activities like prayer, Reiki, and other kinds of energy healing that occur while the practitioner and recipient are geographically distant. This field has been treated using rigorous scientific methods, including controlled experiments meant to eliminate prejudice. Double-blind studies, for example, have sought to assess the impact of remote intentionality on patient outcomes, notably in terms of stress reduction and sickness recovery. Despite not being specifically focused on healing, the Global Consciousness Project provides a tangentially relevant basis by studying connections between collective human desire and changes in random number generators. These associations, however minor, point to an unknown element of non-local phenomena that may explain some therapeutic techniques.

Advanced neuroimaging technologies have transformed the study of consciousness and its link to physical health. Researchers may monitor real-time brain activity during meditation, mindfulness practices, and even placebo reactions using techniques such as functional magnetic resonance imaging (fMRI), positron emission tomography (PET), and magnetoencephalography (MEG). These techniques reveal sophisticated brain networks that light up during concentrated concentration or spiritual experiences, giving old mental discipline methods legitimacy.

Mindfulness has concrete advantages, according to research from organizations such as the University of Wisconsin's Center for Healthy Minds, which shows how continuous meditation may change brain connections, reduce stress, and improve emotional resilience.

Neuroimaging has also proved important in investigating altered states of consciousness. Neuroimaging is used in psychedelic-assisted treatments, which are experiencing a scientific renaissance, to study how chemicals like psilocybin or ketamine alter brain activity. These findings shed light on the brain's default mode network (DMN), which is frequently related with ego and self-referential thought. When the DMN is quiet, people express intense feelings of oneness, which some interpret as glimpses of global awareness. Scientists hope to get a better understanding of the therapeutic potential of these states for treating depression, anxiety, and PTSD by tracking their alterations.

Quantum-coherent biosystems are another frontier in this multidisciplinary investigation. This topic, which is based on quantum biology, investigates how quantum phenomena such as coherence, entanglement, and tunneling arise in biological systems. Photosynthesis, for example, relies on quantum coherence to optimise energy transmission inside chloroplasts. Similarly, bird navigation has been related to quantum entanglement in cryptochromes, which are proteins that are sensitive to Earth's magnetic field. These findings blur the distinction between classical biological processes and quantum physics, implying a deeper oneness in the principles that control life.

With its enormous complexity, the human brain is a perfect candidate for studying quantum-coherent processes. While ideas like Orch-OR (orchestrated objective reduction) by physicist Roger Penrose and anesthesiologist Stuart Hameroff remain speculative, they suggest that quantum coherence occurs inside microtubules, which are structural components of neurons. These microtubules might function as quantum processors, connecting the brain to a larger, non-local realm of information. Although contentious, this idea is consistent with anecdotal stories of heightened awareness during meditation, near-death experiences, and deep states of flow.

The use of quantum-coherent concepts in healthcare has the potential to revolutionize our approach to diagnosis and treatment. Quantum sensors, for example, are being designed to detect minute changes in biological systems, allowing for early identification of illnesses such as cancer and neurodegenerative disorders. These sensors, which rely on quantum entanglement or superposition, provide extraordinary sensitivity when compared to conventional approaches. Similarly, advances in bioinformatics use quantum computing to examine large datasets, revealing genetic and proteomic patterns that have the potential to transform personalized treatment.

The merging of these pioneering fronts has far-reaching ethical consequences. As researchers discover the interconnectivity of the mind, body, and universe, they raise concerns about the moral obligations that come with such knowledge. Non-local healing, for example, calls into question traditional concepts of agency and consent. If ideas or intentions have the potential to impact distant consequences, how should these powers be governed or used? Similarly, neuroimaging studies that uncover the neurological foundations of spiritual experiences may mistakenly reduce these deep moments to mechanical processes, possibly decreasing their subjective importance.

The manipulation of biological processes using cutting-edge technology in quantum-coherent bio-systems raises worries about unforeseen repercussions. The notion of employing quantum computers to improve cognitive or physical capacities, for example, sparks discussions about justice, access, and the possibility of misuse. These concerns highlight the need of multidisciplinary collaboration, with philosophers, ethicists, and spiritual leaders working together to shape policies that promote human dignity and well-being.

Public participation is critical to keeping these pioneering sectors transparent and inclusive. Educational activities, community conversations, and easily accessible materials may all help to demystify science and encourage a feeling of shared discovery rather than elitist exclusivity. Documentaries, podcasts, and interactive displays provide chances to demonstrate the practical applications of non-local healing, neuroimaging, and quantum biology, bridging the gap between scientific discovery and social benefit.

The incorporation of contemplative practices into scientific inquiry is a possible approach to overcoming these problems. Mindfulness and meditation techniques not only improve individual well-being, but they also foster virtues like empathy, patience, and humility. Scientists might approach their job with a greater sense of purpose and responsibility if they base cutting-edge research in ethical norms. This approach is consistent with indigenous beliefs, which emphasize the interdependence of all life and the significance of acting in harmony with nature.

As these pioneering fields advance, they provide glimpses of a future in which the borders between science, philosophy, and spirituality are blurred. Non-local healing studies call into question the boundaries of human potential, improved neuroimaging technologies expand our grasp of the mind's link to reality, and quantum-coherent biosystems reveal the underlying mechanisms that keep life going. These disciplines work together to expose a cosmos that is not only intimately interrelated, but also replete with opportunities for exploration and development. Humanity may continue to study the mysteries of life with collaboration, curiosity, and ethical stewardship, led by scientific and spiritual discoveries.

Open Questions: Maintaining Rigor and Inclusiveness While Pushing Boundaries

The combination of quantum theory and spirituality poses significant concerns beyond the scope of present scientific paradigms. As academics investigate this frontier, they face both exciting opportunities and substantial challenges. Balancing rigorous technique with open-minded inquiry is critical for understanding the intricacies of a topic that straddles the empirical and metaphysical. This delicate balance promotes inclusion by encouraging cooperation across disciplines, beliefs, and cultures while retaining scientific integrity.

One of the most serious outstanding concerns in this field is what awareness is. Despite substantial advances in neuroscience and quantum theory, the fundamental mechanisms of consciousness remain mysterious. Consciousness resists reductionist explanations, prompting some scientists and philosophers to speculate that it is a basic aspect of the cosmos rather than a mere result of brain activity. This concept is consistent with panpsychism, a philosophical viewpoint that holds awareness exists at all levels of matter. Quantum techniques, such as the Penrose-Hameroff Orch-OR theory, propose that microtubules within neurons may work at the quantum level, possibly connecting consciousness to the fabric of reality itself. These hypotheses, however, are theoretical and have been criticized for their lack of empirical support.

Another unsolved issue in quantum physics is the observer effect.

Measurement appears to impact outcomes in quantum systems, sparking disputes regarding awareness' involvement in physical reality. While traditional interpretations credit the observer effect to the interaction of a measuring apparatus and a quantum system, other viewpoints argue that human consciousness may play a more direct role. Experiments like the delayed-choice quantum eraser suggest a complicated link between perception, causation, and time, calling into question linear ideas of cause and effect. The question of whether this occurrence has significance for spirituality or metaphysics is still being debated, necessitating careful experimental design and interpretation.

The idea of non-locality, which is central to quantum entanglement, raises fundamental issues regarding the universe's interconnection. What implications does the fact that particles separated by great distances can impact one another instantly have for our view of space and time? The oneness of existence has always been stressed in spiritual traditions, and the consequences of entanglement reflect this. Researchers are investigating whether non-locality may extend to macroscopic systems like biological beings or awareness itself. While these notions are theoretical, they serve as inspiration for multidisciplinary partnerships that push the limits of physics, biology, and philosophy.

Another set of concerns arises from the ethical implications of investigating quantum-spiritual interactions. As technology improves, especially in fields such as quantum computing and neuroimaging, researchers must consider the societal ramifications of their discoveries. If quantum coherence is discovered to have a role in brain function, it has the potential to transform our knowledge of mental health and cognitive improvement. However, such developments raise questions about privacy, consent, and potential abuse. It is critical to strike a balance between the revolutionary potential of these discoveries and ethical controls to ensure that development benefits all people.

In quantum-spiritual research, inclusivity is critical for developing a comprehensive grasp of the subject. Historically, cultural and philosophical biases have impacted scientific study, frequently marginalizing ideas that threaten established paradigms. Indigenous knowledge systems, for example, provide profound insights into the interconnection of nature and the universe, which are consistent with some interpretations of quantum mechanics. Respect, cooperation, and a willingness to interact with other epistemologies without appropriating or reducing their relevance are required for incorporating these traditions into mainstream study.

Mysticism and spirituality's influence on scientific study is also worth investigating. While science has always placed a premium on scientific evidence and reproducibility, spiritual activities frequently stress subjective experience and individual development. Bridging different methods necessitates a thorough awareness of their strengths and weaknesses. Meditation, for example, has been demonstrated to induce observable changes in brain activity, but its transforming effects on consciousness are very individualized and impossible to measure. Finding ways to combine subjective thoughts with empirical data might lead to new lines of research, enhancing both.

Differentiating real investigation from pseudoscience is a significant difficulty in this sector. The word "quantum" is frequently overused in popular culture to lend undeserved weight to erroneous statements. This approach not only compromises the rigor of quantum research, but it also threatens to alienate serious scientists who might otherwise engage in multidisciplinary inquiry. Creating explicit criteria for evaluating claims at the interface of quantum theory and spirituality is critical for preserving credibility and creating meaningful conversation. This attempt requires peer-reviewed research, transparency in approach, and a dedication to intellectual honesty.

The incorporation of quantum principles into practical applications creates other concerns. Quantum sensors and computing technologies show great potential in sectors ranging from medical to environmental research. However, the entire extent of their potential societal influence remains unknown. Quantum cryptography, for example, might transform data security, whereas quantum algorithms could speed up drug development advances. These innovations have the potential to transform businesses and human experiences, but they must also be carefully considered in terms of ethical and ecological repercussions.

Finally, the philosophical implications of quantum theory call into question long-standing beliefs about reality. Quantum physics' indeterminacy implies that the cosmos is a dynamic, probabilistic system rather than a deterministic machine. This viewpoint is consistent with spiritual traditions that emphasize the impermanence of life and the creative possibilities of uncertainty. To reconcile these notions with standard scientific perspectives, however, one must be willing to accept ambiguity and complexity. Researchers must balance pursuing definite solutions and acknowledging the mysteries that remain beyond our present comprehension.

Maintaining rigor and inclusion while pushing the frontiers of quantum-spiritual research is a tricky but critical endeavor. Scholars may examine these important topics in ways that improve humanity's knowledge of itself and the cosmos by encouraging multidisciplinary cooperation, valuing multiple viewpoints, and upholding the highest standards of scientific honesty. As the voyage progresses, it provides not just the possibility of revolutionary discoveries, but also a chance to ponder the nature of knowledge, connection, and existence.

CHAPTER 30: PHILOSOPHY OF SCIENCE AND SPIRITUAL PRAXIS

"Science without religion is lame, religion without science is blind." – Albert Einstein

The empirical foundation of modern science is based on what is observable, quantifiable, and repeatable. Certain important concerns, like as the nature of consciousness and the possibility of an afterlife, call into doubt the entire foundation of this system. These enigmas, while important to human existence, are difficult to quantify and frequently lie outside the scope of normal scientific instruments. Examining these restrictions highlights the need for alternative techniques and multidisciplinary approaches that recognize the complexities of such topics while maintaining the rigor of empirical research.

Consciousness is one of the most difficult problems in empirical research. Despite decades of neuroscientific investigation, the so-called "hard problem of consciousness" has not been answered. This word, proposed by philosopher David Chalmers, emphasizes the difficulties of describing how subjective feelings, or qualia, emerge from brain processes. While techniques like functional magnetic resonance imaging (fMRI) and electroencephalography (EEG) enable researchers to map brain activity and link it with mental processes, they fail to capture the subjective substance of experience. A scan, for example, may identify the brain correlates of perceiving red, but it cannot explain how one feels to experience redness.

Attempts to overcome this gap sometimes devolve into speculative or philosophical discussions. Some academics argue that consciousness, like space and time, is a basic characteristic of the cosmos rather than just a result of biological systems. This viewpoint is consistent with panpsychism, which holds that every matter has some degree of consciousness. While appealing, such ideas are difficult to evaluate scientifically because they lack observable factors that can be modified or quantified. This constraint emphasizes the difficulty of understanding phenomena that transcend physical observation.

Similarly, the existence of an afterlife defies factual verification. Despite its cultural and spiritual significance, this subject defies research using typical scientific approaches. Near-death experiences (NDEs), which are frequently touted as proof for life after death, have been thoroughly examined, although their interpretation remains debatable. Some studies explain NDEs to neurochemical changes or oxygen deprivation in the brain, while others say that they indicate the continuation of consciousness outside of the body. The subjective and anecdotal quality of NDE experiences hinders scientific interpretation, as does the impossibility to duplicate or research such occurrences in controlled circumstances.

In many fields, the constraints of empiricism are both technological and conceptual. The scientific method is founded on assumptions that may be disproven by observation or testing. However, issues regarding consciousness or the afterlife frequently include non-material components of existence that cannot be seen. For example, the concept of a soul or transcendent self cannot be examined directly since it does not interact in a quantifiable way with physical tools. This epistemological difference emphasises the need for alternative frameworks that may allow the study of immaterial or metaphysical phenomena while maintaining critical rigour.

Interdisciplinary techniques are one potential way to investigate these problems. Philosophy, for example, provides instruments for investigating the conceptual basis of consciousness and the afterlife, as well as insights that supplement scientific evidence. Eastern religions, such as Buddhism, stress experiential knowledge obtained via practices such as meditation, which can lead to deep insights into the nature of consciousness. While these approaches do not meet empirical science requirements, they provide useful insights that can influence and deepen scientific investigation.

Emerging areas, such as contemplative science, are attempting to combine these disparate methods. Researchers want to bridge the gap between subjective experience and empirical assessment by investigating the brain impacts of meditation and other contemplative activities. Long-term meditators, for example, demonstrate changes in brain structure and function, such as greater thickness in areas related with attention and emotional control, according to research. While these findings do not directly address the difficult topic of consciousness, they do show that integrating scientific approaches with experiential practices can help us get a better understanding of the mind.

The conflict between scientific rigor and the examination of metaphysical issues poses ethical concerns. In this period of fast scientific and technological growth, there is a risk of ignoring or marginalizing ideas that do not fit within the mainstream empirical paradigm. Indigenous knowledge systems, for example, frequently feature complex cosmologies and understandings of consciousness that call Western scientific assumptions into question. To engage with these traditions respectfully and inclusively, one must be willing to push the frontiers of inquiry while avoiding cultural appropriation or dilution.

Furthermore, the exploration of these topics has practical consequences for human well-being. A better understanding of consciousness may lead to advances in mental health treatment, cognitive enhancement, and artificial intelligence. Similarly, persons wrestling with existential problems may find peace and purpose in investigating the possibility of an afterlife or the nature of existence beyond the physical. The quest of knowledge must be balanced with its ethical and practical consequences to ensure that scientific advancement benefits mankind as a whole.

Empiricism's limitations also call into question the importance of wonder and mystery in scientific research. While science strives to understand and anticipate occurrences, some may always stay outside its comprehension. Embracing ambiguity may encourage humility and amazement, both of which drive scientific and spiritual inquiry. By accepting our understanding's limitations, we open ourselves up to new ideas and views, allowing for multidisciplinary cooperation and creativity.

To advance our knowledge of consciousness and the afterlife, we must strike a delicate balance between scientific rigor and an openness to alternative techniques. Researchers may push the bounds of inquiry while honoring the unique nature of these fundamental topics by combining insights from neuroscience, philosophy, spirituality, and contemplative practices. This approach not only broadens our comprehension of these puzzling events, but also improves our appreciation for life's richness and beauty.

Introspection and rigorous experimentation are complementary approaches.

The convergence of introspection and rigorous testing provides an exciting frontier in humanity's effort to comprehend the nature of reality. These perspectives, which are sometimes viewed as diverse or even incompatible, instead provide complimentary avenues for exploring deep issues about consciousness, existence, and the cosmos. While scientific testing focuses on concrete facts and observable occurrences, introspection looks into subjective experiences and the inner workings of the mind. They work together to create a more comprehensive picture of the human situation and the universe.

Scientific investigation has traditionally served as the foundation for comprehending the world around us. The scientific method, which focuses on observation, hypothesis, investigation, and reproducibility, has given astonishing insights into natural laws. From gravitational waves to the mapping of the human genome, diligent testing has shed light on previously unknown phenomena. However, this technique has inherent limits, particularly when dealing with topics that go beyond the physical, such as the beginnings of consciousness or the idea of a linked universal essence.

Introspection, which is based on subjective experience, is an essential supplement in this regard. Meditation, contemplation, and self-reflection are all practices that allow you to reach interior levels of consciousness that are not accessible by outward observation. Introspection has long been acknowledged as a valuable technique for investigating the nature of self, consciousness, and reality in ancient spiritual traditions such as Buddhism, Hinduism, and mystical Christianity. Modern neuroscience has begun to verify the transforming benefits of such activities, revealing changes in brain structure and function related with mindfulness and meditation practices.

Contemplative neuroscience is one example of where these methods have come together. This field of study seeks to understand how meditation and other introspective practices affect brain function, emotional control, and general well-being. Long-term meditators, for example, show higher connectivity in the default mode network, a brain area involved with self-referential thinking, according to research utilizing functional magnetic resonance imaging (fMRI). These discoveries link subjective insights received via introspection to objective evidence gathered through rigorous investigation, establishing a conversation between the inner and outside domains of inquiry.

This collaboration is also visible in the study of consciousness. Neuroscientists and philosophers are both concerned with the "hard problem" of consciousness—how and why subjective experiences emerge from physical processes in the brain. Introspection gives first-hand information on the qualitative character of feelings like love, terror, and awe. When these viewpoints are joined with third-person evidence from brain imaging and cognitive trials, they yield a more comprehensive, multifaceted picture of consciousness. For example, studies on the brain correlates of meditation frequently include participant self-reports, combining introspective views with objective data.

The relationship between reflection and exploration is not without its difficulties. The challenge of integrating subjective impressions with objective scientific criteria is a substantial barrier. Introspective ideas are intrinsically personal and non-replicable, rendering them immune to the reproducibility that supports scientific legitimacy. Furthermore, the language of introspection frequently develops from cultural and spiritual backgrounds that may not be consistent with modern science's factual paradigm. Concepts like "enlightenment" and "universal oneness" are difficult to put into practice experimentally, creating impediments to multidisciplinary integration.

Despite these obstacles, new methods are developing to overcome the gap. One intriguing technique is first-person neuroscience, which integrates participants' subjective reports into study design. Researchers can investigate phenomena such as altered states of consciousness, flow states, and mystical experiences by educating participants in introspective approaches and integrating their findings with neuroimaging data. This approach values subjective experience while basing it in the rigors of scientific inquiry.

Quantum mechanics is also an excellent tool for investigating the relationship between introspection and exploration. The observer effect, a fundamental concept in quantum physics, states that the act of seeing affects particle behavior. While this concept has special applications in quantum physics, it is consistent with introspective traditions that stress the observer's involvement in shaping reality. Both theories call into question the concept of an objective, autonomous cosmos, arguing that reality is co-created via interaction and perception.

The benefit of integrating introspection and experimentation goes beyond academic research; it has far-reaching consequences for personal and communal development. Introspective activities build self-awareness, empathy, and emotional resilience, all of which are necessary for managing modern life's difficulties. Simultaneously, rigorous experimentation gives the skills for addressing major global concerns like as climate change and public health crises. By combining these techniques, humankind may tap into both inner wisdom and outward knowledge to promote a more balanced and sustainable future.

This integrated viewpoint is especially important in resolving existential issues regarding meaning, purpose, and interconnectivity. While scientific exploration can unveil the workings of the cosmos, introspection frequently gives the sensation of awe and wonder that stimulates more investigation. They constitute a dynamic interplay, with one enhancing and shaping the others. For example, the discovery of the Higgs boson, popularly known as the "God particle," increased our understanding of particle physics while simultaneously sparking profound philosophical and spiritual questions on the essence of life.

Education and multidisciplinary collaboration are critical in promoting this integration. Curricula that foster both critical thinking and contemplative practices provide students with the tools they need to investigate complicated issues from several perspectives. This approach is exemplified by institutions such as the Mind & Life Institute, which brings together scientists, philosophers, and contemplatives to expand our knowledge of consciousness and wellbeing. Such endeavors show how collaboration may transcend disciplinary borders and create new paradigms of knowledge.

Finally, the merging of introspection and rigorous testing represents a larger movement toward holistic methods to understanding reality. This shift recognizes the limits of any one paradigm and highlights the significance of diverse views when solving complicated issues. By emphasizing both the subjective and objective, mankind may get a better grasp of the universe and its role within it, developing a more inclusive and expansive view of knowledge.

The Role of Awe: Balancing Rational Process with Respect for the Depth and Mystery of Life

Awe is a powerful and transformational feeling that crosses the intellectual and spiritual worlds, providing a unique perspective on life's mysteries. It is a state of expanded awareness in which the borders of self blend with the immensity of the cosmos, whether inspired by the delicate design of a quantum particle, the majesty of a starlit sky, or the profound wisdom hidden in ancient spiritual books. While awe is sometimes dismissed as a subjective sensation, it plays an important role in balancing scientific rationality with the reverence and wonder that inspire humanity's deepest explorations.

Awe is an underrated motivator of invention and understanding in the world of science. Niels Bohr, Werner Heisenberg, and Albert Einstein, the founding fathers of quantum physics, have voiced amazement at the quantum world's paradoxical and unexplained behavior. Bohr compared the difficulties of comprehending quantum mechanics to the paradoxes of Eastern mysticism, while Einstein famously compared the universe's enigmatic workings to "the mind of God." These sentiments reflect how awe can coexist with rigorous intellectual pursuits, fueling curiosity and perseverance in the face of complexity.

Awe is also important in spiritual and philosophical traditions, as it acts as a catalyst for transcendence and connection. In many cultures, awe is seen as the gateway to the holy, allowing humans to perceive the infinite inside the limited. This feeling crosses cultural boundaries, from the Vedic idea of "Rta," the cosmic order, to Abraham's awe at creation. These traditions frequently employ awe as a pathway to insight, emphasizing humility and cultivating an awareness for all existence's interdependence.

Modern neuroscience has begun to delve into the scientific roots of awe, demonstrating its influence on the human brain and behavior. According to research, feelings of awe engage the default mode network, a brain area linked with self-referential thinking, while decreasing activity in the prefrontal cortex, the site of executive control. This dual impact produces a sense of "self-diminishment" as well as an improved awareness of the larger whole, allowing people to transcend ego-driven viewpoints. These findings imply that awe is more than just a brief subjective experience, but a deep shift in awareness with quantitative advantages such as improved mental health, increased empathy, and increased creativity.

The interaction of awe and intellectual inquiry is most visible in the study of the universe. Astronomers and physicists commonly characterize their job as a conversation with the sublime, whether they are studying the complex dance of galaxies or examining the tiny structures of subatomic particles. Astrophysics, in particular, has revealed a world that functions on both strange and elegant principles, with black holes warping spacetime and dark matter shaping the cosmos. These discoveries not only challenge human comprehension, but also inspire wonder by reminding us of the limitations of human vision and the limitless potential of inquiry.

Similarly, the quantum universe provides ideal conditions for generating awe. Entanglement, superposition, and the observer effect contradict traditional reasoning, implying a considerably more complex and interwoven world than previously understood. These principles call into question the linear, deterministic worldview that dominated classical physics, paving the way for a paradigm that values ambiguity and wonder. This change resonates with many spiritual traditions that highlight the limitations of human cognition and the importance of humility in the face of the infinite.

The development of awe has practical consequences for dealing with modern issues. As mankind struggles with concerns like climate change, social injustice, and technology ethics, awe may act as a unifying force that transcends individual differences. According to research, awe promotes prosocial conduct by motivating individuals to prioritize community well-being over personal benefit. Awe may create a sense of stewardship and duty by changing the attention from the ego to the bigger whole, which is necessary for navigating the complexity of today's world.

Despite its deep advantages, the position of wonder in science and spirituality is not without debate. Critics contend that when awe is divorced from intellectual investigation, it can lead to irrationality or blind belief. In quantum mysticism, for example, awe has been used to promote pseudoscientific claims, combining metaphorical insights with factual facts. This emphasizes the necessity of basing awe in critical thinking and evidence-based processes, such that it contributes to rather than detracts from intellectual rigorousness.

A rationalist dismissal of awe as subjective or unscientific, on the other hand, ignores its transforming potential. By dismissing awe, science risks losing the fundamental feeling of wonder that drives inquiry and discovery. To bridge this divide, a nuanced approach is required that acknowledges awe as a real and valuable part of human experience capable of improving both scientific and spiritual pursuits.

Education provides a strong platform for weaving wonder into the fabric of intellectual and psychological development. Programs that combine scientific literacy with experiential learning, such as stargazing programs, nature retreats, or immersive virtual reality explorations of the universe, may foster both a feeling of wonder and critical thinking. Similarly, introducing contemplative practices into academic contexts can assist students and researchers in connecting with the larger concerns underlying their work, developing a more holistic approach to knowledge.

Integrating awe into daily life has the potential to alter people. Simple techniques like careful observation of nature, connecting with art and music, or pondering on the immensity of the cosmos may all help to restore a feeling of wonder and connectivity. These moments of wonder serve as reminders of humanity's place in the universe, providing peace and inspiration in the midst of modern life's demands.

Awe overcomes the binary thinking that frequently separates science and spirituality by combining the rational process with appreciation for wonder. It encourages a mindset that values both accuracy and potential, appreciating the strength of scientific data while staying open to the unknown. By embracing awe, humankind may bridge the gaps between these disciplines, fostering a deeper appreciation for the universe's complexity and beauty.

Finally, awe's job is to broaden the scope of inquiry and imagination, rather than to deliver final solutions. It serves as a reminder that the quest of knowledge is about the journey as much as the goal, an ever-changing dance of comprehension and mystery. Awe, whether viewed through the lens of a microscope, the grandeur of a telescope, or the silence of contemplation, urges us to investigate the limitless possibilities of life with humility, curiosity, and amazement.

CHAPTER 31: CRITIQUES & DEBATES IN QUANTUM SPIRITUALITY

"Doubt is the origin of wisdom." – René Descartes

Skepticism, when used constructively, serves as an important tool in the search of knowledge, ensuring that unproven assertions do not eclipse serious science. Over the course of decades, the combination of quantum physics with spiritual or mystical tales has sparked both inspiration and controversy. While such analogies frequently give understandable metaphors for complicated scientific processes, detractors contend that mixing symbolic interpretations with empirical research can result in fundamental errors, undermining both scientific legitimacy and the integrity of spiritual traditions. This section delves into the opinions of skeptics, underlining the major obstacles and warnings connected with incorporating quantum notions into nonscientific frameworks.

Skeptics frequently criticize the misuse of quantum mechanics in public speech. Quantum theory, with features such as entanglement, wave-particle duality, and the observer effect, contradicts conventional wisdom. However, the terminology employed to describe these phenomena, such as "energy fields," "interconnection," or "observer-dependent reality," is frequently embraced by spiritual and self-help communities without a thorough comprehension of the underlying mathematics or experimental methods. This leads to ambiguous or incorrect assertions that conceal the complexities of quantum physics. For example, claims like "thoughts can influence quantum particles" or "quantum entanglement explains telepathy" lack factual support yet resonate because they correspond to pre-existing mystical ideas.

The observer effect, which defines how the act of measuring changes the state of a quantum system, is a major source of controversy. This phenomena occurs in physics as a result of particle contact with the measurement device, which is frequently at the subatomic level. However, in some spiritual interpretations, the observer effect is misinterpreted as evidence that human awareness directly influences physical reality. While this idea has philosophical merit, physicists say that it oversimplifies a complicated process by confusing the mechanical function of observation with the metaphysical implications of awareness. Skeptics argue that such interpretations jeopardize public comprehension of science by portraying hypothetical concepts as established facts.

Skepticism also applies to the monetization of quantum mysticism. In recent years, quantum language has been used to sell health goods, alternative treatment, and even financial plans. Claims of "quantum healing" or "quantum energy" are usually accompanied by pseudoscientific explanations that use the enigma of quantum physics to provide credence. This phenomena, known as "quantum woo," has sparked strong condemnation from the scientific community, with heavyweights such as physicist Brian Cox and theoretical physicist Sean Carroll publicly condemning such behaviors. Their criticisms underline that utilizing scientific language without supporting evidence not only misleads customers, but also weakens faith in actual scientific research.

Conflation is an issue that arises in academic and multidisciplinary conversations, as well as public discourse. While topics such as quantum biology and consciousness studies provide intriguing pathways for investigating the intersections of quantum physics and life sciences, critics warn against exaggerating preliminary findings. For example, hypotheses positing that quantum coherence has a role in biological processes such as photosynthesis or brain activity are still under inquiry rather than proven science. Critics emphasize the need of differentiating between hypotheses and proven outcomes in order to avoid speculative leaps that might undermine the study.

Skeptics believe that combining science with spirituality risks overshadowing each discipline's essential merit. Science values falsifiability, experimentation, and facts, but spirituality frequently connects with subjective experience, metaphor, and symbolic meaning. When these realms are incorrectly integrated, scientific rigor suffers, and spiritual activities are reduced to pseudoscientific frameworks that fail to represent their depth. Skeptics argue for a peaceful cohabitation of multiple domains, with metaphors from quantum physics recognized as interpretative tools rather than scientific realities.

A particularly sharp criticism develops over the use of quantum notions to legitimize spiritual teachings or ancient knowledge. Proponents of quantum mysticism frequently point out parallels between quantum theories and spiritual ideas, such as the Buddhist concept of "emptiness" or the Hindu concept of "Brahman" as the ultimate truth. While these similarities might provide powerful analogies, critics contend that they risk anachronism by projecting current scientific notions onto historical traditions that emerged independently of quantum physics. Furthermore, the selective application of quantum theory to validate spiritual beliefs ignores the larger scientific background, which may include results that contradict or complicate these interpretations.

Skeptical voices also raise questions about quantum mysticism's epistemological consequences. Proponents of quantum mechanics may unwittingly combine factual investigation with philosophical speculation by portraying it as a pathway to understanding consciousness, free will, or the essence of reality. Critics argue that, while quantum theory presents important philosophical concerns, it does not inevitably give solutions to existential or spiritual quandaries. For example, the notion that quantum uncertainty allows for free will is speculative because it conflates physical indeterminacy with agency. Skeptics advocate for a more disciplined approach, in which the philosophical implications of quantum mechanics are examined with intellectual humility and analytical rigor.

Another issue to consider is quantum mysticism's educational consequences. In a society where scientific literacy is becoming increasingly important, the spread of myths about quantum theory might impede public comprehension of fundamental concepts. Skeptics say that educators and communicators must explain quantum physics, portraying it as a demanding but understandable science rather than an obscure area accessible only through metaphor. Educators may enable individuals to distinguish between reality and fiction by encouraging critical thinking and interaction with primary scientific sources, therefore diminishing the attractiveness of pseudoscientific claims.

Despite these objections, skeptics recognize the constructive potential of quantum-inspired metaphors when utilized wisely. Analogies generated from quantum physics can operate as a link between abstract scientific notions and lived experience, encouraging curiosity and multidisciplinary debate. For example, the concept of entanglement as a metaphor for human interconnectivity might encourage ethical introspection and societal solidarity if presented as an interpretative tool rather than a literal fact. By explicitly defining the boundaries between science and metaphor, such approaches can deepen both scientific and spiritual discussions without jeopardizing their respective foundations.

The conflict between skepticism and quantum mysticism ultimately reflects larger problems about the nature of knowing and the relationship between empirical and experienced understanding. While skeptics warn against uncritically using quantum principles in non-scientific circumstances, they equally acknowledge the human urge for meaning and connection that motivates these interpretations. Balancing skepticism and receptivity necessitates a nuanced approach that upholds scientific integrity while appreciating quantum metaphors' symbolic potential to elucidate life's complexities.

Skeptics contribute to a more informed and fair discussion of quantum mysticism by calling for discernment and intellectual rigor. They contribute to the legitimacy of both fields by criticizing spurious claims and maintaining a clear separation between science and metaphor, ensuring that the awe-inspiring revelations of quantum physics are not undermined by misinterpretation or abuse. As science continues to push the boundaries of the quantum realm, skepticism remains an important antidote, encouraging a culture of curiosity, accountability, and respect for reality's intricacies.

Constructive Critique: Promoting Well-structured Inquiry into Extraordinary Claims

The study of quantum physics and its linkages with spiritual and philosophical ideas has enthralled academics, philosophers, and the general public alike. This merger has resulted in deep concepts, but it has also spawned numerous speculative assertions that defy scientific rigor. While skepticism is an important check on unfounded claims, constructive critique seeks to engage intelligently with unusual claims, encouraging an environment of intellectual rigor, openness, and multidisciplinary cooperation. Constructive critique contributes to the bridge between creative discovery and empirical confirmation by fostering systematic research.

The notion of falsifiability, which is a pillar of the scientific process, is central to constructive criticism. This principle, proposed by philosopher Karl Popper, states that a scientific assertion must be testable and falsifiable. In the context of quantum spirituality, constructive critique requires that theories that link quantum phenomena to metaphysical or spiritual conceptions be tested quantitatively and reproducibly. Claims that awareness impacts quantum states, for example, may inspire novel research, but these tests must comply to stringent evidentiary requirements in order to avoid sliding into pseudoscience.

One of the difficulties in criticizing unusual statements is differentiating between metaphor and empirical assertion. Quantum physics frequently lends itself to interesting analogies, such as entanglement expressing interconnection or the observer effect indicating the influence of perception on reality. While these analogies can elicit philosophical thought, constructive criticism ensures that they are not misinterpreted as real scientific facts. This divide promotes clarity, allowing interdisciplinary conversation to flourish while maintaining the integrity of any area.

Constructive critique stresses peer evaluation and multidisciplinary collaboration. In scientific research, peer review serves as a gatekeeper, ensuring that findings are evaluated by field specialists before being acknowledged as valid. When quantum concepts are applied to fields such as consciousness studies, energy medicine, or metaphysics, bringing together experts from many disciplines can strengthen the investigation process. For example, neuroscientists, physicists, and philosophers working together on the Penrose-Hameroff theory of quantum consciousness can provide insights that individual fields may miss. This collaborative approach creates a mix of skepticism and inventiveness.

Another important part of constructive criticism is avoiding confirmation bias. Confirmation bias, the propensity to favor information that confirms one's prior opinions, is a serious difficulty when investigating remarkable claims. Researchers and theorists who approach quantum spirituality with the goal of verifying their beliefs risk neglecting evidence that contradicts or complicates their assumptions. Constructive critique promotes fair study of data, intellectual humility, and openness to different interpretations.

Constructive critique is especially useful when dealing with statements that mix up correlation and causation. Quantum processes frequently reveal fascinating correlations, such as the immediate interaction between entangled particles. However, interpreting these correlations as proof of causality requires careful consideration, particularly in situations such as mind-body interactions or distant healing. Critics emphasize the need of experimental controls, statistical rigor, and repeatability in assessing such claims. Constructive critique promotes the strength and credibility of scientific investigation by holding unusual claims to these norms.

Education is critical to encouraging constructive criticism. In an age where quantum ideas are frequently popularized through simple explanations or speculative interpretations, increasing scientific literacy is critical. Educational programs that teach fundamental concepts of quantum physics, philosophy of science, and critical thinking can help people engage with remarkable claims rationally. Such programs also inspire the next generation of academics to embrace multidisciplinary research with both interest and methodological rigour.

The significance of constructive criticism extends beyond science, providing insights into how unusual claims might be investigated within spiritual or philosophical contexts. Many spiritual traditions value introspection, contemplation, and experiential inquiry, which are similar to the rigorous approaches used in scientific research. Constructive critique promotes a meaningful interchange of ideas between various fields by encouraging spiritual practitioners to use organized methodologies, such as systematic documentation of subjective experiences or interactions with scientists.

Constructive critique also serves as a foundation for discussing the ethical implications of remarkable claims. Claims about quantum healing, for example, can elicit optimism but can also generate excessive expectations or abuse susceptible people. Constructive critique protects against damage while cultivating trust by requiring practitioners and academics to provide openness, proof, and responsibility. This ethical dimension emphasizes the larger societal importance of well-structured research.

To develop constructive criticism, skepticism and inventiveness must be balanced. While skepticism is useful in avoiding spurious claims, it may also hinder creativity and hastily discard ideas. In contrast, constructive criticism fosters a culture in which unusual ideas are investigated with both inventiveness and discipline. This balance is particularly important in new domains such as quantum biology and quantum approaches to consciousness, where the frontiers of present knowledge are still being established.

The constructive criticism of remarkable claims has important consequences for public communication. Popular scientific media, documentaries, and self-help literature all play an important role in molding popular conceptions of quantum mechanics and its applications. Constructive critique allows communicators to communicate their views with clarity, subtlety, and an acknowledgement of ambiguity. This allows them to pique people's interest without promoting myths.

The ultimate purpose of constructive criticism is not to deny unusual claims outright, but rather to create a framework for their critical consideration. Constructive critique guarantees that the examination of quantum phenomena and their philosophical consequences stays fresh and trustworthy by encouraging discourse, supporting multidisciplinary cooperation, and preserving empirical inquiry standards. This approach recognizes the complexity of the quantum universe while honoring humanity's ability for wonder and discovery.

In an era where the lines between science, philosophy, and spirituality are becoming increasingly blurred, constructive criticism serves as a guiding principle for meaningful research. It encourages academics, philosophers, and the general public to think critically about unusual claims, developing a culture of curiosity, rigor, and respect. By adopting this approach, we may explore the fundamental problems offered by quantum physics with imagination and integrity, ensuring that our quest for knowledge is anchored in both wonder and wisdom.

Respectful discourse: elevating dialogue rather than polarizing science and spirituality.

The convergence of science and spirituality has always been a fruitful arena for discussion, with responses ranging from deeply perceptive to sharply polemical. At its finest, this debate promotes mutual enrichment by presenting new views on age-old issues about life, awareness, and the cosmos. However, it has the potential to polarize, putting the rigor of scientific empiricism against the introspective and interpretative character of spirituality. Respectful conversation, based on openness and intellectual humility, provides a means to bridge this gap, promoting collaborative discovery that transcends entrenched boundaries.

Respectful conversation starts with acknowledging the usefulness and limits of both scientific and spiritual perspectives. Science, with its emphasis on observation, experimentation, and replicability, excels in discovering the mechanisms of the natural world. Spirituality, which is frequently anchored in personal experience, intuition, and interpretative traditions, tackles issues of meaning, purpose, and interconnectivity. While these realms function in diverse ways, they are not always in conflict. Instead, they might complement one another by presenting perspectives that the other may ignore. Respectful discussion necessitates recognition of this complementarity, avoiding the reduction of any position to caricature or dogma.

A major tenet of polite conversation is the desire to actively listen and interact with opposing points of view. In the context of quantum spirituality, this entails taking skeptics' concerns seriously while also giving attention to those who want to combine quantum concepts with spiritual insights. Skeptics frequently highlight the significance of empirical rigor and warn against stretching scientific concepts into realms they were not intended to address. Proponents of quantum spirituality, on the other hand, advocate for a broader understanding of science, one that includes its philosophical and metaphysical implications. Respectful conversation should not strive to settle these conflicts prematurely, but rather views them as opportunities for development and understanding.

Clear and accurate language is vital for promoting polite debate. Miscommunication is sometimes caused by the confusing usage of terminology with multiple meanings in scientific and spiritual contexts. For example, the term "energy" has distinct meanings in physics, referring to a quantifiable feature of systems. In spiritual activities, "energy" may refer to subtle, experiential phenomena that are difficult to quantify scientifically. Participants in the debate can prevent misconceptions and provide the groundwork for meaningful exchange by clarifying the use of terminology and avoiding conflation.

Respectful conversation also implies a commitment to intellectual humility. This entails understanding the provisional nature of knowledge and being willing to reconsider one's own assumptions or interpretations. In the area of quantum spirituality, intellectual humility might emerge as a physicist conceding that the philosophical implications of quantum mechanics are not completely understood, or as a spiritual practitioner understanding that their interpretations may not be consistent with empirical data. Such humility develops a culture of mutual respect, allowing discussion to flourish even in the face of conflict.

Empathy and curiosity are also essential components of respectful debate. Empathy enables individuals to value the opinions and experiences of others, even if they differ greatly from their own. Curiosity fuels the urge to learn from these disparities, viewing them as possibilities for growth rather than impediments. When skeptics approach spiritual ideas with inquiry rather than contempt, they may gain insight into the human yearning for meaning. Similarly, when spiritual philosophers confront scientific criticism, they may improve their interpretations and increase their legitimacy.

Respectful conversation flourishes in situations that promote multidisciplinary cooperation. Universities, research organizations, and think tanks are ideal venues for such discussions, bringing together specialists in physics, philosophy, theology, and other subjects. The different viewpoints offered by these disciplines are beneficial to collaborative initiatives that research themes like as consciousness, quantum physics, and the nature of reality. For example, the study of quantum consciousness has drawn on ideas from neuroscience, physics, and contemplative traditions, proving the power of multidisciplinary methods to solving complicated problems.

Respectful conversation in the public realm may be fostered through media literacy and education. Popular depictions of quantum physics and spirituality frequently oversimplify or sensationalize these concepts, resulting in misunderstandings and heated disagreements. Educational programs that build a greater grasp of both areas can prepare learners to interact with these topics deliberately and critically. Media sites may also help by focusing on detailed, well-researched material rather than clickbait headlines or overblown claims.

Respectful conversation is especially necessary when discussing ethical issues surrounding quantum mysticism. Claims of quantum healing, for example, can frequently generate optimism but can mislead susceptible people if provided with little proof. Practitioners, scientists, and the general public may work together to create ethical principles that strike a balance between openness to new ideas and the need for responsibility and rigor.

One of the difficulties of polite conversation is managing profoundly held ideas and emotions, which frequently underlay talks about science and spirituality. When questioned, these ideas might lead to defensiveness or animosity, preventing real discourse from occurring. One strategy for overcoming these hurdles is to focus on common values, such as a dedication to truth-seeking or a desire to increase human well-being. Participants can establish a feeling of collaborative purpose by stressing similar aims and bridging ideological differences.

The importance of leadership in facilitating polite dialogue cannot be emphasized. Thought leaders, academics, and public celebrities can influence the tone of scientific and spiritual discourse. They can encourage others to follow suit by demonstrating polite involvement and valuing intellectual integrity first. In contrast, when leaders adopt divisive or dismissive attitudes, they risk sustaining conflict and inhibiting development.

Respectful conversation is not without its problems, but the advantages are enormous. It fosters an environment in which varied ideas may coexist and benefit one another, where creativity and curiosity are encouraged, and where the search of knowledge takes precedence above the desire to be correct. In the framework of quantum spirituality, respectful discussion has the ability to increase our understanding of the universe's complexity and our role within it.

Respectful conversation fosters an inquiry culture that appreciates both scientific rigor and the human capacity for wonder, rather than polarizing science and spirituality. It encourages us to tackle difficult problems with humility, sensitivity, and a collaborative attitude, acknowledging that the road to knowledge is just as essential as the goal. This allows for fresh ideas and discoveries that cross traditional boundaries, improving both science and spirituality.

CHAPTER 32: BRIDGING QUANTUM CONCEPTS INTO DAILY LIFE

""What we know is a drop, what we do not know is an ocean." – Isaac Newton

The convergence of quantum physics and mindfulness shows an unexpected yet significant synergy. Both disciplines highlight the value of embracing uncertainty and letting go of strict expectations in order to cultivate a mentality that thrives in the face of complexity and unpredictability. Mindfulness, as a practice based on present and awareness, is perfectly aligned with the quantum view of reality, which is dynamic, probabilistic, and free of deterministic absolutes. Individuals can acquire humility, flexibility, and a greater connection to the present moment by incorporating quantum theory's established principles of uncertainty into everyday mindfulness activities.

Mindfulness begins with accepting the current moment as it is, which is mirrored in the quantum principle that particles remain in a state of superposition until they are noticed. Human experience, like quantum systems, resists easy description. Mindfulness helps people to examine their thoughts, feelings, and experiences without judgment or need for control. This is consistent with the quantum idea that observation does not simplify reality, but rather discloses its underlying complexity. Recognizing the same principle between mindfulness and quantum physics enables practitioners to embrace existence's fluidity, viewing uncertainty as possibilities for progress rather than hurdles to be overcome.

The quantum concept of uncertainty, best represented by Heisenberg's Uncertainty concept, illustrates that some pairings of attributes, such as location and momentum, cannot be known with absolute precision at the same time. This intrinsic constraint draws parallels to the mindfulness notion of nonattachment. Non-attachment in mindfulness refers to letting go of the need to hold closely to results, expectations, or identities. Just as quantum theory embraces uncertainty as a basic component of reality, mindfulness helps practitioners to find calm in the face of life's unpredictability. This strategy not only minimizes stress but also promotes resilience, allowing people to adjust to change more easily.

Recognizing the existence of uncertainty naturally leads to humility. Even the most sophisticated quantum theories admit the limitations of human comprehension. Similarly, mindfulness fosters humility by urging practitioners to approach each experience with curiosity rather than preconceived ideas. This approach allows for ongoing learning and personal progress while removing the ego's urge to establish control or assurance. Humility, as a habit, serves as a link between scientific investigation and spiritual discovery, emphasizing the importance of questions above definite solutions.

Another important skill that results from the interaction of mindfulness and quantum uncertainty is adaptability. Quantum physics demonstrates that systems develop in response to observation, a notion that may be analogously applied to human behavior. Individuals who practice mindfulness gain the capacity to respond intelligently rather than impulsively to environmental stimuli. This adaptability is similar to that of quantum systems, in which results are modified by environment and interaction. Mindfulness therefore becomes a tool for negotiating the intricacies of modern life, allowing people to stay grounded in the face of changing situations.

Practical mindfulness activities make it easier to put these concepts into practice. For example, attentive breathing keeps focus in the present moment, producing a feeling of calm awareness. This simple yet significant approach can be viewed as a symbolic act of "observing" one's own internal quantum system, noting the infinite possibilities contained inside each breath. Similarly, body scans, in which people focus their attention on different regions of their bodies, replicate the quantum process of measuring specific features while being aware of the overall system. These activities promote a holistic awareness that considers the physical, emotional, and cognitive elements of experience.

Mindfulness also fosters a tolerance for ambiguity, which is necessary for both scientific research and everyday living. Ambiguity is not a defect in quantum physics, but rather a part of reality that requires researchers to go beyond binary frameworks. Similarly, mindfulness assists individuals in navigating the grey zones of human experience, where answers are rarely black and white. Rather of trying to resolve ambiguity, practitioners gain a greater sense of patience and confidence in the unfolding of life's processes.

The benefits of combining mindfulness with a knowledge of quantum concepts extend beyond the individual to society as a whole. When people face uncertainty with humility and adaptation, they contribute to a culture of empathy and cooperation. This is especially vital in a society coping with complex issues that resist simplistic answers, such as climate change, social injustice, and global health problems. Mindfulness practitioners may encourage communal action based on shared responsibility and mutual respect by instilling a sense of connectivity and open-ended exploration.

Scientific evidence backs up mindfulness's transforming potential in enhancing mental and emotional well-being. Mindfulness activities have been demonstrated in studies to reduce stress, increase attention, and boost emotional regulation. These results are consistent with the quantum-inspired view that accepting uncertainty leads to increased psychological flexibility. Recognizing the connections between quantum theory and mindfulness allows scholars and practitioners to have a better grasp of how these fields influence and enrich one another.

Education is a strong tool for incorporating mindfulness and quantum ideas into daily life. Mindfulness training may be integrated into scientific education in schools, colleges, and community activities, cultivating a generation that values both critical thinking and introspective awareness. Such multidisciplinary approaches allow people to connect with the world's complexity in a balanced and intelligent way, bridging the gap between abstract theory and practical implementation.

Critics may claim that connecting quantum physics with mindfulness simplifies or misinterprets scientific principles. However, when explored with attention and intellectual honesty, these comparisons can reveal important truths about the human experience. The idea is to keep a clear contrast between metaphor and scientific reality, utilizing quantum theory terminology as a lens to investigate mindfulness rather than proof for its efficacy.

The combination between quantum uncertainty and mindfulness emphasizes the necessity of seeing the unknown as a source of possibilities rather than dread. Both disciplines remind us that the beauty of life comes in its unpredictability, urging us to live completely in the now while keeping open to the future. Mindfulness practitioners may traverse the difficulties of life with grace and resilience if they cultivate humility, flexibility, and a deep awareness for the interconnection of everything. This method not only improves individuals' well-being, but it also helps to create a more compassionate and peaceful environment.

Compassion and Entanglement: Applying Unity Principles to Social and Environmental Issues

The notion of quantum entanglement, which implies that particles may influence each other immediately regardless of distance, is a powerful metaphor for interconnection. Its ramifications extend beyond physics, providing a framework for investigating how compassion might alleviate social and environmental issues. By understanding entanglement as a metaphor of oneness, one may better understand how actions affect the larger world. This interrelated vision creates empathy and a sense of communal responsibility for the planet's and its people' health.

In its most deep form, compassion transcends individual emotions and serves as a guiding principle for behavior. When combined with a quantum-inspired view of interconnectivity, it stresses the fluidity of the boundaries between ourselves and others. This view is essential to many spiritual traditions; the notion that "all is one" is consistent with quantum entanglement's argument that systems are inextricably connected. This unity emphasizes the significance of tackling social inequities and environmental deterioration as interrelated issues that affect the entire society.

The use of quantum entanglement as a metaphor begins with acknowledging that each individual is part of a larger, interconnected system. This perspective of social justice opposes the inclination to consider concerns such as poverty, inequality, and institutional discrimination as isolated problems. Instead, it becomes clear that these inequalities are strongly rooted in larger institutions such as economic systems, cultural norms, and historical legacies. To address one component of injustice, one must consider the complete web of interrelated variables.

Movements for environmental justice provide a tangible example of this. Many underprivileged populations face a disproportionate share of environmental impact, from dirty water supplies to dangerous industrial sites. This inequality highlights an important link: the exploitation of natural resources frequently corresponds with the exploitation of disadvantaged communities. Recognizing this interdependence shifts the emphasis from discrete initiatives to systemic solutions, encouraging collaboration between environmental and social justice activists.

Compassion serves as the driving force behind these initiatives. Unlike pity, which frequently promotes hierarchical relationships, compassion recognizes people' and communities' common humanity and interdependence. Instead of fostering dependency, it stimulates action that uplifts and empowers. This is especially critical when dealing with global concerns like climate change, because the effects of inactivity are felt globally yet disproportionately by the most disadvantaged.

Quantum entanglement also encourages thought about the influence of individual acts within a bigger system. Small acts of kindness or intentional choices can have far-reaching consequences, just as a change in one particle can impact another across great distances. This viewpoint flips the narrative from despair—overwhelmed by the magnitude of world problems—to empowerment. It emphasizes how even apparently little acts, such as eliminating waste or supporting ethical enterprises, may contribute to a greater wave of good change.

The environmental movement provides an engaging backdrop for comprehending this rippling effect. Reducing plastic use, saving energy, and planting trees may appear small in isolation. However, when millions of people adopt similar behaviors, the total impact is dramatic. This is consistent with the quantum principle that, when separate particles are entangled, they display behaviors that defy linear causation, resulting in results greater than the sum of their parts.

This intertwined viewpoint also helps social advocacy. Historically, grassroots movements have caused substantial cultural transformations by using the collective strength of citizens. From civil rights to environmental conservation, these movements show how linked efforts, motivated by compassion and shared purpose, can overcome entrenched oppressive institutions. Quantum entanglement is a scientific metaphor for understanding how seemingly separate events combine to cause systemic change.

The technique of attentive engagement is fundamental to applying unity principles to social and environmental challenges. As previously noted, mindfulness promotes connectivity and empathy. This awareness converts abstract notions into experienced reality, leading people to contemplate how their decisions affect the larger web of existence. Mindful participation is consistent with the quantum measurement principle, which states that observation influences outcomes. Similarly, deliberate understanding of social and environmental challenges affects priorities and actions, resulting in a more compassionate and sustainable society.

Collaboration develops as a logical outgrowth of this integrated worldview. Quantum entanglement implies that the nature of reality is determined by interactions rather than independent things. Similarly, solving global concerns necessitates breaking down barriers and cultivating collaborations across disciplines, cultures, and industries. Environmental sustainability, for example, cannot be achieved without economic policies, technical advancements, and community-based activities. These partnerships exemplify the spirit of entanglement, in which various contributions converge to produce solutions that outperform any individual effort.

Education is critical in developing this attitude. Integrating quantum-inspired concepts into curricula can motivate students to look at the world through an interconnected lens. Teaching the physics of entanglement, as well as its metaphorical implications, promotes critical thinking and empathy, equipping future generations to face difficult situations from a holistic viewpoint. Education promotes a culture that values both intellectual inquiry and compassionate action by highlighting the interrelationship between science, ethics, and social responsibility.

Critics may claim that drawing similarities between quantum physics and social or environmental challenges oversimplifies scientific concepts. While this warning is legitimate, the intention is not to equate metaphors with scientific data, but rather to utilize them as tools for comprehending interrelated systems. Quantum entanglement provides a strong lens for investigating the interrelated aspect of life, reminding people of their place in a wider, interdependent totality. When used correctly, these metaphors deepen debates about compassion and togetherness while maintaining scientific rigor.

In this setting, the principle of humility becomes critical. Quantum physics demonstrates that reality is significantly more complicated than human perception can comprehend. Similarly, solving social and environmental concerns necessitates accepting the limitations of one's own expertise and embracing various viewpoints. Humility promotes openness to cooperation, creativity, and continual learning, all of which are required to navigate the intricacies of global concerns.

The incorporation of compassion and attachment into social and environmental campaigning indicates a significant shift in viewpoint. It encourages people to abandon a fragmented perspective of the world in favor of a holistic vision that acknowledges the interdependence of everything. By growing this knowledge, mankind can confront the problems of the twenty-first century with empathy, resilience, and a common commitment to achieving an equitable and sustainable future. Quantum mechanics courses provide essential insights into the skill of living responsibly in a beautifully interconnected world.

Holistic Synthesis: Quantum-Inspired Perspectives to Improve Well-Being and Ethical Living

While the concepts of quantum mechanics are profoundly established in physics, they provide a rich tapestry of metaphors that broaden our knowledge of human experience, ethics, and well-being. A comprehensive synthesis of various quantum-inspired viewpoints prompts a reconsideration of existence's interconnection and how this understanding might impact individual and community decisions. Individuals and society may create more compassion, resilience, and ethical accountability by incorporating quantum theory concepts into everyday life.

The idea of interconnection, as manifested most clearly by quantum entanglement, is central to this synthesis. In a physical sense, entangled particles show connections that defy traditional explanations, remaining connected regardless of distance. Translated into human terms, this phenomenon highlights the fundamental ways in which acts have far-reaching consequences for people and systems beyond immediate experience. This integrated worldview calls into question the idea of separation and encourages a responsible morality. Recognizing that every choice, no matter how tiny, may have an impact on the larger web of life creates a responsible and caring perspective.

In practice, adopting a quantum-inspired viewpoint entails accepting uncertainty and ambiguity. The indeterminacy at the heart of quantum physics reflects the unpredictability of human experience. Heisenberg's uncertainty principle, which emphasizes the difficulty of knowing a particle's location and momentum with precise precision, is a metaphor for life's inherent unpredictability. Acceptance of uncertainty fosters humility and openness, helping people to approach issues with adaptability and curiosity rather than strict control. This translates into mindfulness, or the ability to stay present and adaptable in the midst of life's changes.

Quantum superposition, which permits systems to be in numerous states at the same time until detected, is another metaphor for human potential and decision-making. This notion encourages thought on the various possibilities that exist in every instant. Instead of perceiving options as binary or fixed, a quantum-inspired mentality embraces the fluidity of possible outcomes. This viewpoint fosters creativity, invention, and the bravery to go along unexplored territory. It fosters resilience by assisting individuals in viewing setbacks as chances for growth rather than insurmountable hurdles.

The holographic principle, which states that each portion of a hologram comprises the entire image, is a great metaphor for holistic existence. It highlights the link between individual well-being and collective health. Just as the health of a single organ affects the entire body, so does the health of a single individual or community affect the larger social and ecological system. This idea is consistent with the increased emphasis on holistic health treatments that consider physical, mental, emotional, and social aspects. Community-based wellness programs, integrative medicine, and environmental sustainability all embody this holistic approach, illustrating how linked activities improve communal well-being.

Quantum analogies have also had a significant impact on ethical life. The observer effect, in which the act of observing changes the behavior of a quantum system, emphasizes the importance of awareness and purpose in affecting outcomes. When applied to ethical decision-making, this concept argues that intentional contemplation on one's principles and behaviors might result in more considered and meaningful decisions. It encourages people to think about the long-term consequences of their actions, establishing an intentionality ethic. Choosing sustainable goods, lowering consumption, or advocating for fair legislation are all examples of activities founded in reflective awareness that demonstrate how human choices contribute to system change.

Quantum-inspired ideas not only promote individual progress, but they also have significant consequences for society systems. The interconnectedness of quantum systems provides a blueprint for redesigning social and organizational processes. Collaborative techniques that embrace variety, inclusion, and common purpose are similar to the interdependent interactions seen in quantum systems. In reality, this can result in the creation of more fair and robust institutions that value communal well-being above hierarchical power. Workplaces that value cooperation and adaptation, for example, are better suited to navigating the complexity of a fast changing environment.

Education is critical in instilling these viewpoints in society. Teaching quantum-inspired notions not only broadens scientific knowledge, but also fosters an interconnection and ethical responsibility. Education may equip students to think critically and behave compassionately by combining interdisciplinary approaches that connect science, philosophy, and social ethics. Students who are exposed to these concepts are more likely to approach global issues with a sophisticated awareness of complexity and a dedication to long-term solutions.

The incorporation of quantum-inspired notions into everyday life is also consistent with spiritual and philosophical traditions that value oneness and interconnectedness. Many wisdom traditions, from Buddhism to Indigenous cosmologies, reflect the quantum truth that everything is interrelated. These traditions provide useful frameworks for putting abstract concepts into practice, such as compassion, gratitude, and respect for the natural world. Individuals may draw from a broad source of wisdom to influence their decisions and build a stronger sense of purpose by combining scientific and spiritual viewpoints.

Critically, the use of quantum analogies must be done with honesty and caution. While these ideas are useful tools for reframing human experience, it is critical to avoid misrepresenting or oversimplifying scientific notions. The idea is not to equate metaphors with empirical data, but to utilize them as lenses through which to investigate new possibilities. The combination of quantum-inspired viewpoints can strengthen both personal and communal undertakings by upholding scientific rigor and ethical thought.

One of the most revolutionary characteristics of this synthesis is its ability to evoke optimism and action in the face of global difficulties. From climate change to social injustice, the interlinked issues of the twenty-first century necessitate solutions that respect complexity and interdependence. According to quantum-inspired viewpoints, tiny, focused activities can lead to substantial systemic transformations. They also promote a resilient and adaptable attitude, allowing people and communities to face uncertainty with bravery and innovation.

Humanity may rethink its relationship with the planet by adopting this comprehensive synthesis. While quantum physics is based in the microscopic level, its principles reveal deep truths about the interconnectedness of reality. Individuals who incorporate these concepts into their daily lives can foster higher well-being, ethical integrity, and a sense of common purpose. This synthesis is more than just an academic exercise; it is a call to action—a reminder that we are all interconnected in the intricate web of life, and our decisions influence the world we live in.

CHAPTER 33: SYNTHESIS: THE EVOLVING TAPESTRY

"We are not human beings having a spiritual experience. We are spiritual beings having a human experience." – Pierre Teilhard de Chardin

The complicated web of linkages between quantum physics and spirituality has resulted in a tapestry of concepts that reflect a developing knowledge of reality. By investigating the interconnections of these domains, from the microscopic events of quantum randomness to the vast tales of cosmic design, a holistic picture emerges—one that combines scientific rigor with profound philosophical inquiry. This synthesis connects seemingly unconnected domains, providing insights into the nature of reality and humanity's position in it.

This topic is founded on the idea of quantum randomness, which challenges conventional physics' deterministic assumptions. The intrinsic unpredictability of occurrences like wave function collapse calls into question the conventional view of the cosmos as mechanical. While randomness may look chaotic, it also allows for creativity, spontaneity, and freedom, making it an ideal setting for addressing concerns like agency, purpose, and even divine will. Spiritual interpretations frequently perceive this ambiguity as an expression of cosmic freedom, a cosmos devoid of fixed causation yet filled with possibilities.

The random but ordered aspect of quantum physics is consistent with spiritual conceptions of balance and contradiction. Many traditions emphasize the interaction of opposites—light and darkness, being and non-being, chaos and order. The wave-particle duality of quantum systems reflects these dualities, indicating that entities may exist in seemingly contradictory states at the same time. This comparison encourages thought on the presence of several facts and the richness of plurality in both the scientific and spiritual elements of existence.

Another deep intersection is seen in the entanglement principle, which states that particles preserve instantaneous interactions despite their spatial separation. This phenomena defies traditional notions of localization and separateness, providing a stunning metaphor for interconnection. The idea that all things are inherently related is key to spiritual traditions, as represented in concepts such as Buddhist interdependent origination, Hindu view of Brahman as global awareness, and Sufi mystical teachings of oneness. Entanglement emphasizes the shared nature of all existence, prompting a reconsideration of individualism and instilling a feeling of social duty.

Beyond entanglement, the holographic concept provides another convincing link. The idea that the complete system might be inscribed in its pieces is consistent with spiritual teachings about wholeness and oneness. For example, in the mystical picture of Indra's Net, every node mirrors and contains all others, much like the holographic world, which holds that the cosmos' information is stored on its edges. This notion evokes not just awe, but also a knowledge of the fundamental interconnectivity of all levels of existence, from microscopic to cosmic.

Cosmic design is an ideal setting for combining quantum science with spirituality. The anthropic principle, which holds that the universe's fundamental constants are precisely calibrated to sustain life, has spurred disputes concerning purpose and intentionality. Some take this as proof of a greater intellect or divine design, while others see it as a natural outcome of a multiverse framework. Regardless of perspective, this debate sheds light on humanity's search for meaning in the cosmos. Spiritual creation myths frequently overlap with scientific ideas, highlighting elements like as emergence, evolution, and harmony.

The observer effect in quantum physics adds another degree of conceptual depth. The argument that measurement influences experiment results implies that awareness actively shapes reality. While the scientific community debates the exact consequences, this theory is consistent with spiritual traditions that emphasize mindfulness, purpose, and the creative power of thinking. The observer effect, whether achieved through meditation awareness or purposeful development of ethical behavior, serves as a metaphor for human consciousness' transforming power.

Synchronicity, or the meaningful alignment of occurrences without a causal relationship, has an intriguing counterpart in quantum correlations. While Jungian synchronicity is more closely related to psychology and spirituality than empirical science, its connection with entanglement provides fruitful fodder for discussion. These linkages serve as a reminder that meaning is frequently produced rather than discovered, and that human experience plays an important part in interpreting cosmic patterns.

Throughout these research, amazement emerges as a unifying thread. Both quantum physics and spirituality elicit tremendous astonishment, pushing the boundaries of human comprehension and fostering humility. Awe bridges the gap between scientific investigation and existential contemplation, reminding us that the search of knowledge is inextricably linked to the enjoyment of mystery. Whether looking at the expanse of the universe or analyzing the behavior of subatomic particles, awe inspires appreciation for the complexities of existence.

This emotion of wonder and connectivity has ethical concerns. Recognizing the relational aspect of reality promotes more inclusive, caring, and sustainable ways of life. Understanding that individual acts have ramifications throughout interrelated systems, both scientific and spiritual viewpoints call for a deeper sense of responsibility. From solving global concerns such as climate change to encouraging interpersonal peace, these thoughts emphasize the importance of collective well-being.

Education and multidisciplinary collaboration are critical for achieving this synthesis. By incorporating quantum principles into larger philosophical and ethical frameworks, society may foster a more holistic worldview. Educational efforts that combine the sciences and humanities can help people interact with complicated subjects critically and creatively. Research institutes and think tanks that focus on these intersections provide valuable venues for innovation, encouraging new ways of thinking about reality and humanity's position in it.

As the distinctions between disciplines become increasingly blurred, the intersections of quantum physics and spirituality provide an ever-expanding range of possibilities. These intersections stimulate not just intellectual inquiry but also practical application, urging people to carry out the concepts of interconnectivity, awareness, and intentionality in their daily lives. The emerging themes examined here show the possibility of a broader, more integrated view of existence—one that values both the rigor of scientific research and the depth of spiritual experience.

Common Ground: Where Scientific Theories of Interconnected Fields Meet Spiritual Experiences of Unity

The search of comprehending the cosmos has frequently taken two parallel paths: one based on factual science, striving to unravel the principles that control reality, and the other based on spirituality, probing the fundamental interconnectivity and oneness of existence. While these methods were previously viewed as distinct or even incompatible, the expanding debate surrounding quantum mechanics has shown areas of convergence in which various viewpoints not only coexist but enrich one another. This investigation of common ground shows a shared language of connectivity, as well as a tapestry that connects science and soul.

At the center of this junction is the notion of oneness, which is a fundamental principle in many spiritual traditions and a repeating subject in quantum physics. Quantum entanglement is an example of how this concept is expressed scientifically. When particles become entangled, their states are coupled regardless of physical distance. This phenomena, which

Albert Einstein memorably described as "spooky action at a distance," calls into question traditional ideas of separation. From a spiritual sense, entanglement resonates well with teachings that emphasize the oneness of all things, such as the Buddhist idea of interdependent origination or the Hindu understanding of Brahman as the ultimate indivisible truth. Both theories emphasize that individuality is an illusion, with everything inextricably linked in a great cosmic web.

The observer effect connects science and spirituality by putting human consciousness at the core of how reality unfolds. In quantum physics, measurement appears to impact the fate of a quantum system by reducing a superposition of states to a single observable reality. This principle calls into question the traditional concept of an objective, observer-independent cosmos and proposes a participation role for awareness. Spiritual traditions, particularly those based on meditation and contemplative practices, have long held that human consciousness influences experience and reality. The convergence of these viewpoints promotes further investigation into the nature of consciousness and its function in the universe.

Another area of convergence is the holographic principle, a scientific idea that proposes that the whole universe's information may be recorded on its borders. This idea echoes spiritual teachings that propose the macrocosm is reflected within the microcosm, as seen in the Hermetic maxim "As above, so below." The holographic principle resonates with mystical traditions that see the universe as a unified whole, with each part containing the essence of the entire system. This alignment provides a deep perspective on existence, eliciting scientific and spiritual awe.

The notion of unity also appears in discussions of the anthropic principle, which holds that the universe's physical constants are precisely calibrated to allow for the presence of life. While scientists disagree on whether this shows a multiverse or an underlying cosmic design, spiritual viewpoints frequently take this fine-tuning as proof of purpose or divine intelligence. Both perspectives address the mystery of existence, promoting musings on humanity's role in the universe and the possible interconnectivity of all life.

The concept of synchronicity serves as another intriguing connection. Carl Jung coined the term "synchronicity," which refers to meaningful coincidences that lack causal explanation but have strong personal relevance. Quantum physics, including entanglement and non-locality, provides a foundation for understanding how such connections may emerge across physical and metaphysical realms. While synchronicity exists largely in the psychological and spiritual worlds, its resonance with quantum concepts encourages multidisciplinary discussion of the nature of meaning, causation, and interconnectivity.

These linked motifs go beyond theoretical alignment to influence ethical and philosophical questions. Recognizing the interdependence of all things promotes a sense of responsibility that is fundamental to both scientific and spiritual worldviews. Quantum physics demonstrates how slight changes in one element of a system may have far-reaching consequences for the entire system, a notion that is reflected in ecological and social systems. Similarly, spiritual teachings frequently highlight the consequences of individual acts, promoting compassion, awareness, and environmental stewardship. The convergence of different viewpoints facilitates the formation of a holistic ethos that combines scientific findings with spiritual ideals.

The integration of science and spirituality has practical consequences for human well-being. Mindfulness meditation, a spiritual tradition-based practice, has been found to improve mental and physical health, with demonstrable impacts on brain function and stress management. These activities are consistent with quantum concepts of intentionality and the observer effect, implying that concentrated awareness may impact both human experience and larger systems. Integrating these ideas into healthcare, education, and public policy can help create more resilient and compassionate communities.

Education and research play critical roles in discovering and developing this common ground. Interdisciplinary endeavors bringing together physicists, philosophers, neuroscientists, and spiritual practitioners create fertile ground for creativity and discovery. Such interactions promote the creation of new frameworks for interpreting reality that combine scientific rigor with meditative insight. They also provide chances to solve difficult global concerns such as climate change and social injustice using integrated methods that recognize both the tangible and immaterial elements of life.

As these discussions go, it becomes evident that the lines between scientific and spiritual inquiry are not set but flexible. Each field provides distinct tools and viewpoints that, when combined, result in a more comprehensive knowledge of reality. Science provides techniques for testing ideas and understanding the physical world's mechanics, whereas spirituality provides insights into the subjective and transcendent components of experience. They offer a complementary framework that acknowledges the complexities and mysteries of reality.

The developing relationship between quantum physics and spirituality reflects a larger cultural movement toward integrative thinking. By accepting both scientific and spiritual viewpoints, humankind may build a more comprehensive worldview that values variety, encourages collaboration, and inspires awe. The intersection of these areas is more than just an intellectual exercise; it represents a revolutionary chance to redefine humanity's connection with the universe and with one another. This synthesis brings the desire for knowledge and the pursuit of meaning together, driving mankind toward a more profound and harmonious understanding of life.

Long-term Potential: How Each Discipline Can Benefit from This Interplay, Fostering Deeper Human Insight

The dynamic interplay between quantum physics and spirituality has shed light not just on the riddles of life, but also on humanity's ability for higher understanding. This convergence acts as a link across disciplines, fostering a comprehensive perspective of reality that combines scientific rigor with spiritual inquiry. By combining the strengths of both viewpoints, humans might unveil transformational possibilities that cut beyond scientific, philosophical, and personal domains.

Quantum mechanics has transformed the scientific perspective by proving that reality is significantly more complex and linked than classical models could describe. Entanglement, non-locality, and superposition are examples of phenomena that call into question the mechanical understanding of the cosmos, showing a dynamic system in which every piece is part of a bigger whole. These discoveries are consistent with spiritual beliefs that emphasize oneness, connectivity, and the transcendent aspect of reality. By presenting these connections in a systematic conversation, both sectors might improve their approaches: science by absorbing larger philosophical ideas, and spirituality by adopting the discipline of empirical investigation.

One of the most fundamental consequences of this interaction is its ability to broaden humanity's knowledge of consciousness. Quantum physics raises basic problems regarding the observer's role in altering reality, a premise shared by spiritual traditions that emphasize the transformational power of consciousness. Recent breakthroughs in neuroscience, reinforced by quantum concepts, show that consciousness may be inextricably linked to the fabric of the cosmos. Collaborative study at the junction of these fields has the potential to solve the secrets of consciousness, leading to advancements in mental health, artificial intelligence, and even spiritual investigation.

The unifying notion of interconnection provides solutions to global concerns. Climate change, social injustice, and resource scarcity necessitate comprehensive methods that cross traditional discipline lines. Quantum physics shows how seemingly unrelated systems are linked, but spirituality stresses the moral obligation that such linkages entail. Together, these viewpoints promote a paradigm change from exploitative practices to sustainable cohabitation, with compassion and stewardship as core concepts.

On a personal level, the intersection of quantum physics and spirituality offers strategies for handling ambiguity. Both schools emphasize that ambiguity and paradoxes are inherent in reality. Quantum physics shows a universe of probability rather than certainty, yet spiritual beliefs promote acceptance of the uncertainty as a component of the human experience. This shared understanding promotes resilience, flexibility, and creativity, allowing people to face life's problems with an open mind and a clear sense of purpose.

This interaction has several practical implications, including medical, education, and technology. Quantum-inspired models of linked systems can help healthcare providers develop holistic therapy approaches that address the physical, mental, and emotional elements of well-being. Mindfulness meditation, a technique derived from spiritual traditions, is increasingly backed by scientific research confirming its effectiveness in stress reduction and cognitive performance. These traditions demonstrate how combining science and spirituality may result in practical advantages for individuals and communities alike.

This synthesis also has the potential to help education. Curriculum that includes both scientific ideas and spiritual philosophies can help pupils develop critical thinking, empathy, and ethical awareness. This method enables students to investigate the interconnections of knowledge, instilling a feeling of wonder and curiosity about the cosmos. By removing artificial borders between disciplines, educators can educate future generations to solve complicated issues with creativity and compassion.

Technological innovation driven by quantum concepts emphasizes the potential of this multidisciplinary conversation. Quantum computing, with its ability to handle massive quantities of information via superposition and entanglement, exemplifies the interrelated aspect of reality that spiritual beliefs highlight. As this technology evolves, it may provide solutions to problems ranging from climate modeling to medical research. However, the ethical consequences of such advancements demand a balanced viewpoint based on the moral frameworks supplied by spiritual traditions.

This synthesis is centered on the transformational power of wonder. Both quantum physics and spirituality evoke a tremendous feeling of awe, allowing humans to interact with the cosmos in ways that go beyond intellectual knowledge. This common experience cultivates humility, allowing people to appreciate their place in the wider cosmic order. By accepting this sensation of wonder, humans may develop a deeper awareness for the interconnectivity of all things, promoting a shared sense of duty and purpose.

The confluence of these disciplines calls into question the tight boundaries that have traditionally divided them. Science, which has traditionally concentrated on the tangible components of existence, is increasingly investigating metaphysical issues. Spirituality, in turn, is growing more willing to include empirical facts into its frameworks. This reciprocal openness fosters communication and collaboration, allowing one sector to learn and enrich the other. Such a dynamic interaction has the potential to yield new discoveries that neither field could attain on its own.

Furthermore, this combination has the ability to shift cultural narratives about development and purpose. Modern civilizations frequently stress technical growth and financial affluence above underlying issues of purpose and interconnectivity. By combining quantum discoveries with spiritual principles, mankind may redefine development in terms of overall well-being, ecological balance, and ethical integrity. This shift in viewpoint promotes a more balanced approach to growth, emphasizing both innovation and contemplation.

As this conversation progresses, it is critical to retain an attitude of inquiry and humility. While the intersections of quantum physics and spirituality have great potential, they must be navigated carefully to avoid mistaking metaphor with scientific proof. Constructive collaboration between various areas necessitates intellectual rigor, ethical responsibility, and a dedication to appreciating other points of view. Humanity may face the intricacies of life by promoting an open and inclusive conversation, combining the best of both disciplines.

Finally, the ability of this interaction to spark greater human knowledge is what gives it long-term value. By combining the analytical accuracy of science with the transforming wisdom of spirituality, mankind may pave the way for greater knowledge, compassion, and creativity. This synthesis not only broadens our understanding of the cosmos, but also deepens our feeling of being a part of it. This integrative method transforms the quest for knowledge into a voyage of connection, exposing the fundamental interconnectedness that underpins all creation.

CHAPTER 34: CONCLUSION: UNRAVELING THE COSMIC WEB

"There are more things in heaven and earth, Horatio, than are dreamt of in your philosophy." - William Shakespeare

As we come to the close of this exploratory journey, it's essential to pause and reflect on the mosaic of ideas we've examined. The tapestry of quantum physics and spirituality is intricate, but like a cosmic web, its individual threads come together to create a unique pattern, offering profound insights into the nature of existence itself.

The Symphony of Two Worlds

It's tempting to think of quantum physics and spirituality as two distinct realms, each with its language and framework. However, as we have observed throughout this book, these two worlds are more like musical genres that share notes, chords, and scales but express them differently. Both speak to the inexplicable mysteries of existence and interconnectedness—quantum physics through equations and experiments, spirituality through metaphors and experiential insight. The marriage of these two disciplines is not just about intellectual stimulation; it speaks to a human yearning for wholeness and a complete understanding of our place in the Universe.

What is more fascinating is that the intersection of quantum physics and spirituality is not a recent occurrence propelled by the New Age movement or even 20th-century discoveries alone. Spiritual traditions dating back millennia have spoken of concepts that echo the puzzling phenomena found in quantum mechanics—whether it be the wave-particle duality reminiscent of mystical dualities, or the interconnectedness experienced in states of spiritual enlightenment resembling quantum entanglement. This suggests a perennial wisdom that cuts across cultures and eras, persistently pushing humanity to reconsider its understanding of reality.

The continuity of Exploration

Scientific inquiries and spiritual quests are evolutionary in nature. New discoveries often lead to more questions, setting the stage for ongoing exploration. For instance, the development of quantum computing might soon provide radical insights into problems once deemed insurmountable, perhaps even offering us a glimpse into the "Mind of God." Similarly, consciousness studies could eventually shed light on why and how observation affects quantum states, and whether this has any implications for spiritual practices like meditation or prayer.

One of the most significant challenges in this field is to establish a methodological framework that respects the strengths and limitations of both quantum physics and spiritual traditions. While empirical evidence is the cornerstone of scientific exploration, spirituality often relies on introspective and phenomenological insights, making it difficult to design experiments that can satisfy the rigors of both. Nevertheless, as interdisciplinary studies become more common and as our tools for understanding both the external and internal worlds become more sophisticated, the potential for revolutionary discoveries increases.

What Lies Ahead?

As we look toward the future, the continued integration of quantum physics with spiritual insights holds the promise of a more nuanced understanding of reality. It also beckons us to be humble and receptive, recognizing that both the scientific and spiritual realms offer valuable perspectives that are part of a greater whole. Could the quantum realm eventually give us a mathematical model for spiritual phenomena like karma or provide empirical evidence for the concept of a life force? Only time will tell.

The ethical implications of merging these domains are not to be overlooked. As we probe deeper into the quantum realm and its applications—whether it's in technology, medicine, or artificial intelligence—we must also consider the spiritual and ethical dimensions of our discoveries. After all, knowledge without wisdom is like a ship without a compass; it may move fast but not necessarily in the right direction.

Unraveling the cosmic web where quantum physics and spirituality intertwine is not a task that can be completed; it is an ongoing journey. Both disciplines offer windows into a larger reality, each illuminating different aspects of the same cosmic landscape. As we have traversed this terrain, we've seen that rather than being at odds, science and spirituality can enrich each other in profound ways, providing a more comprehensive map of existence. It is this larger view that beckons us forward, inviting us to continue exploring, questioning, and marveling at the wondrous complexity of the Universe and our place within it.

BIBLIOGRAPHY

Introduction: Exploring Science and Spirit

Barad, K. (2007). Meeting the Universe Halfway: Quantum Physics and the Entanglement of Matter and Meaning. Duke University Press.

Capra, F. (1975). The Tao of Physics: An Exploration of the Parallels Between Modern Physics and Eastern Mysticism. Shambhala.

Bohr, N. (1987). The Philosophical Writings of Niels Bohr. Ox Bow Press.

Zohar, D., & Marshall, I. (1990). The Quantum Self: Human Nature and Consciousness Defined by the New Physics. William Morrow.

Nicolescu, B. (2002). Manifesto of Transdisciplinarity. SUNY Press.

Chalmers, D. J. (1996). The Conscious Mind: In Search of a Fundamental Theory. Oxford University Press.

Foundations of Quantum Mechanics

Heisenberg, W. (1958). Physics and Philosophy: The Revolution in Modern Science. Harper & Row.

Planck, M. (1932). Where Is Science Going? Allen & Unwin.

Feynman, R. P. (1965). The Character of Physical Law. MIT Press.

Dirac, P. A. M. (1981). The Principles of Quantum Mechanics. Oxford University Press.

Griffiths, D. J. (2016). Introduction to Quantum Mechanics. Cambridge University Press.

Schwinger, J. (2001). Quantum Mechanics: Symbolism of Atomic Measurements. Springer.

Spiritual Frameworks of Interconnection

Eliade, M. (1957). The Sacred and the Profane: The Nature of Religion. Harcourt.

Nhat Hanh, T. (1991). Peace Is Every Step: The Path of Mindfulness in Everyday Life. Bantam.

Kabbalah Centre International. (2004). The Essential Zohar: The Source of Kabbalistic Wisdom. Harmony Books.

Bohm, D. (1980). Wholeness and the Implicate Order. Routledge.

Watts, A. (1975). Tao: The Watercourse Way. Pantheon.

Wilber, K. (1996). A Brief History of Everything. Shambhala.

Wave-Particle Duality and Spiritual Paradox

Young, T. (1804). Experimental Demonstrations of the General Facts of Interference of Light. Philosophical Transactions of the Royal Society.

Barbour, J. B. (1999). The End of Time: The Next Revolution in Physics. Oxford University Press.

Laozi. (2018). Tao Te Ching (Trans. Stephen Mitchell). Harper Perennial.

Pauli, W. (1952). The Influence of Archetypal Ideas on the Scientific Theories of Kepler. Springer.

Greene, B. (2004). The Fabric of the Cosmos: Space, Time, and the Texture of Reality. Knopf.

Klee, P. (1920). Creative Credo. Kunstmuseum Basel.

Quantum Entanglement and Oneness

Einstein, A., Podolsky, B., & Rosen, N. (1935). Can Quantum-Mechanical Description of Physical Reality Be Considered Complete? Physical Review.

Bell, J. S. (1987). Speakable and Unspeakable in Quantum Mechanics. Cambridge University Press.

Varela, F., Thompson, E., & Rosch, E. (1991). The Embodied Mind: Cognitive

Science and Human Experience. MIT Press.

Lanza, R. (2010). Biocentrism: How Life and Consciousness Are the Keys to Understanding the Universe. BenBella Books.

Nadeau, R., & Kafatos, M. (2001). The Non-Local Universe: The New Physics and Matters of the Mind. Oxford University Press.

De Chardin, T. (1959). The Phenomenon of Man. Harper Perennial.

Observer Effect and Consciousness

Wheeler, J. A. (1983). Law Without Law. In Quantum Theory and Measurement. Princeton University Press.

von Neumann, J. (1932). Mathematical Foundations of Quantum Mechanics. Springer.

Rosenblum, B., & Kuttner, F. (2006). Quantum Enigma: Physics Encounters Consciousness. Oxford University Press.

Stapp, H. P. (1993). Mind, Matter, and Quantum Mechanics. Springer.

Penrose, R. (1994). Shadows of the Mind: A Search for the Missing Science of Consciousness. Oxford University Press.

Chopra, D., & Kafatos, M. (2017). You Are the Universe: Discovering Your Cosmic Self and Why It Matters. Harmony Books.

Schrödinger's Cat and Coexisting States

Schrödinger, E. (1935). Die gegenwärtige Situation in der Quantenmechanik. Naturwissenschaften.

Tegmark, M. (2007). The Multiverse Hierarchy. In The New Physics for the Twenty-First Century. Cambridge University Press.

Everett, H. (1957). "Relative State" Formulation of Quantum Mechanics. Reviews of Modern Physics.

Zukav, G. (1979). The Dancing Wu Li Masters: An Overview of the New Physics. William Morrow.

Sartre, J.-P. (1943). Being and Nothingness. Methuen.

Heidegger, M. (1927). Being and Time. Harper Perennial.

Quantum Tunneling and Miraculous Events

Fowler, R. H., & Nordheim, L. (1928). Electron Emission in Intense Electric Fields. Proceedings of the Royal Society of London.

Gamow, G. (1928). Zur Quantentheorie des Atomkernes. Zeitschrift für Physik.

Polkinghorne, J. (1986). One World: The Interaction of Science and Theology. SPCK.

Tipler, F. J. (1994). The Physics of Immortality: Modern Cosmology, God, and the Resurrection of the Dead. Doubleday.

Davies, P. (1995). The Mind of God: Science and the Search for Ultimate Meaning. Simon & Schuster.

Bohm, D., & Hiley, B. J. (1993). The Undivided Universe: An Ontological Interpretation of Quantum Theory. Routledge.

Heisenberg's Uncertainty and Free Will

Heisenberg, W. (1927). Über den anschaulichen Inhalt der quantentheoretischen Kinematik und Mechanik. Zeitschrift für Physik.

Libet, B. (1985). Unconscious Cerebral Initiative and the Role of Conscious Will in Voluntary Action. Behavioral and Brain Sciences.

Smolin, L. (2013). Time Reborn: From the Crisis in Physics to the Future of the Universe. Houghton Mifflin Harcourt.

Kane, R. (2005). A Contemporary Introduction to Free Will. Oxford University Press.

Popper, K. (1972). Objective Knowledge: An Evolutionary Approach. Oxford University Press.

Nagel, T. (1986). The View from Nowhere. Oxford University Press.

Superposition and Multiple Realities

Everett, H. (1957). Many-Worlds Interpretation of Quantum Mechanics. Princeton University Press.

Deutsch, D. (1997). The Fabric of Reality: The Science of Parallel Universes and Its Implications. Penguin.

Zeh, H. D. (1970). On the Interpretation of Measurement in Quantum

Theory. Foundations of Physics.

Susskind, L. (2005). The Cosmic Landscape: String Theory and the Illusion of Intelligent Design. Back Bay Books.

Yogananda, P. (1946). Autobiography of a Yogi. Self-Realization Fellowship.

Targ, R., & Puthoff, H. E. (1974). Information Transfer under Conditions of Sensory Shielding. Nature.

The Holographic Principle and Wholeness

't Hooft, G. (1993). Dimensional Reduction in Quantum Gravity. arXiv preprint gr-qc/9310026.

Susskind, L. (1995). The World as a Hologram. Journal of Mathematical Physics.

Bohm, D. (1980). Wholeness and the Implicate Order. Routledge.

Talbot, M. (1991). The Holographic Universe. HarperCollins.

Laszlo, E. (2007). Science and the Akashic Field: An Integral Theory of Everything. Inner Traditions.

Hawking, S. (1988). A Brief History of Time: From the Big Bang to Black Holes. Bantam.

Quantum Cosmology and Creation Narratives

Linde, A. D. (1983). The Inflationary Universe. Reports on Progress in

Physics.

Guth, A. H. (1981). Inflationary Universe: A Possible Solution to the Horizon and Flatness Problems. Physical Review D.

Hawking, S., & Ellis, G. F. R. (1973). The Large Scale Structure of Space-Time. Cambridge University Press.

Campbell, J. (1949). The Hero with a Thousand Faces. Princeton University Press.

Vilenkin, A. (2006). Many Worlds in One: The Search for Other Universes. Hill and Wang.

Krauss, L. M. (2012). A Universe from Nothing: Why There Is Something Rather Than Nothing. Free Press.

Hidden Variables and Karmic Threads

Bohm, D. (1952). A Suggested Interpretation of the Quantum Theory in Terms of "Hidden Variables". Physical Review.

Bell, J. S. (1964). On the Einstein Podolsky Rosen Paradox. Physics Physique Физика.

Weber, M. (1922). The Sociology of Religion. Beacon Press.

Steiner, R. (1904). Theosophy: An Introduction to the Supersensible Knowledge of the World and the Destination of Man. Anthroposophic Press.

Lanza, R. (2010). Biocentrism: How Life and Consciousness Are the Keys to Understanding the Universe. BenBella Books.

Capra, F. (1996). The Web of Life: A New Scientific Understanding of Living Systems. Anchor Books.

Quantum Healing and Energy Work

Popp, F. A. (1992). Biophoton Emission: New Evidence for Coherence and DNA as Source of Biophotons. Journal of Scientific Exploration.

Chopra, D. (1989). Quantum Healing: Exploring the Frontiers of Mind/Body Medicine. Bantam.

Becker, R. O., & Selden, G. (1985). The Body Electric: Electromagnetism and the Foundation of Life. HarperCollins.

Gerber, R. (2001). Vibrational Medicine: The #1 Handbook of Subtle-Energy Therapies. Bear & Company.

Pert, C. B. (1997). Molecules of Emotion: Why You Feel the Way You Feel. Scribner.

Tiller, W. A. (1997). Science and Human Transformation: Subtle Energies, Intentionality, and Consciousness. Pavior Publishing.

Quantum Chaos and Spiritual Disorder

Gleick, J. (1987). Chaos: Making a New Science. Viking.

Lorenz, E. N. (1963). Deterministic Nonperiodic Flow. Journal of the Atmospheric Sciences.

Prigogine, I. (1980). From Being to Becoming: Time and Complexity in the

Physical Sciences. W.H. Freeman.

Capra, F. (1991). The Tao of Physics: An Exploration of the Parallels Between Modern Physics and Eastern Mysticism. Shambhala.

Kaufman, S. A. (1995). At Home in the Universe: The Search for Laws of Self-Organization and Complexity. Oxford University Press.

Whitehead, A. N. (1929). Process and Reality. Macmillan.

Synchronicity and Quantum Correlations

Jung, C. G. (1952). Synchronicity: An Acausal Connecting Principle. Princeton University Press.

Pauli, W. (1955). The Influence of Archetypal Ideas on the Scientific Theories of Kepler. Journal of Analytical Psychology.

Bohm, D., & Peat, F. D. (1987). Science, Order, and Creativity. Routledge.

Koestler, A. (1972). The Roots of Coincidence. Random House.

Hiley, B. J., & Pylkkänen, P. (2005). Can Mind Affect Matter via Active Information?. Mind and Matter.

Goswami, A. (1993). The Self-Aware Universe: How Consciousness Creates the Material World. TarcherPerigee.

The Anthropic Principle and Purpose

Carter, B. (1974). Large Number Coincidences and the Anthropic Principle in Cosmology. IAU Symposium.

Barrow, J. D., & Tipler, F. J. (1986). The Anthropic Cosmological Principle. Oxford University Press.

Davies, P. (2004). The Goldilocks Enigma: Why Is the Universe Just Right for Life?. Penguin.

Dyson, F. (1979). Time Without End: Physics and Biology in an Open Universe. Reviews of Modern Physics.

Smolin, L. (1997). The Life of the Cosmos. Oxford University Press.

Rees, M. (1999). Just Six Numbers: The Deep Forces That Shape the Universe. Basic Books.

Non-locality and the Akashic Field

Aspect, A., Grangier, P., & Roger, G. (1981). Experimental Tests of Realistic Local Theories via Bell's Theorem. Physical Review Letters.

Laszlo, E. (2004). The Akashic Field: An Integral Theory of Everything. Inner Traditions.

Wheeler, J. A. (1978). The "Past" and the "Delayed-Choice" Double-Slit Experiment. Mathematical Foundations of Quantum Theory.

Sheldrake, R. (1981). A New Science of Life: The Hypothesis of Morphic Resonance. Tarcher.

Bohm, D. (1980). Wholeness and the Implicate Order. Routledge.

Goswami, A. (2001). Quantum Creativity: Think Quantum, Be Creative.

Hampton Roads.

Everett's Many-Worlds and Rebirth

Everett, H. (1957). "Relative State" Formulation of Quantum Mechanics. Reviews of Modern Physics.

Tegmark, M. (1998). The Interpretation of Quantum Mechanics: Many Worlds or Many Words?. Fortschritte der Physik.

Barbour, J. (1999). The End of Time: The Next Revolution in Physics. Oxford University Press.

MacGregor, G. (1983). Reincarnation in East and West: A Comparative Study of Nirvana and Samsara. Philosophical Library.

Wheeler, J. A. (1983). Law Without Law. In Quantum Theory and Measurement. Princeton University Press.

Zurek, W. H. (2003). Decoherence, Einselection, and the Quantum Origins of the Classical. Reviews of Modern Physics.

Quantum Teleportation and Astral Travel

Bennett, C. H., Brassard, G., & Ekert, A. K. (1993). Quantum Cryptography and Teleportation. Physics Today.

Zeilinger, A. (1997). Experiment and the Foundations of Quantum Physics. Reviews of Modern Physics.

Monroe, R. A. (1971). Journeys Out of the Body. Anchor Books.

Barrow, J. D. (1991). Theories of Everything: The Quest for Ultimate Explanation. Clarendon Press.

Bohm, D., & Hiley, B. J. (1993). The Undivided Universe: An Ontological Interpretation of Quantum Theory. Routledge.

Ring, K. (1980). Life at Death: A Scientific Investigation of the Near-Death Experience. Coward, McCann & Geoghegan.

Ethics in the Quantum-Spiritual Realm

Feynman, R. P. (1985). Surely You're Joking, Mr. Feynman!. W.W. Norton.

Capra, F. (1996). The Web of Life: A New Scientific Understanding of Living Systems. Anchor Books.

Bohm, D., & Peat, F. D. (1987). Science, Order, and Creativity. Routledge.

Dyson, F. (1997). Imagined Worlds. Harvard University Press.

Schrödinger, E. (1944). What Is Life? The Physical Aspect of the Living Cell. Cambridge University Press.

Hawking, S. (2010). The Grand Design. Bantam.

Quantum AI and the Divine Mind

Lloyd, S. (2006). Programming the Universe: A Quantum Computer Scientist Takes on the Cosmos. Knopf.

Tegmark, M. (2017). Life 3.0: Being Human in the Age of Artificial Intelligence. Knopf.

Deutsch, D. (1997). The Fabric of Reality: The Science of Parallel Universes—and Its Implications. Penguin.

Kurzweil, R. (2005). The Singularity Is Near: When Humans Transcend Biology. Viking.

Penrose, R. (1989). The Emperor's New Mind: Concerning Computers, Minds, and the Laws of Physics. Oxford University Press.

Floridi, L. (2014). The Fourth Revolution: How the Infosphere Is Reshaping Human Reality. Oxford University Press.

Consciousness Studies: The Next Frontier

Hameroff, S., & Penrose, R. (1996). Orchestrated Reduction of Quantum Coherence in Brain Microtubules: A Model for Consciousness. Mathematics and Computers in Simulation.

Chalmers, D. J. (1995). Facing Up to the Problem of Consciousness. Journal of Consciousness Studies.

Crick, F., & Koch, C. (1990). Toward a Neurobiological Theory of Consciousness. Seminars in the Neurosciences.

Dehaene, S. (2014). Consciousness and the Brain: Deciphering How the Brain Codes Our Thoughts. Viking.

Searle, J. R. (1997). The Mystery of Consciousness. The New York Review of Books.

Tononi, G. (2008). Consciousness as Integrated Information: A Provisional Manifesto. Biological Bulletin.

Metaphysics and Determinism in Quantum Theory

Bell, J. S. (1964). On the Einstein Podolsky Rosen Paradox. Physics Physique Физика.

Heisenberg, W. (1958). Physics and Philosophy: The Revolution in Modern Science. Harper.

Popper, K. R. (1982). Quantum Theory and the Schism in Physics. Hutchinson.

Penrose, R. (2004). The Road to Reality: A Complete Guide to the Laws of the Universe. Knopf.

Rovelli, C. (2016). Reality Is Not What It Seems: The Journey to Quantum Gravity. Penguin.

Ismael, J. T. (2016). How Physics Makes Us Free. Oxford University Press.

Quantum Mysticism in Fiction & Media

Zukav, G. (1979). The Dancing Wu Li Masters: An Overview of the New Physics. HarperOne.

Kaku, M. (2008). Physics of the Impossible: A Scientific Exploration into the World of Phasers, Force Fields, Teleportation, and Time Travel. Doubleday.

Tipler, F. J. (1994). The Physics of Immortality: Modern Cosmology, God, and the Resurrection of the Dead. Doubleday.

Barad, K. (2007). Meeting the Universe Halfway: Quantum Physics and the Entanglement of Matter and Meaning. Duke University Press.

Hawking, S., & Mlodinow, L. (2010). The Grand Design. Bantam.

Rees, M. (2001). Our Cosmic Habitat. Princeton University Press.

Technological Horizons and Spiritual Insight

Harari, Y. N. (2015). Homo Deus: A Brief History of Tomorrow. Harvill Secker.

Kurzweil, R. (2012). How to Create a Mind: The Secret of Human Thought Revealed. Viking.

Bostrom, N. (2014). Superintelligence: Paths, Dangers, Strategies. Oxford University Press.

Floridi, L. (2010). Information: A Very Short Introduction. Oxford University Press.

Lloyd, S. (2006). Programming the Universe: A Quantum Computer Scientist Takes on the Cosmos. Knopf.

Tegmark, M. (2017). Life 3.0: Being Human in the Age of Artificial Intelligence. Knopf.

Cultural and Historical Roots of Quantum Mysticism

Schrödinger, E. (1944). What Is Life? The Physical Aspect of the Living Cell. Cambridge University Press.

Heisenberg, W. (1958). Physics and Philosophy: The Revolution in Modern Science. Harper.

Capra, F. (1975). The Tao of Physics: An Exploration of the Parallels Between Modern Physics and Eastern Mysticism. Shambhala.

Jung, C. G. (1952). Synchronicity: An Acausal Connecting Principle. Princeton University Press.

Laszlo, E. (2004). The Akashic Field: An Integral Theory of Everything. Inner Traditions.

Bohm, D. (1980). Wholeness and the Implicate Order. Routledge.

Reappraising Materialism and Physical Reality

Rovelli, C. (2017). The Order of Time. Riverhead Books.

Barbour, J. (1999). The End of Time: The Next Revolution in Physics. Oxford University Press.

Hawking, S., & Mlodinow, L. (2010). The Grand Design. Bantam.

Schrödinger, E. (1944). What Is Life? The Physical Aspect of the Living Cell. Cambridge University Press.

Kaku, M. (2014). The Future of the Mind: The Scientific Quest to Understand, Enhance, and Empower the Mind. Doubleday.

Goswami, A. (1993). The Self-Aware Universe: How Consciousness Creates the Material World. TarcherPerigee.

Future Directions and Collaborative Research

Laughlin, R. B. (2005). A Different Universe: Reinventing Physics from the Bottom Down. Basic Books.

Wilczek, F. (2015). A Beautiful Question: Finding Nature's Deep Design. Penguin Press.

Tegmark, M. (2014). Our Mathematical Universe: My Quest for the Ultimate Nature of Reality. Knopf.

Penrose, R. (2020). Cycles of Time: An Extraordinary New View of the Universe. Vintage.

Barad, K. (2007). Meeting the Universe Halfway: Quantum Physics and the Entanglement of Matter and Meaning. Duke University Press.

Rovelli, C. (2021). Helgoland: Making Sense of the Quantum Revolution. Riverhead Books.

Philosophy of Science and Spiritual Praxis

Kuhn, T. S. (1962). The Structure of Scientific Revolutions. University of Chicago Press.

Nagel, T. (2012). Mind and Cosmos: Why the Materialist Neo-Darwinian Conception of Nature Is Almost Certainly False. Oxford University Press.

Popper, K. R. (1959). The Logic of Scientific Discovery. Hutchinson.

Barbour, J. (1999). The End of Time: The Next Revolution in Physics. Oxford University Press.

Goswami, A. (1993). The Self-Aware Universe: How Consciousness Creates the Material World. TarcherPerigee.

Searle, J. R. (1997). The Mystery of Consciousness. The New York Review of Books.

Critiques and Debates in Quantum Spirituality

Hossenfelder, S. (2018). Lost in Math: How Beauty Leads Physics Astray. Basic Books.

Stenger, V. J. (2007). Quantum Gods: Creation, Chaos, and the Search for Cosmic Consciousness. Prometheus Books.

Dawkins, R. (2006). The God Delusion. Bantam.

Coyne, J. A. (2015). Faith vs. Fact: Why Science and Religion Are Incompatible. Viking.

Pigliucci, M. (2010). Nonsense on Stilts: How to Tell Science from Bunk. University of Chicago Press.

Shermer, M. (2016). Skeptic: Viewing the World with a Rational Eye. Henry Holt and Co.

Integrative Practices: Bridging Quantum Concepts into Daily Life

Tolle, E. (1997). The Power of Now: A Guide to Spiritual Enlightenment. New World Library.

Kabat-Zinn, J. (1990). Full Catastrophe Living: Using the Wisdom of Your Body and Mind to Face Stress, Pain, and Illness. Bantam.

Chopra, D. (1989). Quantum Healing: Exploring the Frontiers of Mind/Body Medicine. Bantam.

Nhat Hanh, T. (1998). The Heart of the Buddha's Teaching: Transforming Suffering into Peace, Joy, and Liberation. Parallax Press.

Dalai Lama, & Ekman, P. (2008). Emotional Awareness: Overcoming the Obstacles to Psychological Balance and Compassion. Henry Holt and Co.

Wallace, B. A. (2007). Contemplative Science: Where Buddhism and Neuroscience Converge. Columbia University Press.

Synthesis: The Evolving Tapestry

Wilczek, F. (2008). The Lightness of Being: Mass, Ether, and the Unification of Forces. Basic Books.

Penrose, R. (2020). Cycles of Time: An Extraordinary New View of the Universe. Vintage.

Kaku, M. (2014). The Future of the Mind: The Scientific Quest to Understand, Enhance, and Empower the Mind. Doubleday.

Rovelli, C. (2017). The Order of Time. Riverhead Books.

Capra, F. (1975). The Tao of Physics: An Exploration of the Parallels Between Modern Physics and Eastern Mysticism. Shambhala.

Barad, K. (2007). Meeting the Universe Halfway: Quantum Physics and the Entanglement of Matter and Meaning. Duke University Press.

THE END

Printed in France by Amazon
Brétigny-sur-Orge, FR